Study Abroad,
Second Language Acquisition
and Interculturality

SECOND LANGUAGE ACQUISITION

Series Editors: **Professor David Singleton**, *University of Pannonia, Hungary* and Fellow Emeritus, *Trinity College, Dublin, Ireland* and **Associate Professor Simone E. Pfenninger**, *University of Salzburg, Austria*

This series brings together titles dealing with a variety of aspects of language acquisition and processing in situations where a language or languages other than the native language is involved. Second language is thus interpreted in its broadest possible sense. The volumes included in the series all offer in their different ways, on the one hand, exposition and discussion of empirical findings and, on the other, some degree of theoretical reflection. In this latter connection, no particular theoretical stance is privileged in the series; nor is any relevant perspective – sociolinguistic, psycholinguistic, neurolinguistic, etc. – deemed out of place. The intended readership of the series includes final-year undergraduates working on second language acquisition projects, postgraduate students involved in second language acquisition research, and researchers, teachers and policymakers in general whose interests include a second language acquisition component.

All books in this series are externally peer-reviewed.

Full details of all the books in this series and of all our other publications can be found on http://www.multilingual-matters.com, or by writing to Multilingual Matters, St Nicholas House, 31-34 High Street, Bristol BS1 2AW, UK.

SECOND LANGUAGE ACQUISITION: 135

Study Abroad, Second Language Acquisition and Interculturality

Edited by
Martin Howard

MULTILINGUAL MATTERS
Bristol • Blue Ridge Summit

DOI https://doi.org/10.21832/HOWARD4146

Library of Congress Cataloging in Publication Data

A catalog record for this book is available from the Library of Congress.

Names: Howard, Martin- editor.

Title: Study Abroad, Second Language Acquisition and Interculturality /
  Edited by Martin Howard.

Description: Bristol, UK; Blue Ridge Summit: Multilingual Matters, 2019. |
  Includes bibliographical references and index.

Identifiers: LCCN 2019010159 (print) | LCCN 2019022253 (ebook) |
  ISBN 9781788924146 (hbk : alk. paper) | ISBN 9781788924139 (pbk : alk. paper)

Subjects: LCSH: Second language acquisition. | Language and languages—Study
  and teaching. | Foreign study. | Intercultural communication.

Classification: LCC P118.2 .S885 2019 (print) | LCC P118.2 (ebook) |
  DDC 401/.93—dc23

LC record available at https://lccn.loc.gov/2019010159

LC ebook record available at https://lccn.loc.gov/2019022253

British Library Cataloguing in Publication Data

A catalogue entry for this book is available from the British Library.

ISBN-13: 978-1-78892-414-6 (hbk)
ISBN-13: 978-1-78892-413-9 (pbk)

Multilingual Matters

UK: St Nicholas House, 31-34 High Street, Bristol BS1 2AW, UK.

USA: NBN, Blue Ridge Summit, PA, USA.

Website: www.multilingual-matters.com
Twitter: Multi_Ling_Mat
Facebook: https://www.facebook.com/multilingualmatters
Blog: www.channelviewpublications.wordpress.com

The policy of Multilingual Matters/Channel View Publications is to use papers
that are natural, renewable and recyclable products, made from wood grown in
sustainable forests. In the manufacturing process of our books, and to further
support our policy, preference is given to printers that have FSC and PEFC Chain
of Custody certification. The FSC and/or PEFC logos will appear on those books
where full certification has been granted to the printer concerned.

Typeset by Deanta Global Publishing Services Limited.
Printed and bound in the UK by Short Run Press Ltd.
Printed and bound in the US by NBN.

Contents

Acknowledgements

This volume emanates from the transnational 'Study Abroad Research in European Perspective' (SAREP) project, supported in 2016–2020 through the European agency COST (Cooperation in Science and Technology [COST Action 15130]). I am most grateful to COST which supported a range of activities within the project, an outcome of which is the volume presented here. I also wish to thank the contributors who offered their work, along with the reviewers who shared their expertise in reviewing the chapters. Finally, my thanks go to Laura Longworth at Multilingual Matters, and the Second Language Acquisition series editors, David Singleton and Simone Pfenninger, for their support during the process.

Martin Howard
Cork, February 2019

Contributors

Fanny Forsberg Lundell is associate professor of French at Stockholm University. Besides publishing extensively on formulaic language in French and Spanish as L2s with a particular focus on high-level proficiency, she also works on pragmatics, conversation analysis and spoken language in general. Recently, her work includes psychological and social perspectives on high-level L2 attainment in different migratory contexts.

Rozenn Gautier received a PhD in linguistics from Grenoble Alpes University where she studied the role of social network on sociolinguistic competence in second language acquisition. She focuses on American and Chinese learners of French as a second language with a special interest in the social dimensions of the study abroad context in France. She has worked as a researcher and lecturer in Grenoble Alpes University and the University of Lyon 2.

Leah Geoghegan is an EFL teacher. She holds an MA in theoretical and applied linguistics from the Universitat Pompeu Fabra, specializing in language acquisition and learning, and is currently undertaking a second MA in translation studies at Portsmouth University. She was project manager and main writer for the website 'Intclass' (http://intclass.upf.edu/), a multimedia science tool for the promotion of three main foreign language contexts: study abroad, immersion and formal instruction. Her research interests include second language acquisition, English as a lingua franca and study abroad. She has contributed a chapter to the EUROSLA Studies Series monographic volume on learning context effects.

Martin Howard is head of the School of Languages, Literatures and Cultures at University College Cork (Ireland). His research interests lie in second language acquisition with particular reference to study abroad, temporality and (socio)linguistic variation; sociolinguistics; and the French language in Canada. He is founding editor of the journal *Study Abroad Research in Second Language Acquisition and International Education*, and chair of the European COST Action, 'Study Abroad

Research in European Perspective' (SAREP, 2016–2020). He has previously served as vice-president of the European Second Language Association (EUROSLA) and associate editor of the *International Journal of Canadian Studies*.

Noriko Iwasaki is professor of Japanese language pedagogy and second language acquisition at Nanzan University and also research associate at SOAS University of London, where she worked as senior lecturer of language pedagogy until 2018. She is interested in study-abroad students' development of pragmatic competence and changes in linguistic/cultural identities. She also conducts research on literacy and Japanese mimetics. Her recent publications include a co-edited volume *Ido to Kotoba* (*Mobility and Language*) (Kurosio Publishers), a co-authored chapter 'Making It Your Own by Adapting It to What's Important to You: Plurilingual Critical Literacies to Promote L2 Japanese Users' Sense of Ownership of Japanese' in *Reconceptualizing Connections between Language, Learning, and Literacy* (Springer).

Jane Jackson (PhD, University of Toronto) is professor in the English Department at the Chinese University of Hong Kong, where she teaches courses in applied linguistics/intercultural communication. Her research centers on education abroad, intercultural communication, language and identity, and eLearning. Recent Routledge books include *Online Intercultural Education and Study Abroad: Theory into Practice* (2019), *Interculturality in International Education* (2018), *Intercultural Interventions in Study Abroad* (2018, co-edited with Susan Oguro), *Introducing Language and Intercultural Communication* (2014) and *The Routledge Handbook of Language and Intercultural Communication* (2012, editor). She has also authored *Intercultural Journeys: From Study to Residence Abroad* (Palgrave MacMillan, 2010) and *Language, Identity, and Study Abroad: Sociocultural Perspectives* (Equinox, 2008).

Celeste Kinginger is a professor of applied linguistics at the Pennsylvania State University (USA), where she teaches courses in second language acquisition and education as well as advanced seminars, such as narrative approaches to multilingual identity and second language pragmatics. She is affiliated with the Center for Language Acquisition in the university's College of Liberal Arts. Her research has examined telecollaborative, intercultural language learning, second language pragmatics, cross-cultural life writing and study abroad. Her current work includes a nationwide survey and qualitative investigation of language study abroad alumni, funded by the US Department of Education.

Àngels Llanes received her PhD at the Universitat de Barcelona and is currently a lecturer at the English and Linguistics Department at the

Universitat de Lleida (Spain). Her research focuses on the impact that age and learning context (i.e. study abroad) have on second or foreign language (L2) development. She is also interested in the role that reading in English plays on the development of English. Other research interests are the impact of CLIL classes on English (L2) development and the effects of individual differences on L2 outcomes.

Sònia Mas-Alcolea is currently an associate professor at the University of Lleida, where she obtained her PhD in applied linguistics (2017). Her research focuses on the impact of a study-abroad experience on students' learning and use of a foreign language as well as on their perception of cultural difference. More specifically, she is interested in analysing the ways in which Erasmus students (re)construct their identities throughout the three stages of a study abroad experience (pre, during, post) through discourse. She is a member of the CLA (Cercle de Lingüística Aplicada) group, coordinated by Dr Enric Llurda, which investigates multilingualism in higher education.

Carmen Pérez-Vidal is currently an accredited professor of English at the Department of Translation and Linguistic Sciences, Universitat Pompeu Fabra, Barcelona. Her research interests lie within the field of foreign language learning, bilingualism and learning context effects on study abroad, immersion and instructed second language acquisition. She is the leading researcher of the Study Abroad and Language Acquisition (SALA) research group (http://intclass.upf.edu/). In 2004, she was the launching co-coordinator, together with Martin Howard (University College Cork), of the AILA Research Network (ReN) on study abroad.

Tiina Räisänen is a postdoctoral researcher at the Department of Language and Communication Studies, University of Jyväskylä. Her research interests include sociolinguistics, English as lingua franca, intercultural business communication and language and literacy learning at work. Her longitudinal study focuses on the development of professional communicative repertoires and trajectories of socialization across work settings. She has published for example in *International Journal of Applied Linguistics*, *Journal of Business Communication*, *Sociolinguistics Studies*, in an edited volume *Translanguaging as Everyday Practice* (Springer) and in *Dangerous Multilingualism – Northern Perspectives on Order, Purity and Normality* (Palgrave), which she also co-edited.

Rebekah Rast is professor of English and linguistics at the American University of Paris, where she also holds the position of Director of Teaching, Learning and Faculty Development. A member of the French research group *Structures Formelles du Langage* and a country coordinator of the VILLA project, she is the author of *Foreign Language Input: Initial Processing* (Multilingual Matters), co-editor with ZhaoHong Han of *First Exposure to a Second Language: Learners' Initial Input Processing* (Cambridge University Press) and author of numerous book chapters and articles on the initial stages of second/foreign language acquisition.

1 Second Language Acquisition and Interculturality during Study Abroad: Issues and Perspectives. An Introduction to the Volume

Martin Howard

Introduction

Situated within the field of study abroad research, this book reflects the burgeoning interest in study abroad learners who undertake a period of residence abroad, usually but by no means necessarily as part of their academic programme of study. Such study abroad learners constitute an important cohort among our student population not only within a university context, but also at secondary and indeed primary school level. In the former case, a vast range of programmes are available to both language and non-language students, such as the now long-established European Region Action Scheme for the Mobility of University Students (Erasmus) programme in Europe that celebrated its 30th anniversary in 2017 and has seen well over 3 million university students partake, usually for a semester or a full academic year. Beyond Europe, short-term study abroad over a couple of weeks is especially popular in a North American context, with students sometimes accompanied by staff members of their home university through various University of X programmes in city Y especially in Europe and South America. In an Asian context, a number of countries are key sending countries, such as China, South Korea and India, with many students choosing to undertake a full degree programme of study in a host university abroad (for recent statistics, see Plews & Jackson [2017]; for details on the Japanese context, see Grimes-McLellan

[2017] who outlines a number of constraints on levels of participation in that context in spite of government initiatives to facilitate study abroad; Yang [2016] offers interesting perspectives on intra-Asia mobility, focusing on Chinese talent students in Singapore). From the perspective of Australia and New Zealand, research has especially focused on students going to Japan (see Marriott, 1995), with some research on incoming students from Asia, e.g. Benson *et al.* (2013) and Jackson (2017) on Hong Kong students, as well as Patron's (2007) work on French students in Australia. Beyond these geographical regions, there is, however, little information on students from Africa and South America, in spite of initiatives in some countries in the latter context to promote study abroad, such as Brazil's Science without Borders programme. In the Caribbean context, Craig (2016) offers insights into the challenges faced by such universities where the financial and personal investment required on the part of the student is often prohibitive.

Such a diverse range of opportunities and initiatives to get students on the move reflects the significant internationalisation of higher education, where students can avail of study abroad through full degree programmes at a host university, through exchange programmes from within their home university, initiatives to spend time abroad through a work placement, summer language course or indeed simply spending time in another country for a purpose related to their studies such as in a country where the learner's second language (L2) is dominant. At pre-university levels in the case of secondary and primary school pupils, some also participate in organised study abroad as part of their studies such as through attending school in another country for a specific period of time, usually where they are learning the host language. But the primary means of enhancing their language skills is through summer language programmes over a couple of weeks, which are well known across Europe, especially in the UK and Ireland. A further but often forgotten cohort within the study abroad enterprise concerns professionals, especially teachers who avail of inter-university exchange programmes as part of their professional development (for a study in a North American context, see Bournot-Trites *et al.* [2018]), with teachers in a European context benefitting from the European Union COMENIUS programme.

Taken together, such learner cohorts and diversity of programme types reflect the rich array of participants in terms of age and background profiles and the focus and aim of study. Given their importance within our educational institutions, study abroad research has rightly emerged as an independent subfield within the wider field that is contemporary applied linguistics to capture the vast range of issues that study abroad raises, ranging from pre-departure matters such as programme type, timing of study abroad, duration of stay abroad and student preparation, issues during study abroad such as programme structure and make-up, the learner's *raison d'être* abroad and residence type, among others, to post-study abroad matters such as the learner's reintegration and long-term benefits. Across the study abroad literature, such issues are explored through a multifaceted prism that includes linguistic, intercultural, academic, educational, personal, social and professional development and outcomes during study abroad.

The focus of this book is essentially on the former two; while the personal and the social necessarily interact with linguistic and intercultural development, the chapters presented reflect the strong link between study abroad research and second language acquisition (SLA) and interculturality research. We provide a synopsis of issues in both domains in the following.

The Interface Between Study Abroad Research, Second Language Acquisition and Interculturality: Questions and Issues

While study abroad research can be traced back to Carroll's (1967) initial study such that it has emerged relatively contemporaneously to SLA, it is only since the mid-1990s with the publication of Freed's (1995a) seminal volume and especially since the early 2000s that the field has become particularly buoyant. As we noted above, while the focus is multifaceted, the impact of study abroad on the learner's L2 development has given rise to a vast array of empirical studies that highlight not only the challenges faced by the L2 learner but also the significant linguistic gains to be made in a study abroad context. While illuminating in themselves of SLA processes and outcomes, they also contribute to a range of key questions in SLA research such that they serve a dual purpose of informing study abroad research and contributing to debates within SLA. Those issues are threefold, reflecting the scope of SLA research, namely issues underpinning the learner's L2 development, input and interaction issues and, finally, individual factors at play in the acquisition process.

With regard to L2 linguistic development, study abroad research serves to significantly illuminate the relation between learning context and the specificity of such development. In particular, a key question concerns how development may differ across learning contexts, with the traditional dichotomy being made between the foreign language classroom and the naturalistic context. In this regard, with the increasing popularity of study abroad, a mixture of learner experiences between both contexts is increasingly true of many learners, with some also benefitting from immersion experiences outside of the target language community such as through residential summer schools. While early SLA research may have assigned a limited role to the impact of learning context in so far as acquisition processes are believed to be fundamentally the same across learners, more recent approaches that highlight the role of individual, social and contextual factors have enhanced research interest in the relation between such factors and L2 learner development. In this regard, a range of issues have become increasingly pertinent as a wealth of research on linguistic development during study abroad has brought to the fore the complexity of such development.

In particular, questions arise concerning the specificity of linguistic development in so far as development may not be a case of 'all or nothing' (see Howard, 2005). In other words, certain components of the learner's linguistic repertoire in the L2 may be more prone to development with others being more resistant. Questions arise therefore as to why such development may not be uniform, with some researchers suggesting that study abroad lends itself to the development of more social aspects of language use (see Kinginger, 2009), while others suggest that it may impact less marked features than marked ones (see Howard & Schwieter, 2018). While in some ways such questions relate to linguistic outcomes in terms of the use of specific skills and the use of specific linguistic features in learner language, a further question concerns the potential of the learning context to impact processes of learning such that the stages of linguistic development may differ. In other words, study abroad may simply speed up the acquisition process without fundamentally changing the process, such that learners who do not venture abroad may demonstrate relatively similar outcomes at a later stage.

While the study abroad literature on linguistic development provides extensive insight through various longitudinal and control group comparison studies on the scope and specificity of linguistic development, perhaps the more pertinent question for understanding the complex relation between learning context and L2 development that such studies point to concerns the reasons underlying such a complex relation. On this count, Howard and Schwieter (2018) offer some insight in the case of grammatical development, but there is scope in the study abroad literature to move beyond the level of descriptive studies to more adequately consider the role of learning context at a theoretical level in terms of issues that may be at play in linguistic development when learners change learning context. Indeed, here, an interesting perspective for the future would concern the long-term impact of study abroad in terms of learner retention, attrition and further development of the linguistic gains made abroad following their return to the foreign language classroom, and indeed in the longer term thereafter, as well as in areas less subject to development during a sojourn abroad but perhaps more conducive to development in the foreign language classroom (for further discussion, see Howard & Schwieter [2018]).

While linguistic development does not happen independently without language contact, a further key area concerns its relation to the linguistic input available during the learner's stay abroad, with folk belief holding that study abroad represents an ideal combination of instructed exposure in the foreign language classroom followed by naturalistic exposure in the target language community. Such a change in context raises questions of the learner's ability to utilise the specificity of the input available in the target language community whose characteristics are very different from the written input that dominates and the explicit, metalinguistic information available in many instructed learning environments, although some more implicit input is obviously available. In some ways, the instructed learner has been 'trained' to process the input available in a way that may be very different when confronted with the masses of naturalistic implicit input available abroad where learners often humbly realise the limitations of their prior learning. Learners are faced with the challenge of learning to segment, process and comprehend such naturalistic spontaneous streams of speech that are not necessarily subject to the input modifications that they enjoy in the classroom, even if some input and interactional modifications are necessarily present during interaction in real time abroad (for discussion of input and interactional modifications in SLA, see Long [1985]). In many ways, the more controlled input available in the foreign language classroom in terms at least of the input and interactional modifications that it lends itself to may constitute a 'safer' but not necessarily authentic environment for the learner.

Beyond listening and indeed reading comprehension of the input available, a further challenge concerns the need to enhance learners' production skills so as to demonstrate the putative linguistic development that study abroad facilitates. On this count, the challenges are many whereby the learner must learn to increasingly automatise the metalinguistic skills previously learnt across the full range of components that make up the learner's linguistic repertoire in the L2 such as in relation to pronunciation, fluency, vocabulary, grammar and interactional competence, as well as developing some components that may not feature significantly in the instructed input such as sociolinguistic and sociopragmatic skills. As noted, such instructed input is often in the written medium, but the linguistic production development we refer to extends beyond writing to speaking skills. Taken together, the change in learning context and the input exposure conditions that that entails raises significant questions about the potential for study abroad to impact on the full breadth of the learner's linguistic skills across the components constituting that linguistic repertoire.

While the latter issues pertain to the nature of the learner's linguistic development abroad, they necessarily interact with the learner's engagement with the input available in that environment. On this count, several other key issues for SLA researchers are pertinent beyond the input comprehension ones to which we have alluded. A first matter concerns the characteristics of the input in relation to frequency, transparency and salience issues, where questions arise concerning how items that are more frequent, transparent and salient in the input may be more easily acquired than those that are less frequent, less transparent and less salient. In this regard, usage-based approaches to SLA that highlight such matters can gain significant insight (for discussion of such matters, see Howard [in press]; with regard to usage-based approaches, see Ellis [1998]). Beyond those issues, however, there are also key questions concerning the learner's very contact with the language, such as in relation to type, frequency, duration and intensity of contact, as well as the quantity and quality of input exposure (for discussion, see Howard [2011]). In this regard, matters relate to the learner's language activities abroad such as differences between more passive and active activities where the former would be exemplified by watching TV, listening to the radio and reading, in contrast with more interactive activities such as engaging with members of the host community. In the latter regard, a range of questions therefore arise concerning the social networks that learners develop and their social integration abroad. While masses of input exposure are potentially available, the learner has to create and avail of opportunities to engage with that language input through contact with its speakers. Questions arise therefore as to who the learner is interacting with, for what purpose and what the nature of the interaction is, among others. Such questions have recently been explored in relation to social network analysis with a view to illuminating the characteristics of the learner's social networks abroad (see, e.g. Dewey *et al.*, 2013; Mitchell *et al.*, 2017). Some work has also explored the nature of interaction abroad such as in terms of the distinction between transactional interaction as opposed to more communicative interaction, opportunities for which are often more difficult to create (see Devlin, 2014; Wilkinson, 1998). As a key area of SLA, study abroad can obviously contribute enormously to such input and interaction questions.

Beyond input conditions, the change in learning environment also brings with it various cultural differences giving rise to potential culture shock and affective issues concerning how the learner deals with a change in cultural norms. In this regard, various socio-biographical and contextual factors are pertinent, such as the learner's personality, attitudes and motivation. Such factors can be explored in terms of how study abroad impacts on them in themselves, such that they are not stable but rather dynamic and therefore can evolve over the course of study abroad as they interact with issues in the learner's experiences abroad. Other relevant individual, contextual and programmatic factors that have been explored include learner aptitude, age and gender, residence type, the learner's status abroad and proficiency level, as well as factors in the host environment such as relationships with and attitudes towards the host family, other members of the host community and indeed the target language community and culture in general. Taken together, such factors have in the main been explored in terms of how they might condition learner outcomes. On this count, a key finding in the study abroad literature relates to the highly individual experience that is study abroad such that considerable inter-learner variation is seen to underlie the learner's acquisition and experience abroad with some learners having very different experiences to others, and some evidencing greater progress than others. The social turn that has prevailed in the literature since the early 2000s (see Kinginger, 2008) has highlighted such differential experiences and factors and their interface with the learner's input engagement and acquisition outcomes abroad. In so doing, study abroad research fundamentally underlines their importance in SLA in a way that has been less the case in the foreign language classroom where such levels of inter-learner variation are often seen to be less prevalent (see Freed, 1995b).

While our focus thus far has been on language learning issues, study abroad has also been of significant interest to researchers within an intercultural framework where studies have focused on the nature of the learner's intercultural awareness and development during a sojourn abroad. Indeed, some study abroad programmes such as the Erasmus+ programme incorporate such an area within the overarching aims of the underlying outcomes of study abroad. While interculturality and study abroad constitutes a further relevant strand, it is also situated within the much broader area that is interculturality research such as in relation to intercultural communication (see Holliday, 2011, 2013) and education (see Dervin, 2016; Dervin & Gross, 2016). Indeed, a number of institutions have recently produced documents that explore issues of intercultural concepts, descriptors and implementation, such as the Council of Europe's (2018) *Reference Framework of Competences for Democratic Culture* and UNESCO's (2017) *UNESCO Survey on Intercultural Dialogue*. The Organisation for Economic Co-operation and Development (OECD) similarly envisages preparing a Pisa test on global skills and cultural awareness to complement its tests in other areas, used in comparing national education systems.

Given the opportunities that study abroad offers for sojourning in other cultures, a number of studies have more specifically explored the nature of the learner's intercultural development in terms of how learners come to deal with intercultural issues and the skills they gain (see, e.g. Beaven & Borghetti, 2018; Jackson, this volume), while others have drawn on that work to explore potential interventions prior to and during study abroad to support learner development (see Jackson & Oguro, 2018). Such work draws on a range of models available that depict stages of intercultural development, such as Hammer's (2012) Intercultural Development Inventory, Deardorff's (2008) process model of intercultural competence and Byram's (1997) model of intercultural development (see Jackson, this volume).

While an important body of research on interculturality and study abroad exists, such research is seen to be characterised by a Western-centric approach, drawing on Western paradigms of knowledge and frameworks (see Aman, 2017), with the underlying depiction of intercultural development as a deficiency that is to be overcome through study abroad. Indeed, some authors call for a non-centric approach in terms of decentred interculturality (see Amadasi & Holliday, 2018; Li & Dervin, 2018), as well as the need to better capture the specificity of the concept itself and the processes that underlie it such as in relation to self-other(s) awareness and learner reactions. On this count, it can be seen that intercultural development is highly personal, such that it does not necessarily lend itself well to universal treatment, but is situated within the individual. As such, the scope for potential intercultural training to genuinely impact is seen to raise further questions with the implicit premise that it is a personal journey that one undergoes, drawing on inner resources.

Presentation of the Volume

Against this background, the findings from the study abroad literature are rich within this burgeoning field in spite of the relatively short time frame within which the field has emerged. The volume presented here aims to add to the field by offering studies on a range of innovative issues characterising contemporary study abroad research, drawing on quantitative, qualitative and mixed-methods studies of learners of different source and target languages, in different study abroad settings and contexts and also in some cases extending the scope of inquiry to non-language specialists and professionals who have not often come under the spotlight.

The key themes under focus extend to a number of areas. Firstly, they concern linguistic development issues in an 'English as a lingua franca' setting – while the field benefits from a wealth of studies on such issues in the case of language learners, a clear gap concerns students who choose to go to a country where the dominant language is not their target language and who need to operate in an English as a lingua franca context. Given the status of English as a global lingua franca, it is crucial that study abroad research addresses issues in such learners' linguistic development, not only in the case of English, but also in the case of their experience of the host community language.

A second theme relates to the need to add to our existing understanding of input and social network issues where we need to build on existing research to explore questions more specifically related to the link between the characteristics of the linguistic input such as items available and their perception, processing, comprehension and subsequent uptake and use by the learner. In this regard, research from the perspective of first exposure studies would seem to have a lot to offer. Complementing such input issues is the need to explore social network development across individual learners whereby learners may have different experiences of social integration abroad.

As we noted, individual factors have emerged as key in understanding the learner's experience abroad – in this regard, a first issue concerns their relationship not only with developmental outcomes but also with learning processes abroad, while we also need to extend their investigation beyond typical study abroad learners to other learner cohorts. On the latter count, we include 'cultural migrants' as a case of long-term study abroad as a means of exploring the contribution that such a learner cohort can bring.

Finally, related to individual factors and differences are issues of identity and attitudes to cultural differences where some chapters explore learner identity development and intercultural awareness and attitudes. Taken together, the chapters aim to complement existing research by offering both empirical studies as well as timely state-of-the-art overviews of the themes they address as a resource not only for researchers in the study abroad and SLA communities but also for practitioners who can draw upon the material to better understand the complexity of their learners' experiences abroad.

Presentation of the Contributing Chapters

In Chapter 2: '"Cantonese is My Own Eyes and English is Just My Glasses": The Evolving Language and Intercultural Attitudes of a Chinese Study Abroad Student', Jane Jackson offers a longitudinal case study of the experience of a Hong Kong study abroad participant in New Zealand, and the individual and environmental factors that impacted that experience, along with the linguistic, attitudinal and intercultural development the learner evidences. The case study is part of a larger project with ten undergraduate students, whereby the specificity of the experience of the case study participant is explored, thereby highlighting the importance of exploring individual learners as opposed to whole group analyses. The author concludes by offering suggestions for learner intervention in study abroad, as well as prior to study abroad.

Through a longitudinal prism, Sònia Mas-Alcolea's chapter on 'Study Abroad and Students' Discourse on "Cultural Difference": A Longitudinal View' explores the development in the learners' perception of cultural difference. The Catalan learner participants were located in different European countries where they had the opportunity to engage with other international students, as well as their native speaker hosts, thereby observing various cultural differences. Drawing on membership categorisation analysis, the study offers a qualitative investigation of how the learners discursively construct such differences in terms of thematic categories, and how such discourse evolved over time, from prior to, during, to following their study abroad sojourn.

While the participants in Chapter 3 were located in lingua franca contexts, Chapter 4 by Tiina Räisänen more explicitly takes as its focus that context. Titled 'Discursive Identity Work and Interculturality during Blue-Collar Work Practice Abroad: Finnish Engineering Students as

Language Learners and Users', the chapter focuses on a group of Finnish learners engaged in a work placement in Germany who did not speak the target language of that country. Given the specificity of the learners as participants in a work placement, the chapter showcases the scope of study abroad experiences available, and the importance of offering an investigation of such wide-ranging experiences beyond the traditional study abroad university placement. The qualitative longitudinal study explores the interaction between English as a lingua franca and German as the host country language in the participants' experience abroad, and the learners' experiences of managing such linguistic diversity in their everyday lives both as workers in a factory and as members of the wider host community.

The importance of English as a lingua franca in contemporary study abroad experiences is also at the heart of Leah Geoghegan and Carmen Pérez-Vidal's chapter, 'English as a Lingua Franca, Motivation and Identity in Study Abroad'. In this chapter, through a qualitative case study analysis of Catalan participants in different European countries, the authors seek to investigate the roles that English as a lingua franca assumes in their study abroad experiences as well as in their learner identity and motivational development. Six key roles are identified, and compared and contrasted across the learners not only in countries where English is a lingua franca for the learners, but also in the UK where English holds target language status.

In a final chapter that retains a lingua franca perspective, Àngels Llanes' chapter on 'Study Abroad as a Context for Learning English as an International Language: An Exploratory Study' focuses on the potential for linguistic development in such a lingua franca context when the learners could otherwise have been in a genuinely target language community. Given that study abroad participants who are not specialist language learners are the dominant group, at least in a European context, and that they often find themselves in a country where they need to use English as a lingua franca, Llanes' chapter provides important findings on the scope for such a lingua franca environment to impact on their linguistic development. Through a quantitative longitudinal analysis, the author shows that their general linguistic proficiency and spoken development are positively impacted, especially in terms of fluency and lexical complexity. The findings highlight the potential for learners and programme administrators to look towards such lingua franca contexts as destinations for study abroad.

Moving beyond lingua franca issues, the chapter by Fanny Forsberg Lundell, 'Long-Term Residence Abroad and SLA: The Case of Cultural Migrants in France', depicts the broad net that study and residence abroad encompasses in terms of participants and age groups. The chapter moves the focus of inquiry from traditional study abroad participants, even if they have dominated the field, to 'cultural migrants', thereby highlighting the need to explore learners outside of the traditional education sector. Thus, cultural migrants refers to long-term migrants who have specifically chosen to live abroad for personal and sociocultural reasons. Based on a large-scale project, Forsberg Lundell depicts issues in their linguistic development as potential near-native speakers, while exploring various factors in their experience abroad that may have contributed to that enhanced development, such as agency, effort and motivation.

Beyond such individual factors, input matters are a crucial characteristic of a study abroad context in so far as it fundamentally offers the learner extensive opportunities to potentially engage with masses of L2 input and interaction. Rebekah Rast explores such input issues in her chapter titled 'What First Exposure Studies of Input can Contribute to Study Abroad Research'. In particular, she draws on the body of first exposure studies to present a picture of what they tell us about the learner's ability to draw on the input in a relatively short time frame, the role of characteristics of the input such as frequency and transparency issues and methodological considerations of how they might contribute to the study of input exposure, engagement and uptake on the learner's part during study abroad.

While input is hypothetically extensively available during study abroad compared to the more restricted opportunities in the foreign language classroom, we also know that learners need to create opportunities to avail of such extensive input. Such opportunities are not ready-made, and hence issues of who the learners engage with and the extent of their contacts are also important. On this count, social network development has emerged as a key area in study abroad studies, reflecting the difficulty that learners may have in establishing contact with native speakers in particular. Rozenn Gautier explores such social network development in a chapter titled 'Understanding Socialisation and Integration through Social Network Analysis: American and Chinese Students during a Stay Abroad'. Here, the author draws on social network analysis to provide an empirical investigation within a longitudinal framework of developments in the differential types of social networks her American and Chinese participants evidence during a nine-month stay in France. She explores the changes in the characteristics of those networks, as well as offering potential factors at play in the differences characterising the two groups of learner-participants. The chapter highlights the complexity of learner socialisation during study abroad where the challenge of native speaker contact is not easy.

While social networks are one area where individual differences arise, in her chapter titled 'Individual Differences in Study Abroad Research: Sources, Processes and Outcomes of Students' Development in Language, Culture and Personhood', Noriko Iwasaki offers a timely reflection on the breadth of research conducted on diverse individual factors in a study abroad context. Given the considerable individual differences that such a body of research highlights, Iwasaki attempts to collate the insights that such research offers by conceiving of such factors in terms of sources of predictors of different linguistic outcomes, and sources of differing processes such as in relation to individual experiences abroad and the personal and intercultural outcomes that ensue. The chapter further highlights developments in approaches to the study of individual differences, reflecting developments in their wider study and the importance they have assumed within the field of SLA, from within a quantitative paradigm to more qualitative and mixed-method approaches that offer complementary insights into the multifaceted complexity underlying the issue in hand.

Continuing with such an overview perspective on the literature, Celeste Kinginger concludes the volume with a chapter on 'Four Questions for the Next Generation of Study Abroad Researchers'. Kinginger offers a thought-provoking reflection on the direction that study abroad research has taken over the years, and looks to the future by identifying four key areas where future research will be especially fruitful. These reflect changes in the concept of study abroad for many participants and the experiences they have abroad compared to their predecessors such that much of the older literature is not necessarily comparable with studies of the contemporary generation. The four areas highlighted relate to societal changes underpinning the experience of study abroad, the importance of longitudinal studies of study abroad in relation to the long-term impact of study abroad, the need for perspectives other than those provided by learners themselves and, lastly, the relation between research and practice in study abroad programme design and organisation.

Taken together, the chapters highlight developments in the field through empirical studies of a number of innovative issues, while also offering overview reflections on the key developments and insights offered by the field to date across a number of critical areas.

References

Amadasi, S. and Holliday, A. (2018) Interculturality: Learning from the 'non-Western Other'. Presentation at COST Action 15130 Workshop, Study Abroad Research in European Perspective, Lisbon, September.

Aman, R. (2017) *Decolonising Intercultural Education*. London: Routledge.

Beaven, A. and Borghetti, C. (2018) *Study Abroad and Interculturality: Perspectives and Discourses*. London: Routledge.

Benson, P., Barkhuizen, G., Bodycott, P. and Brown, J. (2013) *Second Language Identity Development in Study Abroad*. New York: Palgrave Macmillan.

Bournot-Trites, M., Zappa-Hollman, S. and Spiliotopoulos, V. (2018) Foreign language teachers' intercultural competence and legitimacy during an international teaching experience. *Study Abroad Research in Second Language Acquisition and International Education* 3 (2), 275–309.

Byram, M. (1997) *Teaching and Assessing Intercultural Communicative Competence*. Clevedon: Multilingual Matters.

Carroll, J. (1967) Foreign language proficiency levels attained by language majors near graduation from college. *Foreign Language Annals* 1, 131–151.

Council of Europe (2018) *Reference Framework of Competences for Democratic Culture.* Strasbourg: Council of Europe.

Craig, I. (2016) Overseas sojourning as a socioeconomic and cultural development strategy: A context study of the University of the West Indies. *Study Abroad Research in Second Language Acquisition and International Education* 1 (2), 277–304.

Deardorff, D.K. (2008) Intercultural competence: A definition, model, and implications for education abroad. In V. Savicki (ed.) *Developing Intercultural Competence and Transformation: Theory, Research, and Application in International Education* (pp. 32–52). Sterling, VA: Stylus.

Dervin, F. (2016) *Interculturality in Education. A Theoretical and Methodological Toolbox.* Abingdon: Palgrave Macmillan.

Dervin, F. and Gross, Z. (2016) *Intercultural Competence in Education. Alternative Approaches for Different Times.* Abingdon: Palgrave Macmillan.

Devlin, A.M. (2014) *The Impact of Study Abroad on the Acquisition of Sociopragmatic Variation Patterns. The Case of Non-native Speaker English Teachers.* Frankfurt am Main: Peter Lang.

Dewey, D., Ring, S., Gardner, D. and Belnap, R. (2013) Social network formation and development during study abroad in the Middle East. *System* 41, 269–282.

Ellis, N. (1998) Emergentism, connectionism and language learning. *Language Learning* 48, 631–664.

Freed, B. (1995a) *Second Language Acquisition in a Study Abroad Context.* Amsterdam/Philadelphia, PA: Benjamins.

Freed, B. (1995b) Language learning and study abroad. In B. Freed (ed.) *Second Language Acquisition in a Study Abroad Context* (pp. 3–33). Amsterdam/Philadelphia, PA: Benjamins.

Grimes-MacLellan, D. (2017) Challenges for study abroad in contemporary Japan. *Study Abroad Research in Second Language Acquisition and International Education* 2 (2), 147–174.

Hammer, M.R. (2012) The intercultural development inventory: A new frontier in assessment and development of intercultural competence. In M. Vande Berg, R.M. Paige and K.H. Lou (eds) *Student Learning Abroad: What Our Students are Learning, What They're Not and What We Can Do about It* (pp. 115–136). Sterling, VA: Stylus.

Holliday, A. (2011) *Intercultural Communication and Ideology.* London: Sage.

Holliday, A. (2013) *Understanding Intercultural Communication: Negotiating a Grammar of Culture.* London: Routledge.

Howard, M. (2005) Second language acquisition in a study abroad context: A comparative investigation of the effects of study abroad and foreign language instruction on the L2 learner's grammatical development. In A. Housen and M. Pierrard (eds) *Investigations in Instructed Second Language Acquisition* (pp. 495–530). Berlin: Mouton deGruyter.

Howard, M. (2011) Input perspectives on the role of learning context in second language acquisition. *International Review of Applied Linguistics* 49 (2), 71–82.

Howard, M. (in press) Sur le rôle de l'input dans l'enseignement des langues secondes: perspectives acquisitionnistes. In M. Watorek, R. Rast and A. Arslangul (eds) *Dialogue entre Acquisition et Didactique des Langues.* Paris: Presses de l'INACLO.

Howard, M. and Schwieter, J. (2018) The development of a second language grammar during study abroad. In C. Sanz and A. Morales-Front (eds) *The Routledge Handbook of Study Abroad* (pp. 135–148). London: Routledge.

Jackson, J. (2017) The personal, linguistic, and intercultural development of Chinese sojourners in an English-speaking country: The impact of language attitudes, motivation, and agency. *Study Abroad Research in Second Language Acquisition and International Education* 2 (1), 80–106.

Jackson, J. and Oguro, S. (2018) *Intercultural Interventions in Study Abroad*. New York: Routledge.

Kinginger, C. (2008) Language learning in study abroad: Case studies of Americans in France. *The Modern Language Journal* 92, 1–124 [Monograph Series].

Kinginger, C. (2009) *Language Learning and Study Abroad: A Critical Reading of Research*. Basingstoke: Palgrave Macmillan.

Li, Y. and Dervin, F. (2018) The Beijing-Helsinki model of interculturality: Applications for study abroad. Presentation at COST Action 15130 Workshop, Study Abroad Research in European Perspective, Lisbon, September.

Long, M. (1985) Input, interaction and second language acquisition. *Annals of the Academy of Sciences* 379, 259–278.

Marriott, H. (1995) The acquisition of politeness patterns by exchange students in Japan. In B. Freed (ed.) *Second Language Acquisition in a Study Abroad Context* (pp. 197–224). Amsterdam/Philadelphia, PA: Benjamins.

Mitchell, R., Tracy-Ventura, N. and McManus, K. (2017) *Anglophone Students Abroad. Identity, Social Relationships and Language Learning*. London: Routledge.

Patron, M.-C. (2007) *Culture and Identity in Study Abroad Contexts: After Australia, French without France*. Frankfurt am Main: Peter Lang.

Plews, J. and Jackson, J. (2017) Study abroad to, from and within Asia. Special issue of *Study Abroad Research in Second Language Acquisition and International Education* 2 (2), 137–294.

UNESCO (2017) *UNESCO Survey on Intercultural Dialogue*. Paris: UNESCO.

Wilkinson, S. (1998) On the nature of immersion during study abroad: Some participant perspectives. *Frontiers: The Interdisciplinary Journal of Study Abroad* 4 (2), 121–138.

Yang, P. (2016) *Intercultural Mobility and Educational Desire. Chinese Foreign Talent Students in Singapore*. Abingdon: Palgrave Macmillan.

2 'Cantonese is My Own Eyes and English is Just My Glasses': The Evolving Language and Intercultural Attitudes of a Chinese Study Abroad Student

Jane Jackson

Introduction

In the past decade, we have witnessed a steady rise in the number of qualitative and mixed-method studies that are helping us to better understand what actually happens when study abroad (SA) students are in the host country (Coleman, 2013; Jackson, 2018). With the social turn in applied linguistics (Block, 2007; Kinginger, 2013), more and more SA researchers have been scrutinising the affective variables (e.g. emotions, attitudes, feelings, beliefs) that can influence the way second language (L2) sojourns unfold (e.g. Benson *et al.*, 2013; Jackson, 2018; Jackson & Schwieter, in press). This work is providing much-needed direction for pedagogical interventions in SA (Jackson & Oguro, 2018).

In particular, our field is benefiting from case studies that vividly illustrate the developmental trajectories of students in various SA programmes and contexts. Narrativised accounts have centred on the L2 learning of American students in France (e.g. Kinginger, 2004, 2008; Wolcott, 2013), the European Region Action Scheme for the Mobility of University Students (Erasmus) sojourners in European countries (e.g. Murphy-Lejeune, 2002), American learners of Russian in Russia (e.g. Zaykovskaya *et al.*, 2017), Asian students in English-speaking countries (e.g. Barkhuizen, 2017; Jackson, 2008, 2010, 2013, 2016) and American students in China (e.g. Diao, 2017), among others. These studies offer valuable insight into the affective and environmental variables that can lead to divergent sojourn outcomes.

This chapter presents a case study of Zoe (a pseudonym), an undergraduate from Hong Kong who participated in a semester-long international exchange programme in New Zealand. The data for her case were extracted from a project that investigated the language and intercultural development of students from a Hong Kong university who joined an international exchange programme in Australasia. Zoe's case was selected for this chapter as her data were rich in detail, offering insight into the internal and external elements that can influence L2/intercultural development. The analysis of her journey identified many 'missed opportunities'.

Literature Review

Before tracing Zoe's language and intercultural development, the literature review briefly discusses the theoretical constructs that were salient in her case: language and intercultural attitudes; intercultural competence development; motivation, investment and imagined selves; self-efficacy, self-confidence and willingness to communicate (WTC).

Language attitudes

A number of SA researchers have found that language attitudes may bring about differing degrees of L2 attainment (Jackson, 2017; Kinginger, 2009, 2013). The construct 'language attitudes' refers to the feelings or emotions that people have about their own language variety or the language varieties of others (Garrett, 2010). These learned inclinations are affected by an individual's language experiences and socialisation within particular linguistic, cultural and sociopolitical environments. Language attitudes may range from very favourable to highly unfavourable. To confound matters, within a specific context or language situation, L2 learners may harbour both positive and negative feelings about a language or elements of the language (e.g. accents) (Baker, 1992; Garrett, 2010).

Conscious or unconscious language attitudes can influence students' drive to learn/use their L2 (e.g. Jackson & Schwieter, in press; Wanner, 2009; Yashima *et al.*, 2004). Positive perceptions of the host language and culture, for example, may prompt students to initiate conversations with host nationals, while negative attitudes may reduce their willingness to use their L2 and engage in intercultural dialogue (Isabelli-García, 2006; Jackson, 2017).

Intercultural attitudes and intercultural competence development

Language attitudes are closely associated with the construct 'intercultural attitudes'. In Byram's (1997) model of intercultural competence, the notion of 'intercultural attitudes' (*savoir être*) includes 'curiosity and openness, readiness to suspend disbelief about others' cultures and belief about one's own intercultural attitudes' (Byram *et al.*, 2002: 12). Deardorff's (2008) process model of intercultural competence and Hammer's (2012, 2015) intercultural development continuum (IDC), a modified version of Bennett's (1993) developmental model of intercultural sensitivity, also posit that intercultural attitudes are central to the development of interculturality.

In the IDC, intercultural competence is defined as 'the capability to shift cultural perspective and appropriately adapt behavior to cultural difference and commonalities' (Hammer, 2013: 26). This developmental model 'describes a set of orientations toward cultural difference and commonality that are arrayed along a continuum from the more monocultural mindsets of Denial and Polarization through the transitional orientation of Minimization to the intercultural or global mindsets of Acceptance and Adaptation' (Hammer, 2012: 12). In this model, Denial describes a world view that simplifies and/or avoids cultural difference. Individuals in this ethnocentric orientation usually have had very limited intercultural experience and show little interest in learning about other 'ways of being'. Polarisation: Defence/Reversal refers to a judgmental mindset that views cultural differences in terms of 'us vs. them'. In Defence, 'us' (e.g. one's cultural group) is deemed superior and there is little, if any, recognition of limitations; in Reversal (R), 'them' is considered superior, that is, another cultural group is exalted and one's own cultural group is denigrated. Minimisation (M) is a transitional world view that emphasises cultural commonality and universal values. With limited cultural self-awareness, individuals in this transitional orientation may not be aware of or pay sufficient attention to deeper-level cultural differences (e.g. sociopragmatic norms of politeness, values). Acceptance characterises a world view that can understand and appreciate complex cultural differences, while Adaptation refers to the stage in which individuals have the capacity to modify their behaviour so that it is appropriate and authentic in a particular cultural context or situation.

If student sojourners possess a positive, open mindset and are genuinely interested in their new surroundings and the people they encounter, they are believed to be in a better position to take advantage of intercultural opportunities that arise (Hammer, 2012; Jackson, 2018). More engaged in the host environment, they are apt to experience more growth in language awareness and intercultural sensitivity than students who possess a rigid, ethnocentric mindset and avoid intercultural interactions. Accordingly, interculturalists argue that it is important for SA researchers to pay attention to the language and intercultural attitudes of L2 sojourners, including pre-sojourn dispositions (Deardorff, 2008; Jackson, 2018). SA scholars also point to the need to raise awareness of these elements in pedagogical interventions (Jackson, 2018; Jackson & Oguro, 2018).

Motivation, investment and imagined selves

Within the context of applied linguistics, motivation generally refers to a psychological trait or internal process that drives people to accomplish a language-related goal (e.g. enhanced speaking skills) (Dörnyei & Ushioda, 2013). In relation to language learning, Ellis (1997: 75) defines motivation as 'the attitudes and affective states that influence the degree of effort that learners make to learn an L2'. In SA contexts, motivation is sometimes referred to as expectations, drives, motives, reasons and/or aspirations (Kinginger, 2009; Krzaklewska, 2008).

Psycholinguists maintain that motivation can play a pivotal role in language and intercultural development, influencing the depth of investment, persistence and, ultimately, learning outcomes (Dörnyei *et al.*, 2015; Ginsberg & Wlodkowski, 2015; Jackson, 2017). Studies of language learners have identified several types of motivation, including an instrumental orientation (e.g. the learning of a language to gain admission to a prestigious university abroad) and an integrative orientation (e.g. the enhancement of intercultural communication skills in an L2 to become close to host nationals who speak that language) (Gardner, 1985, 2010; Gregersen & MacIntyre, 2014).

Self-determination research has categorised motivation as intrinsic (e.g. the desire to learn a language because it is pleasurable) or extrinsic (e.g. the learning of an L2 to accrue certain rewards such as admission to an international exchange programme) (Gardner, 2010; Ryan & Deci, 2002; Ushioda, 2014). Building on this notion, Dörnyei's (2009) L2 Motivational Self System raises awareness of learner-specific elements (e.g. emotional state, proficiency level, personality traits, cognitive ability, self-identities) and learning situational factors (e.g. institutional culture, sociopolitical environment, instructor) that can influence an individual's language (and intercultural) learning motivation and shift over time.

Extending the work of social theorist Pierre Bourdieu (1991), Norton (2001, 2013) employs the construct of investment to acknowledge the historically and socially constructed connection that learners have with their L2 and their sometimes limited motivation to master it. She argues that if individuals invest in L2 learning, they expect to acquire symbolic resources (e.g. friendship, education) and material rewards (e.g. financial gains), which will enhance their status. As the value of their cultural capital rises, learners acquire more self-confidence, set more ambitious goals for their future and reassess their imagined selves. In Norton's (2001, 2013) estimation, investment and self-identities are interrelated, with the latter depicted as dynamic, multiple and sometimes contradictory, in accord with a poststructuralist orientation.

Situating the construct of integrativeness within the context of English as a global lingua franca, Dörnyei (2005, 2009) reframed language learning motivation in terms of learner identities and 'possible/ideal selves'. Drawing on psychological theories of the self (Higgins, 1987; Markus & Nurius, 1986), the L2 Motivational Self System consists of the following dimensions: the 'Ideal L2 self', the 'Ought-to L2 self' and the 'L2 learning experience'. Dörnyei (2009: 29) defines the former as 'the L2-specific facet of one's ideal self'; the 'Ought-to L2 self' encompasses 'the attributes that one believes one ought to possess (i.e. various duties, obligations, or responsibilities) in order to avoid possible negative outcomes'. The 'L2 learning experience' refers to 'situation-specific motives related to the immediate learning environment and experience' (Dörnyei, 2009: 29). L2 learning motivation is thought to be driven by the desire to reduce the gap between one's actual self and ideal possible selves (e.g. the wish to become more fluent in an L2 and/or more interculturally competent).

This conceptual model recognises the socially situated, fluid nature of motivation, that is, an individual's degree of investment and type of language learning motivation may change over time due to a range of internal and external elements (Dörnyei et al., 2015; Ushioda, 2014). In the home environment, for instance, an individual's motivation to master an L2 may strengthen after gaining admission to an internship programme in a country where that language is widely used in daily life. Conversely, an L2 learner's desire to become more proficient in the language may wane if examination results are discouraging.

While it is often taken for granted that L2 students who join an SA programme will possess a strong desire to take advantage of affordances in the host community, for a variety of affective and environmental reasons (e.g. unequal relations of power between L2 speakers and first language [L1] host nationals), they may not do so; newcomers may gain much less exposure to the host language and local 'ways of being' than anticipated (Coleman, 2013; Jackson, 2018).

Self-efficacy, self-confidence and willingness to communicate

In addition to motivation, investment and other identity-related issues, the language and intercultural learning of student sojourners may be affected by their degree of self-efficacy and self-confidence. Self-efficacy refers to 'individuals' beliefs about their capabilities to perform well' (Graham & Weiner, 1995: 74). Bandura (1994) discovered that people who possess a high degree of self-efficacy approach difficulties with a positive mindset, which facilitates their learning. In contrast, individuals who have a low self-efficacy tend to perceive challenges as overly threatening. Doubting their ability to succeed, they may withdraw, reducing opportunities for learning and personal growth.

Linking this construct to motivation in L2 learning and use, Ehrman (1996: 144) found that 'enhanced self-efficacy – that is, more expectations of good results – tends to increase motivation. It also increases willingness to take risks'. After reviewing L2 motivation studies, Mercer and Williams (2014: 182) concluded that 'having a positive sense of self, irrespective of how that is defined, is invaluable for successful learning in terms of reducing anxiety, enhancing motivation, developing persistence and promoting autonomy, self-regulation and an effective, flexible use of strategies'. To develop constructive intercultural relationships through the use of an L2, individuals must have enough self-confidence and self-efficacy beliefs to initiate and sustain intercultural interactions in that language (Allen, 2010; Mills, 2014).

SLA research also suggests that self-efficacy beliefs are closely associated with an individual's degree of investment in language learning and the WTC in that language. MacIntyre *et al.* (1998: 547) define the latter as a person's 'readiness to enter into discourse at a particular time with a specific person or persons, using a L2'. Student sojourners may possess a high level of WTC in their L2 in the host environment and expect to greatly enhance their language proficiency and intercultural competence; however, for multiple reasons, they may not initiate or sustain intercultural interactions in their L2. In addition to internal factors (e.g. personality, anxiety, low self-efficacy, L2 and intercultural attitudes), external elements (e.g. low host receptivity, limited access to the host community) can affect the use of the host language and stymy or enhance L2/intercultural learning (Gregersen & MacIntyre, 2014; Sampasivam & Clément, 2014).

All of these elements were taken into account when reviewing the developmental trajectories of the international exchange students who took part in my investigation, including the female participant whose journey is featured in this chapter.

Research Design

The main study employed a longitudinal, mixed-method design, with both quantitative and qualitative data collected from Hong Kong university students who took part in a semester-long international exchange programme in Australasia in the 2016–2017 academic year. Their journeys were tracked from April 2016 (in Hong Kong) through their sojourn in Australia or New Zealand (July–November), until at least six months after their return home.

Method

Participants

Forty-four Australasia-bound students from a bilingual (Chinese–English) university in Hong Kong took part in the main study. All participants were ethnic Chinese students with an upper intermediate to advanced level of proficiency in English (an average score of 7.2 on the International English Language Testing System [IELTS]); all participants had taken some English-medium content courses at their home university. From this cohort, 10 individuals (4 males and 6 females) volunteered to serve as focal case participants: 7 were from the business administration faculty, 2 from the social science faculty and 1 from the Faculty of Arts. Similar to the full cohort, most of the case participants were in their third year of a four-year degree programme. Only one had previous SA experience (a short-term language enhancement programme).

Data collection

In April 2016, at a pre-departure session organised by the Office of Academic Links in the home university, the Australasia-bound students were invited to complete a pre-sojourn questionnaire that gathered demographic information and details about such aspects as: sojourn aims, expectations and concerns; L2 proficiency/use, self-identities; social networks and intercultural competence. Among the survey respondents, ten indicated a willingness to be interviewed and all of them were invited to join the study as case participants.

In addition to the pre-sojourn questionnaire, the case participants shared their views in individual, semi-structured pre-sojourn interviews with a bilingual research assistant (RA) in Cantonese, English or Putonghua (Mandarin), depending on their choice. In these sessions, which lasted 85 minutes on average, they were asked to provide additional details about their impending sojourn. To supplement these data and provide a pre-sojourn measure of their intercultural competence, they completed the Intercultural Development Inventory (IDI) v.3 (Hammer, 2015). This cross-culturally validated psychometric instrument, which consists of 50 statements, measures the orientations that are described in the IDC (Hammer, 2009a, 2009b, 2012) that was described earlier.

While abroad, the case participants responded to monthly email prompts and were interviewed on Skype to provide additional information about their L2/intercultural learning in sessions that lasted around 50 minutes, on average. Photo elicitation was also employed to develop more insight into their international experience. To this end, the case participants were asked to select and describe photos of their sojourn that were significant to them.

Immediately after their semester abroad, all of the students in the main study were asked to complete a questionnaire that solicited information about their sojourn learning and experiences in the host country. Many items were similar to those in the pre-sojourn questionnaire to facilitate a comparison of responses. The case participants also completed the IDI and participated in individual semi-structured interviews to gain more understanding of their sojourn/re-entry. These in-depth sessions, which included photo elicitation, lasted approximately 117 minutes, on average. As in the pre-sojourn phase, these individual sessions were conducted in their L1 or English, depending on their preference.

Six or seven months after their return to Hong Kong, the case participants were again interviewed to gain insight into the longer-term impact of their sojourn experience. These sessions lasted approximately 100 minutes, on average. At this time, the IDI was also administered for the third and final time.

Data analysis

The pre- and post-questionnaire data were processed using SPSS (descriptive statistics), while the IDIs were sent to IDI, LLC for processing (https://idiinventory.com/). The analysis of the IDI reports provided an indication of each case participant's actual and perceived levels of intercultural sensitivity before and after the sojourn, and supplemented the qualitative data.

As soon as the qualitative data were collected (e.g. interview transcripts, email responses), they were entered into an NVivo 11 Pro database and subjected to open, thematic coding (Bazeley & Jackson, 2013; Edhlund & McDougall, 2013; Grbich, 2013). I devised codes to reflect what I saw in the data rather than limit myself to preconceived ideas (Bazeley, 2013). The coded qualitative data were then triangulated with the quantitative measures (e.g. IDI results). In addition to full-group profiles, this process facilitated the construction of narrativised accounts of each case participant's journey. Cross-case comparisons helped to identify elements that led to differing paths and outcomes.

Zoe's Journey

To gain a deeper understanding of the elements that can influence the developmental trajectories of student sojourners, the remainder of this chapter centres on the journey of Zoe, a female case participant who provided a detailed account of her emotions and L2/intercultural experiences (e.g. L2 use, intercultural relations). I begin her story by briefly describing her pre-sojourn family life, education, language proficiency/use, social network, intercultural/international experience and career aspirations. I then reveal her aims, concerns and expectations for the semester-long sojourn in New Zealand. Next, her sojourn experiences and reintegration in Hong Kong are described and discussed, focusing on her language and intercultural goals/attitudes and shifting social network. Thus, her journey was tracked from April 2016 until July 2017.

Profile and family background

When the study got underway, Zoe was a 19-year-old anthropology major at a bilingual (Chinese–English) university in Hong Kong. Ethnically Chinese, Zoe was born and raised in the territory. While her mother was from Mainland China, her father had grown up in Hong Kong. Her parents did not speak English, and Cantonese was used at home. Neither of her parents had completed secondary school and no one in her family had SA experience.

Prior to her sojourn in New Zealand, Zoe had some travel experience, which consisted of short trips in Asia with her family. She had taken two tertiary-level anthropology courses that had included some discussion of cross-cultural communication. At this point, she had no multicultural friends and spent most of her free time with Hong Kong Chinese classmates.

Pre-sojourn

L2/intercultural attitudes and ability

In the pre-sojourn questionnaire, Zoe revealed that she spoke three languages: Cantonese (her L1), English and Putonghua (Mandarin). She began studying English as an additional language in primary school and attended an English-medium secondary school. At university, her anthropology courses were in English or a mixture of Cantonese and English; Zoe had also taken some general education courses in her L1. Shortly before going abroad, she scored 7 on the IELTS (corresponding to 94–101 in the test of English as a foreign language [TOEFL]) (ETS, 2017). In the pre-sojourn questionnaire, using a 5-point Likert scale (1 = poor to 5 = excellent), she rated her English language proficiency as 'very good' (4). She perceived her reading skills in English to be 'excellent', and her listening and writing skills to be 'very good'. Least confident in her speaking ability in English, she rated it as 'good'.

Zoe offered insight into her language use and language/intercultural attitudes in an interview in Cantonese that lasted 64 minutes. Among the three languages she spoke, she felt closest to her L1. With regard to her feelings and perceptions of English, she made a clear distinction between 'academic English' and 'informal, social English'. She was familiar with academic discourse but stressed that she had little experience with using the language in social situations. She largely viewed English as a necessary tool for academic success and had very little confidence in her ability to engage in informal intercultural interactions in the language. In her interview, she discussed her use of English and the desire to enhance her intercultural communication skills through SA:

> Since I grew up in Hong Kong, I learnt mostly formal English and rarely use it in daily life conversations. I want to learn daily life English so when I come back I can communicate better with foreigners [...] My language is a failure. The English I learnt is pretty academic. When it comes to daily life conversations, I have a problem. In Hong Kong, I don't often communicate with foreigners. (Pre-SA interview, 16 May 2016)

At this juncture, Zoe did not use English with 'foreigners' and characterised her 'social English' as a 'failure'. While her home university had more than 1000 inbound international exchange students, including some who attended courses with her, Zoe did not interact with them in or outside of class. This may explain why she rated her intercultural competence much lower than her overall English language proficiency. Using a 5-point Likert scale, ranging from 'poor' to 'excellent', she rated her intercultural communication skills and degree of openness to people from other cultural backgrounds as 'fair' (2). Interestingly, in her interview she expressed the desire to 'communicate better with foreigners'. She expected New Zealanders to be welcoming and hoped to enhance her language and intercultural communication competence while in the host environment.

Pre-SA IDI profile

Similar to the other case participants, Zoe completed the IDI before going abroad. In this instrument, the Perceived Orientation (PO) indicates where an individual places him or herself along the IDC (either Denial, Polarisation [Defence/Reversal], Minimisation, Acceptance or Adaptation) (Hammer, 2009a, 2009b, 2012, 2013). Zoe's pre-sojourn PO was 121.09, in the middle of the Acceptance range, indicating that she believed herself to be very interculturally competent.

The Developmental Orientation (DO) provides an indication of an individual's 'primary orientation toward cultural differences and commonalities along the continuum *as assessed by the IDI*' (Hammer, 2009b: 5). The DO is the perspective that the individual is most apt to draw on in intercultural encounters. Similar to the PO, the DO can be Denial, Polarisation (Defence/Reversal), Minimisation, Acceptance or Adaptation (Hammer, 2009b: 5). Zoe's pre-sojourn DO was 91.64, in the first half of Minimisation, the transitional phase.

The Orientation Gap (OG) is the difference between the PO and the DO. According to Hammer (2009b), a difference of seven points or more indicates a meaningful difference. In Zoe's case, her pre-sojourn OG was 29.45, signifying a great overestimation of her intercultural competence, similar to her peers.

The IDI profile also provides an indication of what Hammer (2009a: 5) refers to as Trailing Orientations (TO), 'orientations that are "in back of" an individual's DO on the intercultural continuum "that are not resolved"'. When embroiled in an intercultural conflict, for example, trailing issues may pull individuals back from their DO for coping with cultural difference. The analysis of the TO indicated that Zoe's world views in relation to Denial and Defence were in transition. Leading Orientations (LO) indicates the orientations immediately 'in front of' the individual's primary (developmental) orientation. As her DO on entry was Minimisation, her LO were Acceptance through Adaptation.

The IDC also provides an indication of the respondent's 'sense of disconnection or detachment' from his or her cultural group. Scores of less than 4.00 indicate that an individual is not 'resolved' and may be experiencing a lack of involvement in core aspects of being a member of a cultural community (Hammer, 2009a). Zoe's pre-sojourn cultural disengagement score was 4.80 out of 5.00, indicating that she felt connected to her cultural group, which she identified as Hong Kong Chinese.

Sojourn aims, expectations and concerns

Before traveling to New Zealand, Zoe offered a window into her sojourn goals, expectations and concerns in her pre-sojourn questionnaire and interview. She also offered to share what she had jotted down in her personal diary. To keep herself on track, Zoe planned to periodically revisit the following list while in the host environment:

Must do's in New Zealand

(1) Travel!!!!!!
(2) Skydive
(3) Camping (star-gazing)
(4) Farm visit
(5) Try local food (kiwis & wine)
(6) Take a course not offered in the home university
(7) Volunteer work
(8) Participate at least once in a social event
(9) Reading for pleasure
(10) Lying on the grass doing nothing to think about what I would like to be in the future

(Pre-sojourn diary)

Nearly all of the items were associated with self-development (e.g. volunteerism, becoming more open) and personal pursuits (e.g. having fun, adventure) rather than academic or professional advancement. In the pre-sojourn questionnaire, using a Likert scale, whereby 1 = 'not at all important' to 5 = 'extremely important', respondents were asked to rate common sojourn aims in relation to their impending international educational experience. They could also add items to the list. Zoe selected the following as most important for her personally:

- to become mature and independent;
- to travel and see many new places;
- to experience life in another culture;
- to increase my ability to cope with new situations;
- to broaden myself.

While academic, language and intercultural communication goals were on the list, none was selected by Zoe as 'extremely important'. Her top aims centred on personal development and enjoyment, offering an image of her idealised sense of self. In the questionnaire, she was also asked who she expected to spend most of her time with abroad (students from her ethnic group, local students from the host culture, international students from other cultures or on her own). Different from most of the case participants, she chose the last option.

In her pre-sojourn interview, which took place at her home university, Zoe spoke about sojourn aims and expectations that differed from what she had mentioned earlier. In keeping with a Minimisation perspective, she said that she would like to interact with people in New Zealand who have a different cultural background from her in order 'to find out our similarities'. She expected host nationals to be friendly, and planned to 'talk to people proactively in English'. She reasoned that intercultural experience would help her to become more open-minded: 'With more experience I'll be willing to accept other things'. Her WTC in English appeared to be high; however, on her home campus she made no effort to gain intercultural experience or use English in informal situations. As Zoe had previously indicated that she planned to spend much of her sojourn alone, her degree of commitment to these interactive goals seemed doubtful. Early in the study, contradictions in her statements and actions raised questions about her investment in language and intercultural learning and WTC in English, especially in social situations.

Level of preparedness and sojourn concerns

In the pre-sojourn questionnaire, the respondents were asked how well prepared they were for the sojourn, using a 4-point Likert scale: 'very well prepared', 'well prepared', 'somewhat prepared' and 'not prepared'. Zoe selected 'somewhat prepared', indicating that she was not very confident about her readiness. The respondents were also provided with a list of challenges that student sojourners may encounter while studying abroad and asked to select the three items that they believed would be the most challenging for them personally. They were also invited to add any items that did not appear on the list. Zoe identified the following as the top three challenges she expected to face:

- interacting with people from other cultures;
- unpredictable situations;
- racial discrimination.

In contrast, most of her peers cited 'homesickness' and 'class participation' among their top three concerns. While Zoe did not indicate that a 'language barrier' would be challenging for her, the linguistic element is related to the items she selected, especially the first one.

Sojourn

In mid-July 2016, Zoe travelled to New Zealand with several students from her home university to begin her semester-long international exchange programme. While abroad, she responded in English to monthly email prompts that elicited information about her language use/attitudes, intercultural interactions, adjustment and self-identities. On Skype, she was also interviewed by an RA in the middle and near the end of her stay to gain more insight into her sojourn life. The first Skype session took place on 4 October 2016 and lasted 37 minutes; the second one was conducted on 18 November 2016 and lasted 68 minutes. During the sojourn, Zoe also shared and discussed digital images of sojourn experiences that were especially meaningful to her.

A promising start

Similar to her Hong Kong peers who had travelled to the same host institution, Zoe opted to live in a hall of residence. She had her own room with six 'floor mates' – two local students and four international exchange students from Korea and India. In the first week, Zoe attended the orientation for international students that was arranged by her host university and joined the 'Study Abroad Network' (SAN). In the mid-sojourn interview, she described the organisation and its activities: 'SAN is a group of local students who guide the international students on trips and tours that usually last two or three days. I went to all of them' (4 October 2016).

As an anthropology major, Zoe was especially keen to learn more about the indigenous culture of New Zealand; and so, she enrolled in a course on Maori culture and joined excursions to cultural sites. In her first email response, she wrote: 'I try to clarify my deep-rooted misunderstandings on other cultures. What I find inadequate in me is all I know is just very little. I still have more and more to hear and learn about'. By the time she wrote her second email, she believed that her grasp of the local culture was being enhanced through the Maori course and SAN excursions. In a very positive, optimistic tone, she wrote: 'My under-standing of the host culture has improved. I got in touch with some local people [...] I am taking courses about New Zealand history, culture and performing arts, and I've joined many cultural activities and tours'.

Several weeks later, in her first Skype interview, she still appeared to be in a very positive frame of mind as she described her smooth adjust-ment to the host environment: 'I adapted better and faster than expected as I met many people in orientation week. The activities I joined were for international students and everyone was eager to meet new people so I quickly formed a social circle'. Zoe's comments and the choices she made suggested that her sojourn would be fruitful and provide many opportu-nities for (inter)cultural learning and the enhancement of her social skills in English. All was not as rosy as these comments suggested.

Language use, ability and attitudes

Throughout the sojourn, Zoe shared information about her language use, ability and attitudes. In her response to the first email prompt, she recounted the linguistic challenges she faced in the host environment in her daily life as well as in class. Prior to the sojourn, she had been quite confident in her academic English but had worried about social discourse. Contrary to her expectations, in an English-speaking environ-ment she felt insecure and inept when using the language in *both* aca-demic and social situations. In the following email, it was evident that her self-efficacy in English had decreased:

> I'm finding my English skills inadequate in both social and academic situ-ations. Some terms have no direct translation from Cantonese to English and it's hard to grasp the English-native way to express feelings and thoughts. This makes it difficult for me in social situations. Although I've used English as a medium of study in Hong Kong, the pace of speaking, accents, and academic terms create difficulties for me to keep up with the lectures. I have to ask for clarification and look up words in the diction-ary very often. (Email #1, 24 August 2016)

Outside of class, when interacting with Asian international students who did not speak Cantonese or Putonghua, Zoe used English as a lingua franca, which enabled her to practice using the language in social situa-tions. As the sojourn progressed, however, she also became more sensi-tive to the gap between her language proficiency and that of L1 speakers. In her second email, she cited a number of linguistic elements that still posed difficulties for her: 'To some degree, I can speak in a faster pace than before, with less hesitation. However, I still find problem of lack-ing vocabularies and expression. It's also hard to hear some foreign accents...' (16 September 2016).

When reflecting on her language attitudes in the third email (16 October 2016), she commented that the gulf between herself and English had grown smaller in an English-speaking environment: 'I feel closer to English. It's better than in Hong Kong because I have more chances to speak English and I listen to the language more'.

Near the end of the sojourn, Zoe took stock of her sojourn goals and English language proficiency. In her last sojourn email she wrote:

> My goals were to experience life, to try everything new as much as possible and to improve myself on English and academic attainment. I think to a large extent I have realized them. I think I have improved my English to some extent. I can read better, but especially speak and listen faster. However, I expected I can get much better. There is always room to improve.

She had not yet realised what Dörnyei (2009) terms her 'Ideal L2 self'. In her estimation, she had experienced gains but had expected to do better. Her social network and the choices she made in the host environment helped to explain her developmental trajectory.

Evolving social network and intercultural attitudes

In the first email response, Zoe stated that she was spending much of her free time with her Korean floor mate in addition to two of the students from her home university. Similar to many newcomers, she found it difficult to make friends with locals as their social ties were already formed; her lack of self-confidence and self-efficacy in English inhibited her interactions with them. By the following month, her social network largely consisted of students from Hong Kong and other parts of Asia.

> My friendship circles are mainly Asians. They include my dorm mates, people from Hong Kong, people I met myself in events, as well as people introduced to me by my friends. I spend most of my time with international students, for example, my Korean and Indian dorm mates, and Asian friends I met in various occasions. (Email #2, 16 September 2016)

The photo elicitation sessions provided more insight into her social network and use of English outside of class. In her first and second sojourn interviews, Zoe shared digital images that were especially meaningful to her. Most were of buildings or landscapes (e.g. her host university, her hostel [dormitory], a museum, farm, garden, night market). While she featured in some images (selfies), only one showed her with a friend (her Korean roommate who accompanied her on a SAN excursion).

In the interview that took place in mid-October, Zoe was asked how she was spending her free time and her response offered a window into her social network and language use. 'I'm closest to my floor mate from

Korea. We communicate in English. Next, I hang out most with Hong Kong students from [my home university], then international students, and local students last'. A few weeks later, in response to the third email prompt she revealed that she was spending most of her time alone, as she had anticipated prior to the sojourn. 'My friendship circle has not changed much since my arrival. I did not meet many new friends or get even closer with my existing friends. I started working on my own. More often I stay in my room or do shopping alone'. Her social network had shrunk, limiting exposure to the host language and culture.

Language, culture and sense of belonging

In an unfamiliar sociocultural environment, Zoe's identity was questioned on multiple occasions and this prompted her to think more deeply about her linguistic and cultural roots and preferred identities. In a Skype interview near the end of the sojourn, she explained:

> It's becoming clearer to me that I'm a Hong Konger. I have a strong sense that Hong Kong is my origin. And I appreciate Hong Kong culture and also the language more. I think that Cantonese is a beautiful language now [...] Not sure why this sense has become stronger. (18 November 2016)

In New Zealand she developed a much stronger sense of belonging to her homeland. Although this is not an unusual phenomenon among student sojourners, she had not expected this to happen. Zoe's connection to Cantonese and Hong Kong culture had strengthened, whereas her feelings about English appeared to have only slightly changed.

Immediate Post-sojourn

After she returned to Hong Kong in December 2016, Zoe shared her views about her international educational experience by way of the post-sojourn questionnaire, her response to the fourth email prompt and an interview that lasted 83 minutes. She also shared more images that depicted meaningful elements in her sojourn.

Perceived sojourn gains

In the post-sojourn questionnaire, Zoe was provided with a list of potential sojourn gains and asked to select the top three that applied to her. As in the pre-sojourn questionnaire, she could add any items that were not on the list. Zoe chose the following:

- increased understanding of my own culture, identities and values;
- more self-confidence, maturity and independence;
- first-hand experience with life in another culture.

She did not select language proficiency as one of her 'top gains'. While she had perceived her openness to other cultures as only 'fair' prior to going to New Zealand, she rated it as 'very good' after spending a semester abroad. Prior to the sojourn, she believed that her intercultural communication skills were only 'fair'; however, after gaining international educational experience, she perceived them to be 'good'. In her post-sojourn interview, she explained that she had had more opportunities to meet people from other cultural backgrounds and this had helped her to become more 'interculturally sensitive', even though she had spent much of her time alone or with other Hong Kongers.

Immediate post-SA IDI profile

Immediately after the sojourn, Zoe completed the IDI for a second time to provide a measure of her intercultural competence after her international educational experience. This time, her PO was 120.27 (still in Acceptance), while her DO was 87.49 (a reduction of 4.15 points but still in the first half of Minimisation, the transitional phase). She continued to significantly overestimate her intercultural competence as her OG was 33.78. As in the pre-sojourn administration, the analysis of TO revealed that her Denial and Defence world views were not fully resolved. Since her DO remained in Minimisation, her LO were still Acceptance through Adaptation. Thus, a comparison of her pre-and post-sojourn IDI profiles indicated that she had regressed slightly in terms of her intercultural competence after her stay in New Zealand. With regard to her identity, her cultural disengagement score was 4.20 out of 5.00. While reduced, it still indicated that her cultural engagement was resolved and she felt some connection or attachment to her cultural group. This was also apparent in the information she provided in her interview and email responses.

Challenges in the host environment

When asked to indicate the most challenging aspects of her exchange experience, Zoe selected 'a language barrier', 'personal safety and security' and 'unpredictable situations'. The last item was the only one that she had selected in the pre-sojourn phase. Even though she cited language as a challenge in the post-sojourn questionnaire, she rated her overall proficiency in English as 'very good'. She had become more assured of her speaking ability, but less confident in her listening skills. In her interview, she revealed that it was still difficult for her to comprehend rapid speech and she found different accents confounding. In her fourth and final email response, she offered further insight into her perception of her language and intercultural skills:

I think my English proficiency is now more comprehensive than before because I learnt more vocabulary and expressions for daily life, but I am always looking for more practice and further improvement. I believe my intercultural communication skills improved to some extent as I had more chances to communicate with people from different cultural backgrounds. It's still hard for me to hear some accents but I am more confident to communicate with foreigners than before. (16 December 2016)

Although she expressed appreciation for opportunities to engage in intercultural interactions, in the second half of her stay, she did not take full advantage of the host environment and tended to spend much of her time alone or with co-nationals. When asked to provide more details about her intercultural learning, she was very vague, suggesting that she still had limited understanding of intercultural elements, and preferred to focus on the linguistic dimension.

'Travel abroad and know yourself'

The well-worn saying 'travel abroad and know yourself' applies to many SA students, including Zoe. While in New Zealand, she became more aware of her potential and sense of self. With more self-confidence, she no longer saw herself as a 'shy person' who was incapable of social interactions in an L2.

I couldn't imagine that I could travel to a place by myself, to an environment where they speak a foreign language [...] And I really interacted with the bus drivers and the owner of the hostel where I stayed. I really liked to chat a little bit, and share. I didn't think that I could do it before. Actually, I'm not the shy person I thought I was so I think people can know more about themselves when they go to a foreign land. (Post-sojourn interview, 15 December 2016)

The above excerpt suggests that she had experienced gains in self-confidence and self-efficacy in relation to her ability and use of English in social situations. In her last email response, she stated that she was using more English in Hong Kong than she had before the sojourn, especially through code-mixing. 'Most of the time I do not speak in English in complete sentences but keep using some terms in English with my friends. I use English for texting my friends. The frequency to use English terms in a sentence increased…'. She also added that she was sometimes thinking in English and this impacted her Cantonese. 'It takes more time for me to translate an English expression into Cantonese in my mind when I talk with my parents now'.

Language and intercultural attitudes

Post-sojourn, Zoe felt more confident using English in social situations and believed that she was 'getting closer' to the language. She still felt much more attached to Cantonese, noting that she could express her ideas and emotions more freely in her L1.

> I think I'm getting closer to English. It doesn't make me feel uncomfortable […] Now that I'm back, I feel like it was quite amazing that I was able to handle everything on my own in English […] I feel like Cantonese is really my language. I can express 100% of what I want to say. And I feel like finally I am in an environment where I share the same things as my friends, my family […] I feel like Cantonese is really lively. It can describe very complicated situations. (Post-sojourn interview, 15 December 2016)

Compared with Cantonese, she did not have the same facility in English and this created a barrier between her and the language. Moreover, she associated Cantonese with her family and friends, whereas English was still primarily for academic discourse or interactions with 'foreigners'. In this interview, she contrasted her feelings about the two languages.

> Cantonese is my own eyes and English is just my glasses. When I put them on, I can see the world […] In New Zealand, I needed to use English every day so I always put on my glasses every day. The glasses are part of me. I still put them on if I need them […] Learning another language is just like putting on contact lenses. (Post-sojourn interview, 15 December 2016)

It is evident from her metaphor and other comments that she still viewed English largely from an instrumental perspective (e.g. as a communication tool to use when needed). After sojourning in the target speech community, some L2 sojourners are convinced that the host language has become an integral part of themselves; however, this did not happen with Zoe.

Early in the sojourn, Zoe used English as a lingua franca with international exchange students who did not speak Cantonese. By the end of her stay, however, she was spending much of her free time alone or engaged in daily communications with Hong Kong friends in New Zealand or back home (via online interactions). The digital images that she chose to share were generally in accord with what she divulged in her interview. They illustrated a night out at a restaurant with Asian friends, a 'Māori performing arts' lecture, an anthropology lecture, a Thai festival and a farewell ceremony for international students. The only image that showed her with friends was the meal that she shared with Hong Kong sojourners and her Korean roommate.

Re-entry and reintegration

Whereas some of the case participants had found it difficult to reintegrate into Hong Kong life, Zoe's re-entry was less troublesome. In her last email, she wrote: 'I am glad that I kept in close contact with family and friends when I was abroad so that it seems our connection has never been stopped, which also help my reintegration'. While frequent contact with home provided socio-emotional support for her while she was in New Zealand and eased her readjustment to Hong Kong, it also meant she had not been fully immersed in the host environment.

The case participants who were more engaged in the host community became more confident in their social English skills; these sojourners believed that they had moved closer to their 'Ideal L2 self' (Dörnyei, 2009) and some even maintained that they had acquired a 'global self' while abroad. After they returned to Hong Kong, these individuals made an effort to seek out opportunities to use English and continued to display more interest in international affairs. In contrast, Zoe appeared to be less invested in mastering social English skills and nurturing a global persona. Interestingly, her time abroad appeared to have strengthened her regional identity, which was tightly bound to her L1 and cultural roots. In the post-sojourn questionnaire, she wrote: 'While in New Zealand, it became clearer to me that I am a Hong Konger. I have a strong sense that Hong Kong is my origin and appreciate more the culture and language of Hong Kong'.

Zoe's lack of deep investment in language and intercultural learning was again apparent in her post-sojourn interview when she candidly disclosed that her social circle had returned to its original form as she no longer had the 'need' to develop multicultural relationships: 'In my home university my identity is different. I'm no longer an exchange student and I have my own local social circle. My need to make new friends with people from different cultures has really dropped a lot'.

Interestingly, in her last email, Zoe expressed the desire to see more of the world and experience cultural diversity. 'I am planning to go on a working holiday before I find a long-term job. I'd like to explore more about the world and different cultures after this exchange experience'. In her mind, intercultural elements appeared to be associated with distant lands and, similar to the pre-sojourn phase, Zoe made little effort to engage in intercultural L2 interactions on her own campus before or after the sojourn.

Post-Post Sojourn (Seven Months after Re-entry)

To gain a sense of the longer-term influence of the sojourn, Zoe was reinterviewed in July 2017 by an RA, around seven months after her return to Hong Kong. This session, which was conducted in English, lasted 105 minutes. Zoe also completed the IDI to provide an additional measure of her intercultural competence at this stage.

Post-post-SA IDI profile

In the third administration of the IDI, her PO was 124.53 (still in Acceptance); her DO was 96.10 (8.61 points greater than the previous administration but still in the first half of Minimisation, the transitional phase). Although her OG was reduced to 28.42, this score indicated that she continued to significantly overestimate her degree of intercultural competence. As in the previous administrations, the analysis of TO revealed that her Denial and Defence world views were not yet fully resolved (e.g. at times, she continued to view cultural differences in terms of a binary 'us vs. them' orientation). Since her DO remained in Minimisation, her LO were still Acceptance through Adaptation. With regard to her identity, her cultural disengagement score was 4.20 out of 5.00, the same as in the previous administration.

A comparison of the three administrations of the IDI showed that although she had regressed slightly in terms of intercultural competence during her sojourn in New Zealand, after she had been back on home soil for around seven months and had had more time to process her experiences, she became more interculturally sensitive. Nonetheless, she had not yet moved into an ethnorelative or 'open mindset' stage, according to the IDC. The last administration of the IDI and the analysis of the qualitative data also indicated that Zoe felt connected to her cultural group (Hong Kong Chinese) throughout the study.

Intercultural competence development

The post-post sojourn interview shed light on Zoe's perception of her intercultural competence development. Interestingly, although she valued the chance to practice 'openness to cultures' during the sojourn, she primarily attributed growth in this area to what she had learned in her anthropology courses rather than her international experience (or reflection on it).

> Even though I learned some facts about people from other cultures and some theories, like we shouldn't be ethnocentric because every culture is the same in the sense that no one is better than the other, and I learned in my anthropology courses that we should respect each other, I needed to practice it [...] I'm not sure if study abroad helped me to become more interculturally competent because my major, anthropology, makes me more sensitive in this sense [...] I already had this sense before I went on exchange. I just had the chance to practice my openness to cultures there. (12 July 2017)

As an anthropology major, most of Zoe's courses explored the similarity and diversity of social, political, economic and religious cultural systems; none centred on intercultural communication or the practical development of intercultural communication skills. In her last interview, she displayed awareness of the importance of cultural knowledge (e.g. customs, history) and the cultivation of an open, respectful mindset to foster intercultural relations; however, she did not demonstrate a sophisticated grasp of intercultural communication skills. When invited to provide detailed examples of the strategies she used to enhance her interactions with individuals from a different cultural background, she remained vague. In line with the IDI findings, she still appeared to overestimate her level of intercultural competence. Further, she did not recognise opportunities to gain practical intercultural experience on her home campus or in the wider Hong Kong community.

L2 attitudes/use

When asked to describe her feelings about the languages she spoke, Zoe explained that she still felt much closer to her L1. While her WTC in English had strengthened, she would still not initiate interactions 'with foreigners' unless she felt the 'need' to do so and this was rare; her English language usage and degree of intercultural contact appeared to have returned to what it was prior to the sojourn. In this part of her interview, she referred to her English as 'broken', indicating a reduced level of self-efficacy and self-confidence in her oral skills, in particular.

> I still feel closest to Cantonese. It's still not a problem for me to read English. I think using English for academic discussions is fine. It's better than before I went on exchange. For daily conversations, it has gone back to how it was before I went on exchange [...] My attitude towards English has improved because before going to New Zealand, I felt like I could talk to foreign people but didn't feel like talking to them. Now, it doesn't matter if I'm talking to people who speak in English or Cantonese, I can still communicate with them. I can express what I want to express but I will still only initiate a conversation with them if I feel like I need to do so, just like talking to professors or during discussions in tutorials, but I seldom talk to people in English about gossip or news. Everyday English is missing [...] My English is still not very good. My English is broken... (12 July 2017)

Similar to the pre-sojourn phase, Zoe was asked to use a metaphor to describe her relationship with Cantonese and English, and she again returned to the glasses image to explain the reduction in her English language ability and her attachment to her L1:

> I feel like I'm more short-sighted now. I can't see as clearly with my glasses. I need to change them. I need to improve them again, find some ways to improve [...] Even though you have a pair of glasses, your eyes may become more short-sighted so you may have to change your glasses [...] When you go from a very cold place to outside in the summer your glasses get fogged up. English is like this. Because I didn't clean my

glasses, because I didn't practice, now when I put on my glasses, it's not as clear as before. I have to keep improving [...] As for Cantonese, it's still my eyes. (12 July 2017)

Throughout the study, Zoe retained an intimate connection to her L1. For her, Cantonese was an integral part of herself (e.g. like her eyes), whereas English was still somewhat removed from her (e.g. like eye glasses that she could put on when needed and then cast aside when not useful). She regretted that her proficiency in English had reverted to the pre-sojourn level as she was no longer using it in daily life. In her interview, she said:

> I think it's a bit sad that my English has gone back to the level it was before I went to New Zealand coz' I really found that there's no chance to practice English in daily conversations [...] Even if I talk to professors or TAs [Teaching Assistants] in English, I only have a few lectures each week. Most of the time, I speak Cantonese with my friends and family who don't know English [...] I really have no chance to speak English in daily conversation and seldom use it outside of class. Most of my friends are from Hong Kong so we speak in Cantonese. Even in tutorials, we speak in an academic tone but in New Zealand I used social English [...] My overall proficiency is still good because I believe that if I immerse myself in a foreign environment again, my oral skills will go back to a very good standard again. (12 July 2017)

Convinced that this attrition was due to the Hong Kong environment rather than her agency, she expressed confidence that her language proficiency, especially her oral skills, would return to 'a very good standard' in an English-speaking environment. Although she had spent much of her free time alone or with Hong Kong friends while in New Zealand, she perceived herself to have been immersed in the sojourn environment.

Social network and cultural (dis)engagement

Zoe also revealed that her social network was the same as in the pre-sojourn phase: 'Basically, I stay with the same group of friends as before my exchange experience. My stay in New Zealand was short and I didn't establish another social circle there'. Her revelation contradicted the descriptions of her social life that she had provided in the first half of her sojourn. While in the host environment, she had spent much of her time chatting with her Hong Kong friends in her L1, whether face-to-face or online. Her last comment in the following excerpt also suggests that she was not as happy or as engaged in activities in the host environment as she had indicated earlier.

I'm now closer to my friends in Hong Kong, the group I originally had connections with before going to New Zealand. Even though I had friends in New Zealand, I was still keeping in touch with my friends in Hong Kong, and we talked more than before during my time in New Zealand. On WhatsApp, I talked to my friends more often than I did in Hong Kong [...] Near the end of my exchange, I was like 'I really want to go home', and my friends were like 'I wish you could come back as soon as possible', topics like that. (12 July 2017)

In New Zealand, like many first-time sojourners, Zoe experienced life as a minority member for the first time. In an unfamiliar environment, she developed a heightened attachment to her preferred identity as a Hong Konger. While she found the host nationals friendly, it was not as easy to approach them or build relationships with them as she had expected. In her last interview, she explained why she drew closer to people who shared her cultural and linguistic roots.

When I was in New Zealand, my sense of being a Hong Konger was stronger than in Hong Kong because I was a minority there. Sometimes I couldn't express the exact meaning in English but I could express the feeling to my friends from Hong Kong. I felt like we shared the same culture so we bore the same identity. We were Hong Kong people. (12 July 2017)

Her comments were in accord with the IDI's measure of cultural (dis)engagement. Feeling like an outsider in the host environment, she preferred to interact with peers from her own ethnic group.

A Cross-Case Comparison: Unique and Common Elements in Zoe's Journey

To better understand the unique elements in Zoe's journey, it is helpful to compare her story with those of the other case participants. A cross-case analysis identified themes, similarities and differences, and contradictions in the participants' stories that might otherwise have been overlooked. In particular, this process drew attention to the role that language and intercultural attitudes and expectations can play in shaping sojourn learning and engagement (e.g. the degree of investment in the diversification of social networks and the enhancement of sociopragmatic skills in English).

Prior to the sojourn, all of the case participants used their L1 in social settings and English was largely limited to the academic arena (e.g. English-medium courses). Most had little intercultural/international experience and only one had previously studied abroad. Their social networks largely consisted of Hong Kong Chinese friends; few interacted with international exchange students on their home campus.

Prior to travelling to New Zealand or Australia, all of the case participants expressed the desire to make international friends, participate in intercultural interactions in English and move closer to their 'Ideal L2 self'. While excited about what lay ahead, Zoe expressed concern about her ability to function in the language in her social life. Her nervousness was shared by some of her peers, who also had doubts about their self-efficacy, especially in relation to their ability to use English effectively and appropriately in informal social situations. Like nearly all of the case participants, Zoe possessed a detached, instrumental orientation towards the language and felt closer to her L1.

In the host country, the case participants differed in terms of their level of engagement in the orientations and social activities organised by their host institution. Zoe initially appeared to benefit from meeting other international exchange students in the SAN excursions and in her dorm; however, she ended up spending much of her free time alone or interacting online with friends and family in Hong Kong. With advances in technology (e.g. email, social media, QQ, WhatsApp), it is now much easier for SA students to remain connected to home. Although beneficial in terms of socioemotional support, it can lessen the need for sojourners to use their L2 and take advantage of affordances in the host community.

Unmet expectations also played a role in the way the sojourns unfolded. In Zoe's case, some of her expectations were not realised and this hampered her degree of intercultural engagement. For example, she had expected it to be much easier to meet and develop relationships with host nationals, but for a variety of reasons (e.g. language barrier, well-established social networks among local students) she found it difficult to do so. This was a common experience among the case participants. In response, some focused on the cultivation of meaningful multicultural relationships with international students who had a different cultural background from them, whereas others spent most of their free time with co-nationals.

While abroad, all of the case participants demonstrated interest in the host environment, to varying degrees. Different from her peers, Zoe, an anthropology major, took a course about the local culture (e.g. Māori performing arts, history). While it enriched her cultural knowledge, it did not appear to enhance her intercultural competence. She could soak up cultural facts and still remain somewhat detached from the host environment. While the other case participants, on average, gained 2.38 points on the IDI by the end of the sojourn, Zoe's degree of intercultural competence was reduced by 4.15 points and she remained in the same phase (Minimisation) in the IDC.

After exposure to English in daily life, most of the case participants, including Zoe, felt closer to the language and believed that their language skills had been enhanced to varying degrees. Zoe stated that she had become more willing to start conversations with 'foreigners' in English while abroad; however, once she returned home, she made little effort to use the language outside of class and her social network reverted to what it was in the pre-sojourn phase. As noted by MacIntyre *et al.* (1998), WTC does not necessarily result in action. If an individual's perception of the cultural capital associated with a language decreases, the investment in L2/intercultural enhancement may also decline (Bourdieu, 1991; Norton, 2001, 2013).

Zoe's re-entry and her experiences in the post-post sojourn phase also differed from the returnees who made a stronger effort to maintain the multicultural ties that they had forged in Australasia. These individuals continued to diversify their social network and mentored inbound and outbound international exchange students. Determined to keep their 'international selves' alive and move closer to their 'Ideal L2 selves', they identified and took advantage of opportunities to use English outside of class. Accordingly, they continued to develop a tighter connection with the language. In contrast, while her language and intercultural attitudes had become more positive, Zoe still viewed English through an instrumental lens. She did not recognise linguistic or intercultural affordances in her home environment.

Summary and Conclusions

Zoe's story, and those of many of her peers, challenge idealistic notions of 'immersion' and the 'automatic personal transformation' of students who participate in an international exchange programme. While this young woman developed a more positive attitude towards English and intercultural interactions, she ended up spending most of her time alone and did not take advantage of affordances in the host country. In the immediate post-sojourn phase, she did not display a higher level of intercultural competence or investment in L2 use/learning. Six months or more after returning to Hong Kong, some of the case participants had taken concrete steps to expand their diverse social networks and gain more L2/intercultural exposure in Hong Kong. Zoe, however, did not feel the need to do so and quickly reverted to her pre-sojourn routine. Her IDI results indicate that she remained in the same transitional phase of intercultural competence development throughout the study and in the post-post sojourn phase did not appear to be deeply invested in either language or intercultural enhancement.

Her journey may have unfolded differently if she had benefited from research-based pedagogical interventions (e.g. structured reflection at strategic intervals). Regular debriefings may have kept her on track and helped her to deal with unmet expectations and barriers to participation in the host environment. An intervention may have bolstered her language and intercultural attitudes and provided the support and encouragement she needed to become more active. In an online intercultural communication course that I developed for international exchange students to take while they are abroad, mentoring encourages the participants to become more engaged and reflective in the host environment, while simultaneously learning about various dimensions of intercultural communication. The analysis of a recent offering found that the group as a whole gained nearly 12 points in DO on the IDI, significantly more than the exchange students from my university who were abroad for the same period without this intervention (Jackson, 2018). Other forms of pedagogical intervention for student sojourners are showcased in Jackson and Oguro (2018).

In Zoe's case, there are also missed opportunities in the immediate post-sojourn phase. Once she was back on home soil, the systematic 'unpacking' of her SA and re-entry experience would have prompted her to reflect more deeply on her experiences and set realistic goals for further L2/intercultural learning. As the re-entry phase is often overlooked, I developed an intercultural transitions course for SA returnees and inbound international exchange students at my institution; through reflective activities, the participants develop a deeper understanding of the dimensions of intercultural competence, critically examine their L2/intercultural experience and set attainable targets for further learning and engagement (Jackson & Oguro, 2018). Similar to the online course, an evaluation of learning outcomes indicates that the participants develop a higher level of intercultural competence and more willingness to use their L2 in intercultural interactions.

A range of internal, affective variables (e.g. language and intercultural attitudes, motivation, investment, personality, self-efficacy) and external factors (e.g. host receptivity, social activities organised by hosts, access to local communities of practice) can lead to divergent sojourn outcomes, including varying degrees of L2/intercultural competence (Jackson, 2012, 2018; Kinginger, 2009; Paige & Vande Berg, 2012). Richly detailed, longitudinal studies, with multiple types of data collected before, during and after SA, can provide direction for pre-sojourn orientations/courses and pedagogical interventions during and after an international educational experience (e.g. intercultural debriefings). Ultimately, however, it will still be up to the students to decide whether or not they take advantage of affordances.

Advantages and Limitations of Case Studies

While large-scale, quantitative studies can provide a broad picture of sojourn experience, mixed-method or qualitative investigations that track the developmental trajectories of SA students have the potential to provide deeper insight into variables that are influencing sojourn learning and intercultural engagement. When robust, SA case studies can raise awareness of issues that have been previously overlooked. Narrativised accounts can also help to demystify the findings of large-scale studies and inspire pedagogical interventions that have the potential to enrich and extend the L2/intercultural learning of student sojourners.

In particular, in-depth case studies can raise awareness of unique and common elements in SA experience. Cross-case analyses can help us to identify and make sense of differences in developmental trajectories and sojourn outcomes. SA research that relies on single pre- and post-sojourn measures may easily overlook the natural twists and turns that characterise international educational experience. In Zoe's case, multiple types of data were collected throughout her journey, including digital images, interviews, questionnaires and a diary. A systematic review of these data brought to light contradictions in her aspirations, expectations and actions, and helped to demystify the multifarious elements that influenced the way her unique story unfolded. Further, since the full impact of a sojourn may not be fully realised until many months or years, as Zoe's case suggests, it would be beneficial for our field to conduct more longitudinal studies.

Case studies are not without limitations. It is important to recognise that they are partial accounts of an international educational experience. They depend on the participants' ability to accurately recall details and may be limited by the researcher's questions or directions. Instead of relying on a single type of data collected at the end of a sojourn, the systematic collection of multiple types of data from the pre-sojourn to post-sojourn phase is essential to grasp the complexity of an SA experience. Member checks (informant feedback or respondent validation) are also important to improve the accuracy, credibility, validity and transferability (also known as applicability or internal validity) of a study. Despite limitations, I believe that cases have much to offer our field.

Acknowledgements

The study was supported by a grant from the University Mobility in Asia and the Pacific (UMAP) organization and the Faculty of Arts at the Chinese University of Hong Kong.

References

Allen, H.W. (2010) Language-learning motivation during short-term study abroad. *Foreign Language Annals* 43, 27–49.

Baker, C. (1992) *Attitudes and Languages*. Clevedon: Multilingual Matters.

Bandura, A. (1994) Self-efficacy. In V.S. Ramachaudran (ed.) *Encyclopedia of Human Behavior* (Vol. 4; pp. 71–81). New York: Academic Press.

Barkhuizen, G. (2017) Investigating multilingual identity in study abroad contexts: A short story analysis approach. *System: An International Journal of Educational Technology and Applied Linguistics* 71, 102–112.

Bazeley, P. (2013) *Qualitative Data Analysis: Practical Strategies*. London: Sage.

Bazeley, P. and Jackson, K. (2013) *Qualitative Data Analysis with NVivo* (2nd edn). Thousand Oaks, CA: Sage.

Bennett, M.J. (1993) Towards ethnorelativism: A developmental model of intercultural sensitivity. In R.M. Paige (ed.) *Education for the Intercultural Experience* (2nd edn; pp. 21–71). Yarmouth, ME: Intercultural Press.

Benson, P., Barkhuizen, G., Bodycott, P. and Brown, J. (2013) *Second Language Identity in Narratives of Study Abroad*. Basingstoke: Palgrave.

Block, D. (2007) *Second Language Identities*. London: Continuum.

Bourdieu, P. (1991) *Language and Symbolic Power*. Boston, MA: Harvard University Press.

Byram, M. (1997) *Teaching and Assessing Intercultural Communicative Competence*. Clevedon: Multilingual Matters.

Byram, M., Gribkova, B. and Starkey, H. (2002) *Developing the Intercultural Dimension in Language Teaching: A Practical Introduction for Teachers*. Strasbourg: Council of Europe.

Coleman, J.A. (2013) Researching whole people and whole lives. In C. Kinginger (ed.) *Social and Cultural Aspects of Language Learning in Study Abroad* (pp. 17–46). Amsterdam/Philadelphia, PA: Benjamins.

Deardorff, D.K. (2008) Intercultural competence: A definition, model, and implications for education abroad. In V. Savicki (ed.) *Developing Intercultural Competence and Transformation: Theory, Research, and Application in International Education* (pp. 32–52). Sterling, VA: Stylus.

Diao, W. (2017) Between the standard and non-standard: Accent and identity among transnational Mandarin speakers studying abroad in China. *System: An International Journal of Educational Technology and Applied Linguistics* 71, 87–101.

Dörnyei, Z. (2005) *The Psychology of the Language Learner: Individual Differences in Second Language Acquisition*. Mahwah, NJ: Lawrence Erlbaum Associates.

Dörnyei, Z. (2009) The L2 motivational self system. In Z. Dörnyei and E. Ushioda (eds) *Motivation, Language Identity and the L2 Self* (pp. 9–42). Bristol: Multilingual Matters.

Dörnyei, Z. and Ushioda, E. (2013) *Teaching and Researching Motivation* (2nd edn). Abingdon: Routledge.

Dörnyei, Z., MacIntyre, P. and Henry, A. (2015) Introduction: Applying complex dynamic systems principles to empirical research on L2 motivation. In Z. Dörnyei, P. MacIntyre and A. Henry (eds) *Motivational Dynamics in Language Learning* (pp. 1–7). Bristol: Multilingual Matters.

Edhlund, B. and McDougall, A. (2013) *NVivo 10 Essentials*. Stallarholmen: Form and Kunskap.

Ehrman, M.E. (1996) *Understanding Second Language Acquisition*. Oxford: Oxford University Press.

Ellis, R. (1997) *The Study of Second Language Acquisition*. Oxford: Oxford University Press.

ETS (Educational Testing Service) (2017) Compare TOEFL scores. See https://www.ets.org/toefl/institutions/scores/compare/ (accessed 10 August 2017).

Gardner, R.C. (1985) *Social Psychology and Second Language Learning: The Role of Attitudes and Motivation*. London: Edward Arnold.

Gardner, R.C. (2010) *Motivation and Second Language Acquisition: The Socio-Educational Model*. New York: Peter Lang.

Garrett, P. (2010) *Attitudes to Language*. Cambridge: Cambridge University Press.

Ginsberg, M.B. and Wlodkowski, R. (2015) Motivation and culture. In J.M. Bennett (ed.) *The Sage Handbook of Intercultural Competence* (Vol. 2; pp. 634–637). Los Angeles, CA: Sage.

Graham, S. and Weiner, B. (1995) Theories and principles of motivation. In D. Berliner and R. Calfee (eds) *Handbook of Educational Psychology* (pp. 63–84). New York: MacMillan.

Grbich, C. (2013) *Qualitative Data Analysis: An Introduction* (2nd edn). London: Sage.

Gregersen, T. and MacIntyre, P.D. (2014) *Capitalizing on Language Learners' Individuality: From Premise to Practice*. Bristol: Multilingual Matters.

Hammer, M.R. (2009a) The Intercultural Development Inventory: An approach for assessing and building intercultural competence. In M.A. Moodian (ed.) *Contemporary Leadership and Intercultural Competence: Exploring the Cross-Cultural Dynamics within Organizations* (pp. 203–217). Thousand Oaks, CA: Sage.

Hammer, M.R. (2009b) Intercultural development inventory v. 3 (IDI) education group profile, report. See http://idiinventory.com/pdf/idi_sample.pdf (accessed 6 August 2017).

Hammer, M.R. (2012) The intercultural development inventory: A new frontier in assessment and development of intercultural competence. In M. Vande Berg, R.M. Paige and K.H. Lou (eds) *Student Learning Abroad: What Our Students Are Learning, What They're Not and What We Can Do about It* (pp. 115–136). Sterling, VA: Stylus.

Hammer, M.R. (2013) *A Resource Guide for Effectively Using the Intercultural Development Inventory (IDI)*. Berlin, MD: IDI, LLC.

Hammer, M.R. (2015) Developmentally appropriate pedagogy. In J.M. Bennett (ed.) *The SAGE Encyclopedia of Intercultural Competence* (Vol. 2; pp. 483–486). Thousand Oaks, CA: Sage.

Higgins, E.T. (1987) Self-discrepancy: A theory relating self and affect. *Psychological Review* 94, 319–340.

Isabelli-García, C. (2006) Study abroad social networks, motivation, and attitudes: Implications for second language acquisition. In M.A. DuFon and E. Churchill (eds) *Language Learners in Study Abroad Contexts* (pp. 231–258). Clevedon: Multilingual Matters.

Jackson, J. (2008) *Language, Identity, and Study Abroad*. London: Equinox.

Jackson, J. (2010) *Intercultural Journeys: From Study to Residence Abroad*. Basingstoke: Palgrave Macmillan.

Jackson, J. (2012) Education abroad. In J. Jackson (ed.) *Routledge Handbook of Language and Intercultural Communication* (pp. 449–463). Abingdon: Routledge.

Jackson, J. (2013) The transformation of 'a frog in the well': A path to a more intercultural, global mindset. In C. Kinginger (ed.) *Social and Cultural Aspects of Language Learning in Study Abroad* (pp. 179–204). Amsterdam/Philadelphia, PA: Benjamins.

Jackson, J. (2016) Breathing the smells of native-style English: A narrativised account of a L2 sojourn. *Language and Intercultural Communication* 16 (3), 332–348.

Jackson, J. (2017) The personal, linguistic, and intercultural development of Chinese sojourners in an English-speaking country: The impact of language attitudes, motivation, and agency. *Study Abroad Research in Second Language Acquisition and International Education* 2 (1), 80–106.

Jackson, J. (2018) *Interculturality in International Education*. London/New York: Routledge.

Jackson, J. and Oguro, S. (eds) (2018) *Intercultural Interventions in Study Abroad*. London/New York: Routledge.

Jackson, J. and Schwieter, J.W. (in press) Study abroad and immersion. In J.W. Schwieter and A. Benati (eds) *Cambridge Handbook of Language Learning*. Cambridge: Cambridge University Press.

Kinginger, C. (2004) Alice doesn't live here anymore: Foreign language learning and renegotiated identity. In A. Pavlenko and A. Blackledge (eds) *Negotiation of Identities in Multilingual Contexts* (pp. 219–242). Clevedon: Multilingual Matters.

Kinginger, C. (2008) Language learning in study abroad: Case studies of Americans in France. *Modern Language Journal* 9 (1), 1–124.

Kinginger, C. (2009) *Language Learning and Study Abroad: A Critical Reading of Research*. Basingstoke: Palgrave Macmillan.

Kinginger, C. (2013) Introduction: Social and cultural aspects of language learning in study abroad. In C. Kinginger (ed.) *Social and Cultural Aspects of Language Learning in Study Abroad* (pp. 3–16). Amsterdam/Philadelphia, PA: Benjamins.

Krzaklewska, E. (2008) Why study abroad? An analysis of Erasmus students' motivations. In M. Byram and F. Dervin (eds) *Students, Staff and Academic Mobility in Higher Education* (pp. 82–98). Newcastle: Cambridge Scholars Publishing.

MacIntyre, P.D., Clément, R., Dörnyei, Z. and Noels, K.A. (1998) Conceptualizing willingness to communicate in a second language: A situational model of second language confidence and affiliation. *The Modern Language Journal* 82 (4), 545–562.

Markus, H. and Nurius, P. (1986) Possible selves. *American Psychologist* 41, 954–969.

Mercer, S. and Williams, M. (2014) Concluding reflections. In S. Mercer and M. Williams (eds) *Multiple Perspectives on the Self in SLA* (pp. 177–185). Bristol: Multilingual Matters.

Mills, N. (2014) Self-efficacy in second language acquisition. In S. Mercer and M. Williams (eds) *Multiple Perspectives on the Self in SLA* (pp. 6–22). Bristol: Multilingual Matters.

Murphy-Lejeune, E. (2002) *Student Mobility and Narrative in Europe: The New Strangers*. London: Routledge.

Norton, B. (2001) *Identity and Language Learning: Gender, Ethnicity and Educational Change*. Harlow: Pearson Education.

Norton, B. (2013) *Identity and Language Learning: Extending the Conversation* (2nd edn). Bristol: Multilingual Matters.

Paige, R.M. and Vande Berg, M. (2012) Why students are and are not learning abroad. In M. Vande Berg, R.M. Paige and K.H. Lou (eds) *Student Learning Abroad: What Our Students Are Learning, What They're Not and What We Can Do about It* (pp. 29–58). Sterling, VA: Stylus.

Ryan, R.M. and Deci, E.L. (2002) Overview of self-determination theory: An organismic dialectical perspective. In E.L. Deci and R.M. Ryan (eds) *Handbook of Self-Determination Research* (pp. 3–33). Rochester, NY: The University of Rochester Press.

Sampasivam, S. and Clément, R. (2014) The dynamics of second language confidence: Contact and interaction. In S. Mercer and M. Williams (eds) *Multiple Perspectives on the Self in SLA* (pp. 23–40). Bristol: Multilingual Matters.

Ushioda, E. (2014) Motivational perspectives on the self in SLA: A developmental view. In S. Mercer and M. Williams (eds) *Multiple Perspectives on the Self in SLA* (pp. 127–141). Bristol: Multilingual Matters.

Wanner, D. (2009) Study abroad and language: From maximal to realistic models. In R. Lewin (ed.) *The Handbook of Practice and Research in Study Abroad: Higher Education and the Quest for Global Citizenship* (pp. 81–98). New York/London: Routledge.

Wolcott, T. (2013) An American in Paris: Myth, desire, and subjectivity in one student's account of study abroad in France. In C. Kinginger (ed.) *Social and Cultural Aspects of Language Learning in Study Abroad* (pp. 127–154). Amsterdam/Philadelphia, PA: Benjamins.

Yashima, T., Zenuk-Nishide, L. and Shimizu, K. (2004) The influence of attitudes and effect on willingness to communicate and second language communication. *Language Learning* 54, 119–152.

Zaykovskaya, I., Rawal, H. and De Costa, P. (2017) Learner beliefs for successful study abroad experience: A case study. *System: An International Journal of Educational Technology and Applied Linguistics* 71, 113–121.

3 Study Abroad and Students' Discourse on 'Cultural Difference': A Longitudinal View

Sònia Mas-Alcolea

Introduction

The flagship student exchange programme of the European Union (EU), the European Region Action Scheme for the Mobility of University Students (Erasmus), is nowadays still deemed as 'one of the most visible and popular initiatives' of the EU (Feyen & Krzaklewska, 2013: 9). Spain has long been its leader in participant numbers, reaching 37,235 outgoing students in the academic year 2013–2014 (European Commission, 2015). Despite the difficult economic situation in the last years and the cuts that the Erasmus programme has undergone in this country, every year the number of higher education students who decide to participate in this academic mobility programme is growing. The decision of mobile students to study abroad appears to be influenced by various circulating discourses that praise academic mobility and discursively construct it as entailing benefit not only relating to the learning of a foreign language, but also to undergoing a 'transition from one culture to another' (Koskinen & Tossavainen, 2004: 111). The Erasmus student exchange programme, in particular, has been claimed to foster greater intercultural awareness by promoting 'understanding and cohesion among members belonging to different cultures and, thus, by raising the students' sense of European citizenship' (Pozo-Vicente & Aguaded-Gómez, 2012: 441).

Most research on SA has examined the impact of the SA experience based on quantitative and/or qualitative pre-post data (e.g. Llanes & Muñoz, 2009; Tracy-Ventura et al., 2016); on qualitative post-only retrospective data (e.g. Krzaklewska, 2013; Krzaklewska & Skórska, 2013; Murphy-Lejeune, 2002; Papatsiba, 2006); or only on data collected during the stay (e.g. Jackson, 2010; Kalocsai, 2014; Wood, 2013). The current study aims to contribute to a greater understanding of the process the students undergo, by comparing their experiences in three different contexts (the

UK, Denmark and Italy), and by collecting observational and elicited verbal data longitudinally during the three different stages of the study abroad (SA) experience (pre-sojourn, during and post-sojourn). In this sense, the purpose of the present chapter is not to assess the students' 'intercultural competence' (IC) but to examine whether and how the Erasmus SA experience has an impact on the development of the students' perception of 'cultural difference/sameness' over time; and, ultimately, on their 'culturespeak' (Hannerz, 1999) or the 'uncritical and systematic use of the word culture in discourse' (Dervin, 2011: 39). Following the chronological order of the stay, the research questions this study attempts to answer are the following:

(1) Prior to departure, how do the students express their expectation and motivation to encounter 'cultural difference'?
(2) Once abroad, do the students report encountering cultural difference? Is the SA experience changing their evaluation and perception of 'cultural difference'? In what way(s) do the students' social networks abroad trigger this change?
(3) After the stay, how do the students discursively construct the impact that the stay had on their identities as regards their visions of the Self and 'the Other'?

Both 'culture' and 'identity' constitute two concepts that are central in this study and which the students (re)negotiated and (re)constructed over the course of their SA experience. Following a social constructivist perspective, the notion of 'culture' will be conceived in this study as a discursive product that is constantly being '[re]produced by people, rather than being [something] that explain[s] why they behave the way they do' (Phillips, 2007: 45). Similarly, the analysis of the students' discourse supports a post-structuralist view of identity that conceives it as being fluid, dynamic and subject to change or, following Kouhpaeenejad and Gholaminejad (2014: 200), as 'socially organized, reorganized, constructed, co-constructed, and continually reconstructed through language and discourse'.

Study Abroad and (Inter)culturality

[...] you will strengthen your aptitudes like your adaptability to new environments, [...] which will improve your curriculum in a labour market that is becoming more global every day. Getting to know other cultures, other ways of doing and of thinking will enrich you. A lot of students who have participated in an international mobility programme consider that this has been one of the best experiences in their life.

(Excerpt taken from a leaflet about mobility at the participants' home university; my translation.)

The above excerpt comes from one of the means used by the home university of the participants in this study to promote mobility among its students by praising and presenting it as undoubtedly entailing cultural (and linguistic) benefits, in any of the destinations chosen. Indeed, this institutional discourse could be claimed to be part of the SA marketing consumed by many students who absorb 'the [attractive] images and rhetoric of international education advertisements' (Zemach-Bersin, 2009: 303).

As various studies (e.g. Murphy-Lejeune, 2002; Papatsiba, 2006) have shown, many students – and this is also the case of the participants in this study – see an SA experience as an escape from 'cultural sameness' and thus as a window that allows them to somewhat uniquely experience 'cultural diversity'. They want to participate in an SA programme with a clear expectation and desire to encounter 'cultural difference' and/or to 'know other cultures' – this is something they do not seem to imagine as happening among people of the same nationality. In this sense, students – and also various circulating (institutional) discourses – seem, on the one hand, to present 'a view of the world where crossing a national border signifies selecting those who are different', as Dervin (2016: 38) posits. And, on the other hand, they seem to reproduce discourses where the term 'culture' corresponds to the notion of 'national culture', although the nation often acts as 'an external force which is in conflict with a wide variety of layered cultural realities which collect around personal life trajectories (including religion, family history, community, occupation, politics and language) often in multiple national locations' (Holliday, 2010: 165). Besides, students tend to leave with the motivation to be immersed in the 'local culture' of the host country and to interact with 'the locals' who they initially imagine 'as being homogeneous and [as having] clearly identifiable attributes' (Piller, 2011: 7) because of where they are from. In this sense, I concur with Dervin (2016: 28) who claims that 'while the word diversity should refer to multiplicity, it often means difference and "oneness"'. This is, in turn, related to Holliday's (2016) notion of 'cultural blocks and threads', which has to do with two existing modes of thinking and talking about cultural difference. On the one hand, talking about cultural blocks implies the view of national cultures as different entities and as clearly marked boundaries that 'remain uncrossable and [that] confine interculturality to observing and comparing the practices and values of one's own and the other's national cultures' (Holliday, 2016: 319). On the other hand, talking about and focusing on threads implies the awareness of, and sensitivity to, similarities between people despite coming from different countries and/or despite having a different nationality. In brief, while cultural blocks are used to 'build boundaries and [to] restrict cultural travel', threads are used to actually 'cross [these] boundaries' (Holliday, 2016: 321, emphasis added). In this sense, even though individuals tend to switch from one mode of thinking to the other, focusing on threads can help us create 'a common ground for sharing and enabling interculturality' (Holliday, 2016: 320).

In any case, the students' development of IC is one of the various benefits SA has often been portrayed to entail and which presumably helps people perform 'effectively and appropriately when interacting with others who are linguistically and culturally different from oneself' (Fantini & Tirmizi, 2006: 12). This outcome has generally been examined from a rather quantitative perspective in studies which conclude that the students' intercultural sensitivity and/or competence – two terms that are often used interchangeably – increase after their SA experiences (e.g. Anderson *et al.*, 2006; Clarke *et al.*, 2009; Cots *et al.*, 2016; Elola & Oskoz, 2008). By way of illustration, Anderson *et al.* (2006: 467), who used Hammer and Bennett's (2002) Intercultural Development Inventory (IDI) questionnaire, concluded that 'put[ting] out students in face-to-face contact with people of different cultures' improves their understanding and acceptance of cultural diversity. In a similar vein, Pozo-Vicente and Aguaded-Gómez (2012), who followed a mixed-methods approach, claimed that the Erasmus SA experience constitutes a complex process of acquisition and implementation of knowledge (sociolinguistic awareness), skills (the fact of overcoming stereotypes and prejudices) and attitudes (acceptance and respect for other 'cultures'), which clearly 'fosters the development of intercultural competence' (Pozo-Vicente & Aguaded-Gómez, 2012: 456; my translation). Similarly, Cots *et al.* (2016) carried out a mixed-methods study with the objective of examining the impact of academic mobility on the development of the IC of students from two universities in Catalonia (Spain). This study, which used a pre-stay and a post-stay questionnaire following Byram's (1997) three different components of IC (attitudes, knowledge and behaviour), concluded that 'the clearest impact of an academic mobility [...] is an increase in knowledge about other cultures' (Cots *et al.*, 2016: 318). These are but some of the many studies that have used standardised instruments (Hammer & Bennett, 2002) and/or models (e.g. Byram, 1997; Deardorff, 2009) with the objective of quantifying the students' (inter)cultural learning as a result of their SA experience.

However, despite Convey's (1995: 142, cited in Jackson, 2005: 165) claim that 'the experience abroad cannot be fully quantified [and that] the outcome has to be measured in terms of the quality of the experience', studies that rely on qualitative data in order to examine the impact of an SA experience on the students' intercultural learning are scarce. Edmonds (2010), for instance, employed qualitative methods (semi-structured interviews and written reflective travel journals) in order to assess the impact of mobility programmes on the development of intercultural competence among nursing students, and concluded that they benefitted from their international experiences as regards their awareness of diverse 'cultures' and their ability to adapt to an unfamiliar environment, among other aspects. Similarly, Murphy-Lejeune's (2002) study, for which 50 'European student travellers' were interviewed, centred on the analysis of the narratives of these students with the objective of gaining a retrospective view of their experiences. This qualitative approach, the author underscores, certainly allowed for 'a first-hand in-depth picture of student travellers and their experience [...] in all its ambiguity and complexity' (Murphy-Lejeune, 2002: 43). Concerning the intercultural dimension of the stay, the analysis of the students' discourse showed that academic mobility did trigger personal change and/or development that had to do with the fact that 'over time, interest in other people's difference wanes' and that 'categorical judgements lose their power and are replaced by a more personal approach to others' (Murphy-Lejeune, 2002: 211).

The emerging discourse from interviews and other tools for self-report, which 'transforms the internal experience into an outside reality' (Murphy-Lejeune, 2002: 44), is a similar object of study in Jackson's (2005) work, focusing on the diaries written by 15 Hong Kong Chinese students who spent five weeks abroad (in England). Through the analysis of these diaries, which provide 'unique insights into the sojourn through the eyes of the students themselves' (Jackson, 2005: 179), Jackson aimed to examine the students' 'versions of reality' (Ochs & Caps, 1996) in relation to the development of their intercultural communicative competence. This analysis unveiled the development in the students' identities as regards their understanding and acceptance of various cultural practices encountered abroad, which they initially deemed to be different and even difficult to adapt to, and which 'finally became "treasures" in their eyes' (Jackson, 2005: 176).

Following this qualitative trend, the present study, which combines both textual and observational data, is intended to contribute to the body of research on student mobility within Europe, not by quantifying the students' intercultural learning, but by bringing to the fore the change in their discourses in relation to their social links with different and not-so-different 'others'. Indeed, the social networks a student establishes while abroad have been claimed to be 'crucial to [linguistic and cultural] learning outcomes' (Coleman, 2013: 29). This is also supported by Geeraert et al. (2014: 86) who asserted that 'who sojourners have contact with, matters for both cultural adjustment and intergroup affect' and that 'travel may not always broaden the mind, especially if one does not choose their international contacts wisely'.

Taking into account that one of the aspects that 'matters more for ERASMUS students is social life' (Krupnik & Krzaklewska, 2013: 213) and that there is a strong sense of community among Erasmus students (Tsoukalas, 2008), the present study centres on this specific variable – the students' social fabric (Murphy-Lejeune, 2002) abroad – and particularly on the ways in which this has an impact on their understanding of 'culture' and, ultimately, on their construction of their and of the Others' identities. As will be suggested in the analysis of the data, this chapter takes a critical stance towards (a) the essentialist, uncritical and systematic use of the term 'culture' (Piller, 2011) present in many circulating discourses and which is generally presented as defined by nationality; and (b) the fact of presenting the SA experience as a somewhat unique opportunity to 'meet other cultures' – as the excerpt starting this section illustrates. Concerning the latter, I align myself with some scholars who have questioned this 'credo' about SA by suggesting that 'in practice (...) the picture is less rosy' (Fabricius *et al.*, 2016: 580) and that intercultural competence, one of the potential benefits of an international experience, does not automatically increase by simply being in a foreign country. Instead, as Behrnd and Porzelt (2012) suggest, there are many variables affecting its development, such as the students' personal factors, the length of time spent abroad, the fact of going abroad with and without preparation and, as will be highlighted in this chapter, their social networks while abroad.

Research Design: Undertaking a Qualitative Multiple Case Study

The present chapter reports on a qualitative multiple case study which has been defined as being based on a 'detailed, in-depth data collection involving multiple sources of information rich in context' (Creswell, 1998: 61). This allowed me, on the one hand, to capture the complexity of the participants' diverse experiences and, on the other hand, to seek out and present the multiple, and even contradictory, perspectives on the way(s) in which participants discursively constructed their identities while reflecting upon the impact that the Erasmus experience had on their sense of self.

Participant selection

The focal participants of this study were nine undergraduate students from a university in Catalonia (Spain), who participated in the Erasmus exchange programme in the academic year 2013–2014, in three different contexts: the UK, Denmark and Italy. Table 3.1 provides the students' profiles, ranging in age from 22 to 26 years.

As shown in Table 3.1, all participants were born in Catalonia and all but two had previous international travel experience. At the study's onset, the participants were in their third year of study at university. The majority of them spent one semester abroad, with the exception of two students (Verònica and Marina) who went to Italy and the UK, respectively, for one year.

Table 3.1 Participant profiles

Students' names	Home country	Age	Degree	Previous experience abroad	Length of Erasmus (months)	Host country
Amanda	Catalonia	22	Law	✓	5	UK
Marina	Catalonia	22	English studies	✓	10	UK
Roger	Catalonia	22	Law	✓	5	UK
Ariadna	Catalonia	26	Social education	✓	5	Denmark
Mònica	Catalonia	22	Education	✓	5	Denmark
Joan	Catalonia	24	Industrial engineering	✓	5	Denmark
Patrícia	Catalonia	23	Law	×	5	Italy
Verònica	Catalonia	22	Business administration	✓	10	Italy
Josep Miquel	Catalonia	23	Law	×	6	Italy

Note: Names are pseudonyms.

Data collection and analysis

As a longitudinal multiple case study, this project is based on multiple and complementary kinds of data collected over a period of two years, which include focus group interviews, a short questionnaire with six open-ended questions concerning their expectations about their SA experience, a series of written experiential accounts, a semi-structured interview on site and a narrative interview (see Figure 3.1). Through this data collection, the participants were asked about their language learning/use experiences as well as their understanding of 'cultural difference', given that these were not only the students' main motives for going abroad, but also the two main interests of the larger research project to which this study belongs. In this sense, the data collected in this study are conceived as intersubjective, interactional processes in which both the researcher and the participants became co-constructors, co-tellers or co-narrators (Norrick, 2000).

The aim in collecting data from multiple sources and at different times (pre-, during and post-stay) was to help illuminate the development (if any) of the focal students' identity over time, mostly by obtaining first-hand accounts of their experiences through interviews and elicited written and oral reflections. These were also complemented with the method known as shadowing, which has been described as 'entail[ing] a researcher closely following a subject over a period of time to investigate what people actually do in the course of their everyday lives, not what their roles dictate of them' (Quinlan, 2008: 1480). Accordingly, I spent approximately four days with each of the participants, following them into their classes and in any other non-academic activities that were part of their life abroad. Indeed, this allowed me not to rely solely on the

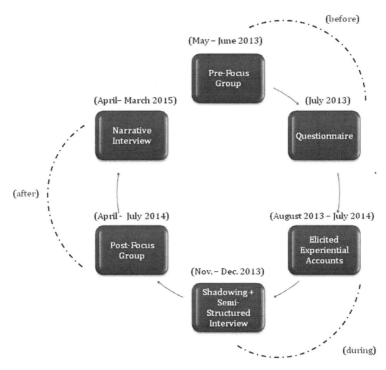

Figure 3.1 The process of data collection

participants' recounting of events, but to become a co-narrator and co-construct the meaning of each of their Erasmus experiences.

The fact of tracking the students longitudinally allowed a focus not only on the outcomes of the stay, but also on the students' journey and on their ongoing construction of their identity, which can be seen as a process in which they took into account their initial motives for going abroad and the things that actually happened once there. The process of data collection finished with narrative interviews with selected participants one year after they had returned, which proved to be useful for hearing their voices individually and not as a group, and for rounding out the data previously collected while co-constructing their Erasmus storied experiences.

In relation to this study's data analysis, and from a discourse-analytic perspective, the ethnomethodologically oriented method known as Membership Categorization Analysis (MCA) (Fitzgerald & Housley, 2015; Sacks, 1972; Stokoe, 2012) and the analytical tool of stance (Du Bois, 2007; Jaffe, 2009) were used. On the one hand, MCA allowed an examination of the ways in which students brought into play self- and other-categorisations of those involved in their storied Erasmus experiences and how these evolved as a result of the SA experience. Excerpt 1 exemplifies some categorial analysis by drawing on the narrative interview that I held with Verònica (IT). The open-ended question at Line 1, 'and how did it all end', initiates a new sequence about how her experience abroad ended.

Excerpt 1: Exemplifying categorial analysis

(Excerpt taken from the narrative interview with Verònica)

1 Sònia:[1]   and how did it all end/

2 Verònica: we··ll_ * good\ I mean_ I le·ft happily\ I mean_ <u>everybody</u> when they
3   leave * when he leave··s his Erasmus_ says aw·· (...) I won't be able to
4   go back home_ (...) they were sad\ but I·_ but I was happy\

5 Sònia: to go back/

6 Verònica: yes\ the problem with this is that I expected one thing and it has been the
7   opposite\ bu··t for me_ * I myself think that the people_ * I mean_ once
8   there_ * I mean_ partying and doing nothing and living life\ which_ I find
9   good but_ * I don't know\ +er·m+ one year like this_

Verònica used the term 'everybody' in Line 2 to classify what she conceived as the general behaviour of all Erasmus students. According to Verònica, 'sad' was a common category-bound predicate (Stokoe, 2012) of Erasmus students, when having to return home, and 'partying and doing nothing and living life' (Line 8) were invoked as category-bound activities (Stokoe, 2012) that Erasmus students normally engage in.

On the other hand, and as Figure 3.2 visually illustrates, Verònica's words in Excerpt 1 also allow us to see how she displayed her stance towards the social reality she was discursively constructing. Indeed, the

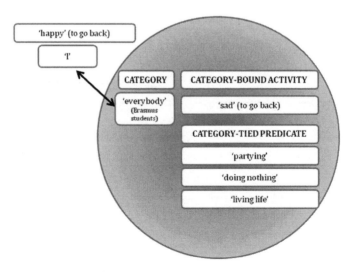

Figure 3.2 The interplay of MCA and Stance

behaviour of Erasmus students became a stance object (Du Bois, 2007) which she evaluated and towards which she positioned herself.

Verònica clearly positioned herself as being outside of this 'everybody', and thus suggested that she was an atypical Erasmus student who engaged with different, and even opposite, category-bound activities and to whom she would assign different category-bound predicates. Therefore, even though Verònica had gone to Italy as an Erasmus student, in her first turn, she explicitly made a distinction between 'everybody' and the pronominal form 'I', and made it clear that she did not feel part of the Erasmus community by appealing to, among other resources, opposite emotions, as in 'they were sad\ but I·_ but I was happy\'. This instance underscores Jaffe's (2009: 9) claim that, 'personal stance is always achieved through comparison and contrast with other relevant persons and categories'.

In brief, the analysis of this excerpt serves to illustrate the complementarity of the two instruments used in the current study (MCA and Stance), which provide a richer account of two discursive practices that participants constantly engaged with, in and through their discourse(s): categorisation and evaluation of social 'reality'.

Findings

Pre-stage. 'Meeting a different culture': An expected activity of Erasmus students

Before departure, most participants constructed their imagined identities as Erasmus-students-to-be who would forge social relationships mainly with 'the locals' and with other international exchange students. By way of illustration, the students expected to 'meet people from other cultures_ from other countries'[2] (Verònica, IT) and/or to 'see how another culture lives which in spite of being close, we are very different' (Ariadna, DK). Indeed, it is as members of the category 'Erasmus student' and, at the same time, also probably influenced by the 'imagineering of study abroad' (Härkönen & Dervin, 2016: 41), that they saw this category as 'carr[ying] a [...] set of category-bound activities, predicates, or rights and obligations that are expectable for an incumbent of that category to perform or possess' (Stokoe, 2012: 282). Apart from the learning and use of a foreign language, the activity of 'meeting a different culture' is part of the expected and 'common knowledge' about the SA experience. This is in line with Papatsiba (2006: 108), who equally stresses that 'for the majority of individuals who deliberately decide to experience a stay abroad, a certain curiosity and desire of encounter with the culturally different Other exist'.

However, it is important to note how the participants of this study seemed to use the term 'culture' as 'an explanation for everything that a representative of another country does, thinks, etc. while ignoring the fact that other reasons might apply' (Dervin, 2016: 113); as 'nothing more

Table 3.2 Categorisation of 'the locals' prior to departure

Category	Category-bound predicate	Category-bound activity
'British people'	'cold' (Marina, UK) 'not so open or as friendly as Catalans' (Amanda, UK) 'not so expressive'/'less impulsive if we compare them to the typical Spanish/Catalan' (Roger, UK)	
'Danish people'	'more developed and formal' (Ariadna, DK) 'more responsible in all aspects' (Joan, DK)	'have different values from the ones here (...): legality, doing one's work well, etc'. (Joan, DK) 'have a different mentality as regards eating habits: more natural products' (Joan, DK)
'Italian people'	'quite similar' (Verònica, IT) 'very similar to the Catalan personality'; 'quiet'; 'carefree' (Josep M., IT)	'have similar customs to ours' (Patrícia, IT)

than a convenient and lazy explanation' (Piller, 2011: 172); and, ultimately, as if it were common knowledge and/or self-explanatory. When asked to expand on this so longed-for contact with cultural difference, most participants, for instance, came up with culturalist or essentialist category-implicative descriptions (Stokoe, 2009) mainly about 'the locals'. Table 3.2 provides a summary of the participants' categorisations of these others prior to departure, appearing in the data collected from the short written questionnaire and the (pre) focus group.

In connection with the students who went to the UK, Marina expected to find 'cold people' and, yet, admitted that this was a 'stereotype I would like to change once I get to know them'. These category-bound features of 'British people' generated by Marina were somehow shared by Amanda, who wrote that she thought the British 'are not so open or as friendly as Catalans', and by Roger, who contended that the main difference between Catalan and British societies has to do with the fact of expressing emotions – a category-bound activity that Roger treated as not tied to the category 'British people' (see Excerpt 2).

Excerpt 2: British versus Catalan society

(Excerpt taken from the written questionnaire of Roger – UK)

1 While we Spaniards/Catalans tend to be very expressive and gesticulate quite a lot, I
2 believe that it is undeniable that the British (most of them) are not so [expressive]. It
3 is what is known as the British phlegm which, as I understand it, consists in showing
4 [...] a balanced and rational self (or, better said, less impulsive if we compare it to the
5 typical Spanish/Catalan).

As can be seen in their comments, the three students who went to the UK assigned different, and even opposite, category-bound predicates (Stokoe, 2012) ('very expressive'/'less impulsive'; 'friendly'/'cold', 'not so friendly'; 'open'/'not so open') and activities ('gesticulate a lot'; 'show a balanced self') that, according to them, defined and made the British and Catalan/Spanish people different societies. Notice that there is a stance token produced by Roger, in Lines 1–2, through the use of the epistemic verb 'believe' (Line 2) and the adjective 'undeniable' (Line 2), which indexes the high certainty with which Roger claimed that the British are not so expressive. Roger also seemed to accept, though, that these were nothing but 'biased descriptions' which are often difficult to avoid. This is actually related to Dervin's (2016: 81) claim that othering and, specifically, essentialism is 'a universal sin' and that, although we should be aware of the fact that we inhabit a world with diverse diversities (Dervin, 2009, 2016), 'no one is immune to it' (Dervin, 2016: 81).

In respect of those students who went to Denmark, two of them shared a similar stance towards Danish people, while highlighting positive aspects that Catalans somehow lack. On the one hand, Ariadna ascribed to Danish society the predicates 'more developed and formal', although she did not specify in what aspects. On the other hand, being 'more responsible in all aspects' appeared to be the category-bound description (Stokoe, 2012) assigned by Joan to Danish nationals. Besides, as he wrote in the questionnaire, the members that form the category 'Danish people' were also defined by 'activities' such as having 'different values from the ones here [...]: legality, doing one's work well, etc.'; and a 'different mentality as regards eating habits: more natural products'. In this case, although the participants did idealise 'the Other', their categorisation of the 'locals' as expectably 'different' did not seem to trigger ethnocentrism or the belief that 'one's culture, country, or group is better than others' (Dervin, 2016: 114). Yet, the comparison between the host and home societies does sometimes 'create dichotomies between the "good" and "bad", the "civilized" and "uncivilized", and the "same" and the "other"' (Dervin, 2016: 11) and this is clearly seen in the discourse of the students who went to Denmark, prior to their departure.

Unlike the students who went to the UK and Denmark, the three participants who decided to go to Italy did not seem to be '"victims" of the differentialist bias' (Dervin, 2016: 36) and asserted that they expected Italian society to be quite similar to Catalan society. For instance, Verònica (IT) stated that she thought 'there are no big differences between the Spanish society and the Italian because they are quite similar societies' and Patrícia used the same predicate – 'similar to ours' – to describe 'Italian customs'. Josep Miquel's categorisation of Italians was in line with Verònica's and Patrícia's descriptions, to which he added the predicates 'quiet' and 'carefree'. Additionally, he claimed that the Italian character is 'very similar to the Catalan [personality]'.

To sum up, the analysis of the students' discourses of Othering prior to departure shows that they focused on cultural blocks (Holliday, 2016:

318) which, despite acknowledging diversity, 'reinforce the notion of uncrossable cultural boundaries' defined by the nation state. At this stage, the students' discourse, which is characterised by their generalising about the Other, is somehow 'solidify[ing] culture and community, bounding them together (I am a Pakistani so I do it this way)' (Dervin, 2011: 40). In brief, through the students' discourse analysed in this section, we can grasp a sense of the term 'culture' as explanatory of all behaviours, as an agent and/or entity on its own, as a *passepartout* term (self-explanatory and justified by itself), and as homogenising and equivalent to national culture, and thus corresponding to categories defined by the nation state.

During the stay. Navigating between 'cultural' differences and similarities

During the stay, the students reported that 'local students' were not part of their social fabric (Murphy-Lejeune, 2002) and that they tended to socialise more with other Erasmus students and/or compatriots within and outside the university context. The following excerpts constitute three examples of the many instances in which most participants claimed that their relationship with the locals was almost non-existent.

Excerpt 3: 'Erasmus make Erasmus friends'

(Excerpt taken from the semi-structured interview while shadowing Verònica – IT)

1	Verònica:	I thought I would make Italian friends but I haven't even made one\ (...) this
2		is how it goes\ the Erasmus make Erasmus friends but not with the people of
3		the host country\ they look at us but ignore us\

Excerpt 4: '[the Danish students] ignored us'

(Excerpt taken from the semi-structured interview while shadowing Ariadna – DK)

1	Ariadna:	our [university] (...) was small\ one could see that we were the foreigners
2		because they were·· all from there_ and we were the small group\ at the
3		beginning the Danish students looked at us but then it was like··_ * well_
4		they ignored us\

Excerpt 5: 'they weren't willing to keep on talking'

(Excerpt taken from the narrative interview with Amanda – UK)

1	Amanda:	(...) here [in our home country] (...) they say we ignore the Erasmus
2		students_ but there [in the UK] twice as much\ you know/ and sometimes
3		you asked something_ they answered_ but they weren't willing to keep on
4		talking\ I mean_ I found them very_ ve··ry_ very very cold\

Verònica, Ariadna and Amanda coincided in presenting the local students of the host country as 'ignoring' the Erasmus students. The predicate 'cold' and the activities 'ignoring Erasmus students' and 'not being willing to socialize with them' were treated as category-bound features of 'local students'. The limited contact of exchange students with the locals has also been noted by different scholars (e.g. Harrison & Peacock, 2010; Tsoukalas, 2008; Van Mol, 2014; Waters & Brooks, 2011). For instance, Van Mol (2014: 81) also contends that 'mobile and local students might cross each other's paths at university, but [that] social interaction likely remains limited'.

Despite limited interaction with the locals, most students formulated categorisations of them while highlighting some small 'cultural differences' (see Table 3.3). It is worth noting, though, that these categorisations did not result from interactions with host residents but from the participants' observations and, thus, from their interpretations of what they normally did and/or of the way they dressed.

Table 3.3 Categorisation of 'the locals' during the stay

Category	Category-bound predicate	Category-bound activity
'the British'		'when they get to university_ they say I leave the··_ the city_ (...) during the four years at university they do no·t_ +uh·+ they do not live at home\' (Marina, UK) 'when· they start university they want to leave home and they just go home to·· ask for money\ ' (Amanda, UK)
'the Danish'	'very nationalist' (Ariadna, DK) 'more advanced' (Ariadna, DK)	'they all have a flag pole' (Ariadna, DK) 'they are more civilised' (Ariadna, DK) 'the only thing that surprises me is that the girls dress super elegantly and wear trainers\ (...) they wear a * they normally wear a tracksuit' (Ariadna, DK) 'they normally give a hug [when they greet someone]' (Ariadna, DK) 'when they go out they wear trainers\ always\ they wear a dress_ they are very well-dressed and wear make up_ with their dress and trainers\ all of them\ right/' (Mònica, DK)
'the Italians'	'well-dressed' (Josep M., IT)	

The analysis of these categorisations about the locals that the students formulated during their stay denotes that the 'local culture' is described from a position of an external observer (often from superficial and/or visual aspects, such as the way certain people dressed and/or the national flags on the balconies). This is obvious if we take into account that the students' contact with the host residents was anecdotal, if not non-existent.

However, as pointed out earlier, the participants of this study did form relationships with, on the one hand, compatriots – a relationship which some of the participants presented as inevitable. On the other hand, the students also formed relationships with other international students or 'equal strangers' (Murphy-Lejeune, 2002: 202), who had the same 'Erasmus status' (Bracke & Aguerre, 2015: 140), who had also moved from a familiar to an unfamiliar milieu, and who were, therefore, also concerned with 'building a level of fitness that is necessary for their daily functioning' (Kim, 2012: 229). This finding resonates to some extent with the finding of scholars such as Waters and Brooks (2011) who highlight the common isolation of international students. In the interviews held with the participants in this study during their stay and based on my observations of them on site, I actually used the term 'bubble' to share with the participants my view of them as living in a sort of 'self-contained enclave' (Tsoukalas, 2008: 144) and of their little contact with the host residents.

Although some of the participants in this study had more contact with international students than others, we can generally see that the students' evaluation of these 'others' (of non-Spanish Erasmus students) – based on either their interaction with them or on their mere observation of them resulting from sharing the same classroom space – is somewhat different from the one they displayed prior to departure. During their SA experience, when asked about whether their contact with other international students involved their adaptation to and/or their learning about different 'cultures', most of them displayed a sense of togetherness through utterances such as 'at the end you realize that we are all young people·· and we are all looking for the same\ having fun and that's it\' (Josep M., IT); or 'I think we aren't so different because_ at the end of the day_ +uh··+ we are a·ll_ the same age_ (...) I don't know\ we were all comfortable_ we didn't encounter so much difference\' (Marina, UK). The students' constant use of the pronoun 'we' underlines the broadening and inclusive nature of their utterances, by suggesting that they are all members of the same category ('Erasmus student') who, in spite of not sharing the same nationality and/or language, would share many category-bound features (such as their age and motivations) as evidenced in Josep Miquel's utterance 'we are all looking for the same things'. This is in line with Papatsiba's (2006: 119) work on the SA experience of French Erasmus students for whom 'encountered cultural differences [...] finally became less important in their eyes, because of the emergence of similarities linked to age and student status, between initially [perceived] culturally different partners'. Indeed, there seems to be a 'transition from the phase of strangeness towards a feeling of familiarity' (Papatsiba, 2006: 119); yet, some of them acknowledged some perceived 'small' differences between them and the rest of the international students, as summarised in Table 3.4.

As evidenced in Table 3.4, some students mentioned the way of greeting students from Northern Europe who they had met abroad and for whom kissing each other twice was presented as not being a

Table 3.4 Perceived differences among international students

Category	Category-bound features	
	Category-bound predicate	Category-bound activity
'the Germans'	'cold' Patrícia, IT	–
'the Dutch'	–	'kiss each other three times' Roger – UK 'kiss each other three times' Amanda – UK
'Brazilians and the Spanish'	–	'kiss each other twice [when greeting someone]' Marina – UK
'people from northern Europe'	'not used to kissing each other twice' Marina, UK	–
'all the [international] students'	–	'eat inside the class, during [...] lessons' Mònica – DK

category-bound activity (Marina, DK) and who were thus perceived and categorised as 'cold' (Patrícia, IT). In fact, as illustrated in Excerpt 6, Marina was asked to do an assignment on non-verbal communication, in which she stressed the differences she had perceived among other international students as regards greetings.

Excerpt 6: 'personal space_ depends very much_ on the·· _ on the cultu·re\'

(Excerpt taken from the semi-structured interview with Marina – UK)

1	Marina:	we did an activity o··n {(ENG) body language} because we were precisely
2		very interested in it because * of course_ since we were··· _ * well_ +uh+ we
3		got together_ two Brazilian girls and two Spanish girls\ right/ and then when
4		we got here_ +uh··+ * well_ we were shocked that we would directly kiss
5		each other twice and that everybody seemed very shocked\ right/ (...) and
6		they shook hands\ mainly those fro··m the Northern countries_ because they
7		are not used to this\ and in fact_ we made them do a kind of activity_ where
8		we told them_ first of all we need you to_ to sit a···t the back of the class\
9		okay/ and it turned out that_ there was one from Norway and one from
10		Germany_ and both of them sat one next to the other_ leaving a lot of space\
11		and there were two Spanish who sat super close to each other and we said to
12		them_ look_ +uh··+ with this exercise the only thing we wanted to show you
13		is_ tha··t personal space_ depends very much_ on the·· _ on the cultu·re\

The affective stance predicate 'shocked', in Line 4, indexes Marina's evaluation of and position towards the different way(s) of greeting and towards the personal space her Norwegian and German classmates required, which she saw as being determined by (national) 'culture' (Line 13). In spite of only having had contact with one German and one Norwegian student – as she mentioned on another occasion in the semi-structured interview – she seemed to assume that shaking hands (instead of kissing) and 'leaving a lot of space' (Line 10) were two category-bound activities that define all members of the category 'German' or 'Norwegian'. Indeed, Marina's words generally present 'the other' as 'imprisoned in the strait-jackets of a homogenized "diversity"' and, thus, somehow imply that diversity means 'oneness' (Dervin, 2016: 28) and not multiplicity.

Apart from the different ways of greeting that some of the partici-pants had perceived and that they attributed to a specific 'culture' defined by the nation state, Mònica also treated the activity of 'eating in class' as a category-bound feature of all exchange students in Denmark, no matter their nationality, which she evaluated as 'unusual' in Spain (see Excerpt 7).

Excerpt 7: Eating in class: An 'unusual' practice in Spain

(Excerpt taken from the third experiential report written by Mònica)

1   Another thing that is unusual in Spain is that here all the pupils eat inside the class, during
2   lessons. I didn't do it till now. But now I usually eat my lunch in the class or maybe an
3   apple, etc. Even some of the students go to the canteen, buy their lunch and go upstairs
4   with the plate and eat there!! AMAZING!!

Mònica was not used to eating inside the classroom but, while abroad, this is a practice she changed, as evidenced in Lines 2–3 where she wrote that 'now I usually eat my lunch in the class or maybe an apple'. The student's affective stance towards this difference she encountered in Denmark is clearly reinforced through the adjective 'amazing' (Line 4), which she wrote in capital letters, and through the final exclamation marks.

It is also interesting to note, though, that during their stay two stu-dents highlighted the 'cultural' differences, not among the international students they had met, but among fellow compatriots. In this sense, they did seem to differentiate between the two groups (us and them) in terms of nationality (Catalans and Spaniards), for which they seemed to indi-cate that being Catalan means not being Spanish. This is something none of them expected before departure.

Excerpt 8: 'I don't identify with this posse at all\'

(Excerpt taken from the semi-structured interview while shadowing Joan – DK)

1   Joan: where I find differences is {(@) between Catalans and Spaniards\} and they are
2   evident\ I see them * at the beginning when we went to Denmark with Ramón_
3   we found more similarities between us [(@) and the Danish than with the
4   Spaniards\} (...) I don't know\ the Spa& * I * of course_ there are a lot of
5   students from southern Spain\ right/ when we went out in Denmark with
6   Ramón_ we looked at each other and said_ +wow+ I don't identify with this
7   posse at all\ {(SPA) hey chap_ what's up/} boisterou··s\

During his stay, as seen in Excerpt 8, Joan (DK) did not categorise the other non-Spanish exchange students he met abroad as 'different'; instead, he used this evaluative adjective to refer to Spanish (non-Catalan) Erasmus students, to whom he referred as 'the posse' (Line 6). According to Joan, the category-bound predicate 'boisterous' (Line 7) was the feature that distinguished Spanish from Catalan Erasmus students, in spite of sharing the same passport. In this sense, although Joan still presents a homogenising view of people by using labels (Spaniards, Catalans), the SA experience somehow allowed him to realise that cultural homogeneity may not always be defined by the nation state (Spain, in this case), given that he did not 'identify with this posse at all'; instead, he seemed to acknowledge the existence of diverse diversities (Dervin, 2009, 2016), even within the same nation state. Similar to Joan, Verònica (IT), who mostly interacted with other compatriots, claimed that she found cultural differences among them and expressed her surprise at 'learning a lot about Spain' during her SA experience.

In brief, we have seen how prior to departure, the students expressed their desire to live an adventure characterised by encountering 'cultural' differences, thereby creating boundaries between 'sameness' and 'difference' or between 'us' and 'them', based on prejudices mainly about non-compatriots. During the stay, we have seen how this initial feeling of detachment from the host residents and non-Spanish Erasmus students blurred and was eclipsed by a feeling of 'togetherness' and 'sameness' based on shared category-bound features of Erasmus students, such as the fact of being the same age and/or sharing activities (e.g. going to university and/or partying). In relation to those participants who interacted with non-compatriots, 'cultural' differences did not disappear but were presented as 'small differences'. Indeed, during the stay we can see how 'proximity [among other internationals] surreptitiously gain[ed] the upper hand' (Murphy-Lejeune, 2002: 131). However, for the participants who interacted with Spanish (non-Catalan) Erasmus students, the shock came from discovering and perceiving a feeling of detachment from this group, in spite of their co-nationality. What was perceived and thus evaluated as sameness prior to departure, was transformed into 'difference' during their stay. Boundaries were thus constructed within the same nation state.

Post-stage. Reconstructing cultural difference

After their sojourn abroad, most participants presented the Erasmus experience as having been a transformative one in respect of their visions of Self and of Others. See, for example, Excerpt 9 taken from the last elicited written report, in which Marina (UK) commented on the way(s) in which she felt this experience had changed her perception of 'culture' and 'cultural difference'.

Excerpt 9: 'I've changed my viewpoint of people in general'

(Excerpt taken from the last experiential written report, Marina – UK)

1 I also used to have lots of stereotypes about the cultures and I've seen they aren't always
2 true. I've also changed my viewpoint of people in general. (...) I've become more open-
3 minded and I made friends not only from all the UK but also from Brazil, China, Africa,
4 USA and all of us have things in common.

This excerpt illustrates how a student's lack of previous experience or direct contact with people from other countries may be crystallised into preconceived images about them that emerge from stereotypes or from '"collective meta-attitudinal" discourses that lay boundaries between [national] groups' (Dervin, 2012: 186). For Marina (UK), although she still talked about 'national cultures' as a relevant construct, the Erasmus programme had an impact on her 'viewpoint of people in general' (Line 2) and thus on her preconceived ideas about people coming from different countries. In fact, as also shown in Excerpt 10, it is interesting to see how, one year after her SA experience, she still recalled how that experience helped her learn that all humans have things in common, despite coming from different countries.

Excerpt 10: 'I come to the conclusion that_ we are all humans'

(Excerpt taken from the narrative interview with Marina – UK)

1 Marina: I was a person that_ * well_ * I mean_ I will not say I was racist but I was
2   very narrow-minded\ a··nd_ and *no way\ I have made friends from
3   everywhere\

4 Sònia: by narrow-minded you mean you probably had some pre-conceived ideas
5   about certain people/

6 Marina: yes\ stereotypes\ of course\ whi··ch_ * I mean_ * until you don't know the
7   person you don't see that_ that * I mean_ that you are much more similar
8   tha·n_ tha··n_ than you thought\ (...) I would have never imagined that I
9   would have friends * the thing is that I have friends fro·m_ Africa_ I have
10   a friend from Malawi and another fro·m_ from Gambia\
11

12 Sònia: who you have met in Wales/

13 Marina: yes_yes_yes_yes\ I mean_ (...) I come to the conclusion that_ we are all
14   humans and tha·t * I mean_ it is a matter of adaptation\ because· * I don't
15   know\ these girls cooked us some food fro·m_ from their country and I
16   loved it\ when I got here to the UK * I mean_ I started to feel anger
17   towa·rds_ towards Hindus_ because of their way of being and everything_
18   * well_ they are very chauvinist_ and yet I have a friend who is Hindu\ so_
19   * with whom I get on very_ very_ very_ very well_ and who is a totally
20   different person from_ from those [Hindu] people who_ who I· * I mean_
21   that * well_ who I thought were like this\

The impact of the SA experience on Marina's sense of self is underlined by the change of verb tenses (she moves from using the past tense to using the present tense) and the way she categorised her two different selves: the one prior to departure, which she presented as 'very narrow-minded' (Line 2); and the self upon return, which she implicitly evaluated as open-minded or as enjoying 'cultural' diversity (Line 16). Marina expressed her surprise (Lines 9–10) at the fact that she made friends with people from non-European countries about whom she had formed stereotypes or preconceived ideas, and at the fact that 'you are much more similar tha·n_ tha··n_ than you thought' (Lines 8–11). The interaction with other students from different countries allowed her to position herself as now having learnt that, beyond national borders, 'we are all humans' (Lines 13–14) and that we should know the person first before grouping him or her into a category, while suggesting that that person behaves and/or thinks the same way as would all people with the same nationality. As another example, we can also see how, before studying abroad, Marina boxed Hindu people into the same national category and categorised them as 'very chauvinist' (Line 18). After the stay, she realised that she should not use the same category-bound features to describe and generalise about the behaviour and/or way of thinking of all Hindu people. Her new Hindu friend was presented as being 'totally different' and, therefore, as not matching what she admitted was a preconceived idea of a cultural difference defined by the nation state: 'I thought [they] were like this' (Line 21).

Something similar was reported by Roger (UK) and Amanda (UK) who asserted that, prior to departure, they had an idealised vision of 'British people' and of the UK as a country. Although their contact with 'the locals' was almost non-existent, Excerpt 11 shows how the SA experience changed their preconceived ideas about the UK and 'British people'. In this case, though, they did not display a positive stance towards the host country and people.

Excerpt 11: 'I had also idealized it\'

(Excerpt taken from the post-focus group with Roger and Amanda – UK)

1 **Roger:**   I was a little disappointed\ before_ I_ I had an image about the UK and *
2   oh my God\ the_ the knowledge centre_ (...) very_ very idealized
3   probably a··nd well_

4 **Amanda:** yes_ I had also idealized it\ and they are not that perfect\

5 **Roger:**   the streets are so dirty\

6 **Amanda:** they are not so * I had an idea about them like·· very courteous and very
7   perfect\ they are very perfect during the day_ but when they go out at
8   night they don't have control\ (...) I didn't like the party there because of
9   this_ because people lose control\

Roger's negative stance towards the stance object – the UK – is displayed through the adjective 'disappointed' (Line 1), thereby indexing his affect towards the country which, prior to departure, he asserted he had idealised (Line 3). Amanda took a clear convergent position to Roger's previous stance utterance by the stance marker 'yes' and by repeating the same stance utterance 'I had (also) idealized it' (Line 4). While Roger displayed a negative evaluation of the streets in the city where he was living as 'dirty' (Line 5), Amanda tied the predicate 'not that perfect' (Line 4) and the activity of 'losing control [when partying]' (Line 9) to the category 'British people'. The way Amanda generalised about 'British people' reinforces once more that 'the nation-state is still often regarded as the default signifier of cultural identification' (MacDonald & O'Regan, 2012: 553).

Regarding those students who went to Denmark, similarly to Marina (UK), Mònica and Joan displayed a very positive stance towards interacting with students from different countries. On the one hand, Mònica contended that she was 'very happy about the Erasmus experience_ (...) for helping [her] be in contact with people from abroad_ and respect_ respect other customs\'. Although initially it was not easy for Mònica to socialise with the other exchange students, towards the end of the stay she displayed a positive stance towards the 'cultural' diversity she had encountered abroad and for which she asserted that the stay had awoken her interest in travelling around the world and meeting 'different' people: 'I am willing to travel more_ to··_ to be in contact with people_ who do not necessarily have my customs\'. On the other hand, Joan (DK) asserted that 'going abroad (...) and seeing other ways of_ o·f living_ new ways of thinking_ (...) opens your mind\'. In fact, in the narrative interview, he reported doing a lot of group work mainly with two other exchange students (one from Romania and one from Germany). Excerpt 12 shows an instance where Joan (DK) commented on how the stay changed his perceptions of 'cultural difference'.

Excerpt 12: 'we have the same sense of humour'

(Taken from the narrative interview with Joan – DK)

1 Sònia: and has this Erasmus broken down any·· * any stereotypes that you had/

2 Joan: (...) well_ I think they [German people] have··_ in general_ I think they have a
3   little bit o··f_ * because I also met a German girl in Serbia and more or less *
4   they are similar\ they have another sense of humour\ (...) sometimes we made
5   jokes_ the Romanian boy and I laughed and he didn't\ you know/ and
6   sometimes he made jokes and the Romanian boy and I thought_ what/ you
7   know/ so_ I have realized that (...) Romanians and us have a lot of things in
8   common\ (...) not with the Germans but with Romanians_ (...) we have the
9   same sense of humour\

In this excerpt, we see how Joan presented two opposite category-bound features of, on the one hand, German people, whom he described as having a different sense of humour (Line 4); while, on the other hand, grouping Spanish and Romanian people into the same category-bound description as having a lot of things in common (Lines 7–8) in spite of not sharing the same nationality. Despite the fact that Joan also realised that he can share certain aspects with people from other countries, and despite the fact that he only interacted with one student from Romania during his stay, we see how he formulated generalisations about Germans, Romanians and even Spaniards as if their 'particular' sense of humour was marked by their very same nationality.

Ariadna (DK) differed from Joan in that she did not resort to essentialist comments, or what Gee (2008: 29) calls 'simplifications of reality'. Instead, she contended that, at the residence where she lived with Erasmus students from different countries, the 'country labels' were not made relevant in their daily interactions (see Excerpt 13).

Excerpt 13: 'at the end_ you didn't think in terms of country labels'

(Excerpt taken from the post-focus group with Ariadna – DK)

```
1  Ariadna:  I lived_ * we were twelve at home·_ * at the beginning it is true that you
2            were the Belgian girl or whatever_ but at the end you didn't think in
3            terms of country labels _ instead we were all_ * I don't know_ * you
4            didn't think that that girl was from another place\ since we spoke the
5            same language which was English_ you were already_ you were already
6            seen as one more\ I mean_ (...) you didn't_ you didn't think of country
7            labels\ but rather as all the same\
```

Ariadna (DK) presented a change as regards the use of 'country labels' (Line 3), which were made relevant in the initial interactions among the exchange students, but which eventually shifted to the background. She stressed the use of the English language as establishing a strong bond among the students with whom she lived and that each of them, regardless of their country of origin, was considered as 'one more' (Line 6) and/or as being 'all the same' (Line 7).

Finally, regarding those students who went to Italy, when asked to reflect on the impact of their Erasmus experience upon return, just as in the case of Mònica (DK), two of them (Patrícia and Josep M.) mentioned that the stay had triggered their willingness to travel abroad; yet, they did not present it as having changed the ways in which they perceived and dealt with cultural differences. This could be due to the fact that these students remained within their network of compatriots. In brief, the students who went to Italy did not present their Erasmus experience as being a transformative one regarding the intercultural dimension of the stay.

To sum up, at the post-stage, those students who went to the UK and Denmark confirmed the tendency observed during the stay with regard to their 'culturespeak'. That is, at these two stages their discourse showed variation with respect to the pre-stage, in the sense that the Erasmus experience appeared to have increased their awareness of cultural sameness and decreased their sense of difference. In this sense, although nationality labels were for most participants still valid as significant categories to describe the people they had encountered abroad, the majority of them mentioned that the SA had enhanced their desire to travel and have new experiences abroad.

Discussion and Conclusion

This study offers original findings about SA not previously reported, by longitudinally tracking (pre-, during and post-stay) the change in the students' perceptions/discourses of cultural difference/sameness, thereby underscoring the dynamicity and performativity of identities (Butler, 1988) and, ultimately, presenting it as an important outcome of SA. The following questions were addressed: prior to departure, how do the students express their expectation and motivation to encounter 'cultural difference'?; during the stay, is the SA experience changing their evaluation and perception of 'cultural difference', and in what way(s) do the students' social networks abroad trigger this change?; and after the stay, how do the students discursively construct the impact that the stay had on their identities in respect of their visions of the Self and 'the Other'?

With regard to the first research question, the students participated in the Erasmus programme with a clear expectation and desire to encounter cultural difference and/or the exotic Other – a difference they saw as being defined by the nation state. Indeed, before leaving, and also probably influenced by other circulating discourses on SA, the students boxed this Other into solid national categories (Dervin, 2016) and built categorial descriptions always marked by their national mask, which they considered to be presumed common-sense knowledge. Their essentialist and stereotypical mode of thinking before and at the beginning of their stay was characterised by a belief in national cultures as 'the prime units of cultural identity' (Holliday, 2016: 319) and thus, by grouping members who could be defined under the same features (e.g. 'the Danish eat more natural products' – Joan, DK; 'the British are not so open and friendly as Catalans' – Amanda, UK). Indeed, their initial use of categorisation acted as a form of prejudice (Allport, 1954) about the people with whom the students expected to interact – mostly host nationals and other exchange students. To a certain extent, this corroborates Allport's (1954: 20–21) claim that 'the human mind must think with the aid of categories [which] are the basis for normal prejudgement' and which 'saturate all that [they] contain with the same ideational and emotional flavour'.

The analysis of the students' discourse during the stay, however, and this relates to the second research question, shows that the Erasmus experience undoubtedly had an impact on their initial stereotypical thinking or discourses of Othering (Dervin, 2016), given that they started to emphasise the similarities – not so much the differences – with other students from different countries whom they had met abroad. On the one hand, those students who formed relationships with non-Spanish/non-Catalan internationals moved from 'distance-maintaining judgements' (Murphy-Lejeune, 2003: 111) about the Other to finding commonalities that, in spite of having a different nationality, their international networks may share. Once abroad, they became aware of the fact that their initial preconceived ideas about members of a given nationality somehow 'mar[red] the game prior to departure' (Murphy-Lejeune, 2003: 111) and that lack of familiarity often leads to a vision of culture that does not necessarily match 'reality' (e.g. Marina [UK] finally concluded that the category-bound predicate 'chauvinist' did not apply to all 'Hindus', as she would have claimed prior to departure; Joan [DK] expressed his surprise at the fact that Romanians had a similar sense of humour to Spanish people; and Josep M. [IT] concluded that 'at the end you realize that we are all young people·and we are all looking for the same\').

On the other hand, the students' link with other co-nationals allowed some of them to gain awareness of the fact that there may also be diverse diversities (Dervin, 2009, 2016) among people who have the same nationality. Although they still employed or associated themselves with certain nationality labels or blocks, they seemed to recognise that there may be heterogeneity within these (e.g. although he associated himself with 'Catalans', Joan [DK] expressed his disalignment as regards the way some Spanish students behaved, despite sharing the same home country).

In this sense, despite highlighting the similarities that they shared with other international students, and/or the differences with co-nationals, none of the participants (except Ariadna – DK) forewent the use of national(ity) labels to refer to their social networks and, thus, they still showed a solid and generalising understanding of 'culture' (Dervin, 2016). Yet, they refused the idea that certain category-bound features apply to all members belonging to a particular national(ity) category, as they did in the pre-stage. Thus, we can observe that there was a certain change, a positional move along the essentialist–non-essentialist continuum view of (national) 'culture', from a mainly essentialist, block-based positioning to a positioning where, although still essentialising, cultural blocks and threads (boundaries and similarities) were combined (Holliday, 2016).

Besides the fact that most students showed an enhanced willingness to travel abroad and to meet and/or to live with people from other countries, such a change (relating to the third research question) evidenced the dynamic and flexible nature of identity and simultaneously could place these 'Erasmus students' closer to the ideal of the 'intercultural speaker' (Byram *et al.*, 2001): a language learner who is at the same time open to diverse perspectives and capable of mediating among them; and for whom national labels, although still employed, are no longer presented as 'uncrossable cultural boundaries' (Holliday, 2016: 318). Accordingly, the fact that they highlight and talk about cultural threads could be interpreted as a way of building bridges with people from different countries and, thus, of approaching the Other in a renewed way: not based on preconceived cultural differences, but on the assumption of the existence of commonalities. For instance, it is interesting to note how, at the post-stage, Marina (UK) groups herself and her social networks abroad, not into a national(ity) category, but into the category 'humans', thus highlighting the similarities that they all shared despite coming from different countries. This is also corroborated by other students like Ariadna (DK) who finally described herself and all her social networks abroad under the predicate 'all the same' and asserted that 'at the end you didn't think in terms of country labels'.

If we acknowledge this shift in the students' intercultural behaviour, it could be claimed that this study's results align to some extent with the 'new' tenor that the Erasmus programme is acquiring: from a mere 'education policy towards an identity policy' (Striebeck, 2013: 198), aimed at increasing social cohesion within Europe.

To finish, this study has a number of limitations. First of all, its longitudinal approach, combined with time constraints, made it impossible to pilot the data collection methods, and consequently some of them may not have been fully effective, being either too general and not sufficiently focused, or not tackling core but peripheral issues. Finally, given that interculturality was one of the interests of the larger research project to which this study belongs, some concepts and related ideas were indirectly mentioned to the participants, who, in turn, were encouraged to (re)negotiate them.

Acknowledgements

This research was supported by Grant 2017 SGR1522. I would like to thank Àngels Llanes, Martin Howard and Helena Torres-Purroy for their insightful comments on this chapter. Finally, I am also very grateful to the anonymous reviewers for their detailed feedback and suggestions.

Notes

(1) Sònia is the researcher/interviewer.
(2) Most of the data presented in this chapter were originally in Catalan and have been translated into English.

References

Allport, G.W. (1954) *The Nature of Prejudice*. New York: Addison.
Anderson, P.H., Lawton, L., Rexeisen, R.J. and Hubbard, A.C. (2006) Short-term study abroad and intercultural sensitivity: A pilot study. *International Journal of Intercultural Relations* 30 (4), 457–469.
Behrnd, V. and Porzelt, S. (2012) Intercultural competence and training outcomes of students with experiences abroad. *International Journal of Intercultural Relations* 36 (2), 213–223.

Bracke, A. and Aguerre, S. (2015) Erasmus students: Joining communities of practice to learn French? In R. Mitchell, N. Tracy-Ventura and K. McManus (eds) *Social Interaction, Identity and Language Learning during Residence Abroad* (pp. 139–168). Amsterdam: The European Second Language Association (EUROSLA).

Butler, J. (1988) Performative acts and gender constitution: An essay in phenomenology and feminist theory. *Theatre Journal* 40 (4), 519–531.

Byram, M. (1997) *Teaching and Assessing Intercultural Communicative Competence*. Clevedon: Multilingual Matters.

Byram, M., Nichols, A. and Stevens, D. (2001) Introduction. In M. Byram, A. Nichols and D. Stevens (eds) *Developing Intercultural Competence in Practice* (pp. 1–8). Clevedon: Multilingual Matters.

Clarke, I., Flaherty, T.B., Wright, N.D. and McMillen, R.M. (2009) Student intercultural proficiency from study abroad programs. *Journal of Marketing Education* 31 (2), 173–181.

Coleman, J.A. (2013) Researching whole people and whole lives. In C. Kinginger (ed.) *Social and Cultural Aspects of Language Learning in Study Abroad* (pp. 17–44). Amsterdam/Philadelphia, PA: Benjamins.

Convey, F. (1995) The stay abroad: Objectives, strategies, outcomes. In G. Parker and A. Rouxeville (eds) *'The Year Abroad': Preparation, Monitoring, Evaluation* (pp. 127–152). London: CILT.

Cots, J.M., Aguilar, M., Mas-Alcolea, S. and Llanes, À. (2016) Studying the impact of academic mobility on intercultural competence: A mixed-methods perspective. *The Language Learning Journal* 44 (3), 304–322.

Creswell, J.W. (1998) *Qualitative Inquiry and Research Design: Choosing among Five Approaches*. London: Sage.

Deardorff, D.K. (2009) Synthesizing conceptualizations of intercultural competence: A summary and emerging themes. In D. Deardorff (ed.) *The SAGE Handbook of Intercultural Competence* (pp. 264–270). Thousand Oaks, CA: Sage.

Dervin, F. (2009) Transcending the culturalist impasse in stays abroad: Helping mobile students to appreciate diverse diversities. *Frontiers: The Interdisciplinary Journal of Study Abroad* 18, 119–141.

Dervin, F. (2011) A plea for change in research on intercultural discourses: A 'liquid' approach to the study of the acculturation of Chinese students. *Journal of Multicultural Discourses* 6 (1), 37–52.

Dervin, F. (2012) Cultural identity, representation and othering. In J. Jackson (ed.) *The Routledge Handbook of Language and Intercultural Communication* (pp. 181–194). London: Routledge.

Dervin, F. (2016) *Interculturality in Education: A Theoretical and Methodological Toolbox*. Berlin: Springer.

Du Bois, J.W. (2007) The stance triangle. In R. Englebretson (ed.) *Stancetaking in Discourse: Subjectivity, Evaluation, Interaction* (pp. 139–182). Amsterdam/Philadelphia, PA: Benjamins.

Edmonds, M. (2010) The lived experience of nursing students who study abroad: A qualitative inquiry. *Journal of Studies in International Education* 14 (5), 545–568.

Elola, I. and Oskoz, A. (2008) Blogging: Fostering intercultural competence development in foreign language and study abroad contexts. *Foreign Language Annals* 41 (3), 454–477.

European Commission (2015) *ERASMUS: Mobility Creates Opportunities – European Success Stories*. Luxembourg: Publications Office of the European Union. See https ://data.europa.eu/euodp/repository/ec/dg-eac/erasmus-data-2013-2014/erasmus-fft-brochure_online_en_FINAL.pdf (accessed 18 September 2017).

Fabricius, A.H., Mortensen, J. and Haberland, H. (2016) The lure of internationalization: Paradoxical discourses of transnational student mobility, linguistic diversity and cross-cultural exchange. *Higher Education* 73, 577–595.

Fantini, A. and Tirmizi, A. (2006) *Exploring and assessing intercultural competence*. World learning publications. Paper 1. See http://digitalcollections.sit.edu/worldlearning_publications/1 (accessed 18 February 2017).

Feyen, B. and Krzaklewska, E. (eds) (2013) *The ERASMUS Phenomenon – Symbol of a New European Generation?* Frankfurt am Main: Peter Lang.

Fitzgerald, R. and Housley, W. (eds) (2015) *Advances in Membership Categorisation Analysis*. London: Sage.

Gee, J.P. (2008) *Social Linguistics and Literacies: Ideology in Discourses* (3rd edn). New York: Routledge.

Geeraert, N., Demoulin, S. and Demes, K.A. (2014) Choose your (international) contacts wisely: A multilevel analysis on the impact of intergroup contact while living abroad. *International Journal of Intercultural Relations* 38, 86–96.

Hammer, M.R. and Bennett, M.J. (2002) *The Intercultural Development Inventory (IDI) Manual*. Portland, OR: Intercultural Communication Institute.

Hannerz, U. (1999) Reflections on varieties of culturespeak. *European Journal of Cultural Studies* 2 (3), 393–407.

Härkönen, A. and Dervin, F. (2016) Study abroad beyond the usual 'imagineering'? The benefits of a pedagogy of imaginaries. *East Asia: An International Quarterly* 33 (1), 41–58.

Harrison, N. and Peacock, N. (2010) Cultural distance, mindfulness and passive xenophobia: Using Integrated Threat Theory to explore home higher education students' perspectives on internationalisation at home. *British Educational Research Journal* 36 (6), 877–902.

Holliday, A. (2010) *Intercultural Communication and Ideology*. London: Sage.

Holliday, A. (2016) Difference and awareness in cultural travel: Negotiating blocks and threads. *Language and Intercultural Communication* 16 (3), 318–331.

Jackson, J. (2005) Assessing intercultural learning through introspective accounts. *Frontiers: The Interdisciplinary Journal of Study Abroad* 11, 165–186.

Jackson, J. (2010) *Intercultural Journeys: From Study to Residence Abroad*. Basingstoke: Palgrave Macmillan.

Jaffe, A. (2009) *Stance: Sociolinguistic Perspectives*. Oxford: Oxford University Press.

Kalocsai, K. (2014) *Communities of Practice and English as a Lingua Franca: A Study of Students in a Central European Context*. Berlin: Mouton deGruyter.

Kim, Y.Y. (2012) Beyond cultural categories: Communication, adaptation and transformation. In J. Jackson (ed.) *The Routledge Handbook of Language and Intercultural Communication* (pp. 229–243). London: Routledge.

Koskinen, L. and Tossavainen, K. (2004) Study abroad as a process of learning intercultural competence in nursing. *International Journal of Nursing Practice* 10 (3), 111–120.

Kouhpaeenejad, M.H. and Gholaminejad, R. (2014) Identity and language learning from post-structuralist perspective. *Journal of Language Teaching and Research* 5 (1), 199–204.

Krupnik, S. and Krzaklewska, E. (2013) Researching the impact of ERASMUS on European identification – Proposal for a conceptual framework. In B. Feyen and E. Krzaklewska (eds) *The ERASMUS Phenomenon – Symbol of a New European Generation?* (pp. 207–228). Frankfurt am Main: Peter Lang.

Krzaklewska, E. (2013) ERASMUS students between youth and adulthood: Analysis of the biographical experience. In B. Feyen and E. Krzaklewska (eds) *The ERASMUS Phenomenon – Symbol of a New European Generation?* (pp. 79–96). Frankfurt am Main: Peter Lang.

Krzaklewska, E. and Skórska, P. (2013) Culture shock during ERASMUS exchange – determinants, processes, prevention. In B. Feyen and E. Krzaklewska (eds) *The*

ERASMUS Phenomenon – Symbol of a New European Generation? (pp. 105–126). Frankfurt am Main: Peter Lang.

Llanes, À. and Muñoz, C. (2009) A short stay abroad: Does it make a difference? *System* 37 (3), 353–365.

MacDonald, M. and O'Regan, J.P. (2012) A global agenda for intercultural communication research and practice. In J. Jackson (ed.) *The Routledge Handbook of Language and Intercultural Communication* (pp. 553–567). London: Routledge.

Murphy-Lejeune, E. (2002) *Student Mobility and Narrative in Europe: The New Strangers*. London: Routledge.

Murphy-Lejeune, E. (2003) An experience of interculturality: Student travellers abroad. In G. Alred, M. Byram and M. Fleming (eds) *Intercultural Experience and Education* (pp. 101–113). Clevedon: Multilingual Matters.

Norrick, N.R. (2000) *Conversational Narrative: Storytelling in Everyday Talk*. Amsterdam/Philadelphia, PA: John Benjamins.

Ochs, E. and Capps, L. (1996) Narrating the self. *Annual Review of Anthropology* 25, 19–43.

Papatsiba, V. (2006) Study abroad and experiences of cultural distance and proximity: French Erasmus students. In M. Byram and A. Feng (eds) *Living and Studying Abroad: Research and Practice* (pp. 108–133). Clevedon: Multilingual Matters.

Payrató, L. and Alturo, N. (2002) *Corpus oral de conversa colloquial. Materials de treball* (Vol. 11). Barcelona: Edicions Universitat Barcelona.

Phillips, A. (2007) *Multiculturalism without Culture*. Princeton, NJ: Princeton University Press.

Piller, I. (2011) *Intercultural Communication: A Critical Introduction*. Edinburgh: Edinburgh University Press.

Pozo-Vicente, C. and Aguaded-Gómez, J.I. (2012) El programa de movilidad ERASMUS: motor de la adquisición de competencias interculturales. *Revista de Investigación Educativa* 30 (2), 441–458.

Quinlan, E. (2008) Conspicuous invisibility: Shadowing as a data collection strategy. *Qualitative Inquiry* 14 (8), 1480–1499.

Sacks, H. (1972) On the analyzability of stories by children. In J. Gumperz and D. Hymes (eds) *Directions in Sociolinguistics: The Ethnography of Communication* (pp. 329–345). New York: Holt, Rinehart and Winston.

Stokoe, E. (2009) Doing actions with identity categories: Complaints and denials in neighbor disputes. *Text & Talk* 29 (1), 75–97.

Stokoe, E. (2012) Moving forward with membership categorization analysis: Methods for systematic analysis. *Discourse Studies* 14 (3), 277–303.

Striebeck, J. (2013) A matter of belonging and trust: The creation of a European identity through the ERASMUS programme? In B. Feyen and E. Krzaklewska (eds) *The ERASMUS Phenomenon – Symbol of a New European Generation?* (pp. 191–206). Frankfurt am Main: Peter Lang.

Tracy-Ventura, N., Dewaele, J-M., Köylü, Z. and McManus, K. (2016) Personality changes after the 'year abroad'? *Study Abroad Research in Second Language Acquisition and International Education* 1 (1), 107–127.

Tsoukalas, I. (2008) The double life of Erasmus students. In F. Dervin and M. Byram (eds) *Students, Staff and Academic Mobility in Higher Education* (pp. 131–152). Newcastle: Cambridge Scholars Publishing.

Van Mol, C. (2014) Erasmus student mobility as a gateway to the international labour market? In J. Gerhards, S. Hans and S. Carlson (eds) *Globalisierung, Bildung und grenzüberschreitende Mobilität* (pp. 295–314). Berlin: Springer.

Waters, J. and Brooks, R. (2011) 'Vive la différence?': The 'international' experiences of UK students overseas. *Population, Space and Place* 17 (5), 567–578.

Wood, L. (2013) Social ERASMUS? Active citizenship among exchange students. In B. Feyen and E. Krzaklewska (eds) *The ERASMUS Phenomenon – Symbol of a New European Generation?* (pp. 127–139). Frankfurt am Main: Peter Lang.

Zemach-Bersin, T. (2009) Selling the world: Study abroad marketing and the privatization of global citizenship. In R. Lewin (ed.) *The Handbook of Practice and Research in Study Abroad: Higher Education and the Quest for Global Citizenship* (pp. 303–320). New York: Routledge.

Appendix: Transcription Conventions

(Based on Payrató and Alturo's [2002] transcription system)

Laughter: Laughter particles are indicated with the @ symbol between the '+' symbol, approximating syllable number; utterances spoken laughingly appear between square brackets.

Lengthening: Dots (·) indicate prolongation of the immediately prior sound.

Repetition: All voluntary and involuntary repetitions of words and phrases are transcribed.

Terminal pitch movement: Rising pitch movement is marked with a slash (/); falling pitch movement is marked with a backslash (\); continuing or level pitch movement is marked with an underscore (_).

Reformulation of an idea: An asterisk (*) indicates that the speaker has reformulated an idea.

Omissions: Words omitted are indicated with three dots between square brackets [...]; a word that was started but left unfinished is indicated by the ampersand symbol &.

Non-Catalan speech: Utterances in languages that are not the speaker's first language (Catalan) appear between square brackets with the language indicated.

4 Discursive Identity Work and Interculturality during Blue-Collar Work Practice Abroad: Finnish Engineering Students as Language Learners and Users

Tiina Räisänen

Introduction

The focus of this chapter is on questions of identity and interculturality during work practice abroad. It complements earlier applied linguistic research on study abroad (SA) that has largely documented second language (L2) learning outcomes (Benson *et al.*, 2013: 35; see Kinginger, 2009 for an overview). The present study concentrates on engineering students who intend to learn about their field of study in Germany, where English has the role of a foreign language. Although the students have their first extensive experience of using English as a lingua franca (ELF) with speakers of different first languages (L1s) while working abroad, they cannot manage only with English but instead need to use other communicative resources, develop their repertoires and (re)negotiate their identities. Importantly, although the students have little or no earlier experience in the local language, German, they are expected to learn and use it at work (cf. Benson *et al.*, 2013: 35–36). Such situations represent contemporary, late-modern working life, increasingly characterized by migration, mobility and hybridity (Canagarajah, 2013a; Duchêne *et al.*, 2013; Messelink *et al.*, 2015). As people need to work with others with different biographies and histories of socialization, and different values and norms, competence in dealing with interactions becomes a key issue. People from different linguacultural backgrounds may not have very much knowledge about cultural, linguistic and religious diversity in general (Ladegaard & Jenks, 2015: 2; see also Jackson, 2014) and therefore working in such environments poses various challenges and requires a particular kind of professional communicative repertoire (Räisänen, 2013; see also Louhiala-Salminen & Kankaanranta, 2011).

Student mobility can take various forms, among them student exchange, study visits, practical training and different types of internships. All of these share the element of a 'stay abroad', which is used here as an umbrella term to refer to various types of programs involving students studying, working and living outside their countries of origin as part of their education. Staying abroad is a temporary form of migration and a site for identity development, socialization and the learning of various linguistic, cultural, social, personal, intercultural and professional skills (Benson et al., 2013: 35; Messelink et al., 2015). Migration here refers to any 'mobile citizen who migrates or is mobile for various reasons' such as work and leisure (Duchêne et al., 2013: 6–7). Staying abroad is commonly seen as an essential tool to develop various competences needed in professional life (e.g. Kinginger, 2009; Lewis, 2009; Paige et al., 2009). In particular, a stay abroad is part of the education of future professionals to face the demands of competitive job markets, to become global citizens in the multicultural world (Jackson, 2008) and to earn 'mobility capital' (Murphy-Lejeune, 2002). As a learning context within higher education, it has grown in popularity over recent decades as part of institutions' internationalization attempts (OECD, 2015). For instance, student mobility within the European student exchange program, Erasmus, has increased enormously. For example, the number of students in higher education leaving Finland for a period of more than three months' mobility was fewer than 7,000 in 2000, while in 2015 that number had increased to over 10,000 students (CIMO, 2016).

Language and intercultural learning during a stay abroad have been popular topics of applied linguistic research. The following section outlines the major foci of earlier research and situates this chapter in the tradition.

Stay Abroad Research: Language Learning and Intercultural Communication

A brief outline of earlier research

Within applied linguistics, research on staying abroad as part of educational studies, labelled 'study abroad', has developed rapidly over the past few decades along with the increasing popularity of various SA programs. Since the first studies were published in the 1990s (Freed, 1995; Pellegrino, 1998; Polanyi, 1995), SA research has been concerned with capturing language learning outcomes and the kind of personal and social factors that contribute to the (non-)success of the stay (e.g. Dewey *et al.*, 2013; Isabelli-García, 2006; Llanes *et al.*, 2012). Increasing attention has also been targeted at individual students' different and unique development and changes during the stay abroad; for example, how students construct diversity (Dervin & Layne, 2013), identities (Benson *et al.*, 2013; Jackson, 2008, 2010) and an intercultural mindset (Jackson, 2016). On the research agenda have also been intercultural learning (see Beaven & Borghetti, 2016) and the development of intercultural competence (e.g. Holmes & O'Neill, 2012) and intercultural communicative competence (e.g. Boye, 2016). For example, Bennett's (1993, 2004) Developmental Model of Intercultural Sensitivity has been utilized to capture student sojourners' trajectory of intercultural development along the continuum of ethnocentrism and ethnorelativism (Anderson *et al.*, 2006; Jackson, 2009, 2010, 2011).

Most SA research on language learning and intercultural development has focused on students in target language contexts and host cultures (e.g. DeKeyser, 2010; Jackson, 2008, 2009, 2010, 2011; Kinginger, 2009, 2013; Martinsen, 2011). Findings have revealed major variation between individuals and their learning outcomes (Beaven & Spencer-Oatey, 2016: 350). Fewer studies have looked at students with little or no knowledge of the host language but with a history of learning English as a foreign language. Moreover, previous studies have principally been interested in students of an L2 and students studying through the medium of an L2 abroad. This study adds a new dimension to research by focusing on non-language specialists whose primary purpose in their stay abroad is to do a compulsory internship, and to do this partly in a language that they had not previously studied. It is important to study such contexts because they also shed light on the communicative challenges faced by transnational workers (see e.g. Ladegaard & Jenks, 2015; Roberts, 2010; Zhu, 2014), who need to get their job done regardless of their level of language proficiency (cf. Louhiala-Salminen *et al.*, 2005; Räisänen, 2013). As this chapter shows, workers require a particular kind of communicative repertoire and need to reconstruct their identities.

Competence, culture and interculturality

In SA research, students' encounters with locals and other students during a stay abroad are usually viewed as intercultural, and in relation to these, students' intercultural (communicative) competencies and their development have been of interest. This has given rise to two important notions in terms of the present study: competence and culture.

Intercultural competence is a popular concept used to refer to the skills and attitudes needed to communicate successfully with people from different backgrounds.[1] These skills include the ability to interact with others, mediate between different perspectives, acceptance and sensitivity towards other people and cultures and their perceptions of the world, and awareness of one's own cultural positioning (Byram *et al.*, 2001; Wilkinson, 2012). However, the notion of competence is somewhat problematic because it presupposes knowledge of a set of dispositions, attitudes, abilities and skills that can be compartmentalized and evaluated and that progress neatly, linearly and cumulatively (Canagarajah, 2018: 35). This dominant assumption of competence as perfect mastery of a set of skills has been challenged with a call for a more practice-based and spatial approach and a view of 'competence' as success in situated encounters with the use of one's full repertoire (Canagarajah, 2018). This includes translanguaging, that is, the process of making meaning and producing knowledge by moving not only between languages but also beyond them and beyond semiotic modes and modalities (Blackledge & Creese, 2017; Li, 2016: 3–4). The notions of translanguaging and translingual practice (Canagarajah, 2013b) highlight the use of a whole range of resources (linguistic, embodied, material) used by people when communicating and aiming at achieving their goals, and at work, to handle their everyday tasks. Moreover, competence in this framework relates to being sensitive to communicative resources needed in a particular context. Knowing how to do this in an intercultural encounter where one needs to use a foreign language is particularly important in working life.

Before elaborating on interculturality, we need to look at the second notion, culture. Static and essentialist conceptualizations of culture and cultural membership, which characterize much of traditional intercultural communication research (e.g. Hofstede, 1983), have been challenged by scholars influenced by the poststructuralist paradigm (e.g. Dervin, 2014; Holliday, 2010). A great deal of intercultural communication research has sought to compare distinct cultural groups' behavior and communicative practices (the term 'cross-cultural communication', see Scollon & Scollon, 2001), or has studied cultural differences between distinct groups from an interactional perspective (labelled as 'intercultural communication' – Scollon and Scollon [2001]). Studies have taken as a starting point that intercultural communication occurs between distinct cultural groups and, as Piller (2011: 14–15) notes, in such studies culture and cultural identity are treated as something that people have, and which thus inherently influence how they approach communication and actually communicate.

The concept of interculturality problematizes the static notions of culture and cultural identity and emphasizes the *inter* nature of interactions.[2] In communication, individuals produce and interpret subjective and intersubjective constructions of cultural identities (e.g. Dervin & Liddicoat, 2013). Interculturality refers to individuals' cultural affiliations as emergent in interactions – the core idea is that cultural differences are salient only if participants make them relevant during interaction (Higgins, 2007; see also Mori, 2003; Zhu, 2015). Therefore, cultural identities are not necessarily relevant if the focus is on other identities (e.g. professional and gender). Cultural identities are avowed, ascribed, reworked or resisted at the level of interpersonal interaction and relationships. They are situated, practical accomplishments in interactions and emerge through both the interplay of self-orientation and ascription-by-others, and the interplay of language use and sociocultural identities (Zhu, 2015). As cultural identities and cultural memberships are discursively constructed, 'culture thus exists only insofar as it is performed, and even then its ontological status is that of a pointedly analytical abstraction' (Baumann, 1996: 11). Hence, culture in intercultural communication should not be seen as something that people have, but rather as something that people construct, do and make relevant (see also Piller, 2011: 15). According to Dervin (2010), the notion of interculturality highlights the presence of the other (her/his language proficiency, age, gender, etc.) in intercultural competence; it does not solely focus on the individual and measure her/his abilities.

In interactions, then, individuals orient to identities and cultural frames of reference in different ways and co-construct their understanding together by managing and working through not only their differences but also their similarities, using processes of adequation and distinction (Bucholtz & Hall, 2003). In ELF interactions in particular, which are relevant for this chapter, people are seen to bring together their own linguacultural backgrounds and repertoires in order to achieve their goals in whatever activity they are engaged (Baker, 2009: 581–582). In his study, Baker (2009, 2011, 2016) focused on conceptualizations of culture in ELF by drawing on empirical data from L2 learners and users of English at a university in Thailand. His findings show that ELF users draw on multiple cultural frames of reference, moving between and across local, national and global contexts in dynamic ways (Baker, 2009). In another study, Kalocsai (2009) studied Erasmus exchange students' socialization into newly emerging ELF communities of practice. The students successfully learned to use ELF but experienced challenges in socializing with locals due to problems in their language proficiency and language choice (Kalocsai, 2009: 42–43). Virkkula and Nikula's (2010) and Räisänen's (2016) studies on Finnish engineering students' identity construction before and after staying abroad show that as a result of their increased contact with other ELF speakers, students' identities change from English as a foreign language (EFL) learners to ELF users, with national culture an important resource for identity construction. This highlights the constructed nature of culture and identities as situated, fluid and changing, as understood in social constructionism (e.g. Gergen, 1999; Hall, 1996). The present study sheds further light on foreign language learners' and users' identity work as they orient to discourses of sameness and difference during work practice abroad where they need to use ELF.

The Study

Participants

This chapter draws on a longitudinal study that has followed a group of Finnish engineers for over 15 years, since 2003 when, as students at a university of applied sciences,[3] they enrolled in a four- to six-month internship at a factory in Germany. Their work consisted of working on machines, assisting the permanent personnel and handling manufactured material. The students' L1 is Finnish, they were born in Finland between 1977 and 1981, and they had lived in Finland all their lives before the stay abroad. They had studied English as a school subject (a foreign language) for over ten years since third grade, and Swedish since eighth grade, and some of them had taken a course in German either in high school or higher education.

Before their stay abroad, all except one of the students had travelled abroad for a holiday for only two weeks; only one had been abroad for a month. They reported having used English very little in Finland apart from at school, reading news on the internet and occasional encounters with tourists on the street. The students saw the use of English principally in terms of speaking and mentioned the lack of opportunities to speak English in Finland (Virkkula & Nikula, 2010). Thus, for them the stay abroad manifested itself as an opportunity to use English in out-of-school contexts because English was the only foreign language they knew before going to Germany.

The students lived in a student dorm in a small town in Germany, where they interacted with local residents and other students from Germany, Greece, China and India. The students had blue-collar jobs in a factory, and colleagues from Germany and Portugal. Company policy advocated the learning and use of German on the job rather than English. Since the students had little or no knowledge of German, they preferred English but over time learned some German. This chapter focuses on five participants: Pete, Tero, Oskari, Risto and Simo (the names are pseudonyms). As a researcher, I was able to gain an ethnographic and insider's perspective on the participants' lives, experiences and communicative situations since at the same time I was doing my own compulsory period of language practice as a student of German; I travelled with them, worked in the same factory, and lived in the same dorm.

Ethnographic and discursive approach

This chapter combines ethnographic and discursive perspectives to try to find out what discourses the students draw on, how they orient to sameness and difference, and what identities they make relevant in these discursive processes.

Here, ethnography functions both as a methodology and an approach; it is 'a way of seeing the world'. Ethnography makes it possible to see connections between specific micro-level instances and macro-level societal issues, policies, practices and ideologies (Blommaert & Dong, 2010). Combined with a longitudinal approach, it makes it possible to trace how individuals' prior socialization to discourses, learning biographies and histories plays a role in their current practices, such as orientations to sameness and difference (cf. Duff, 2008; Garrett & Baquedano-López, 2002). Thus, ethnography can account for the important historical aspect of a stay abroad, as biographies and individual histories facilitate understanding of the changes that occur (Benson *et al.*, 2013: 3). Ethnography also ensures that the place and space of practices will be incorporated into understanding both human practices and their development (see e.g. Weisner, 1996), as findings are contextualized, situated and conceptually and empirically connected to the properties of the social settings in which they are studied.

When individuals talk about their experiences and language use abroad, they draw on discourses. Discourses are people's 'socially accepted association[s] among ways of using language, of thinking, feeling, believing, valuing and of acting [...]' (Gee, 1990: 143). They offer individuals resources for identity work (Bamberg *et al.*, 2011; Georgakopoulou, 2007), that is, ways to understand one's relationship to the world. Hence, by drawing on discourses, individuals position themselves as certain kinds of people and project a certain identity. A discursive approach makes it possible to explore individuals' interculturality because, in drawing on discourses, people construct their reality, and reject and embrace aspects of that reality and their own (changing) place within it.

Discourses are not merely handed down to individuals, but individuals have agency to orient to certain discourses and identities in talk (Bamberg *et al.*, 2011). From a non-essentialist standpoint, identities are discursive, dynamic, changing and context dependent. Thus, identities and discourses do not just exist as given notions, but they are discursively constructed by individuals and made relevant by them (see also Piller, 2011: 3; Zhu, 2015). As Bamberg *et al.* (2011: 188) argue, 'it is typically through discursive choices that people define a sense of (an individual) self as different from others, or they integrate a sense of who they are into communities of others'. In interactions, participants do contextualization work, establishing relationships between the context and identifications (Gumperz, 1982). According to Piller (2011: 172), a key question in intercultural communication is: 'who makes culture relevant to whom in which context for which purposes?'. It is thus of interest to see how culture is drawn on in our participants' interviews to define the self and the other and to explain behavior.

Interviews as interaction

The study presented here utilizes interview data and my ethnographic knowledge to study the participants' discursive identity work and interculturality. Interviewing is a key method in qualitative research (e.g. Potter & Hepburn, 2012; Rapley, 2001). Often, however, the interviewee's talk is taken as the sole focus of analysis and is isolated from the local context of interaction in which the talk originally occurred, i.e. the interaction between interviewee and interviewer. This silences the interviewer's talk, questions, comments and requests, which are not considered in the analysis (Rapley, 2001: 304). However, in solely extracting the interviewees' accounts as versions of reality, we may actually misinterpret that reality since it may have been introduced or invoked by the interviewer, not the interviewee. It is, after all, the interviewer who introduces topics and guides the interview in the desired direction, thus inevitably influencing the interviewees' answers (Dervin, 2011: 47). Interviews should be seen as interactions in which the interlocutors co-construct reality (Dervin, 2013: 92, citing Shi-xu, 2001: 285; Rapley, 2001) and jointly orient to interculturality.

In this study, the thematic interviews were conducted in Finnish (see Appendix A and B). Each participant was first interviewed in May 2003 (at the beginning of the stay abroad) and then for the second time either in August or November 2003 (after the stay) depending on the length of each participant's stay abroad (four to six months). The interviews each lasted about one hour and they were transcribed and analyzed in their totality to identify emergent themes across the interviews and participants' orientations to interculturality. Based on close reading of the transcripts, recurrent themes emerged and were grouped together into codes: language learning, language use, surviving with English at work, language competence, English as a global language, German as a local language and adjustment to German culture. Based on these codes, the following main categories were identified: language policy at work, discourses of global vs. local language, translanguaging and identity struggle.

The extracts in this chapter include the interviewer's questions and feedback in order to illustrate the co-construction of reality. In addition, pauses, stress and laughter are included since analysis should consider not only what the participants say but also how they say it (see Appendix C). Due to space restrictions, the extracts are translations from Finnish to English but the analysis draws on the original versions. I acknowledge that translations are never full presentations of the original data but representations by the researcher. Moreover, some expressions and word choices are difficult to translate; therefore, transparency in the research report is important. As an illustration, Appendix D includes two samples of the original Finnish versions.

Findings

Language learner and user identities

This section provides an overview of earlier studies on the participants' identity construction in relation to using English (Räisänen, 2012, 2013, 2016; Virkkula & Nikula, 2010). This is complemented with a focus on their identities in the framework of interculturality. Before their stay abroad, these students had constructed language learner identities by drawing heavily on discourses of schooling and education, which is understandable, given their background and histories. They felt that opportunities for speaking English in Finland were rare, which partly explains their feelings of anxiety and fear about using English. At that time, they held a very compartmentalized view of language as consisting of specific elements to be learned, such as grammar, vocabulary and pronunciation, and they considered native speaker competence the target of learning. Their discursive work points to their backgrounds in very monolingual towns in the 1990s and early 2000s, where they would encounter foreign languages mainly through the media and at school where they focused largely on learning language structures.

The stay abroad contributed to changes in students' identity construction, moving them toward a view of themselves as legitimate (Norton, 2000) users of ELF in relation to other ELF speakers with whom they interacted abroad. They all described increased confidence in speaking English. A collective aspect of linguaculture strengthened in their identity work, as the participants talked about themselves as Finnish users of English and drew on their national culture.

While earlier studies have focused on participants' identity construction in relation to learning and using English abroad, this chapter focuses on their identities in the framework of interculturality, also in relation to German and from the point of view of overlapping themes: language policy at work, discourses of global vs. local language, translanguaging and identity struggle.

Language policy at work

This section addresses the role of the official language policy and situation at work in the participants' orientations to interculturality and identity work. Most of the permanent workers followed the company's language policy, according to which everyone must speak German. Those who knew some English but did not want to speak it may have been afraid of their German boss and possible sanctions. Some of the workers showed little knowledge of English while others spoke it despite the policy (mostly workers of Portuguese origin). This situation caused major challenges for the students who did not know enough German. In Example 1, Pete elaborates on the challenge.

Example 1: Pete (May 2003)

Tiina: well do you think you'll survive with your English proficiency here in Germany?
if you think about how you felt before leaving and maybe now? [---]
Pete: no I'll <u>survive</u> no problem (.)
but I've noticed that (.) with <u>English</u> yes there's no problem
but then you imagine that (.) you hear your colleagues
and almost none of them are speaking English and only you are speaking it
so it is (.) it would be nice to work with a guy (.) in the same workstation
who speaks English
so it would be good (xxx)
Tiina: yeah
Pete: but I would like to learn German (.) it would help after all

First, I ask Pete's opinion about how well he will survive with his English skills in Germany. Pete's position as a competent English speaker is rather obvious as he says that he will survive with English without any problems (the words survive and English are stressed). However, this identity is challenged at work. Pete first makes a contrastive move ('but') and then verbalizes his experience: hearing his colleagues not speaking English and only himself speaking it. There is a clash between his expectations and reality as English skills do not guarantee success in workplace communication. Although Pete would like to communicate in English at work, he would also like to learn German. Risto expressed similar challenges and drew on a discourse of life without language, positioning himself as speechless. In Example 2, Simo draws on the same discourse and an undesirable identity as someone willing to speak but unable to do so, thereby feeling 'stupid' (*tyhmä*).

Example 2: Simo (May 2003)

Tiina: so how does it feel at work when you can't survive with English?
Simo: heheheheh <u>stupid</u> (.) I would like to talk <u>all</u> the time
I have the kind of personality who kind of talks all the time
Tiina: mm
Simo: and then you can't (.) or you <u>can</u> talk there but they label you as <u>crazy</u>
if you start speaking Finnish or English to yourself and they don't understand

Simo is forced to align to a new identity, which prevents him from being true to himself. This identity is also ascribed to him by others, as Simo illustrates when referring to being 'labelled as crazy' (*leimaa hulluksi*) if he starts speaking English to people who do not know it. Interculturality and orientations to difference emerge both from the company's language policy and from the workers' differing language proficiency. For the students, just as for mobile people and migrants in general, knowing the local language may be crucial for fitting in, and it has symbolic power in identity construction processes (see also Angouri, 2013).

As previously mentioned, not all workers followed the German-only rule during the Finnish students' work practice. Tero (Example 3) explains that initially his colleagues did not speak English at all and demanded that Tero should learn German, but by the end they had started to say a few words. This could have been the result of a change either in their attitude toward the language policy or in their actual English proficiency.

Example 3: Tero (August 2003)

Tiina:	do they like speaking English with you?
Tero:	well they do now (.)
	but at first they wouldn't speak it at all
	but now they have started to say a few words
	and those who know English do speak now
Tiina:	yeah
Tero:	<u>yes</u> at <u>first</u> they thought that I have to learn German
Tiina:	right so they noticed that
Tero:	that it's better to speak English
Tiina:	yeah
Tero:	since that guy will never learn German heheh

In the final part of the extract, we jointly construct an explanation for the Germans' willingness to speak English in the end: after Tero's colleagues had noticed that 'that guy will never learn German', they decided that they had better speak English. Also, Pete explicitly mentions how local workers changed their orientation to the Finnish students' repertoires by starting to speak English after claiming for five months that they could not speak it at all. Hence, a grassroots policy gradually emerges that challenges official policy (see also Angouri, 2013). Interestingly, as shown in Virkkula and Nikula (2010), nationality is given as one reason for people's (un)willingness to speak English: Pete, for instance, said that the threshold to speak English was probably lower for Finns than for the locals. This relates to discourses of global and local language.

Discourses of global vs. local language

In discussions on language policy and proficiency, a dichotomy emerges between discourses of English as a global language and German as a local language. This global–local distinction closely relates to interculturality and the participants' construction of themselves and Germans as speakers of English.

In Example 4, when I ask Simo to explain what language proficiency means to him, he mentions communication 'with people in different languages', for instance Finns using English.

Example 4: Simo (May 2003)

Tiina:	so then the term language proficiency (.) something that is used <u>a lot</u>
Simo:	mm

Tiina: so what do you think it means? can you explain?
Simo: language proficiency (2.0) well to be able to communicate (2.0)
         with people in different languages (2.0)
         like (.) Finns in English
Tiina: mm
Simo: and also that (.) in quite many countries it surely is taught so that
         people can communicate through it
         so that they don't have to (2.0)
         like I haven't studied any German so (2.0)
         I can speak with Germans a little bit
         although they don't seem to be very willing to speak English heh

English is offered as an example of a global language, taught in 'quite many countries' and utilized by people in communication. After this, Simo begins with 'so that they don't have to', interrupts himself and gives himself as an example of one who has not studied any German. Therefore, for Simo, English seems to be the best foreign language for people to choose to learn: since it is a global language, one does not have to use and learn other languages. Interestingly, Simo positions Germans as rather unwilling to speak English. Thus, by drawing on a discourse of English as a global language, he orients to differences between Finns and Germans, assigns them different English-speaker identities and identifies himself as a Finnish person speaking English more willingly than Germans do.

In Example 5, Pete draws on the same discourse. Before the following exchange occurs, Pete has described his feelings about learning German with the adjective 'hopeless' (*toivotonta*). Then I ask him whether he thinks he should know German or other people should know English. I thus topicalize the aspect of difference between Pete's and local people's language proficiency, which then forces Pete to continue with that orientation. His word choices reveal his position.

Example 5: Pete (May 2003)

Tiina: well do you think that you should know German here or that (.)
         other people should know English? now?
Pete: (3.0) it is really that when in Rome you do as the Romans do (2.0)
         so I should know German (.)
         but since I don't I of course hope that they would speak English hehe
Tiina: yeah so after all you're <u>here</u> so the language too
Pete: yeah yes and at least a little bit
Tiina: mm
Pete: but after all English in my opinion is the kind of language that everyone
         should know (2.0)
         <u>at least a little</u> bit

Pete draws on a popular, shared discourse of 'When in Rome, do as the Romans do' (*maassa maan tavalla*), which is linked to both acculturation to Germany and respect for local customs. Here, Pete orients to the language of the nation and newcomers' need to adopt, learn and use the national language, and he shows sensitivity toward other people's culture and language. However, after this, a contrastive discourse, English as a global language, is introduced (a language 'everyone should know, at least a little'). Judging by these two representative examples, a definite tension exists between local and global discourses, which then plays a role in how interculturality emerges. Interculturality has to be understood in relation to both micro-level matters, such as the individual's language skills, attitudes and opportunities to speak, and macro-level ideologies and widely circulating discourses. While for Pete, English has value as a global language, his interlocutors align with more locally valued discourses.

Oskari in Example 6 demonstrates similar discursive work. Before our discussion, Oskari has explained how he should have taken some German classes before coming to Germany. Then I ask the same question I asked Pete earlier.

Example 6: Oskari (May 2003)

Tiina:	well do you feel that you should know German here?
	or should people here know English?
	so that you could survive with English
Oskari:	well (6.0)
	well I should know basic things in German too
	I can't require them to know English
	but English is after all such a common language and it is taught here
	so yes (.)
	I think it is not <u>rude</u>
	I mean kind of <u>arrogant</u> to demand that they speak English <u>if</u> they can (.)
	so (.) it's difficult to understand if they are insulted by it
	at least for me it feels quite odd

Here Oskari, too, demonstrates sensitivity toward the local language, the basics of which he thinks he should know, and expresses the opinion that he cannot require Germans to know English. Then Oskari's orientation changes. He draws on a discourse of English as a global language, including notions of a common language and a language taught in German schools. This, then, works to justify Oskari's views: he says that it is not rude (*töykeätä*) or arrogant (*röyhkeää*) to demand that Germans should speak English if they know it. Finally, Oskari puts himself in the same position as someone required to speak English and not feeling offended by that. Interculturality lies in these discourses and in identity work as Oskari ascribes identities to himself and Germans as speakers of a local language and a global language. These co-constructed discourses and orientations in the interview provide a window to processes involving interculturality.

Although the dichotomy between the discourses is obvious, contextual factors need to be acknowledged in understanding interculturality. Whether English should be spoken by everyone is a situated notion.

For instance, Simo refers to his workstation colleagues (older than him, approximately in their fifties and sixties) who do not speak English. Due to their being 'old men', they cannot be expected to know English. While it may be difficult for the students to accept a situation in which a global language has no currency, they are able to show alignment and sensitivity toward the other.

The students' stories from the shop floor naturally raise an important question: how were they able to handle their work without any knowledge of German?

Translanguaging

The interviews illustrate that in the face of diversity people are creative in inventing survival strategies, orienting to similarity and aiming to find common ground. This points to the importance of interpersonal relations in interculturality. Strategies for coping include humor and playfulness, learning German and using one's full communicative repertoire, including translingual practices (Canagarajah, 2013b) and translanguaging (García, 2009; García & Li, 2014; Li, 2016), which draws on spatial repertoires. A spatial repertoire refers to the resources available in the particular space–time in which the activity occurs (Canagarajah, 2018; Pennycook & Otsuji, 2015: 84). These resources include the use of languages, ways of speaking, semiotic resources and modalities (e.g. Räisänen, 2018; Virkkula-Räisänen, 2010).

Example 7 points to the use of one's full repertoire at work. Risto explains how he has been able to solve issues at work so far by resorting to embodied resources, as shown by his reference to 'hands-on' activity. However, this is not a long-term solution, since Risto feels that he cannot accomplish a great deal of the work (work 'is left undone', *jää tekemättä* in Finnish), and thus tasks are not learned because of Risto's failure to understand his co-workers' language. In responding to the question about his colleagues' reactions, Risto confirms their positive attitude although he is embarrassed (*nolona*) by his inability to speak.

Example 7: Risto (May 2003)

Tiina: well have you been able to handle your issues or kind of-?
Risto: well yes so far at least I have
    if not in any other way then hands-on
Tiina: mm
Risto: but yeah a lot of work is left undone (.)
    jobs not learned since you just simply can't <u>understand</u> so
Tiina: mm
    so how have your colleagues taken it now at the beginning?
Risto: <u>ye:ah</u> they have taken it really nicely (.)
    although I can't help but be <u>embarrassed</u> since I just can't speak

This example shows how the availability of non-linguistic resources does not necessarily overcome any embarrassment caused by a lack of language proficiency. Language is a powerful device in identity work and in excluding and discriminating others at work (Lønsmann, 2014). For example, Simo described how one colleague would use gestures to facilitate meaning making, and another showed dislike of Simo's lack of German proficiency. Simo was able to 'read' this immediately from people's looks and their way of speaking, which was 'sort of snapping' (*semmosta tiuskimista*). Interestingly, Simo justifies this and shows his intercultural awareness by pointing out that everybody is entitled to their own opinion. Interculturality in relation to language choice is also illustrated by Tero (Example 8).

Example 8: Tero (August 2003)

Tiina: how about in those offices have you been able to survive in English or?
Tero: well yes after all in English
very seldom have there been situations in which I haven't been able to (.) speak or been able to solve things (.)
I can't think of anything now (.)
only in English and then I've tried to say a few German words in between
Tiina: yeah (.) have there been situations that you just haven't survived at all or have they always been somehow?
Tero: (3.0) yeah well (.) maybe at work if a colleague has come and spoken German or (.) asked
me to do something so then it hasn't necessarily been solved until he has come along to show me
Tiina: yeah right (.) have you learned German?
Tero: well yeah I've been forced to learn a bit although I haven't necessarily always wanted to learn it heh
Tiina: yeah
Tero: but yeah I have learned <u>some</u>

At work, Tero's strategy has been to use English along with a few German words. Elsewhere, he describes this as 'a kind of mixed language' (*semmosta sekakieltä*). The choice of using German indicates Tero's sensitivity and respect toward the local language and an orientation to mutual alignment and sameness. He also refers to embodied resources at work when there is no shared language: a work matter was solved only after the co-worker himself demonstrated the task. However, when I ask Tero about his German learning, he says laughingly how he has been forced to learn it. Tero thus treats the matter humorously. Nevertheless, compared to his orientation to sameness, here, by adopting a humorous and somewhat reluctant stance to learning German, he orients to difference. While translanguaging and using a full repertoire demonstrate mutual alignment and joint construction of meaning, reluctance to learn a local language points toward resistance to alignment. Thus, a tension exists between these orientations.

Oskari's talk, too, points to translanguaging in Example 9. He explains that he has tried to explain things in English 'mixing it up with a few German words' that he knows. Learning German and translanguaging indicate an orientation to sameness. However, the Finnish word choice *sotkea* ('mix up') has a somewhat negative connotation and indicates slight resistance toward mixing languages. Possibly, for Oskari, using one language at a time would be more appropriate, and the right way to perform as a competent language user. Despite using all he knows, Oskari has 'encountered a wall', by which he means the inability to communicate and running out of resources. Oskari describes this as 'frustrating' (*turhauttavaa*).

Example 9: Oskari (May 2003)

Tiina:	can you think of situations in which you had to spend a long time explaining something
	or has it just been that you haven't
Oskari:	well yeah a few times
	at work there have been kind of situations in which I've tried to explain something in English
	mixing it up with a few German words that I know
	but then I've encountered a wall that I just couldn't
	that I ran out of means so that it was just better (.) to let it be
Tiina:	so how does it make you feel when you really want to say
Oskari:	well it's frustrating
	so that you just couldn't (.)
	but you can't do anything about it
Tiina:	mm
Oskari:	because they know it so poorly at work

During their stay abroad, all the participants developed their individual repertoires and learned some German. Risto even said that his German dictionary was probably his most read book during the past five years. Overall, the spatial repertoires, in which co-workers' linguistic repertoires did not meet those of the students, initially posed a major threat to the students' identities.

Identity struggle

Piller (2011: 146) notes that '[w]ho we are in intercultural communication is to a large extent a function of our linguistic proficiency. You cannot "be" an educational expert or a competent shopper if you do not sound like one'. This is reflected in the participants' identity work in relation to the languages they needed during their stay abroad. They constructed different identities in relation to different foreign languages (see also Beaven & Spencer-Oatey, 2016); for example, in using English, one of them had difficulty participating in a conversation in English because thinking what to say takes time and he did not know how to use fillers. Another student when speaking English asked for and received information without making any small talk. Pete explicitly frames small talk as a feature that is somewhat foreign for Finns in general. As discussed in Räisänen (2016), this points to Sajavaara and Lehtonen's (1997) study reflecting on a discourse of Finns' national, and stereotypical, perception of themselves as untalkative northerners.

As regards the German language, the participants first aligned with identities as outsiders. They were asked about how they felt living in a country without any knowledge of the local language. Pete (Example 10) claims to be like 'Alice in Wonderland', for example in stores where everything is labelled only in German. This creates a barrier, influencing one's daily life and shopping practices. In such a situation, knowing and learning German are essential.

Example 10: Pete (May 2003)

Pete:	well yeah you are kind of Alice in Wonderland even when visiting stores when you don't (.)
	if you don't see that it is cheese so no although it is packed somehow and so forth
	so that it says in German only that it includes cheese
Tiina:	mm
Pete:	there are certain difficulties
Tiina:	mm
Pete:	and (.) threshold to buy things when you don't speak German
Tiina:	do you feel that you sort of have to know or learn it?
Pete:	well really I have to sort of in order to handle these daily errands

Pete's stressed 'really' in response to the question about learning German shows his strong orientation: he really has to (*pakko*) know German in order to handle daily life. Like Risto, Pete also used dictionaries to learn the German words he needed at work and to communicate with colleagues. Tero also aligns to an outsider identity, describing his life without any knowledge of German as 'a bit of an orphan' (*tuntuu vähä orvolta*). What helps Tero to survive is the large number of Finns around, the gradual establishment of a daily routine and simply getting used to life in Germany. When explicitly asked about their adjustment to Germany and German culture, the students hold different viewpoints. Although the interviewer orients to the existence of a German culture to which the students need to adjust, the students themselves choose to adopt a particular position. Risto and Pete describe their adjustment in positive terms, despite the language problem they face at work. Particularly helpful for Risto is culture, which is 'after all similar to that in Finland', and thus he did not experience any 'culture shock'. Risto thus draws on the popular discourse and potential difference between one's own and the target culture (Furnham, 2012). Although language complicated Risto's adjustment, he was always able to overcome any problems and move on.

In contrast, Tero explicitly says that he had not anticipated such big differences between the Finnish and German culture. When elaborating on the differences, Tero mentions shopping, handling issues in offices and people's behavior, and comments that 'it just doesn't seem to work' because of 'the language barrier' or because 'the culture is a bit different' (this example is discussed in Räisänen [2016: 168]). In Example 11, I invite Tero to discuss his overall journey and his satisfactions and dissatisfactions with his experiences in Germany.

Example 11: Tero (August 2003)

Tiina: well what are the things you are satisfied with and what you are not and why during this trip?
        can you give some examples?
Tero: mmm (.) well I'm satisfied with the fact that I came here
        I would certainly have regretted it if I hadn't come and
        saw that Finland is after all a good place to live
        worldview expanded a little
        then of course a little (2.0)
        got bored by the way things are handled here in Germany
        here not everything goes the way it does in Finland necessarily (.)
        nothing works for the first time you always have to do it at least twice
        preferably maybe six times (2.0)

First, Tero explains his satisfaction with having gone to Germany. Then he contrasts life in Germany with life in Finland: things are handled differently in Germany, not solved on one's first attempt, and one has to work at something at least twice, even six times. For this reason, Finland and life there are framed as better, life in Germany as poorer (for similar results, see Kinginger [2015]). This kind of ethnocentrism is also visible in Example 12, where Simo discusses his adjustment to German culture.

Example 12: Simo (November 2003)

Tiina: well if we think about adjustment to this German culture so how did it succeed?
Simo: (3.0) heh yeah can you adjust to it heheh
        I don't know (.) quite well
Tiina: what helped for example and what hindered it?
Simo: (3.0) hhh. yeah well it was at first an overall culture shock when going there (2.0)
        I don't know how to take it
Tiina: did language proficiency affect it?
Simo: it did affect it heh

Tiina:	how?
Simo:	well first of all since I didn't know <u>any</u> German
	and then well <u>with English</u> of course (.) I coped (.) to some extent but (2.0) not <u>too</u> well
	mainly because (.) Germans didn't really (.) feel at all enthusiastic about speaking English (.)
	do they have some kind of firm belief stuck <u>in their head</u> that their own language is
	the most important language

Simo's way of speaking is significant here. My question is followed by silence, then Simo laughs and asks whether one can adjust to German culture. His laughter implicitly signals a somewhat negative stance toward German culture, which is portrayed as distant from Simo's own culture. After this, Simo continues on a more serious note: 'I don't know, quite well' and then explicitly illustrates how moving to Germany was overall a culture shock partly because of his lack of German proficiency. Although Simo coped with English to some extent, he did not cope too well. Interestingly, in the discourses of culture shock, Simo draws not only on his own language proficiency but also on that of the other, positioning Germans as not enthusiastic about speaking English. Simo clearly distinguishes Germans as a cultural group and as people with a possibly immovable belief (*iskostuma päässä*) that their own language is the most important one. This view was indeed shared by all the participants. As mentioned earlier, Germans' reluctance to use English was partly attributed to people's age. Willingness to speak also explains this reluctance, as is shown in Example 13, where Oskari is asked to discuss the differences between young and old people's language proficiency.

Example 13: Oskari (May 2003)

Oskari:	well yeah young people clearly
	they do <u>know</u> English
	but some people seem to have a threshold for speaking but
Tiina:	mm
Oskari:	here if you ask do you speak English
	they are kind of uncomfortable and say <u>a little</u>
	[---]
	then then during the conversation you notice that after all they understand everything
Tiina:	yeah
Oskari:	so I don't know (.)
	I guess so I am kind of
	so it is not necessarily
Tiina:	mm
Oskari:	easy I mean if you think about situations <u>in Finland</u> that I've encountered so I'm not very keen to engage in conversations in English either

In Oskari's view, young people clearly know English but seem to find it difficult to start speaking it; they feel embarrassed and reluctant to speak. Nevertheless, they seem to understand everything. Interestingly, Oskari uses the same strategy as in Example 6: by imagining himself in past situations at home in Finland, Oskari aligns to the identity he ascribes to others, as also being not very keen to speak English. Here he is somewhat hesitant in his orientation ('I guess I don't'), but elsewhere he explicitly constructs the identity of an incompetent speaker, someone who is very reluctant to start speaking it (Räisänen, 2012, 2013, 2016; Virkkula & Nikula, 2010). This example illustrates discursive work in finding similarities between intercultural encounters abroad and those at home.

The examples reveal how the participants establish a clear relationship between nationality, culture and language, which functions as a resource for ascribing identities to oneself and others (see also Räisänen, 2016). Participants' identity work thus emerges as associated with interculturality and discourses of difference and sameness. Importantly, the participants' discursive work must be related to the context: the interview, the interactions to which the participants orient and spatial repertoires at work, and the macro context of place, language policies, ideologies, attitudes and societal discourses.

Discussion and Conclusion

This chapter has discussed Finnish engineering students' discursive identity work and orientations to interculturality in the context of blue-collar work practice abroad. The students begin to use ELF abroad after having learned it as a foreign language at school. Using interviews, this chapter has given voice to the students and contextualized their voices in the interview interaction. The voices reflect the challenges that mobile workers encounter in contemporary, transnational working life. Despite the role of English as a global language, the findings point to the need for local languages, use of one's full repertoire and alignment to new identities in order to manage an internship abroad. The students' stay abroad manifested itself as a 'potentially "critical" experience' that contributed to changes in their identities as language users (Benson *et al.*, 2013: 3; Kinginger, 2015).

The participants' earlier socialization was visible in their discursive work when they constructed English language learner identities at the beginning of their stay abroad, drawing on discourses of English as a global language to justify their own repertoires and language choice. Although legitimate ELF user identities were available for the students who, as a result of being abroad, no longer felt any anxiety about speaking English or resorted to native-speaker models (Räisänen, 2013, 2016; Virkkula & Nikula, 2010), discourses of English as a global language lacked the expected currency in the workplace. At work, the local language and company language policy functioned as resources that enabled the hosts to retain power (see also Dervin & Layne, 2013; Lønsmann, 2014), strongly affecting the students' identity work and interculturality. Toward the end, however, some of the students could communicate with their colleagues in English.

The findings show how discourses about language use, proficiency and choice contributed to orientations to difference and sameness that were important in defining the self and other. Interculturality emerged in these discourses, being related to both widely circulating discourses and everyday encounters and spatial repertoires at work. Nationality was a valuable resource in collectivist identity work and the participants constructed themselves as Finnish speakers of English with symbolic power.

The outcomes of the stay abroad were both positive and problematic. The stay did not lead to all of the imagined outcomes (see also Härkönen & Dervin, 2015) and automatic success (see Kinginger, 2009). For example, the students had expected to learn more English and some of them would have liked to have had a more demanding job, which led them to downplay the gains of their stay abroad. In many ways, the period was emotionally demanding for them and provoked feelings of anger and frustration. They experienced challenges both at work and in their leisure time, and some of them found it difficult to adjust to German culture.

The findings indicate that despite the problems, the students were able to work out coping strategies at work, such as learning German and engaging in translanguaging. In situations where they had no shared language, embodiment, gestures and the material environment were important resources (see also Blackledge & Creese, 2017). Also, through working in a multicultural environment the students became more aware of the strengths of their language competence. They also became aware of the similarities and differences between people and other ways of doing and thinking, and were able to position themselves in relation to the other, which in turn led to their engaging in processes of developing intercultural competence (see Byram *et al.*, 2001; Wilkinson, 2012). They also learned about effective and appropriate communication in intercultural interactions, were able to approach others and critically discuss what works and what does not (see Deardorff, 2016: 121–122). Overall, they seemed to move toward a more global mindset, becoming aware of the need to know languages in working life. As a result, many students wanted to continue their language learning in the future – something they had not considered before the stay.

This study has implications for both research and practice. Research on SA and the education of future professionals should acknowledge the relationships between identity work and interculturality and macro and micro discourses. Students should be provided with tools both to critically assess essentialist discourses about cultures and to encounter the situated nature of interculturality. This chapter has sought to make clear that in a study of this kind it is important to know the participants, their backgrounds and the stay abroad context. A critical lens is required, one that incorporates ethnography, acknowledges the researcher's position in meaning-making processes and considers the participants' trajectories over time.

Acknowledgments

This research was funded by the Academy of Finland and the University of Jyväskylä. I wish to thank Tarja Nikula-Jäntti and the two anonymous reviewers for their insightful and helpful comments and suggestions on earlier drafts, and Christina Higgins for hosting my research visit at the University of Hawai'i at Manoa during this project. I would also like to thank Eleanor Underwood for providing suggestions for enhancing readability and the editor for his support and feedback. All remaining weaknesses are my own responsibility.

Notes

(1) Intercultural competence has been defined in various ways but due to space restrictions, the reader is advised to consult, for example, Deardorff (2016).
(2) For similar approaches and discussion on more dynamic views of culture in relation to workplace communication, see for example Schnurr and Zayts (2017).
(3) At that time, the institution in Finland was called 'polytechnic'.

References

Anderson, P., Lawton, L., Rexeisen, R. and Hubbard, A. (2006) Short-term study abroad and intercultural sensitivity: A pilot study. *International Journal of Intercultural Relations* 30, 457–469.
Angouri, J. (2013) The multilingual reality of the multinational workplace: Language policy and language use. *Journal of Multilingual and Multicultural Development* 34 (6), 564–581.
Baker, W. (2009) The cultures of English as a lingua franca. *TESOL Quarterly* 43 (4), 567–592.
Baker, W. (2011) Intercultural awareness: Modelling an understanding of cultures in intercultural communication through English as a lingua franca. *Language and Intercultural Communication* 11 (3), 197–214.
Baker, W. (2016) Culture and language in intercultural communication, English as a lingua franca and English language teaching: Points of convergence and conflict. In P. Holmes and F. Dervin (eds) *The Cultural and Intercultural Dimensions of English as a Lingua Franca* (pp. 70–92). Bristol: Multilingual Matters.
Bamberg, M., De Fina, A. and Schiffrin, D. (2011) Discourse and identity construction. In S. Schwartz, K. Luyckx and V. Vignoles (eds) *Handbook of Identity Theory and Research* (pp. 177–200). New York: Springer.
Baumann, G. (1996) *Contesting Culture: Discourses of Identity in Multi-Ethnic London*. Cambridge: Cambridge University Press.
Beaven, A. and Borghetti, C. (2016) Interculturality in study abroad. *Language and Intercultural Communication* 16 (3), 313–317.

Beaven, A. and Spencer-Oatey, H. (2016) Cultural adaptation in different facets of life and the impact of language: A case study of personal adjustment patterns during study abroad. *Language and Intercultural Communication* 16 (3), 349–367.

Bennett, M. (1993) Towards ethnorelativism: A developmental model of intercultural sensitivity. In R.M. Paige (ed.) *Education for the Intercultural Experience* (pp. 21–71). Yarmouth, ME: Intercultural Press.

Bennett, M. (2004) Becoming interculturally competent. In J. Wurzel (ed.) *Toward Multiculturalism: A Reader in Multicultural Education* (2nd edn; pp. 62–77). Newton, MA: Intercultural Resource.

Benson, P., Barkhuizen, G., Bodycott, P. and Brown, J. (2013) *Second Language Identity in Narratives of Study Abroad*. Basingstoke: Palgrave.

Blackledge, A. and Creese, A. (2017) Translanguaging and the body. *International Journal of Multilingualism* 14 (7), 250–268.

Blommaert, J. and Dong, J. (2010) *Ethnographic Fieldwork: A Beginner's Guide*. Bristol: Multilingual Matters.

Boye, S. (2016) *Intercultural Communicative Competence and Short Stays Abroad: Perceptions of Development*. Münster/New York: Waxmann Verlag.

Bucholtz, M. and Hall, K. (2003) Language and identity. In A. Duranti (ed.) *A Companion to Linguistic Anthropology* (pp. 369–394). Oxford: Blackwell.

Byram, M., Nichols, A. and Stevens, D. (2001) Introduction. In M. Byram, A. Nichols and D. Stevens (eds) *Developing Intercultural Competence in Practice* (Vol. 1; pp. 1–8). Clevedon: Multilingual Matters.

Canagarajah, S. (2013a) Skilled migration and development: Portable communicative resources for transnational work. *Multilingual Education* 3 (8), 1–19.

Canagarajah, S. (2013b) *Translingual Practice. Global Englishes and Cosmopolitan Relations*. London: Routledge.

Canagarajah, S. (2018) English as a spatial resource and the claimed competence of Chinese STEM professionals. *World Englishes* 37, 34–50.

CIMO (2016) Tilastoja korkeakouluopiskelijoiden tekemistä ulkomaanjaksoista vuodelta 2015. Tietoa ja tilastoja −raportit 4. See http://www.cimo.fi/instancedata/prime_product_julkaisu/cimo/embeds/cimowwwstructure/110951_Tietoa_ja_tilastoja_4_2016.pdf (accessed 4 December 2017).

Deardorff, D.K. (2016) How to assess intercultural competence. In H. Zhu (ed.) *Research Methods in Intercultural Communication. A Practical Guide* (pp. 12–135). London: Wiley-Blackwell.

DeKeyser, R. (2010) Monitoring processes in Spanish as a second language during a study abroad program. *Foreign Language Annals* 43 (1), 80–92.

Dervin, F. (2010) Assessing intercultural competence in language learning and teaching: A critical review of current efforts in higher education. In F. Dervin and E. Suomela-Salmi (eds) *New Approaches to Assessing Language and (Inter-)Cultural Competences in Higher Education* (pp. 157–174). Bern: Peter Lang.

Dervin, F. (2011) A plea for change in research on intercultural discourses: A 'liquid' approach to the study of the acculturation of Chinese students. *Journal of Multicultural Discourses* 6 (1), 37–52.

Dervin, F. (2013) Making sense of education for diversities: Criticality, reflexivity and language. In H. Arslan and G. Raţă (eds) *Multicultural Education: From Theory to Practice* (pp. 85–102). Newcastle upon Tyne: Cambridge Scholars Publishing.

Dervin, F. (2014) Exploring 'new' interculturality online. *Language and Intercultural Communication* 14 (2), 191–296.

Dervin, F. and Layne, H. (2013) A guide to interculturality for international and exchange students: An example of hospitality? *Journal of Multicultural Discourses* 8 (1), 1–19.

Dervin, F. and Liddicoat, A. (2013) Introduction. In F. Dervin and A. Liddicoat (eds) *Linguistics for Intercultural Education* (pp. 1–25). Amsterdam/Philadelphia, PA: Benjamins.

Dewey, D.P., Belnap, R.K. and Hillstrom, R. (2013) Social network development, language use, and language acquisition during study abroad: Arabic language learners' perspectives. *Frontiers: The Interdisciplinary Journal of Study Abroad* 22, 84–110.

Duchêne, A., Moyer, M.G. and Roberts, C. (eds) (2013) *Language, Migration and Social Inequalities: A Critical Sociolinguistic Perspective on Institutions and Work*. Bristol: Multilingual Matters.

Duff, P. (2008) Language socialization, higher education, and work. In P. Duff and N. Hornberger (eds) *Encyclopedia of Language and Education* (Vol. 8; pp. 257–270). New York: Springer.

Freed, B. (ed.) (1995) *Second Language Acquisition in a Study Abroad Context*. Amsterdam/Philadelphia, PA: Benjamins.

Furnham, A. (2012) Culture shock. *Journal of Psychology and Education* 7 (1), 9–22.

García, O. (2009) *Bilingual Education in the 21st Century: A Global Perspective*. Oxford: Wiley-Blackwell.

García, O. and Li, W. (2014) *Translanguaging: Language, Bilingualism, and Education*. London: Palgrave Macmillan.

Garrett, P. and Baquedano-López, P. (2002) Language socialization: Reproduction and continuity, transformation and change. *Annual Review of Anthropology* 31, 339–361.

Gee, J. (1990) *Social Linguistics and Literacies: Ideology in Discourses*. London: Falmer Press.

Gergen, K.J. (1999) *An Invitation to Social Construction*. London: Sage.

Georgakopoulou, A. (2007) *Small Stories, Interaction and Identities* (Vol. 8). Amsterdam/Philadelphia, PA: Benjamins.

Gumperz, J. (1982) *Discourse Strategies*. Cambridge: Cambridge University Press.

Hall, S. (1996) Introduction: Who needs 'identity'? In S. Hall and P. du Gay (eds) *Questions of Cultural Identity* (pp. 1–17). London: Sage.

Härkönen, A. and Dervin, F. (2015) 'Talking just about learning languages and getting to know cultures is something that's mentioned in very many applications': Student and staff imaginaries about study abroad. In F. Dervin and R. Machart (eds) *The New Politics of Global Academic Mobility and Migration* (pp. 101–118). Frankfurt-am-Main: Peter Lang.

Higgins, C. (2007) Constructing membership in the in-group: Affiliation and resistance among urban Tanzanians. *Pragmatics* 17 (1), 49–70.

Hofstede, G. (1983) National cultures in four dimensions: A research-based theory of cultural differences among nations. *International Studies of Management & Organization* 13 (1–2), 46–74.

Holliday, A. (2010) *Intercultural Communication and Ideology*. London: Sage.

Holmes, P. and O'Neill, G. (2012) Developing and evaluating intercultural competence: Ethnographies of intercultural encounters. *International Journal of Intercultural Relations* 36 (5), 707–718.

Isabelli-García, C. (2006) Study abroad social networks, motivation and attitudes: Implications for second language acquisition. In M. DuFon and E. Churchill (eds) *Language Learners in Study Abroad Contexts* (pp. 231–258). Clevedon: Multilingual Matters.

Jackson, J. (2008) *Language, Identity, and Study Abroad: Sociocultural Perspectives*. London: Equinox.

Jackson, J. (2009) Intercultural learning on short-term sojourns. *Intercultural Education* 20 (suppl. 1), S59–S71.

Jackson, J. (2010) *Intercultural Journeys: From Study to Residence Abroad*. Basingstoke: Palgrave Macmillan.

Jackson, J. (2011) Host language proficiency, intercultural sensitivity, and study abroad. *Frontiers: The Interdisciplinary Journal of Study Abroad* 21, 167–188.

Jackson, J. (2014) *Introducing Language and Intercultural Communication.* London: Routledge.

Jackson, J. (2016) 'Breathing the smells of native-styled English': A narrativized account of an L2 sojourn. *Language and Intercultural Communication* 16 (3), 332–348.

Kalocsai, K. (2009) Erasmus exchange students: A behind-the-scenes view into an ELF community of practice. *Apples – Journal of Applied Language Studies* 3 (1), 25–49.

Kinginger, C. (2009) *Language Learning and Study Abroad: A Critical Reading of Research.* Basingstoke: Palgrave Macmillan.

Kinginger, C. (ed.) (2013) *Social and Cultural Aspects of Language Learning in Study Abroad.* Amsterdam/Philadelphia, PA: Benjamins.

Kinginger, C. (2015) Student mobility and identity-related language learning. *Intercultural Education* 26 (1), 6–15.

Ladegaard, H.J. and Jenks, C.J. (2015) Language and intercultural communication in the workplace: Critical approaches to theory and practice. *Language and Intercultural Communication* 15 (1), 1–12.

Lewis, R. (ed.) (2009) *The Handbook of Practice and Research in Study Abroad: Higher Education and the Quest for Global Citizenship.* New York: Routledge.

Li, W. (2016) New Chinglish and the post-multilingualism challenge: Translanguaging ELF in China. *Journal of English as a Lingua Franca* 5 (1), 1–25.

Llanes, À., Tragant, E. and Serrano, R. (2012) The role of individual differences in a study abroad experience: The case of Erasmus students. *International Journal of Multilingualism* 9 (3), 318–342.

Lønsmann, D. (2014) Linguistic diversity in the international workplace: Language ideologies and processes of exclusion. *Multilingua* 33 (1–2), 89–116.

Louhiala-Salminen, L. and Kankaanranta, A. (2011) Professional communication in a global business context: The notion of global communicative competence. *Professional Communication* 54 (3), 244–262.

Louhiala-Salminen, L., Charles, M. and Kankaanranta, A. (2005) English as a lingua franca in Nordic corporate mergers: Two case companies. *English for Specific Purposes* 24 (4), 401–421.

Martinsen, R. (2011) Predicting changes in cultural sensitivity among students of Spanish during short-term study abroad. *Hispania* 94 (1), 121–141.

Messelink, H.E., Van Maele, J. and Spencer-Oatey, H. (2015) Intercultural competencies: What students in study and placement mobility should be learning. *Intercultural Education* 26 (1), 62–72.

Mori, J. (2003) The construction of interculturality: A study of initial encounters between Japanese and American students. *Research on Language and Social Interaction* 36 (2), 143–184.

Murphy-Lejeune, E. (2002) *Student Mobility and Narrative in Europe.* London: Routledge.

Norton, B. (2000) *Identity and Language Learning: Gender, Ethnicity and Educational Change.* Harlow: Pearson Education.

OECD (2015) *Education at a Glance 2015: OECD Indicators.* Paris: OECD.

Paige, R.M., Fry, G.W., Stallman, E.M., Josić, J. and Jon, J.E. (2009) Study abroad for global engagement: The long-term impact of mobility experiences. *Intercultural Education* 20 (Suppl 1), S29–S44.

Pellegrino, V. (1998) Student perspectives on language learning in a study abroad context. *Frontiers: The Interdisciplinary Journal of Study Abroad* 4, 91–120.

Pennycook, A. and Otsuji, E. (2015) *Metrolingualism: Language in the City.* London: Routledge.

Piller, I. (2011) *Intercultural Communication: A Critical Introduction.* Edinburgh: Edinburgh University Press.

Polanyi, L. (1995) Language learning and living abroad. Stories from the field. In B. Freed (ed.) *Second Language Acquisition in a Study Abroad Context* (pp. 271–291). Amsterdam/Philadelphia, PA: Benjamins.

Potter, J. and Hepburn, A. (2012) Eight challenges for interview researchers. In J.F. Gubrium and J.A. Holstein (eds) *Handbook of Interview Research* (pp. 555–570). London: Sage.

Räisänen, T. (2012) Discourses of proficiency – endangering aspects of English in an individual's biography of language use. In J. Blommaert, S. Leppänen, P. Pahta and T. Räisänen (eds) *Dangerous Multilingualism: Northern Perspectives on Order, Purity and Normality* (pp. 207–227). Basingstoke: Palgrave Macmillan.

Räisänen, T. (2013) Professional communicative repertoires and trajectories of socialization into global working life. PhD thesis, University of Jyväskylä.

Räisänen, T. (2016) Finnish engineers' trajectories of socialisation into global working life: From language learners to BELF users and the emergence of a Finnish way of speaking English. In P. Holmes and F. Dervin (eds) *The Cultural and Intercultural Dimensions of English as a Lingua Franca* (pp. 157–179). Bristol: Multilingual Matters.

Räisänen, T. (2018) Translingual practices in global business – a longitudinal study of a professional communicative repertoire. In G. Mazzaferro (ed.) *Translanguaging as Everyday Practice* (pp. 149–174). New York: Springer.

Rapley, T.J. (2001) The art(fulness) of open-ended interviewing: Some considerations on analysing interviews. *Qualitative Research* 1, 303–323.

Roberts, C. (2010) Language socialization in the workplace. *Annual Review of Applied Linguistics* 30 (2), 211–227.

Sajavaara, K. and Lehtonen, J. (1997) The silent Finn revisited. In A. Jaworski (ed.) *Functions of Silence* (pp. 263–283). Berlin: Mouton de Gruyter.

Schnurr, S. and Zayts, O. (2017) *Language and Culture at Work*. London: Taylor & Francis.

Scollon, R. and Scollon, S.W. (2001) Discourse and intercultural communication. In D. Schiffrin, D. Tannen and H. Hamilton (eds) *The Handbook of Discourse Analysis* (pp. 538–547). Oxford: Blackwell.

Virkkula, T. and Nikula, T. (2010) Identity construction in ELF contexts: A case study of Finnish engineering students working in Germany. *International Journal of Applied Linguistics* 20 (2), 251–273.

Virkkula-Räisänen, T. (2010) Linguistic repertoires and semiotic resources in interaction: A Finnish manager as a mediator in a multilingual meeting. *Journal of Business Communication* 47 (4), 505–531.

Weisner, T.S. (1996) Why ethnography should be the most important method in the study of human development. In R. Jessor, A. Colby and R. Shweder (eds) *Ethnography and Human Development. Context and Meaning in Social Inquiry* (pp. 305–324). Chicago, IL: University of Chicago Press.

Wilkinson, J. (2012) The intercultural speaker and the acquisition of global/intercultural competence. In J. Jackson (ed.) *The Routledge Handbook of Language and Intercultural Communication* (pp. 296–309). London: Routledge.

Zhu, H. (2014) *Exploring Intercultural Communication: Language in Action*. Abingdon: Routledge.

Zhu, H. (2015) Interculturality: Reconceptualising cultural memberships and identities through translanguaging practice. In F. Dervin and K. Risager (eds) *Researching Identity and Interculturality: Towards a More Reflexive and Critical Methodology* (pp. 109–124). London: Routledge.

Appendices

Appendix A: Interview thematic structure before the stay abroad

Background information
Work
Feelings before leaving
Expectations concerning living and staying in Germany
Language proficiency, conceptions about your own language proficiency
    and proficiency in particular
Speaking English

Appendix B: Interview thematic structure after the stay abroad

Feelings about working and living in Germany
Adjustment to the culture
Surviving with English
Discussions in English
Speaking
Conceptions about language proficiency
Germans
Aims and expectations
Future

Appendix C: Transcription conventions

[--]	omitted text
-	cut-off word
text	emphasis
(.)	micro pause
(1.0)	silence marked in tenths of seconds
(xxx)	unclear speech/transcriber's interpretation

Appendix D: Interview samples in their original version (Finnish)

Example 1: Pete (see corresponding Example 1 in the text)

Tiina: no uskotko sitte selviytyväs englannin kielen taidoillasi täällä Saksassa?
mitä just jos ajatellaan et miltä susta tuntu ennen lähtöä ja ehkä nyt? [---]
Pete: ei kyllä mä selviän ei siinä mitään..
mutta oon huomannu sen että (.) englannin suhteen kyllä ei siinä oo mitään
ongelmaa
mutta se että ku kuvittelee että.
sää kuulet ku työkaverit ku juuri kukaan ei puhu englantia ja itse vaan puhut
niin se että (.) ois mukavampi olla sellasen tyypin kanssa tekemisissä (.)
samassa työpisteessä joka puhuu englantia
että siinä ihan hyvä (xxx)
Tiina: joo
Pete: mut saksaa tekis mieli oppia (.) se kuitenki helpottas

Example 3: Tero (see corresponding Example 3 in the text)

Tiina: puhuuko ne <u>mielellään</u> englantia sun kans?
Tero: no kyllä ne nyt (.)
         mut aluksihan ne ei ruvennu puhhuu sitä ollenkaan
         mutta kyllä ne nyt sitte muutaman sanan on ruvennu sannoo
         ja sitte ketkä osaa englantia niin kyllä ne nyt sitte puhuu englantia
Tiina: Joo
Tero: <u>kyllä</u> ne <u>aluksi</u> meinas että pittää mun opetella saksaa
Tiina: niin just ne huomas sitte että
Tero: että parempi puhua englantia
Tiina: joo
Tero: ku tuo ei opi saksaa ikinä heheh

5 English as a Lingua Franca, Motivation and Identity in Study Abroad

Leah Geoghegan and Carmen Pérez-Vidal

English as a Lingua Franca, Motivation and Identity in Study Abroad: Mapping the Ground

The global spread of English as the newest lingua franca has been one of the most significant developments of this century (Albl-Mikasa, 2010) and, as can be expected, this surge in its importance has had a considerable effect on language learners worldwide. In the past, 'the ultimate goal or standard has been the (unrealistic) ideal of a native speaker' (Ke & Cahyani, 2014: 1). However, as Seidlhofer (2001) suggests, the emergence of English as a lingua franca (ELF) validates the reconsideration of traditional native speaker models whereby, rather than aspiring to reach native-like competence, learners would aim instead towards becoming proficient, international English users.

This shift in focus is likely to affect English language learners, reshaping the way they identify with the language, as well as affecting their motivation to learn. Firstly, regarding identity, ELF may provide a more appealing identity to non-native speakers, given that instead of being 'perennial, error-prone *learners* of [English as a Native Language], they can be competent and authoritative *users* of ELF' (Seidlhofer, 2004: 229) (emphasis added). As for motivation, according to Dörnyei and Ushioda (2013), the spread of English as a global language and international lingua franca appears to have at least two repercussions on the theorisation of language learning motivation. Firstly, there is likely to be a qualitative difference between the motivation for learning English compared with other languages, given that English is increasingly being seen as a basic educational skill, imperative to professional advancement. Secondly, given the role of ELF among non-native speakers, traditional concepts such as integrativeness and attitude towards the target language (TL) community become somewhat hazy, whereas the concept of the international posture of students or professionals has been gradually taking shape (Yashima, 2009: 145). This concept concerns the learners' identification with an international community, rather than a specific second language (L2) group, and is thus extremely relevant in an ELF context.

In recent years, research into such individual factors as identity and motivation within the field of second language acquisition (SLA) and study abroad (SA) has flourished. As Mitchell *et al.* (2015b: 8) have highlighted, 'given the social dislocation inevitably attaching to the experience of study/residence abroad, it is not surprising that qualitative research traditions investigating its impact on sojourners' personality, identity and intercultural awareness has flourished strongly in this particular domain'. The international role of ELF in SA and higher education contexts has also received increasing research attention over the last decade (Jenkins, 2015), in part due to the increase in English-medium instruction in tertiary education outside English-speaking countries. Consequently, English has become a well-established language of communication, being used as a vehicular language to connect students with different linguistic backgrounds (Smokotin *et al.*, 2014). Such a context will evidently affect the language process to a large extent, not only for those learning English, but also for those learning other foreign languages (Mitchell *et al.*, 2015a).

What remains to be seen, given the above, is how exactly ELF affects the learning experience of those learning both English and other languages such as French and German. Against such a backdrop, the aim of this chapter is to investigate the identity and motivation of such language learners in the context of SA. This is done through an examination of learners' views following a sojourn spent on a European Region Action Scheme for the Mobility of University Students (Erasmus) exchange in four different countries in Europe: England, France, Belgium and Germany, so as to be able to draw a profile of each student as an ELF or non-ELF user. It thus adopts a European multilingual perspective, whereby not only English is in focus, but also French and German, and their interaction with ELF. In order to do so, the study explores the differences between language learning in an English-speaking country compared to a French- or German-speaking country. It focuses on ELF, as opposed to French, German or Spanish as a lingua franca, given the tendency for English to be used in this context. Building on a quantitative study (Geoghegan, 2018), which investigated the same issues in a larger group of students, the study uses qualitative research tools with a subgroup of the same participants so as to gain a more detailed picture of the role of ELF in SA (Rezaei, 2012).

We open the chapter by first introducing key concepts and providing background to the study. Next, we give an overview of the existing empirical research on the connections between identity, motivation, SA and ELF. Then, we present the empirical study, its research question and hypothesis, the methodology, participants and procedure. Results and discussion follow, with the chapter finishing with a summary and conclusion.

Identity and Motivation during Study Abroad in the New ELF Paradigm: Consequences for SA Learner Practices

This chapter aims to investigate the connections between the internationalised context of ELF in SA and individual factors such as identity and motivation, so as to be able to create a profile of the participants as ELF users or non-users on the basis of their own self-reported data. The following sections address the relevant literature for this study, beginning with the issues of identity and motivation, and then moving on to the field of SA and ELF.

Identity

Identity has been described as one's 'meaning in the world', a description that includes where the individual is in relation to those around them, their perspective on the world around them and their understanding of their value to others (Eckert, 2000: 41). In relation to SLA, both the learners' individual identity and how they identify with the TL culture are of particular interest. Researchers as early as Schumann (1978) highlighted the importance of these issues, recognising identification with the TL to be a prerequisite for successful SLA. Informal language learning, such as in SA, is thus of particular interest, given that 'the sustained immersion in a new cultural and linguistic milieu seemingly cannot but impact on the individual's sense of self' (Block, 2007: 109). As Jackson (2008) discusses, SA students often struggle with their sense of identity, having been taken out of their comfort zone and thrown into an entirely different linguistic milieu. Furthermore, the value of SA as a learning environment may depend, among other factors, on 'whether [the student's] encounters lead to frustration or to the desperate, creative longing to craft a foreign language-mediated identity' (Kinginger, 2009: 202). That is to say, how students manage the impact on their sense of self may ultimately determine how successful their language acquisition is during SA.

This issue is all the more important in the case of ELF usage during SA, where English has become a well-established language of communication among students with different linguistic backgrounds, even among groups of non-native English speakers (Kalocsai, 2011). While these ELF social groups may provide ample opportunities for practising English, they may also make it more difficult to use and practise other languages. For example, Mitchell *et al.* (2015a) highlight the case of native English speakers who, while studying abroad with the intention of improving their L2, find that many locals may prefer to take advantage of their linguistic capital and speak English with them instead, much to the detriment of developing a French or German language-mediated identity. This problem may also be evident in the case of non-native English speakers who study abroad in countries such as France, Belgium or Germany where, instead of being given opportunities to practise their French or German, they find themselves embedded in an ELF context, using English instead of their other TLs. Even those who study abroad in an English-speaking country may find themselves in such a situation, using ELF with other non-natives, rather than forming bonds with native English speakers. To our knowledge, the above issue, where English appears to thwart the practice of other L2s, has yet to be explored in relation to non-native English speakers learning languages other than English, e.g. a Spaniard learning French.

Motivation

In addition to these challenges regarding identity, language acquisition may also be affected by the learner's motivation. Motivation is one of the most common terms used by teachers and students to explain the success or failure of an individual's learning (Hadfield & Dörnyei, 2013) and, as Dörnyei (2009) points out, even learners with the most remarkable abilities will be unable to accomplish long-term goals if they lack the necessary motivation to do so.

Over the last decade, foreign language motivational research has entered the sociodynamic period, a stage that is concerned with dynamic systems and contextual interaction (Ushioda & Dörnyei, 2012). This stage has given rise to three new conceptual approaches (Ushioda & Dörnyei, 2012), namely, Ushioda's (2009: 218) person-in-context relational view of L2 motivation, motivation from a complex dynamic systems perspective (Waninge et al., 2014) and Dörnyei's (2009: 29) L2 Motivational Self System (L2MSS), which will be central to the current study.

Fusing together aspects of Markus and Nurius' (1986) theory of possible selves and Higgins' (1987) theory of 'ought selves', Dörnyei's L2MSS draws on the idea that an individual's motivation is made up of the following three key parts:

(1) The 'Ideal L2 self', which typically fosters integrative and internalised motives, is the image one has of one's future self as an L2 user according to one's own wishes.
(2) The 'Ought-to L2 self', which reflects more extrinsic types of instrumental motivation, is the image one has of one's future self as an L2 user according to external expectations. It deals with attributes that the learner believes she/he ought to possess in order to meet expectations and avoid negative outcomes.
(3) The 'L2 learning experience' is concerned with 'executive' motives; for example, the impact of the language teacher, curriculum, peer group and experience of success or failure.

With the increase in sociodynamic research in L2 motivation research, it is becoming increasingly evident that research needs to take into account the dynamic individuality of learners, as well as the fact that they, and their motivation, are constantly changing (Guerrero, 2015). Qualitative studies are especially conducive to capturing such dynamics in so far as they are more descriptive and may be able to offer a more detailed picture of students' motivation and identity. Given this, it seems even more imperative that motivational research takes a qualitative approach, in order to gain a thorough understanding of the development and negotiation of the learner's ongoing motivational process (Kim, 2009).

Study abroad

Issues of identity and motivation are particularly pertinent within the context of SA. According to the Organisation for Economic Cooperation and Development (2013), the number of internationally mobile tertiary education students increased from 800,000 in the mid-1970s to 4.3 million in 2011, and the United Nations Educational, Scientific and Cultural Organisation (UNESCO) estimates that the number of students enrolled in higher education outside their home countries will increase to almost 8 million by 2025 (Davis, 2003). As highlighted by Pérez-Vidal (2017), this upward trend in student mobility comes as a result of internationalisation and economic globalisation, and is paralleled by an increased interest in exploring SA effects within the field of SLA. However, a great deal of this research to date has been largely statistical (Jackson, 2008), focusing on linguistic outcomes and grammatical development, while fundamental issues such as sociocultural and intercultural competence have been largely overlooked (Coleman, 1998). This issue is also highlighted by Collentine and Freed (2004: 165), who call for a better definition of 'the social conditions surrounding, affecting and perhaps impeding learner gains'.

This call has led to a shift in SA research from 'identifying and quantifying linguistic gains (or lack of) to exploring the experience of SA from an ethnographic perspective' (Devlin, 2014: 6). Thus, in order to better understand the processes that are involved in language learning, recent research has seen an increase in a more learner-centric approach, using introspective techniques such as diaries, first-person narratives and interviews, as well as case studies and ethnographies (Jackson, 2008). Providing a contextualised view from the participants' perspective, such approaches have allowed researchers to investigate the specific factors that aid and inhibit language acquisition, and the learners' access to both native and non-native speakers.

With the aim of explaining the variation in language development during SA, Mitchell *et al.* (2015a: 134) have called for a 'more refined analysis of students' personal motivations and characteristics, multilingual language practices, and emerging social relations'. Thus, by investigating individual differences such as identity and motivation among learners in SA, we may be better able to understand why there is 'no evidence that one context of learning is uniformly superior to another for all students' (Collentine & Freed, 2004: 164).

English as a lingua franca

The emergence of ELF as a new reality in international communications, and clearly so in SA learning contexts, adds a further argument for gaining a new perspective on how such motivations, relations and practices take place and develop. ELF has been defined as 'a "contact language" between persons who share neither a common native tongue nor a common (national) culture, and for whom English is the chosen foreign language of communication' (Firth, 1996: 240). According to Jenkins *et al.* (2011), interest in ELF research has erupted over the last decade, at least to some extent due to two publications at the start of the millennium. The first was Jenkins (2000), who reported on an empirical study of ELF pronunciation and argued that in ELF communication contexts, native English pronunciation is not optimum. The second was a conceptual piece by Seidlhofer (2001), which highlighted that, due to the lack of description of ELF, native English norms continued to be the only viable target for language learners.

The role of ELF is largely related to language learners' motivation and identity. Firstly, regarding motivation, it has been suggested that language learning and communication skills that are demanded by globalisation influence the learners' motivation towards instrumentality (Block & Cameron, 2002). Regarding Dörnyei's L2MSS, the Ought-to L2 self will likely play a key role, in that students may feel they ought to learn English in order to help them in their future careers. The rise of ELF has also been partly responsible for the reconsideration of traditional concepts such as integrative motivation. Dailey (2009: 7) explains that 'due to the change in global languages, there is no model community to identify with, consequently leading to a broader classification of integrative motivation'. In other words, in an international context where students use English as a language of communication, it makes little sense to gauge the extent to which these students wish to integrate with a native English-speaking community. In such instances, it may make more sense to speak of international posture, rather than integrative motivation; an idea that captures the learners' tendency to relate themselves to an international community rather than a specific L2 group (Yashima, 2009). Regarding the L2MSS, this would affect learners' Ideal L2 self in that, instead of visualising themselves as becoming integrated within a specific L2 community, they may instead visualise themselves as relating to an international ELF community.

Secondly, in the case of identity, Jenkins *et al.* (2011: 307) have highlighted 'the extent to which the young continental Europeans [...]

identify with their own use of English rather than with a standard [native speaker] variety'. Given Norton's (2000) argument that a key aspect of identity in language learning is the way in which the person understands possibilities for the future, it is not surprising that 'where younger ELF users are found in research to identify positively with their own English, it is because they see ELF (not necessarily by name) as likely to enhance rather than deny their future success in a globalized world' (Jenkins *et al.*, 2011: 307).

As mentioned above, Seidlhofer (2004) proposes the term 'ELF users', rather than having learners identify themselves as learners of English, which evidently implies deficiencies. In this way, English users aim towards becoming proficient, international speakers, rather than the unrealistic goal of speaking like a native speaker (Ke & Cahyani, 2014).

It can thus be expected that the role of ELF will greatly affect the experience a language learner has during SA. One factor within SA that has been seen to account for the student's linguistic development and variation is the social networks that are formed during the student's time abroad (Isabelli-García, 2006). Isabelli-García (2006) found that students' motivational orientation changed during their SA, depending on the ability of the learner to interact in social networks. With this in mind, it can be expected that the type of social networks that are formed by SA students, particularly in relation to international ELF communities, will be related in some way to their motivational orientation.

The Empirical Study

As highlighted by Kinginger (2009: 218), 'one of the most pressing questions for study abroad researchers is the relationship between language learning and changing communicative practices and worldviews brought on by intensified globalization'. This study investigates this very issue in relation to ELF usage during SA. While the original orientation of ELF research focused heavily on linguistic form (Jenkins, 2015), the current study examines the connection between the role of ELF and students' personal motivations and changing identities during SA. The aim of the present study is twofold. We first aim to identify the variables that seem to characterise different uses (or non-uses) of ELF. This we do through a data-driven analysis based on the participants' reports. The emergent categories help to illustrate how ELF fulfils different roles in communication while abroad, in relation to the issues of identity and motivation. Secondly, we subsequently apply those same categories to create an individual profile for each of our four participants.

The study builds on our earlier work (see Geoghegan, 2018) where we examined 68 university learners (25 pre-SA and 43 end-of-SA), and aimed to investigate the effect of SA on the motivation and identity of learners of English, as well as of either German or French, sojourning in an English-, German- or French-speaking country using a quantitative approach. On comparing those in an English-speaking country with a French- or German-speaking country, differences were found in the Ideal L2 self, International Posture, International Contact and Intended Learning Effort. Such differential findings call for a more detailed, qualitative investigation to be carried out in order to gain a more thorough understanding of the processes at hand. This is the goal of the study presented in this chapter, which aims to further investigate the language learning motivation and identity of the students, as well as to clarify their connection with the new ELF paradigm. The current qualitative study was conducted using interviews with a subgroup of those advanced EFL undergraduates in Geoghegan (2018), who were additionally asked to reflect on their experiences abroad upon return from their stay.

The study was based on the following research question: What connection is there between ELF and its different roles, and the language learning motivation and identity of higher education students who are sojourning in English- compared with German- or French-speaking countries? We expect that in non-English-speaking countries, ELF may both help and hinder the language acquisition process. In English-speaking countries, it is expected that ELF will also have an effect, possibly offering students a more accessible alternative to communicating with native speakers, namely, by using ELF to communicate with other non-native speakers of English.

Participants

The participants are four Spanish–Catalan bilinguals in the second year of their undergraduate degree. They were selected from Geoghegan's (2018) corpus, based on homogeneous sampling (Dörnyei, 2007). All 43 end-of-SA students who had taken part in the quantitative study were contacted; of these, seven students showed an interest in taking part in the next stage of the study. Due to timetabling restrictions, it was only possible for four of these students to be interviewed. These students were all learning English as a major language, as well as either French or German as a minor language in their undergraduate degree. As part of their curriculum, the students completed a first year of formal instruction, followed by a compulsory three-month SA academic period in a TL country. This SA was organised by the university at the beginning of the second year of their degree and counted towards credit in their home university (see Beattie [2014] for a full account of the programme). Of the four participants in the study, each had spent their SA in a different country (one in the UK, one in Belgium, one in France and one in Germany). Thus, only one student was spending her SA sojourn in an English-speaking country where her major language was spoken.

It was explained in writing to all participants that steps would be taken to ensure their anonymity, including keeping the data in a safe location, not allowing anyone else to access the data and not using the names of individuals in reporting the findings (Macksoud, 2010). It was also specified that collaboration in the study was completely voluntary, following which participants were asked to sign a consent form. Upon their return from SA, the participants took part in face-to-face interviews conducted by one of the authors (see Table 5.1 for a summary of the participants' details).

Table 5.1 Summary of participants and details of interviews

	Participants (pseudonyms used throughout)	Details of interviews
	Four second-year post-SA higher education students of English, and French or German who had studied abroad in England, France, Belgium and Germany	Semi-structured interviews concerning motivation, identity and ELF
Interview	Alex, 21, male, SA in France	Transcript: 5,970 words
Pair 1	Raquel, 19, female, SA in Germany	Length: 48.12
Interview	María, 19, female, SA in England	Transcript: 7,070 words
Pair 2	Laura, 19, female, SA in Belgium	Length: 57.05

Paired depth interviews, whereby two people were interviewed together (Wilson *et al.*, 2016), were conducted for this study, first and foremost to foster a more relaxed environment for the interviewees. In addition, as Highet (2003) points out, frequent and sustained dialogue between participants, while possible in larger focus groups, is much more possible in pair depth interviews. Furthermore, given that the interviewees had spent their SA in different countries, being interviewed in pairs allowed them to compare and contrast their experiences, leading to a more fruitful discussion. However, it should be pointed out that, as with any group interview, there is always the danger of the 'domination of more talkative members of the group and member influence on individual responses' (Riazi, 2016: 123). These potential problems were anticipated so that they could be managed during the interviews. This was done, for example, by addressing each participant in turn and ensuring that both had equal opportunity to answer the questions and express themselves.

Data collection: Instruments and procedure

The interviews were conducted following the students' return from their SA (see Figure 5.1). The sojourn had taken place during term one of year two.

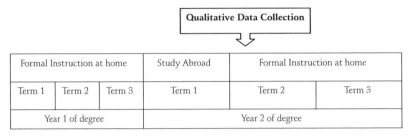

Qualitative Data Collection					
Formal Instruction at home			Study Abroad	Formal Instruction at home	
Term 1	Term 2	Term 3	Term 1	Term 2	Term 3
Year 1 of degree			Year 2 of degree		

Figure 5.1 Design of the study

The instrument used for data collection was an interview guide, or 'set of questions' (Friedman, 2012: 188), created specifically for the purposes of this study (see Appendix A). It consisted of 16 topics, each dealt with by one, two or three questions. Following guidelines set out by Friedman (2012), questions were created that were open-ended and comprehensible, and that were not leading or complex. The number included for each topic depended on the complexity of the question (see Table 5.2 for a list of topics and some sample questions, as explained in the section titled 'Analysis').

The opening topics in the interview guide (1–4) were designed to help the interviewees to relax and to encourage them to open up (Dörnyei, 2007), and dealt with general issues concerning their SA: their classmates, accommodation, classes and work while abroad. The remaining topics (5–16), adopted from questionnaires carried out by Ryan (2009) and Yashima (2009), were used to investigate the Ideal L2 self of English learners in tertiary educational institutions. Feedback was received on the guide from three colleagues prior to its implementation in order to ensure the suitability of the instrument and check for researcher bias in the questions (Berg, 1995). Before carrying out the main interviews, one student was interviewed to pilot the interview guide, in order to identify potential problems and to revise the questions as needed before conducting further interviews (Friedman, 2012).[1] Following the pilot interview, the interview guide was revised and edited accordingly, focusing on the emergent themes of the study. This involved adding a number of sub-questions in order to gain further information relevant to the study. For example, in the pilot study, it became apparent that although the student spent time with other Spaniards, she reported that they often spoke to each other in English. Thus, in the first topic 'Classmates from the home university', an additional question was included to inquire as to what language was used. Other such additions were made in topics 4, 7, 8, 11 and 12.

This interview guide was used as the basis for the study's two semi-structured interviews (total lengths 48.12 and 57.05 minutes each), both conducted in English and with two students taking part in each interview. A semi-structured approach was conceived to allow deviation from the interview guide in order to pursue topics that arose during the

Table 5.2 Categories and sample questions from the interview guide

Topics	Sample questions
(1) Classmates from the home university	Were there other Spanish students on Erasmus there? Did you spend much time together? What language(s) did you speak in?
(2) Accommodation	What were your living arrangements while abroad?
(3) Classes	What kind of classes did you take while abroad?
(4) Work	Did you have a part-time job while abroad?
(5) Use of English/German/French	Did you spend time using English/German/French in your spare time?
(6) Language anxiety/L2 self-confidence	How did you feel when communicating in English/German/French?
(7) Fear of assimilation	Did you find it difficult being away from your home and family?
(8) International contact	Think about the new people you met while abroad. Are there any people who you see yourself staying in contact with?
(9) Intended learning effort	What kinds of things did you do to help you improve your language while abroad?
(10) Contact with family	How much contact did you have with your family and friends from home while on Erasmus?
(11) Ease of learning experience	In what ways do you think being abroad helped you learn the language?
(12) Ability/perceived improvement	In which areas do you think you improved the most (reading/writing/speaking/listening/pronunciation)?
(13) Ideal L2 self	After being abroad, do you think it's easier to imagine yourself as a competent and natural speaker of the language?
(14) Interest in foreign languages	What is it that appeals to you about English/German/ French?
(15) Instrumentality	Do you think that most people want to learn English/French/German simply because it's important for their future careers?
(16) International posture	What place do you see English/German/French having in your future?

course of the interview, yet still enable some degree of cross-case comparison (Friedman, 2012; Robson, 2002). The interviews were recorded using a Sony ICD-MX20 digital voice recorder, which was placed in the middle of the table. Students who took part were subsequently contacted by email in Term 3, in order to ask follow-up questions that had emerged from the analysis and to ensure that their views were accurately taken into account (Friedman, 2012) (see Appendix B). These questions were formulated based on issues that arose over the course of the analysis. For example, in one case, the data suggested that one participant felt more comfortable communicating in English with non-native speakers than with native speakers. Consequently, the question 'Do you prefer speaking English with native speakers or with other non-native speakers?' was included in the follow-up. In such cases, the students' responses were cross-referenced with the data from the interview in order to ensure that the researchers were accurately interpreting the students' responses.

Analysis

For this qualitative analysis, the approach adopted was content analysis where the three-tier coding component of grounded theory was employed (Friedman, 2012). First, 'open coding', wherein data were broken down into manageable segments and assigned conceptual categories; second, 'axial coding', whereby interrelationships between the categories were identified; and third, 'selective coding', where selected codes were applied to the remaining data and further developed and refined (Dörnyei, 2007).

The coding strategy was designed based on suggestions in the literature on qualitative data analysis (Lincoln & Guba, 1985; Miles & Huberman, 1994), and the research questions were used to create a general framework for the analysis (Macksoud, 2010). Within this framework, an interpretive approach was used in order to classify pertinent themes in the data. The categories are presented here before the results, as is conventional; however, they were generated as a result of a bottom-up, data-driven exercise involving different steps and stages, which proceeded as follows, based on guidelines from Baralt (2012).

Step 1: Following data collection, the interviews were subsequently transcribed and coded using the qualitative data analysis software QDA Lite. The interviews were transcribed in full, including all filler words, overlapping speech and pauses, using the CHAT transcription format (MacWhinney, 2009) (see Appendix C).

Step 2: After preparing the data, a project journal was started. This journal was used throughout the coding process to record all coding decisions, questions and reflections (Baralt, 2012) (see Appendix D). Journal entries were guided by the following questions suggested by Bazeley (2007: 29–30):

(1) Why are you doing this project?
(2) What do you think it's about?
(3) What are the questions you're asking, and where did they come from?
(4) What do you expect to find and why?
(5) What have you observed so far?

Step 3: The responses were then coded (open coding), a process that involved assigning a code to represent a concept shown in the data (Baralt, 2012). Under the category of ELF, five tentative codes were established, namely 'Bridge of Communication'; 'Crutch', 'Easier Access to Input', 'Impediment' and 'Language User'. In addition to these five codes under the category of ELF, eight other codes were assigned based on the questions in the interview that tapped into them (see Appendix A), namely L2 Self Confidence and Language Anxiety (6.1–6.2), Fear of Assimilation (7.1–7.3), International Contact (8.1–8.2), Intended Learning Effort

(9.1–9.2), Ideal L2 self (13.1), Interest in Foreign Languages (14.1), Instrumental Motivation (15.1–15.2) and International Posture (16.1–16.2).

Step 4: Following the open coding, axial coding was carried out. The constant comparative method was performed (Bogdan & Biklen, 1998), in which the data were reviewed across transcripts in order to cross-examine the codes that had been used. For example, one of the categories that had emerged during open coding was that of 'Impediment'. At this stage, this category was further broken down into two subcategories (intrinsic and extrinsic) in order to generate more detailed findings (Macksoud, 2010). In addition, the eight codes mentioned above were reanalysed in relation

Table 5.3 Summary of codes with description and sample data

Code	Subcategory	Description	Sample data
ELF as a Bridge of Communication		English linking speakers who do not share a common language	'with the international students I just spoke in English because there were lots of internationalities and maybe they didn't know how to speak German so we spoke in English'
ELF as a Crutch		Using English as an aid to help communication in German/French	'I tried to speak in German and at certain points if we didn't get what the other was saying maybe we just changed to English'
ELF as an Impediment	Intrinsic	Student using English instead of German/French	'it was like really nice I could practise French in the beginning but as soon as I knew how good they spoke English I just said, hey, let's switch to English'
	Extrinsic	Interlocutor using English despite student's attempt to practise German/French	'they just thought, hey, well this guy does not speak French like French people so let's just speak English, let's establish it as a lingua franca'
ELF for Easier Access to Input		Practising English with other international students appears easier than trying to communicate with native speakers, thus ELF is a way to increase amount of exposure	'well my classes were mostly for Erasmus students so I didn't get to know a lot of people from London'
ELF as a Language User		ELF is a more appealing goal than that of a perfectly fluent native speaker. Students can see themselves as language users rather than language learners	'it's not it's not comfortable so I dunno I prefer to speak with foreigners so it's easier to engage and if you make a mistake and someone corrects it's friendly'
ELF non-use		Student studying in a non-English-speaking country using that country's language rather than ELF	'I was all the time with my roommates and they speak French all the time. I had conversations with them and I asked them questions about Belgium and France and we talked about politics and I could practise with them'

to ELF. For example, issues of 'Language Anxiety' were found to be particularly pertinent in ELF as a 'Language User', while 'International Contact' was extremely related to 'Bridge of Communication'.

Step 5: In the selective coding phase, six core categories were selected (see Table 5.3), 'systematically connecting [each] to other categories, validating those similarities and relationships and then completing categories […] that need further refinement and development' (Kolb, 2012: 84). Researcher-denoted codes were used throughout, meaning that the researchers determined the code names that best represented what the data showed (Baralt, 2012).

Step 6: When the coding process was completed, the issue of reliability was addressed by asking two fellow researchers to recode the data using the list that had been generated (Macksoud, 2010). The codes the individuals assigned to the data were then compared with the original ones in order to see how closely we agreed, resulting in an inter-rater reliability value of 95%. The data were then recoded by the researchers of this study, in order to examine how closely our coding decisions overlapped with the original coding decisions. This resulted in an intra-rater reliability value of 100%.

Results

The analysis of the data resulted in six different categories that represented the roles of ELF, as outlined in Table 5.4.

Table 5.4 Coding categories of the role of ELF

Category	Subcategory	Country	Student
(1) ELF as a Bridge of Communication	–	English-speaking and non-English-speaking	Alex, María and Raquel
(2) ELF as a Crutch	–	Non-English-speaking	María
(3) ELF as an Impediment	(3.1) Intrinsic	Non-English-speaking	Alex
	(3.2) Extrinsic	Non-English-speaking	Alex
(4) ELF for Easier Access to Input	–	English-speaking	Alex, María and Raquel
(5) ELF as a Language User	–	English-speaking	María
(6) ELF non-use	–	Non-English-speaking	Laura

We will first discuss each category in turn, drawing from the interview data to analyse the effect of each category on the motivation and identity of the four students: Alex (France), Raquel (Germany), María (UK) and Laura (French-speaking part of Belgium). Following that, an individual profile will be presented for each of the four participants.

ELF as a Bridge of Communication: Raquel, María and Alex

By far the highest use of ELF appeared to be as a common language between non-native English speakers who did not share a common tongue. Much of the time, the students reported that, due to a friend not speaking Spanish, French or German, they would communicate instead in English:

Raquel (Germany):	With the international students I just spoke in English because there were lots of internationalities and maybe they didn't know how to speak German, so we spoke in English.
María (UK):	In my residence they were mostly Spanish or French but we used to speak in English because, like, the group was very mixed, so if you just speak in Spanish or French the others wouldn't understand.
Alex (France):	[We talk in] English actually, you know, like, we understand each other, like, really, really better, and one [friend] doesn't understand French.

Each of the interviewees explained their use of ELF by the fact that in not doing so, there would be one or more individuals who did not understand. The interviewees refer to SA students in France and Germany, who have no knowledge of the country's native language, highlighting the fact that despite not speaking French or German, these students can survive as long as they have English. In the case of the UK, María points out that in the case where there are students with different native languages, English is the language of choice, which appears to encourage the students not to communicate in their native tongue in order not to isolate other international students.

In the foregoing situations, the motivation to speak English is not driven by a need to become integrated into the local community, but rather by a necessity to communicate with other non-native English speakers. This usage exemplifies Yashima's (2009) International Posture as an alternative to traditional concepts such as integrative motivation, given that it captures the learners' tendency to relate themselves to an international community rather than a specific L2 group.

ELF as a Crutch: Raquel

In one case, the role of ELF actually served to aid the students in the acquisition of another TL, with English being used as a crutch to support them at times when they experienced difficulties in communication. One student reported using English as a Crutch at times when she had difficulties communicating in German:

Raquel (Germany): I tried to speak in German to the local people even though they can speak good English but at certain points if we didn't get what the other was saying maybe we just changed to English, but I tried to speak in German.

In such situations, it appears that the learner can rely on English to disentangle miscommunications during conversations, even while focusing on improving a different TL such as German. In this scenario, the student was quite proud to be able to use both her main TL, German, as well as English, using ELF to support her language acquisition and allowing her to present herself as a multilingual individual. It is possible that such multilingual exchanges could help to reinforce the individual's Ideal L2 self as a plurilingual individual, giving the student the needed motivation to continue the development of both languages.

ELF as an Impediment: Alex

While in the previous case it is clear that the role of ELF is constructive, this was not always the case. The following excerpt comes from Alex, who is referring to meeting friends at an international quiz:

Alex (France): I just met several people there and they became, like, my best friends. It was, like, really nice, I could practise French in the beginning, but as soon as I knew how good they spoke English I just said, hey, let's switch to English. I just didn't want to be perceived as someone who barely speaks the language he wants to communicate with, and I just said, hey, let's switch to English.

In this case, Alex does not use English to clear up some misunderstanding, but rather switches to it rather than losing face by speaking a language in which he is less proficient. Rather than portray himself as an incompetent language learner, he quickly identifies himself as a competent international English user.

While in this case the impediment is clearly intrinsic, in other cases, it appeared that it came from other people, much to the frustration of the student:

Alex: The fact is that every time I tried to speak in French, local people tried to speak English because they just thought, hey, well this guy does not speak French like French people so let's just speak English, let's establish it as a lingua franca.

Interviewer: And what did you do in those situations?

Alex: Ah, getting pissed off mostly, well from the inside, actually. I just tried to get by and speak English as well because I didn't want to lose out on those situations.

In this extract, it can be seen that ELF impedes the student's access to his main TL, French. However, given that these situations are still language learning opportunities for English, the student simply accepts it. Such instances can be seen to be seriously demotivating for the learner, with any efforts on the student's part to adopt a French-speaking identity being immediately rebuffed by the native speaker.

In the two cases of ELF as an Impediment, Alex appears to struggle to negotiate between his dynamic language identities, at times choosing to use English himself with his interlocutors, and at others becoming quite angry at those who deliberately switch to English, impeding his exposure to French input.

ELF as a Language User: María

Previous studies have shown that the use of ELF may offer students a more appealing identity, in the sense that they are no longer learners, but language users (Seidlhofer, 2004). This idea was found to be particularly pertinent for one student in the study, María, whose TL was English and who was studying in the UK. In the first excerpt, María explains how she avoided enrolling in certain classes so as not to be tempted to speak Spanish with her colleagues:

María (UK):   [I had to enrol in] Spanish translation but I switched it for French translation so I wouldn't be with Spanish people. I didn't want to be in the Spanish-English translation class because I knew I would just speak in Spanish.

It appears that the student portrayed a high level of intended learning effort, trying to avoid situations in which she would use her first language (L1). She also enrolled in a course in which she was the only Erasmus student, among only British students. However, the scenario did not lead to the intended learning environment expected:

María: Well my classes were mostly for Erasmus students so I didn't get to know a lot of people from London, but there was a course on culture and they were all British people and I was, like, the only Erasmus student. I didn't really speak because I was, like, ashamed of my, I don't know, and they were like 'come on speak, speak'. In the end they just ignored me and I was fine with that.

It can be seen here that, despite attempts to become integrated into a situation where she would be able to practise her TL with native speakers, the student's language anxiety prevented her from taking advantage of the language learning situation. The student later explains how she feels when communicating with native speakers:

María: When I speak with native speakers I feel like I'm being judged because they [...] I don't know, it's like a false impression but I feel like they know the language better than I do, that it's completely ok but every time I make a mistake they make a face like *cringe*, and it's not comfortable, so I dunno. I prefer to speak with foreigners so it's easier to engage and if you make a mistake and someone corrects, it's friendly.

Throughout the interview, this student reported having very little contact with native speakers as compared with international English users. When asked whether meeting native people was something she had wanted to do before arriving, she responded that meeting native people had been on her 'bucket list'. It appears that, while initially having the desire to become integrated into the local community and having an Ideal L2 self that was very much concerned with speaking like a native, upon arriving, the student at times felt insecure or anxious in situations where she was communicating with native speakers. In many SLA scenarios such as this, language acquisition could be seriously affected. However, the student at hand has a perfect alternative: ELF. The student readjusts her expectations and takes advantage of a different group of English users among whom she feels more comfortable:

María: I wanted to improve my skills but then I realised that if I just meet people that are better than me at speaking I would improve anyway. I don't need, like, native speakers to do that.

María: I think it's impossible to achieve, like, a native level in that language so I would be happy if I can just be fluent and competent in that language, if I understand because I think that's the goal to have a language.

Reflecting on her time abroad, María appears to have developed a realisation of the opportunities that contact with non-native speakers can provide, having readjusted her learning practices and expectations accordingly, and aligning them more towards that of the ELF speaker than the native English speaker. Following her time abroad, her Ideal L2 self is no longer restricted to that of a native-like speaker, but instead has shifted to a more accessible, competent, non-native speaker; in other words, a language 'user' rather than a 'learner' (Seidlhofer, 2004).

ELF for Easier Access to Input: María, Alex and Raquel

In keeping with the last section, reports from three of the four interviewees also highlighted the fact that, in certain cases, it was simply easier to form social networks with other non-native English speakers than with native speakers. In some cases, this was for reasons such as the language anxiety described in the previous sections. In others, it was simply because of the context in which students found themselves. For example, María, in the UK, discusses how she was surrounded by other international students, which meant that it was simply more convenient to socialise with them rather than seek out native speakers.

It appears to be the case that in English-speaking countries, students have a choice to become integrated into both the international group of English speakers and the local community, with the former appearing more accessible for the various reasons previously outlined. This is not to say that students will not become integrated to a certain extent in both groups, but rather in the data collected here there is an indication that students may be inclined towards the ELF group rather than native English speakers.

This tendency was not unique to those studying in an English-speaking country, as it was also reported by Alex and Raquel, who were studying in France and Germany:

Alex (France): I did not feel integrated in the society in any moment actually. I felt like integrated in the context because I don't know I'm an Erasmus student I need to, you know, get used to it but, well, I did not feel integrated, you know, just because of them. I don't know, it was kind of a strange feeling.

Raquel (Germany): In my point of view it wasn't for the language [that I didn't feel integrated] it was because you are more with other students and maybe other international students, not that much with local people, and then if you do just some months there you actually do not meet that many people from the city or whatever and that's why for me it's difficult to integrate in this sense. But it's more difficult to know them than the people you are with so that's the problem for me.

These findings are consistent with research by Papatsiba (2006) and Tragant (2012) who found that Spanish and French sojourners, respectively, reported weak interaction with natives, instead forming an international Erasmus community. Thus, though students may initially view their future L2 selves as being surrounded by native speakers, they perhaps find on arrival that it is easier instead to become integrated into this international community, and alter their expectations accordingly.

As suggested by Raquel, it may be due to the fact that these students spent only around three months abroad that it was difficult to become integrated into the local community. Indeed, a recent study by Dewaele *et al.* (2015) found that length of stay was positively linked to difference in willingness to communicate (WTC), suggesting that students may exhibit greater WTC the longer they spend abroad, an attribute that may in turn lead to more integration into the local community. This issue is also raised by Sasaki (2011) who shows that when it comes to motivational factors, longer SA periods of at least four months are often needed in order to reveal changes, and in the case of intrinsic motivation, an even longer period of up to eight months may be required. In addition to the length of SA, it is also possible that self-efficacy was a significant factor. A recent study by Hessel (2017) highlighted the significant effect of self-efficacy on how students exploit the linguistic affordances of SA. The findings showed that students' 'perceptions of self-efficacy at programme entry affected whether they chose to use the L2 in their informal social interactions abroad and with whom' (Hessel, 2017: 49).

ELF non-use: Laura

One of the participants, Laura, did not report using ELF at any time. Instead, she reported a great deal of interaction with native French speakers. She lived with both native French speakers and other Spanish speakers, but communicated with all of them in French; she had a language exchange partner with whom she practised her French and did various activities; and she showed a deep interest in Belgian and French culture and politics. Unlike the other students who, regardless of staying in an English- or non-English-speaking country, reported high usage of ELF, Laura's goals were very clearly aligned towards learning French rather than English, and her Ideal L2 self was very much concerned with being a proficient French speaker:

Laura (Belgium):	In my case, I don't know, but I love French, it's my passion, and if there is a day that I don't hear a word of French it's very sad for me, I need French in my life. I have a special thing with French and I don't know how to explain it but it's like a person to me, I don't know, it's strange.
Laura:	French is not the lingua franca but I think, I don't know, in each time there is a language that is more important than the rest and now it's English, but in my opinion, there are many countries where French is the official language and it's important too. Maybe in another time [French] will be more important.

It is suggested that in this case, Laura's passion for French allows her first to breach the native speaker barrier reported by the other students, and also to avoid the 'ELF as an Impediment' experienced by other students. It should also be noted that having lived with native speakers, the student reported meeting other natives very easily by meeting friends of friends.

Given that Laura was the only student interviewed who lived with native speakers the same age as her, it is plausible that this, combined with her high level of integrative motivation, led to her increased language use with native French speakers.

Learner profiles

Following the presentation of the above categories, a profile for each learner can be drawn on the basis of those that can be ascribed to them (see Table 5.5), these categories becoming then a sort of learning or communication strategy.

Table 5.5   Details of participants and relevant categories/strategies

Participant	Relevant categories/strategies
Alex, 21, male, SA in France	ELF as a Bridge of Communication ELF as an Impediment ELF for Easier Access to Input
Raquel, 19, female, SA in Germany	ELF as a Bridge of Communication ELF as a Crutch ELF for Easier Access to Input
María, 19, female, SA in England	ELF as a Bridge of Communication ELF as a Language User ELF for Easier Access to Input
Laura, 19, female, SA in Belgium	ELF non-use

Firstly, Alex, who studied abroad in France, reports a high amount of ELF usage, adopting English to communicate with other non-native English speakers. This usage can be seen at times to impede opportunities to practise what, in theory, should be his main TL during his SA: French. However, it appears that he found it easier to become integrated into an ELF community rather than a native or non-native French-speaking one. Raquel, in Germany, had a similar experience to Alex with regard to using ELF to facilitate communication, also reporting that at times it was easier for her to find opportunities to speak English than German. That said, she also reported using English to support her acquisition of German, and appeared to have quite a positive experience in being able to use the two languages simultaneously. Thirdly, María, like Alex and Raquel, used ELF to facilitate communication. However, this case is quite different, given that María was living in an English-speaking country. That is to say, despite having access to native English speakers, she still reported a tendency to socialise with other non-native speakers, using English. This was particularly relevant to the issue of identity, as discussed in the section titled 'ELF as a Language User: María'. Finally, Laura, in Belgium, does not report needing to use ELF, discussing instead her integration with native French speakers.

Discussion

The results of the qualitative data were consistent with the hypothesis that in non-English-speaking countries ELF would both hinder and aid in the acquisition of these students' TL, while in an English-speaking country it would provide a more accessible way to practise the language. The results highlight the roles that ELF plays during SA in connection with the individual's identity and motivation. Of the students interviewed, only one, Laura, reported penetrating the native speaker barrier and, perhaps consequently, reported no ELF usage, forming social networks only with native French speakers. It appears that her success in this regard may be a combination of her living arrangements as well as a high level of integrative motivation. While previous research has found no association between housing arrangements and the development of proficiency (Kinginger, 2009), it is perhaps important to point out that in this situation, it is not specifically the type of housing that may be important, but rather the people with whom the student shared her accommodation (native French speakers of a similar age). The other three interviewees, while having contact with native speakers to a lesser degree, reported a high amount of interaction with other non-native English speakers, using ELF as a means of communication. This is consistent with research that has discussed the formation of ELF communities during SA (e.g. Kalocsai, 2011; Kaypak & Ortaçtepe, 2014; Llanes *et al.*, 2016). These students, while having expressed a desire to have contact with native speakers upon arrival, often shifted their learning expectations and aspirations and adopted the identity of the competent non-native English speaker (Seidlhofer, 2004). When met with actions that may have demotivated them, such as in the case of Alex, native speakers switching from the TL to English, or, as in the case of María, language anxiety in the face of native speakers, instead of being discouraged, the students adopted coping mechanisms, shifting between their dynamic language learner identities. In many cases, this could mean manoeuvring towards a possibly more global identity, providing students with ELF exposure and allowing them to become integrated within an international ELF-speaking community, rather than the expected native-speaking one. Such communities were shown to be at times not only easier to access, but in some cases even provided students with a learning environment in which they could feel less anxious compared to that with native speakers. This finding is consistent with research by Papatsiba (2006) and Tragant (2012), which highlighted how Spanish and French sojourners experienced weak interaction with native speakers, and thus instead formed an international ELF community, adopting an international, global identity.

In the case of the English-speaking country, ELF offered the students a kind of safety net, allowing them to overcome challenges to their motivation and identity. It also featured a great deal in the case of non-English-speaking countries, at times aiding communication in the TL and at others impeding it. In the case of Alex, TL input was impeded both by himself in order to present himself as a competent language user, as well as by others, challenging the student's motivation to practise his TL, French, with native speakers.

Summary and Conclusions

This study has investigated the connection between ELF and its different roles, and language learning motivation and identity among higher education students. The results of the qualitative data suggested six key ways in which ELF is related to the motivation and identity of SA students: ELF as a Bridge of Communication, ELF as a Crutch, ELF as an Impediment, ELF for Easier Access to Input, ELF as a Language User and ELF non-use. The first, ELF as a Bridge of Communication, matches the definition of ELF given by Firth (1996), i.e. a contact language between individuals who do not share a common tongue. The second and third categories deal specifically with the effect that English, when learned as a foreign language, has on the learning of other foreign languages like French or German, as in this study, and whether it aids in its acquisition (ELF as a Crutch) or impedes it (ELF as an Impediment). While the issue of English impeding the acquisition of other languages has been addressed in previous research with regard to native English speakers learning an L2 (e.g. Mitchell *et al.*, 2015a), there appears to be a lack of research in respect of non-native speakers of English learning other foreign languages. Similarly, more research is needed to understand how English may be used as a 'crutch' to support learning an additional foreign language. Regarding the fourth category, it was found that ELF offered easier access to opportunities in which students could practise English. This was relevant in situations where the students found it difficult to form links with native speakers, but could instead rely on ELF communities to practise the language. Fifth, regarding ELF as a Language User, results are consistent with the idea that ELF can offer a more appealing language identity, in that rather than an error-prone learner, the student can adopt the identity of a competent and authoritative language user (Seidlhofer, 2004). Finally, one of the three students in a non-English-speaking country did not report any ELF usage, focusing instead on using French, the language of her SA country. As mentioned above, this may have been due to a combination of her living arrangements and a high level of integrative motivation, reporting a great interest in French and Belgian culture and politics. These categories have also allowed us to draw the profile of our participants with respect to their specific use of ELF and the roles it fulfils in their own motivation and identity vis-à-vis the language and the culture behind ELF and their other respective TLs, French or German.

Concerning the limitations of the study, it should be noted that due to time restraints, it was not possible to conduct a longitudinal study, as the students were already abroad when the project commenced. It was thus not possible to conduct face-to-face interviews before the students went abroad. A future study would benefit from testing the same group of students both prior to and following the SA period. Furthermore, when identifying the category 'ELF as a Crutch', it became apparent that future research should investigate further the role that English as an L2 has in the learning of an additional language, particularly in the case of ELF. In this case, particularly interesting data arose from questions in the category 'Use of English/German/French'. When reflecting on the situations in which they used each of their languages, the students discussed the various reasons why they switched from one language to the other, which provided extremely useful data. However, future studies would benefit from creating and including new interview questions that specifically tap into these issues related to ELF as a Crutch and ELF as an Impediment.

Within an SA context, research to date has increasingly acknowledged the importance of the learners' language identity and motivation, with more and more research taking a qualitative approach in order to gain a deeper understanding of the processes at hand. This study has adopted this necessary qualitative approach in order to investigate the connection between ELF and the identity and motivation of the language learner. It has pinpointed some of the issues that arise when learning English, as well as other foreign languages, in the context of SA where ELF is often used extensively. The results of this study further stress the importance of pre-departure preparation, as has been highlighted by researchers such as Collentine (2009), Paige *et al.* (2002) and Pérez-Vidal (2017). Given the surge in ELF in recent years, it is apparent that it cannot be expected that all students simply arrive in their host country and automatically slot in with the local native speakers. ELF offers an alternative that must be taken into account by SA students and administrators alike. It is suggested that institutions take the necessary measures to adequately prepare students for these scenarios, supporting each situation and encouraging students to make the most of the different sources of input available. Students sojourning in an English-speaking country should be encouraged to take advantage of each group, in order to fully immerse themselves in as many language learning situations as possible. Students sojourning in a non-English-speaking country should be adequately prepared to be able to negotiate their multilingual usage while abroad, to allow them to reap the benefits of these learning opportunities, rather than have them be a source of linguistic impediment.

This chapter concludes with the words of Raquel, reflecting on the effect that her SA had on her sense of identity:

> I think this experience helped me understand myself in a deeper level. I was 'lost in translation', and I believe I still am, but now I am aware of the fact that there's different cultures coexisting inside of me, and that all of them make me who I am. I did not feel less Spanish, Catalan or French: I think I felt more 'myself'.

Acknowledgement

This work was supported by the Agència Universitària de Recerca (AGAUR) in Catalonia [2014 SGR 1568], and by the Ministry of Economy and Competitiveness [FFI2013-48640-C2-1-P].

Note

(1) Data from the pilot interview with Sara will also be discussed briefly in the analysis.

References

Albl-Mikasa, M. (2010) Global English and English as a lingua franca (ELF): Implications for the interpreting profession. *Trans-Kom* 3 (2), 126–148.

Baralt, M. (2012) Coding qualitative data. In A. Mackey and S.M. Gass (eds) *Research Methods in Second Language Acquisition: A Practical Guide* (pp. 222–244). Oxford: Wiley-Blackwell.

Bazeley, P. (2007) *Qualitative Data Analysis with NVivo*. London: Sage.

Beattie, J. (2014) The 'ins and outs' of a study abroad programme: The SALA exchange programme. In C. Pérez-Vidal (ed.) *Language Acquisition in Study Abroad and Formal Instruction Contexts* (pp. 59–87). Amsterdam/Philadelphia, PA: Benjamins.

Berg, B. (1995) *Qualitative Research Methods for the Social Sciences*. Needham Heights, MA: Allyn & Bacon.

Block, D. (2007) *Second Language Identities*. London/New York: Continuum.

Block, D. and Cameron, D. (2002) Introduction. In D. Block and D. Cameron (eds) *Globalization and Language Teaching* (pp. 1–10). London: Routledge.

Bogdan, R. and Biklen, S.K. (1998) *Qualitative Research in Education: An Introduction to Theory and Methods* (3rd edn). Boston, MA: Allyn & Bacon.

Coleman, J.A. (1998) Language learning and study abroad: The European perspective. *Frontiers: The Interdisciplinary Journal of Study Abroad* 4 (2), 167–203.

Collentine, J.G. (2009) Study abroad research: Findings, implications and future directions. In M.H. Long and C.J. Doughty (eds) *The Handbook of Language Teaching* (pp. 218–233). New York: Wiley.

Collentine, J.G. and Freed, B.F. (2004) Learning context and its effects on second language acquisition: Introduction. *Studies in Second Language Acquisition* 26 (2), 153–171.

Dailey, A. (2009) Key motivational factors and how teachers can encourage motivation in their students. Master's dissertation, University of Birmingham. See https://www.birmingham.ac.uk/Documents/college-artslaw/cels/essays/secondlanguage/DailySLA KeyMotivationalFactorsandHowTeachers.pdf (accessed 28 March 2019).

Davis, T. (2003) *Atlas of Student Mobility*. New York: Institute of International Education.

Devlin, A.M. (2014) *The Impact of Study Abroad on the Acquisition of Sociopragmatic Variation Patterns: The Case of Non-native Speaker English Teachers*. Bern: Peter Lang.

Dewaele, J-M., Comanaru, R. and Faraco, M. (2015) The affective benefits of a pre-sessional course at the start of study abroad. In R. Mitchell, N. Tracy-Ventura and K. McManus (eds) *Social Interaction, Identity and Language Learning during Residence Abroad* (EUROSLA Monograph Series 4; pp. 33–50). Amsterdam: European Second Language Association. See http://www.eurosla.org/monographs/EM04/Dewaele_etal. pdf (accessed 28 March 2019).

Dörnyei, Z. (2007) *Research Methods in Applied Linguistics*. Oxford: Oxford University Press.

Dörnyei, Z. (2009) The L2 Motivational Self System. In Z. Dörnyei and E. Ushioda (eds) *Motivation, Language Identity and the L2 Self* (pp. 9–42). Bristol: Multilingual Matters.

Dörnyei, Z. and Ushioda, E. (2013) *Teaching and Researching: Motivation*. London: Routledge.

Eckert, P. (2000) *Language Variation as Social Practice: The Linguistic Construction of Identity in Belten High*. Oxford: Blackwell.

Firth, A. (1996) The discursive accomplishment of normality: On 'lingua franca' English and conversation analysis. *Journal of Pragmatics* 26 (2), 237–259.

Friedman, D.A. (2012) How to collect and analyze qualitative data. In A. Mackey and S.M. Gass (eds) *Research Methods in Second Language Acquisition: A Practical Guide* (pp. 180–200). Oxford: Wiley-Blackwell.

Geoghegan, L. (2018) International posture, motivation and identity in SA. In C. Pérez-Vidal, S. López-Serrano, J. Ament and D. Thomas Wilhelm (eds) *Learning Context Effects: Study Abroad, Formal Instruction and International Immersion Classrooms*. Amsterdam: European Second Language Association (EUROSLA).

Guerrero, M. (2015) Motivation in second language learning: A historical overview and its relevance in a public high school in Pasto, Colombia. *HOW* 22 (1), 95–106.

Hadfield, J. and Dörnyei, Z. (2013) *Motivating Learning*. Harlow: Longman.

Hessel, G. (2017) A new take on individual differences in L2 proficiency gain during study abroad. *System* 66, 39–55.

Higgins, E.T. (1987) Self-discrepancy: A theory relating self and affect. *Psychological Review* 94 (3), 319–340.

Highet, G. (2003) Cannabis and smoking research: Interviewing young people in self-selected friendship pairs. *Health Education Research* 18 (1), 108–118.

Isabelli-García, C. (2006) Study abroad social networks, motivation and attitudes: Implications for second language acquisition. In M. DuFon and E. Churchill (eds) *Language Learners in Study Abroad Contexts* (pp. 231–258). Clevedon: Multilingual Matters.

Jackson, J. (2008) *Language, Identity, and Study Abroad: Sociocultural Perspectives*. London: Equinox.

Jenkins, J. (2000) *The Phonology of English as an International Language*. Oxford: Oxford University Press.

Jenkins, J. (2015) Repositioning English and multilingualism in English as a Lingua Franca. *Englishes in Practice* 2 (3), 49–85.

Jenkins, J., Cogo, A. and Dewey, M. (2011) Review of developments in research into English as a lingua franca. *Language Teaching* 44 (3), 281–315.

Kalocsai, K. (2011) The show of interpersonal involvement and the building of rapport in an ELF community of practice. In A. Archibald, A. Cogo and J. Jenkins (eds) *Latest Trends in English as a Lingua Franca Research* (pp. 113–137). Newcastle: Cambridge Scholars Press.

Kaypak, E. and Ortaçtepe, D. (2014) Language learner beliefs and study abroad: A study on English as a lingua franca (ELF). *System* 42, 355–367.

Ke, I.C. and Cahyani, H. (2014) Learning to become users of English as a Lingua Franca (ELF): How ELF online communication affects Taiwanese learners' beliefs of English. *System* 46, 28–38.

Kim, T. (2009) The dynamics of L2 self and L2 learning motivation: A qualitative case study of Korean ESL students. *English Teaching* 64 (3), 49–70.

Kinginger, C. (2009) *Language Learning and Study Abroad: A Critical Reading of Research*. New York: Palgrave Macmillan.

Kolb, S. (2012) Grounded theory and the constant comparative method: Valid research strategies for educators. *Journal of Emerging Trends in Educational Research and Policy Studies* 3 (1), 83–86.

Lincoln, Y.S. and Guba, E.G. (1985) *Naturalistic Inquiry*. Beverly Hills, CA: Sage.

Llanes, À., Arnó, E. and Mancho-Barés, G. (2016) Erasmus students using English as a lingua franca: Does study abroad in a non-English-speaking country improve L2 English? *The Language Learning Journal* 44 (3), 292–303.

Macksoud, R. (2010) Using interview data in case studies. In S. Hunston and D. Oakley (eds) *Introducing Applied Linguistics: Concepts and Skills* (pp. 153–159). London: Routledge.

MacWhinney, B. (2009) The CHILDES Project Part 1: The CHAT transcription format. Department of Psychology, Carnegie Mellon University, Paper 181. See http://repository.cmu.edu/psychology/181 (accessed 28 March 2019).

Markus, H. and Nurius, P. (1986) Possible selves. *American Psychologist* 41 (9), 954–969.

Miles, M.B. and Huberman, A.M. (1994) *Qualitative Data Analysis: An Expanded Sourcebook*. Thousand Oaks, CA: Sage.

Mitchell, R., McManus, K. and Tracy-Ventura, N. (2015a) Placement type and language learning during residence abroad. In R. Mitchell, N. Tracy-Ventura and K. McManus (eds) *Social Interaction, Identity and Language Learning during Residence Abroad* (EUROSLA Monograph Series 4; pp. 95–115). Amsterdam: European Second Language Association. See http://www.eurosla.org/monographs/EM04/Mitchell_etal.pdf (accessed 28 March 2019).

Mitchell, R., Tracy-Ventura, N. and McManus, K. (2015b) Introduction. In R. Mitchell, N. Tracy-Ventura and K. McManus (eds) *Social Interaction, Identity and Language Learning during Residence Abroad* (EUROSLA Monograph Series 4; pp. 7–13). Amsterdam: European Second Language Association. See http://www.eurosla.org/monographs/EM04/EM04Introduction.pdf (accessed 28 March 2019).

Norton, B. (2000) *Identity and Language Learning*. London: Longman.

Organisation for Economic Cooperation and Development (2013) *Education at a Glance 2013: OECD Indicators*. Paris: OECD Publishing.

Paige, R.M., Cohen, A.D., Kappler, B., Chi, J.C. and Lassegard, J.P. (2002) *Maximizing Study Abroad: A Students' Guide to Strategies for Language and Culture Learning and Use*. Minneapolis, MN: Center for Advanced Research on Language Acquisition, University of Minnesota.

Papatsiba, V. (2006) Making higher education more European through student mobility? Revisiting EU initiatives in the context of the Bologna Process. *Comparative Education* 42 (1), 93–111.

Pérez-Vidal, C. (2017) Study abroad and ISLA. In S. Loewen and M. Sato (eds) *The Routledge Handbook of Instructed Second Language Acquisition* (pp. 339–360). London: Routledge.

Rezaei, S. (2012) Researching identity in applied linguistics. *Language, Society and Culture* 35, 45–51.

Riazi, A.M. (2016) *The Routledge Encyclopedia of Research Methods in Applied Linguistics*. London: Routledge.

Robson, C. (2002) *Real World Research*. Oxford: Blackwell.

Ryan, S. (2009) Self and identity in L2 motivation in Japan: The ideal L2 self and Japanese learners of English. In Z. Dörnyei and E. Ushioda (eds) *Motivation, Language and the L2 Self* (pp. 120–143). Bristol: Multilingual Matters.

Sasaki, M. (2011) Effects of varying lengths of study-abroad experiences on Japanese EFL students' L2 writing ability and motivation: A longitudinal study. *TESOL Quarterly* 45, 81–105.

Schumann, J.H. (1978) *The Pidginization Process: A Model for Second Language Acquisition*. Rowley, MA: Newbury House.

Seidlhofer, B. (2001) Closing a conceptual gap: The case for a description of English as a lingua franca. *International Journal of Applied Linguistics* 11 (2), 133–158.

Seidlhofer, B. (2004) Research perspectives on teaching English as a lingua franca. *Annual Review of Applied Linguistics* 24, 209–239.

Smokotin, V.M., Alekseyenko, A.S. and Petrova, G.I. (2014) The phenomenon of linguistic globalization: English as the Global Lingua Franca (EGLF). *Procedia – Social and Behavioral Sciences* 154, 509–513.

Tragant, E. (2012) Change or stability in learners' perceptions as a result of study abroad. In C. Muñoz (ed.) *Intensive Exposure Experiences in Second Language Learning* (pp. 161–190). Bristol: Multilingual Matters.

Ushioda, E. (2009) A person-in-context relational view of emergent motivation, self and identity. In Z. Dörnyei and E. Ushioda (eds) *Motivation, Language Identity and the L2 Self* (pp. 215–228). Bristol: Multilingual Matters.

Ushioda, E. and Dörnyei, Z. (2012) Motivation. In S. Gass and A. Mackey (eds) *The Routledge Handbook of Second Language Acquisition* (pp. 396–409). New York: Routledge.

Waninge, F., Dörnyei, Z. and De Bot, K. (2014) Motivational dynamics in language learning: Change, stability, and context. *The Modern Language Journal* 98 (3), 704–723.

Wilson, A.D., Onwuegbuzie, A.J. and Manning, L.P. (2016) Using paired depth interviews to collect qualitative data. *The Qualitative Report* 21 (9), 1549–1573.

Yashima, T. (2009) International posture and the ideal L2 self in the Japanese EFL context. In Z. Dörnyei and E. Ushioda (eds) *Motivation, Language Identity and the L2 Self* (pp. 144–163). Bristol: Multilingual Matters.

Appendices

Appendix A: Interview guide

Introduction: Tell us about how your stay was organised: you were at _____university? And you were there for _____ weeks?

(1) University classmates
  (1.1) Were there other Spanish students on Erasmus there?
  (1.2) Did you spend much time together?
  (1.3) What language/s did you speak in?
(2) Accommodation
  (2.1) What were your living arrangements while abroad?
  (2.2) How did you organise it/did you experience any issues?
(3) Classes
  (3.1) What kind of classes did you take while abroad?
  (3.2) How many were full courses?
  (3.3) How many through English?
  (3.4) Were you assessed on those courses? In what way?
  (3.5) Did you like them? Why/why not?
(4) Work
  (4.1) Did you have a part-time job while abroad?
  (4.2) Did you try?
  (4.3) Any other periodical activity besides your courses? Sports? Singing/theatre/dance…?
(5) Use of English/German/French
  (5.1) Did you spend time using English/German/French in your spare time?
  (5.2) Did you do activities with Erasmus socialising groups? What were they like?
(6) Language anxiety/L2 self-confidence
  (6.1) How did you feel when communicating in English/German/French?
  (6.2) And in your classes… did you often volunteer to speak in your classes?

(7) Fear of assimilation
    (7.1) Did you find it difficult being away from your home and family?
    (7.2) Did you find it difficult to become integrated with the local community while on Erasmus? Did language have something to do with it?
    (7.3) Were there also different stages in how integrated you felt?

(8) International contact
    (8.1) Think about the new people you met while abroad. Are there any people who you see yourself staying in contact with? Where are they from? What language do you normally speak together?
    (8.2) Did you spend more time with an international group of friends, or with natives? Why? Do you think it's easier to make friends with other Erasmus students (international students) or natives? Why?

(9) Intended learning effort/things done to improve language
    (9.1) What kinds of things did you do to help you improve your language while abroad? (Was contact with people one of them? The media? Shows? Music?)
    (9.2) What did you do to improve your language skills that you couldn't do at home? (Did you use books? Grammars? Dictionaries?)

(10) Contact with family
    (10.1) How much contact did you have with your family and friends from home while on Erasmus? Did you use social networks for that?
    (10.2) And did you use English for communication via social networks?

(11) Ease of learning experience
    (11.1) In what ways do you think being abroad helped you learn the language?
    (11.2) Did you find that in some ways it was more difficult learning abroad than at home?
    (11.3) Did you find that there were differentiated periods or stages in your command of the English language, in the three months you were abroad?

(12) Ability/perceived improvement
    (12.1) In which areas do you think you improved the most (reading/writing/speaking/listening/pronunciation)? How did you achieve this improvement?
    (12.2) Is there an area which you think you did not improve? Why?

(13) Ideal L2 self
    (13.1) After being abroad, do you think it's easier to imagine yourself as a competent and natural speaker of the language?

(14) Interest in foreign languages

    (14.1) What is it that appeals to you about English/German/French?

(15) Instrumentality

    (15.1) Do you think that most people want to learn English/French/German simply because it's important for their future careers?

    (15.2) Why do you want to learn it?

(16) International posture

    (16.1) What place do you see English/German/French having in your future? Do you think you would like to work or live abroad, or do you see yourself using it to work here in Spain?

    (16.2) Do you think that being on Erasmus made you more interested in international affairs?

Wrap-up: Is there anything you'd like to add?

Appendix B: Follow-up questions

Participants in an English-speaking country

(1) In what way do you think being on Erasmus affected your motivation to learn English? Was this what you expected before arriving?

(2) How do you think your Erasmus affected your sense of identity? Did you feel less 'Spanish' or more 'international' while abroad? Was this what you expected?

(3) While abroad, did you socialise more with native English speakers, other native Spanish speakers or an international group using English? (If you spent equal time with more than one group, you can answer the following in relation to each group.)

    (3.1) What were your reasons for this? (e.g. choice or convenience?)

    (3.2) Was this what you expected before arriving?

    (3.3) Do you think one group aided you in your language acquisition more than other groups did/would have? Why/why not?

    (3.4) Did you find it more difficult to become integrated with some groups? Why?

(4) Do you prefer speaking English with native speakers or with other non-native speakers? What appeals to you about using English with other non-native speakers?

Participants in a French- or German-speaking country

(1) In what way do you think being on Erasmus affected your motivation to learn French or German? Is this what you expected?

(2) How do you think your Erasmus affected your sense of identity? Did you feel less 'Spanish' or more 'international' while abroad? Is this what you expected?

(3) While abroad, did you socialise more with native French/German speakers, other native Spanish speakers or an international group using English? (If you spent equal time with more than one group, you can answer the following in relation to each group.)

    (3.1)   What were your reasons for this?

    (3.2)   Was this what you expected before arriving?

    (3.3)   Do you think one group aided you in your language acquisition more than other groups did/would have? Why/why not?

    (3.4)   Did you find it more difficult to become integrated with some groups? Why?

(4) In what way(s) did English (as a lingua franca) help you to learn French/German while abroad? Is this what you expected?

(5) In what way(s) did English (as a lingua franca) make it difficult for you to learn French/German while abroad? Is this what you expected?

Appendix C: Sample interview transcript

@Begin

@Languages: eng

@Participants: CAT Student pseudonym María, ALI Student pseudonym Laura

@ID: eng|geoghegan|CAT

@ID: eng|geoghegan|ALI

[…]

*GEO: ok and what about the classes in your university what kind of classes did you take?

*CAT: well my classes were mostly for Erasmus students so I didn't get to know a lot of people from London um but there was a course on culture that they were all British people and I was like the only Erasmus student I didn't really speak because I was, like, ashamed of my, I don't know, and they were like 'come on, speak, speak' in the end they just ignored me and I was fine with that.

*GEO: you were happy?

*CAT: mostly yes

*ALI: I have done some classes for Erasmus students which were more easy than the other from the test of students from the university and I have been in American culture class which was all in English with students from Brussels the rest of my classes were French and um linguistic and culture French and culture.

*GEO: ok and overall did you like the classes?

*ALI: yes

*CAT: yeah

*GEO: and what about the languages were they mostly, you said already you had one in English?

*CAT: well all my courses were in English I tried to take the French course but they didn't allow me to because I am native French speaker.

*GEO: ah ok

*CAT: so there wasn't any of my level so they said well we'd be happy to have you but you would be like bored the course so they didn't allow me so instead I had to take a spoken communication skills and change like three courses so I could have all the credits.

[...]

@End

Appendix D: Sample interview analysis

Questions to keep in mind (Bazeley, 2007)

(1) Why are you doing this project?
(2) What do you think it's about?
(3) What are the questions you're asking, and where did they come from?
(4) What do you expect to find and why?
(5) What have you observed so far?

Segment under analysis

*CAT: well my classes were mostly for Erasmus students so I didn't get to know a lot of people from London um but there was a course on culture that they were all British people and I was like the only Erasmus student I didn't really speak because I was, like, ashamed of my, I don't know, and they were like 'come on speak, speak' in the end they just ignored me and I was fine with that

Researcher Notes

26.02.2016

The things to bear in mind here are how the student's motivation and identity are effected depending on the context of their

English usage. Here, it seems there is a certain amount of isolation of Erasmus students. While there is the option for students to take classes with native speakers, this student reports that most of her classes are with non-native speakers. While catering for Erasmus students by providing classes specifically for Erasmus students, this may help them with the content but perhaps serve to take away an opportunity for students to mingle with natives. How does this experience compare with the student's interaction with non-native speakers? Here, the reaction appears to be quite negative. It should be noted if there are similar trends elsewhere in the data.

13.03.2016

There seems to be an issue here regarding MOTIVATION and LANGUAGE ANXIETY. The student deliberately seeks out a class of only British students, but reports being 'ashamed'. British students seem initially interested to engage but when met with shyness they get bored and give up? How do other students report how native speakers behave? Do they also feel that native speakers show a lack of interest? I expect that while many speakers want to seek out native speaker interactions, they may also find it difficult to do so. Is this the case? From this segment, it seems that the student experiences a change to her motivation, caused by her language anxiety. In another segment, she has reported enrolling in this class specifically to seek out native speaker interaction, however when it becomes a reality, it appears to be more difficult than she anticipated.

05.04.2016

This segment ties in with the code ELF as a LANGUAGE USER. It shows the perspective of what this student experiences when confronted with native speakers. This should be compared with the same student's reports on speaking with non-native speaker: how does this behaviour tie in with the student's other behaviours? Is there a distinction between her actions in the two situations? It appears so. From the other quotes analyzed so far, it appears that this student's story using ELF as a language user should have its own section in the analysis.

6 Study Abroad as a Context for Learning English as an International Language: An Exploratory Study

Àngels Llanes

Introduction

The potential linguistic benefits of a study abroad (SA) experience are well known as several studies have documented the second or foreign language (L2) gains of students participating in SA programs. These findings are not surprising given that the SA setting offers a combination of formal (in the classroom) and informal (out-of-class) learning, unlimited exposure to the L2 and multiple opportunities to practice the L2 with various interlocutors (Freed, 1995; Llanes & Muñoz, 2013). However, most of these SA studies on L2 development have been conducted with participants going to countries where the language they use for everyday conversations is also the official language of the community (i.e. Spanish students of English going to the UK, or British students of French going to France). The impact of an SA experience in an English as a lingua franca (ELF) country has been relatively unexplored (Durham, 2014). This lack of research is surprising given that nowadays globalization has imposed the need to function in global working environments (Blumenthal & Laughlin, 2009); and as many college students recognize, SA experiences play an essential role in preparing for a successful career in a global world. For students from non-English-speaking countries, mastering at least one L2 is essential in order to function in global environments. Thus, millions of students participate in SA programs every year around the world (European Commission for Education and Training, 2014); the majority of European programs involve a number of countries where English is used by SA learners as a lingua franca. Mobility experiences in English-speaking countries or in ELF countries are supposedly different, mostly because participants in ELF countries will presumably be exposed to more reduced target language (TL) input than participants in English-speaking countries due to the presence of other languages (the official language/s of the host countries) and also because most interactions occur between L2 speakers (as some research on social networks has shown, SA participants lament few interactional opportunities with members of the local community and tend to interact with international students [Coleman, 2015]). In order to fill the gap regarding the lack of research on the impact of SA in ELF countries, the objective of the present study is to examine the L2 oral skills and general proficiency development of a group of Catalan/Spanish learners of English engaging in an SA program in non-English-speaking European countries, where they use ELF to communicate.

Additionally, the present study also attempts to fill another gap in the literature relating to the role of using the same or a different task in data collection. Since researchers are often faced with the problem of using the same or a different task between the pre- and the post-test (both have advantages and disadvantages), and there is little evidence on the consequences of using the same or a different task, the present study attempts to address this issue by administering the same oral narrative in the pre- and in the post-test to a group of students, and a different oral narrative between the pre- and the post-test to another group of students.

Literature Review

Research on the effects of SA experiences has gained popularity in the field of second language acquisition (SLA) because it is believed that this context provides rich and authentic input as well as intensive exposure to the L2, factors that supposedly positively influence L2 development (Llanes & Muñoz, 2013; Muñoz, 2012). However, SA experiences do not lead to equal improvement in all L2 areas. Whereas the effects of SA on some areas are quite clear, for others they are still unclear, either because they have been underexplored or because of inconclusive results. This is not the case for oral skills, which have often been the focus of research because of the assumption that this is the area that benefits most from an SA experience. The studies that have examined the impact of SA on L2 oral skills have mostly found that this area improves significantly after a period abroad. This development has been found in measures underlying different aspects of oral fluency such as speech rate, mean length of run and breakdown fluency (Freed, 1995; Huensch & Tracy-Ventura, 2017; Leonard & Shea, 2017; Llanes & Muñoz, 2009; Segalowitz & Freed, 2004). Likewise, vocabulary acquisition during an SA experience has also been examined. Studies have often found that vocabulary can significantly improve after spending some time in the host country (Foster, 2009; Milton & Meara, 1995; Zaytseva, 2016). Another area that also seems to benefit from an overseas experience is listening comprehension. Despite the fact that L2 listening comprehension development after an SA experience has received comparatively less attention, the results seem to be positive (Cubillos *et al.*, 2008; Llanes & Prieto, 2015; Rodrigo, 2011).

Nevertheless, the impact of SA on other skills such as writing and grammar is still unclear. With regard to writing, whereas some studies have found a significant improvement in L2 writing skills as a result of SA (Pérez-Vidal & Juan-Garau, 2009; Sasaki, 2004, 2009), other studies have reported either comparable gains for SA and 'at-home' (AH) groups or higher scores for the AH students in perceived written fluency (Freed *et al.*, 2003). This lack of consensus regarding the role that SA plays when it comes to improving writing skills might be explained by differences in the measures used, or differences in the programs themselves (e.g. Sasaki's participants spent a much longer time abroad than those of Freed *et al.*). Additionally, participant individual differences might also account for these differences. Llanes and Muñoz (2013), for example, found that age played a significant role in L2 development. More specifically, these authors found that while child SA participants significantly improved on almost all the oral and written measures under study, adult SA participants only improved on a few oral measures and no written ones, while adult AH participants significantly improved on some written measures and no oral measures.

Similarly, research on the impact of SA on L2 grammar development is also unclear. While some researchers have observed clear gains in grammar emerging from an SA experience (Howard, 2006; Ryan & Lafford, 1992), others have not (Collentine, 2004; DeKeyser, 1991), suggesting that more studies are needed to clarify the role of SA in this area. Another area that also needs to be further investigated is reading as there is very little research on the role that the SA context plays in L2 reading development, and existing results are inconclusive as some studies have found positive outcomes (Kinginger, 2008), while others have not (Davidson, 2010; Dewey, 2004). Finally, in the case of L2 pronunciation, studies showing the positive impact of a period abroad (George, 2014; Højen, 2003; Llanes *et al.*, 2016b; Muñoz & Llanes, 2014; Stevens, 2011) outnumber those that have not found improvement after an SA experience (Díaz-Campos, 2004; Mora, 2008).

Despite the efforts to document the impact of SA on the different L2 areas, the aforementioned studies have examined the impact of SA experiences in countries where the participants' L2 is the native or official language (i.e. Spanish learners of English studying in England, or English learners of French studying in France). To the best of our knowledge, only three studies have documented the linguistic impact of SA in a country where the L2 is not the official language but is used as a lingua franca, and only two of them (Köylü, 2016; Llanes *et al.*, 2016a) focused on L2 development; the third one (Glaser, 2017) focused on the metapragmatic self-perceptions of students engaging in SA either in a traditional setting where the participants' L2 is the official language or in an ELF setting.

Glaser found that whereas traditional SA offers more opportunities to apply the strategies learned in class, the ELF setting offers more room for negotiation. Llanes *et al.* (2016a) investigated the impact of a semester-long SA experience in several non-English-speaking countries on L2 written development. Thirty-nine Catalan–Spanish bilinguals, learners of English, were asked to draft a text in English and to complete a placement test. The results showed that participants significantly improved on two of the four measures examined, namely the scores in the placement test (a test of general English proficiency) and lexical complexity. In other words, participants significantly improved their general level of English and their vocabulary after spending a semester in a non-English-speaking country. The authors considered this finding positive given that several studies have explored the role of an SA experience in a country where the L2 of the participants is the native language and no significant differences before and after SA have been found (Freed *et al.*, 2003). Additionally, Llanes *et al.* (2016a) examined whether pre-departure L2 level influenced L2 development, finding that it only affected one measure, grammatical complexity (participants with a higher L2 level at the outset of SA produced more sophisticated sentences in the post-test).

In a similar vein, Köylü (2016) examined the linguistic impact of SA in non-English-speaking countries where English was used as a lingua franca (*n* = 24), namely Austria, Czech Republic, Denmark, Finland, Germany, Greece, Italy, Poland, Portugal and the Netherlands. Köylü included two comparison groups: one group of students learning English in an English-speaking country, namely England (*n* = 7), and a group learning English in their home country, Turkey (*n* = 15). Köylü examined the effects of a 16-week SA experience in the above-mentioned countries on the participants' oral and written linguistic complexity, accuracy and fluency. In order to obtain the oral data, Köylü's participants were provided with the prompt 'What would you like to do during your free time? Why?', and were given ten seconds to prepare; to obtain the written data, participants were given 15 minutes to write an essay titled 'My life: past, present and future expectations'. Köylü's (2016) results indicate that both types of SA are equally beneficial in terms of L2 development, but SA in ELF countries had the added advantage of impacting linguistic identity as an ELF speaker.

Given the scarcity of research on the effects of mobility programs in countries where the native language is not English, the aim of the present study is to shed further light on the role that an SA experience in non-English-speaking countries plays in the participants' English (L2) oral development measured through fluency, lexical and grammatical complexity, and accuracy on the one hand, and on the participants' general L2 proficiency, measured through a general English proficiency test, on the other hand. The present study is a follow-up to Llanes *et al.* (2016a), but with a focus on oral skills. More specifically, the present study seeks to explore what has been found for writing skills in the case of oral skills.

Given that the results of previous research on the development of English writing skills in ELF countries are not negative, it is speculated that the same or better results will be found for the development of oral skills.

Method

Research questions

The research questions (RQs) that guided the present study are the following:

(1) Do English oral skills and English proficiency level improve after spending a semester in an ELF environment, namely a non-English-speaking country?
(2) Is students' L2 pre-departure level related to their L2 development in an ELF environment?

   Since researchers conducting this type of research are usually confronted with the dilemma of using the same or different tasks/instruments in the pre- and post-test (using the same task/instrument may bias the results in favor of the post-test due to possible task-repetition effects, whereas using a different task/instrument may invalidate the research if there is no guarantee that the two tasks/instruments are comparable), the present study also set out to examine whether using the same or a different oral narrative task made a difference in L2 development, as formulated in the third RQ:

(3) To what extent is using the same or a different narrative task related to the participants' L2 gains?

Participants

Participants in this study were selected from a larger pool of participants ($n = 104$) on the basis of the destination country (participants going to English-speaking countries were excluded) and length of stay. The final sample of participants included in the present study is 18 ($n = 8$ males, $n = 10$ females). The students come from a small university in Catalonia and are Catalan–Spanish bilingual. They are all learners of English (L2) pursuing different degrees such as law, primary education, mechanical engineering, agricultural engineering or nursing. These students spent a semester abroad as part of a European Region Action Scheme for the Mobility of University Students (Erasmus) exchange program in an ELF country: Italy ($n = 2$), Denmark ($n = 10$), Germany ($n = 1$), Belgium ($n = 2$), Finland ($n = 1$) and the Netherlands ($n = 2$). The exchange program took place in either the autumn term or the spring term of the academic year.

The participants' mean age was 21.38. Their pre-test mean score on the Oxford Quick Placement Test (OPT) was 34.89, which corresponds to a B1 level according to the Common European Framework of Reference for Languages (CEFR) or to intermediate high/advanced low according to the American Council on the Teaching of Foreign Languages (ACTFL).

Instruments and measures

Participants completed a battery of tests including an oral narrative, a written composition, a placement test and a questionnaire. However, for the present study only the oral data and the placement test were considered. With regard to the oral narrative, participants were shown a story comprising six vignettes. They were given one minute to look at the story and make sure they understood it; they were informed that they were not allowed to ask any language-related questions and that they were only allowed to ask content-related questions. The instructions were given in Catalan/Spanish to make sure that they understood what they were asked to do. Next, they were asked to explain what they saw in the pictures. These were recorded and then analyzed to examine L2 oral development. Since one of the goals of the present study was to see whether using the same or a different narrative had an effect on L2 development, the participants in the pre-test were asked to describe a story about four children playing football (football story), whereas in the post-test seven students were asked to describe the same story and eleven of the students were asked to describe a different story about two children going on a picnic (picnic story). As mentioned, both stories contained six pictures and the procedure was the same for the participants both at the pre- and post-test. The placement test was a general language proficiency test (the OPT), that comprised 60 multiple-choice questions targeting the accurate choice of grammatical and lexical items. The result of this test determined the English proficiency level of participants at both testing times.

Regarding the measures, several measures were analyzed to account for L2 oral development. Oral fluency was measured through words per minute (WPM), whereas Guiraud's (1954) Index of Lexical Richness (GUI) was used to investigate lexical complexity (this measure was calculated by dividing the total number of types by the square root of the total number of tokens). To account for grammatical complexity, the measure of Clauses per T-unit (CL/TU) was computed, which was obtained by dividing the total number of clauses by the total number of T-units. A T-unit is 'one main clause with all subordinate clauses attached to it' (Hunt, 1965: 20). Finally, two measures of accuracy were computed: Error-free T-units per total T-units (EFTU) and the total number of errors per T-unit (Err/TU). The former was calculated by dividing the total number of Error-free T-units by the total number of T-units, whereas the latter was computed by dividing the total number of errors by the total number of T-units. The reason for including two measures of accuracy is because they provide information on two different aspects of accuracy, given that the former provides information on the number of correct sentences, and the latter on the number of errors made. For all the measures included in this study with the exception of one (Err/TU), higher values in the post-test would show improvement. For Err/TU, a decrease in the number of errors in the post-test is expected for improvement to have occurred. All the oral measures included in this study were pruned, which means that false starts, repetitions, self-corrections, words in a language other than English and unfinished sentences were eliminated. These measures were chosen because they have been successfully used in previous studies with participants of similar ages and using the same instruments (Llanes & Muñoz, 2013; Llanes & Serrano, 2014).

Procedure

The international office responsible for student mobility provided information about the students' mobility. Once this information was available, students were selected on the basis of their destination country and length of stay as mentioned above.

The present study has a pre-/post-test design. The pre-test was administered during a specific session organized by the international office and scheduled a few months before the students' departure, given that the students came from different schools and campuses. While the written test, the placement test and the questionnaire were administered to all the participants in the same room, the oral test was administered individually in a quiet room. Regarding the post-test, participants took all the tests individually a week after their return from the host country because of their varying return dates.

The data were transcribed and coded using CLAN (MacWhinney, 2000). Intra-rater reliability was calculated by recoding 15% of the data and comparing the initial coding and the second one. Intra-rater agreement was high (99.1%). Inter-rater reliability was calculated by having another expert code 15% of the data and comparing the coding of the author and that of the second expert. In this case, there was 96.4% coding agreement and the few cases where there was disagreement (mostly regarding accuracy measures) were discussed until agreement was reached.

Next, preliminary assumption testing of the pre-test scores was conducted to check for normality and none of the measures violated the assumption of normality. Therefore, parametric statistics were used to answer the RQs. Three different statistical analyses were used: a paired-sample t-test was run to answer RQ1, bivariate correlations to answer RQ2 and an independent-sample t-test to answer RQ3.

Results

In order to answer the first RQ, which inquired whether English oral skills and English proficiency improve after spending a semester in a non-English-speaking country, a comparison between the scores of the pre- and post-test was done through a paired-samples t-test. The results of the t-test showed that out of the five oral measures, two turned out to be statistically significant, namely WPM ($t(17) = -4.618$, $p = 0.000$, $d = 0.75$) and GUI ($t(17) = -3.817$, $p = 0.001$, $d = 0.93$), and CL/TU was approaching significance ($t(17) = -1.962$, $p = 0.066$). The d of the WPM and GUI measures show that the effect sizes were large. Regarding English general proficiency, the difference between the pre- and post-test in the OPT scores was also significant ($t(17) = -2.775$, $p = 0.013$, $d = 0.27$), but the effect size indicates that the difference was medium. As can be seen in Table 6.1, participants improved on all the measures from the pre- to the post-test, although this improvement was only significant for three of them: WPM (speech rate), GUI (lexical richness) and OPT (general proficiency level).

Table 6.1 Descriptive statistics

	Pre-test		Post-test	
	M	SD	M	SD
WPM	107.07	24.83	126.96*	28.05
GUI	5.04	0.67	5.80*	0.94
CL/TU	1.68	0.31	1.89	0.36
EFTU/TU	0.41	0.22	0.53	0.24
Err/TU	0.85	0.52	0.73	0.58
OPT	34.89	8.14	37.06*	7.90

* Significant difference between the pre- and post-test.

The second RQ aimed to investigate whether students' pre-departure L2 level can affect their L2 development, and in order to answer this question, bivariate correlations between the students' pre-departure L2 level (the OPT scores in the pre-test) and the gains in each of the measures were run. Before running the correlations, gains were calculated by subtracting the score in the post-test from the score in the pre-test (Table 6.2 shows the pre- and post-test OPT scores as well as the gains in this measure for each of the participants).[1] No significant correlations were found between proficiency level and gains in the measures used. Hence, initial proficiency level was not found to play a role when learning the L2 in an international setting in the case of the areas under investigation in this particular study.

Finally, in order to answer RQ3, which inquired about the effects of using the same or a different narrative, an independent-sample t-test was run, with 'same/different narrative' as the independent variable and gains on each of the measures as the dependent variables. Unexpectedly, it was found that participants narrating a different story in the post-test showed greater gain in lexical complexity than participants who described the

Table 6.2 OPT scores

Participant	OPT pre	OPT post	OPT gains
1	36	37	+1
2	33	36	+3
3	31	33	+2
4	26	29	+3
5	48	48	0
6	35	42	+7
7	41	42	+1
8	18	18	0
9	51	50	−1
10	35	38	+3
11	26	31	+5
12	35	41	+6
13	34	29	−5
14	35	38	+3
15	38	36	−2
16	44	49	+5
17	25	33	+8
18	37	37	0

same story ($t(16) = 2.485$, $p = 0.024$). More specifically, participants describing the same story experienced a mean lexical complexity gain of 0.21, whereas participants describing a different story experienced a mean gain of 1.09. Given that using a different narrative was found to significantly influence gains in lexical complexity, another paired-samples t-test was conducted, but this time for the two groups separately (one for the group who performed the same story between the pre- and post-test and another for those who performed a different story). It was found that both groups experienced significant gains in lexical complexity from the pre- to the post-test, but the p level was lower for those performing a different story: $t(10) = -5.697$, $p = 0.000$ for participants narrating a different story, and $t(6) = -0.655$, $p = 0.050$ for those narrating the same story.

Discussion

The first RQ aimed to analyze the effect of an SA experience in an ELF country on oral skills and overall proficiency, and it was found that participants improved on all the measures from the pre- to the post-test. However, only three of these six measures showed a statistically significant improvement, namely WPM (fluency), GUI (lexical complexity) and OPT (general proficiency). This finding confirms the positive findings that previous research in traditional SA experiences has found for L2 oral development (Llanes & Muñoz, 2013; Mora & Valls-Ferrer, 2012), and it also confirms the positive results of previous studies that have looked at oral L2 development in an international setting, where English is used as a lingua franca (Köylü, 2016). In fact, participants in the present study significantly improved on two out of the five oral measures examined (see Appendix). This ratio is promising since several studies examining the impact of SA in a country where the L2 of the participants is the native language have found lower significant-improvement ratios (i.e. 3/12 in Lennon [1990], 1/8 in Freed [1995], 2/10 in Juan-Garau & Pérez-Vidal [2007]).

The fact that students improved their speech rate and their lexical complexity as opposed to the other measures used in the present study might be attributed to the fact that these two areas are more sensitive to the learning context. Previous research shows that these are the two areas most likely to be improved during an overseas experience (Llanes, 2011). However, it could also be the case that the measures used to account for these two L2 areas are more susceptible to gains than the other measures used.

Either way, gains in these two domains can be tentatively explained by three predominant theories in the field of SLA. One of them is the role of practice, based on Anderson's (1983, 1992, 1993) ACT* theory and supported by DeKeyser (2007), which claims that participants have three different types of knowledge (declarative, procedural and automatic) and that automaticity is only possible after extensive L2 exposure and practice. It is speculated that SA participants may enroll with certain declarative knowledge, and once abroad they have multiple opportunities to practice the L2. Therefore, they can avail of opportunities for learning and automatizing. For participants in the present study, the mean pre-test score in the OPT was 34.89, which corresponds to a B1 level. Given that these participants come from a country where the L2 is mostly taught in schools and language schools for a few hours per week through explicit instruction, it is likely that they had some declarative knowledge. Therefore, it is not unreasonable to think that the SA setting offers them the possibility of massive practice that can later lead to the automatization of certain L2 aspects.

Another hypothesis that could explain these results is the Interaction Hypothesis (Long, 1981, 1996), which posits that L2 learning is facilitated through learners' interaction with other speakers. SA participants have many opportunities for interaction and also a wide range of interlocutors, such that this might also explain the improvement in the oral fluency and lexical complexity of SA participants. And finally, another hypothesis that could explain these findings is Swain's (1995) Output Hypothesis, which suggests that by pushing learners to produce output, learners become aware of their linguistic deficiencies and also test hypotheses about the structures of the L2. It is hypothesized that SA participants have many opportunities to produce output and therefore to realize where their linguistic gaps lie. Additionally, previous studies have found that SA participants not only learn more L2 words and expressions, but also try to make greater use of the L2 and less use of the first language (L1) by using approximations that may result in greater vocabulary knowledge and fewer communication breakdowns (Llanes & Muñoz, 2009). These three hypotheses seem to make similar predictions for the two learning contexts under study (traditional SA vs. SA in ELF countries), since it is mostly quality of input that distinguishes between them (although quantity can also be a difference depending on the target country).

A tentative explanation as to why these three hypotheses would predict gains in speech rate and lexical complexity but not in grammar complexity may relate to the type of interlocutors. Given that the participants' interlocutors were often non-native speakers (NSs) of English, it could be the case that their production was less grammatically complex than that of NSs. The same reason could also explain the lack of significant progress in accuracy as the interlocutors' English may not have been as beneficial as NS English. Another plausible explanation for the lack of development in accuracy (and maybe also complexity) is that previous research has found that participants in ELF countries prioritize fluency over accuracy (Köylü, 2016), and the same is true for participants in English as an L2 contexts (Bardovi-Harlig & Dörnyei, 1998).

In terms of general English proficiency, the significant improvement in the OPT is in line with previous research that found overall L2 proficiency improvement as a result of SA in the TL country (Brecht & Robinson, 1995; Lapkin et al., 1995). The significant improvement in the OPT scores also confirms the finding of Llanes et al. (2016a), whose participants' general L2 proficiency improved after a semester-long SA experience in an ELF country. This result points to the beneficial nature of SA on L2 English even when the SA occurs in an ELF country. Nevertheless, improvement in the OPT was not uniform across students, which suggests that other factors such as individual differences or program differences may have played a role.

One could speculate that destination of stay may affect exposure to the language during the sojourn. A qualitative analysis of these data suggests, again, that the host country might not explain L2 development either, because among the learners with the greatest gains in all the measures we find a student whose SA occurred in Belgium, followed by a student whose experience took place in Denmark and another whose experience took place in Italy. And among the students making the fewest gains, we find a participant studying in Italy, followed by another one studying in the Netherlands and another one studying in Denmark.

Another aspect to be highlighted here is the role of the quality of input. If further research confirms the results obtained in the present study and also by Köylü (2016) in that SA in ELF countries can be seen to be as beneficial as SA in English-speaking countries, the role of the quality of input, which is one of the main differences between the two types of SA, should be questioned. In fact, Köylü (2016) found that one of the main differences between participants whose SA occurred in an ELF country and in the TL country related to their tendency to prioritize fluency over accuracy, a common finding in ELF settings (Kaypak & Ortaçtepe, 2014; Mauranen, 2007; Vettorel, 2014). And the present study, in line with Köylü (2016), shows that SA participants in ELF countries significantly improved on some measures such as fluency, lexical complexity and general English, but not on other measures of accuracy or grammar complexity.

The second RQ aimed to analyze whether students' pre-departure L2 level was related to their L2 development. The answer to this question is negative since no significant correlations were found between the participants' pre-departure level and the gains in the measures examined here. This finding corroborates Llanes *et al.* (2016a), who found that pre-departure level did not play a prominent role in the development of L2 written skills when the SA experience occurred in an international setting. This finding also suggests that pre-departure proficiency level does not play a role in improving oral skills in a non-English-speaking country. Previous findings regarding the role of pre-departure proficiency level are unclear: whereas some studies have found that participants with a lower proficiency level experience the greatest gains (Brecht & Robinson, 1995; Llanes & Muñoz, 2009), others have found the opposite, that it is participants with a higher pre-departure level who benefit most from their SA experience (DeKeyser, 2010). The lack of significance of pre-departure level in the present study could be explained by the low number of participants at certain proficiency levels (A2: $n = 4$, B1: $n = 10$, B2: $n = 2$; C1: $n = 2$); nevertheless, because the correlations were run with raw OPT scores and not with corresponding CEFR levels, this seems less likely. After a qualitative exploration of the data regarding proficiency level, it was determined that the student who made the greatest gains in the OPT had an initial L2 level of 25/60 (an A2 level according to the CEFR), followed by a student who had 35/60 (a B1 level) and another student who scored 44/60 (a B2 level); and among the students who did not improve their OPT scores (in fact some of them obtained a lower score in the post-test), the student with the fewest gains had a pre-departure L2 level of 34/60 (a B1 level according to the CEFR), followed by a student with a pre-test OPT score of 38/60 (a B1 level), followed by another one with a score of 51/60 (a C1 level). Hence, a quick look at these data suggests that pre-departure proficiency level did not explain L2 development for the participants in the present study.

Finally, RQ3 inquired to what extent using the same or a different narrative task is related to the participants' L2 gains. Significant differences between participants using a different story were only found for lexical complexity. Surprisingly, participants narrating a different story in the post-test surpassed those narrating the same story as the pre-test in lexical complexity. One tentative explanation is that participants were more familiar with the type of vocabulary elicited by the picnic story (i.e. basket, excursion, picnic, map) as opposed to the type of vocabulary elicited by the football story (i.e. snake, gap, bucket, float), and for this reason they had an advantage over participants who narrated the football story. It could also be the case that the nature of the participants' SA experience led them to learn vocabulary that was more related to the picnic story than to the football story. This finding questions the often-alleged task-repetition effects. If task repetition had played a role, it makes sense to think that it would have been those students narrating the same story in the pre- and post-test who would have shown an advantage in the measures examined. However, only one measure was found to be significantly impacted by using the same/different story, and it was in the opposite direction.

Conclusion and Further Research

The present study has explored the effects of a semester-long SA experience in countries where the L2 of the participants was not an official language, but instead where English was used as a lingua franca. More specifically, the study looked at the impact of such SA experiences on the participants' L2 oral skills and L2 general proficiency, and it was found that two out of the five oral measures as well as the only measure of L2 proficiency examined showed a significant improvement as a result of the overseas experience. Therefore, the results of the present study are quite positive (or at least not negative) as they are comparable to, or sometimes even better than, the results of similar studies where the SA occurred in a country where the L2 of the participants was the native or official language. Additionally, we examined whether participants' pre-departure L2 level was related to the gains they experience, finding that it was not. Finally, the study investigated whether using a different story between the pre- and the post-test would affect the results, and it was found that in general the two stories were comparable, but using a different story significantly favored the scores in lexical complexity. Thus, this finding suggests that piloting the tests and instruments before collecting data, a practice sometimes neglected by scholars because of time constraints, is of paramount importance; otherwise, results could be biased and therefore unreliable. It was speculated that the results of this study would be as positive as or even better than the results of our work examining the effects of an SA experience in an ELF country on L2 written development. This hypothesis was confirmed given that our previous work found improvement in one written variable (syntactic complexity) and the proficiency test, while the study here found improvement in two oral variables (fluency and lexical complexity) and the proficiency test.

Nevertheless, several limitations of the present study can be listed here. One is the relatively low number of participants, which does not allow results to be generalized. Another limitation is the low number of participants going to certain countries, making it impossible to run any inferential statistics tests, and the same holds true for participants of different proficiency levels. The fact that participants had different backgrounds (they majored in different degrees) is also a limitation, but one that reflects the diversity of SA participants today. Another limitation is that the pre-test was administered some time before the participants' departure to the host country, and their L2 development between the pre-test and the time of their departure was not controlled. Finally, in the present study the benefits of a traditional SA setting and an ELF setting are based on a number of measures that show significant development between the pre- and post-tests. The results were considered to be positive because participants in an ELF setting seem to improve in as many areas as those in a traditional SA setting. However, it could be the case that the difference between these two types of SA resides in the extent of the development of each of these measures. Certainly, further research should investigate this issue as it would provide more compelling findings.

Clearly, more research documenting the impact of SA in countries where the participants' L2 is used as a lingua franca is needed. An in-depth comparative project of ELF and SA learners that explores linguistic development would undoubtedly be insightful. This points to a very interesting and fruitful line for further research.

Despite these limitations, the present exploratory study contributes to the area of SA since it reports on L2 oral and general proficiency development in the context of an SA experience in an ELF context. The results suggest that spending time abroad in countries where the participants could use the L2 was enough for gains in oral skills to occur, undermining the role that NSs might play, at least for the three variables that were found to be significant (it could be that quality of the input is important for other variables such as accuracy and complexity). If further research confirms these findings, English L2 learners engaging in SA programs whose aim is to improve their oral skills and general L2 proficiency should consider mobility programs offered by universities in non-Anglophone countries. Since the only two English-speaking countries in Europe are the UK and Ireland, these countries are often the most requested and consequently make it more competitive to obtain funding to study there (in countries such as Spain some students forgo participating in mobility programs if they are not in an English-speaking country). Hence, stakeholders should consider increasing the quota in non-Anglophone countries.

Finally, a research implication also emerges with regard to the use of different instruments/tasks to elicit data. Researchers should be extremely careful when designing or choosing the instruments that are going to be used to examine L2 development, since the use of different (although apparently comparable) materials might bias the results and therefore invalidate the study.

Acknowledgments

This research was supported by grants 2017 SGR1522 and FFI2015-67769P. I would like to thank Martin Howard for his valuable comments and his patience. I would also like to thank the anonymous reviewers, whose insightful comments helped to improve this chapter. Finally, I would like to thank my colleague Enric Llurda for his help with the ELF literature.

Note

(1) Although gains were calculated for all the measures, only those for the OPT are reported due to space constraints.

References

Anderson, J. (1983) *The Architecture of Cognition*. Cambridge, MA: Cambridge University Press.

Anderson, J. (1992) Automaticity and the ACT* theory. *American Journal of Psychology* 105 (2), 165–180.

Anderson, J. (1993) *Rules of the Mind*. Hillsdale, NJ: Lawrence Erlbaum Associates.

Bardovi-Harlig, K. and Dörnyei, Z. (1998) Do language learners recognize pragmatic violations? Pragmatic vs. grammatical awareness in instructed L2 learning. *TESOL Quarterly* 32, 233–259.

Blumenthal, P. and Laughlin, S. (2009) Promoting study abroad in science and technology fields. New York: International Institute of Education. See http://www.iie.org (accessed 15 October 2011).

Brecht, R.D. and Robinson, J.L. (1995) On the value of formal instruction in study abroad: Student reactions in context. In B.F. Freed (ed.) *Second Language Acquisition in a Study Abroad Context* (pp. 317–334). Amsterdam/Philadelphia, PA: Benjamins.

Coleman, J.A. (2015) Social circles during residence abroad: What students do, and who with. In R. Mitchell, N. Tracy-Ventura and K. McManus (eds) *Social Interaction, Identity and Language Learning during Residence Abroad* (EUROSLA Monographs Series 4; pp. 33–51). Amsterdam: European Second Language Association.

Collentine, J. (2004) The effects of learning contexts on morphosyntactic and lexical development. *Studies in Second Language Acquisition* 26 (2), 227–248.

Cubillos, J.H., Chieffo, L. and Fan, C. (2008) The impact of short-term study abroad programs on L2 listening comprehension skills. *Foreign Language Annals* 41 (1), 157–185.

Davidson, D.E. (2010) Study abroad: When, how long, and with what results? New data from the Russian front. *Foreign Language Annals* 43 (1), 6–26.

DeKeyser, R.M. (1991) Foreign language development during a semester abroad. In B.F. Freed (ed.) *Foreign Language Acquisition Research and the Classroom* (pp. 104–199). Lexington, MA: D.C. Heath.

DeKeyser, R.M. (2007) *Practice in a Second Language. Perspectives from Applied Linguistics and Cognitive Psychology*. New York: Cambridge University Press.

DeKeyser, R.M. (2010) Monitoring processes in Spanish as a second language during a study abroad program. *Foreign Language Annals* 43, 80–92.

Dewey, D.P. (2004) A comparison of reading development by learners of Japanese in intensive domestic immersion and study abroad contexts. *Studies in Second Language Acquisition* 26 (2), 303–327.

Díaz-Campos, M. (2004) Context of learning in the acquisition of Spanish second language phonology. *Studies in Second Language Acquisition* 26, 249–273.

Durham, M. (2014) *The Acquisition of Sociolinguistic Competence in a Lingua Franca Context*. Bristol: Multilingual Matters.

European Commission for Education and Training (2014) Erasmus+: Fact sheet. European Commission Education & Training. See https://ec.europa.eu/programmes/erasmus-plus/about/factsheets_en (accessed 10 September 2018).

Foster, P. (2009) Lexical diversity and native-like selection: The bonus of studying abroad. In B. Richards, M. Daller, D. Malvern, P. Meara, J. Milton and J. Treffers-Daller (eds) *Vocabulary Studies in First and Second Language Acquisition* (pp. 91–106). Basingstoke: Palgrave Macmillan.

Freed, B.F. (1995) What makes us think that students who study abroad become fluent? In B.F. Freed (ed.) *Second Language Acquisition in a Study Abroad Context* (pp. 123–148). Amsterdam/Philadelphia, PA: Benjamins.

Freed, B.F., So, S. and Lazar, N.A. (2003) Language learning abroad: How do gains in written fluency compare with gains in oral fluency in French as a second language? *ADFL Bulletin* 34 (3), 34–40.

George, A. (2014) Study abroad in Central Spain: The development of regional phonological features. *Foreign Language Annals* 47 (1), 97–114.

Glaser, K. (2017) Metapragmatic perceptions in native language vs. lingua franca settings. *Study Abroad Research in Second Language Acquisition and International Education* 2 (1), 107–131.

Guiraud, P. (1954) *Les Caractères Statistiques du Vocabulaire. Essai de Méthodologie*. Paris: Presses Universitaires de France.

Højen, A. (2003) Second language speech perception and production in adult learners before and after short-term immersion. Unpublished PhD thesis, University of Aarhus.

Howard, M. (2006) The expression of number and person through verb morphology in French interlanguage. *International Review of Applied Linguistics* 44 (1), 1–22.

Huensch, A. and Tracy-Ventura, N. (2017) L2 utterance fluency development before, during, and after residence abroad: A multidimensional investigation. *The Modern Language Journal* 101 (2), 275–293.

Hunt, K.W. (1965) *Differences in Grammatical Structures Written at Three Grade Levels. Research Report No. 3*. Urbana, IL: National Council of Teachers of English.

Juan-Garau, M. and Pérez-Vidal, C. (2007) The effect of context and contact on oral performance in students who go on a stay abroad. *VIAL (Vigo International Journal of Applied Linguistics)* 4, 117–134.

Kaypak, E. and Ortaçtepe, D. (2014) Language learner beliefs and study abroad: A study on English as a lingua franca (ELF). *System* 42, 355–367.

Kinginger, C. (2008) Language learning in study abroad: Case histories of Americans in France. *Modern Language Journal* (Monograph Series 1) 92, 1–124.

Köylü, Z. (2016) The influence of context on L2 development: The case of Turkish undergraduates at home and abroad. *Graduate Theses and Dissertations*, University of Florida.

Lapkin, S., Hart, D. and Swain, M. (1995) A Canadian interprovincial exchange: Evaluating the linguistic impact of a three-month stay in Quebec. In B.F. Freed (ed.) *Second Language Acquisition in a Study Abroad Context* (pp. 67–94). Amsterdam/Philadelphia, PA: Benjamins.

Lennon, P. (1990) Investigating fluency in EFL: A quantitative approach. *Language Learning* 40, 387–417.

Leonard, K. and Shea, C. (2017) L2 speaking development during study abroad: Fluency, accuracy, complexity, and underlying cognitive factors. *The Modern Language Journal* 101 (1), 179–193.

Llanes, À. (2011) The many faces of study abroad: An update on the research on L2 gains emerged during a study abroad experience. *International Journal of Multilingualism* 3, 189–215.

Llanes, À. and Muñoz, C. (2009) A short stay abroad: Does it make a difference? *System* 37 (3), 353–365.

Llanes, À. and Muñoz, C. (2013) Age effects in a study abroad context: Children and adults studying abroad and at home. *Language Learning* 63 (1), 63–90.

Llanes, À. and Serrano, R. (2014) The effectiveness of classroom instruction 'at home' vs. study abroad for learners of English as a foreign language attending primary, secondary school and university. *Language Learning Journal* 45 (4), 434–446.

Llanes, À. and Prieto, G. (2015) Does listening comprehension improve as a result of a short study abroad experience? *Revista Espanola de Linguistica Aplicada* 28 (1), 199–212.

Llanes, À., Tragant, E. and Serrano, R. (2012) The role of individual differences in a study abroad experience: The case of Erasmus students. *The International Journal of Multilingualism* 9 (3), 318–342.

Llanes, À., Arnó, E. and Mancho, G. (2016a) Is a semester abroad in a non-English-speaking country beneficial for the improvement of English? The case of Erasmus students using English as a Lingua Franca. Special issue of *Language Learning Journal* 44 (3), 292–303.

Llanes, À., Mora, J.C. and Serrano, R. (2016b) Differential effects of SA and intensive AH courses on teenagers' L2 pronunciation. *International Journal of Applied Linguistics* 27 (2), 470–490.

Long, M.H. (1981) Input, interaction and second language acquisition. *Annals of the New York Academy of Sciences* 379, 259–278.

Long, M. (1996) The role of the linguistic environment in second language acquisition. In W.C. Ritchie and T.K. Bhatia (eds) *Handbook of Second Language Acquisition* (pp. 413–458). San Diego, CA: Academic Press.

MacWhinney, B. (2000) *The CHILDES Project: Tools for Analyzing Talk* (3rd edn). Mahwah, NJ: Lawrence Erlbaum Associates.

Mauranen, A. (2007) Investigating English as a lingua franca with a spoken corpus. In M.C. Campoy and M.J. Luzón (eds) *Spoken Corpora in Applied Linguistics* (pp. 33–56). Berlin: Peter Lang.

Milton, J. and Meara, P. (1995) How periods abroad affect vocabulary growth in a foreign language. *ITL Review of Applied Linguistics* 107–108, 17–34.

Mora, J.C. (2008) Learning context effects on the acquisition of a second language phonology. In C. Pérez-Vidal, M. Juan-Garau and A. Bel (eds) *A Portrait of the Young in the New Multilingual Spain* (pp. 241–263). Clevedon: Multilingual Matters.

Mora, J.C. and Valls-Ferrer, M. (2012) Oral fluency, accuracy, and complexity in formal instruction and study abroad learning contexts. *TESOL Quarterly* 46 (4), 610–641.

Muñoz, C. (2012) *Intensive Exposure Experiences in Second Language Learning*. Bristol: Multilingual Matters.

Muñoz, C. and Llanes, À. (2014) Study abroad and changes in degree of foreign accent in children and adults. *Modern Language Journal* 98 (1), 432–449.

Pérez-Vidal, C. and Juan-Garau, M. (2009) The effect of study abroad on written performance. *EUROSLA Yearbook* 9, 269–295.

Rodrigo, V. (2011) Contextos de instrucción y su efecto en la comprensión auditiva y los juicios gramaticales: ¿Son comparables cinco semanas en el extranjero a un semestre en casa? *Hispania* 94 (3), 502–513.

Ryan, J.M. and Lafford, B.A. (1992) Acquisition of lexical meaning in a study abroad environment: *Ser* and *estar* and the Granada experience. *Hispania* 75 (3), 714–722.

Sasaki, M. (2004) A multiple-data analysis of the 3.5-year development of EFL student writers. *Language Learning* 54 (3), 525–582.

Sasaki, M. (2009) Changes in English as a foreign language students' writing over 3.5 years: A sociocognitive account. In R. Manchón (ed.) *Writing in Foreign Language Contexts: Learning, Teaching, and Research* (pp. 49–76). Bristol: Multilingual Matters.

Segalowitz, N. and Freed, F.B. (2004) Context, contact, and cognition in oral fluency acquisition: Learning Spanish in at home and study abroad contexts. *Studies in Second Language Acquisition* 26, 173–199.

Serrano, R., Tragant, E. and Llanes, À. (2012) A longitudinal analysis of the effects of one year abroad. *The Canadian Modern Language Review* 68 (2), 138–163.

Stevens, J. (2011) Vowel duration in second language Spanish vowels: Study abroad versus at-home learners. *Arizona Working Papers in SLA & Teaching* 18, 77–104.

Swain, M. (1995) Three functions of output in second language learning. In G. Cook and B. Seidlhofer (eds) *Principle and Practice in Applied Linguistics: Studies in Honour of H.G. Widdowson* (pp. 125–144). Oxford: Oxford University Press.

Vettorel, P. (2014) *English as a Lingua Franca in Wider Networking. Blogging Practices.* Berlin: Mouton deGruyter.

Zaytseva, V. (2016) Vocabulary acquisition in study abroad and formal instruction: An investigation on oral and written lexical development. Unpublished doctoral thesis, Universitat Pompeu Fabra, Barcelona.

Appendix

The following table presents a summary of the most relevant studies that have examined the effects of an SA experience on oral skills with adult participants. Only studies meeting the following criteria were considered: a term- or semester-long SA experience in a country where the L2 of the participants is the official/native language of the country and the participants are only adults. For studies including multiple data collection times, only the results of a comparable length of time to the one in the present study have been considered. Additionally, for studies including participants with different ages, only the results concerning adults are reported in this table. Finally, for studies looking at more than one L2 domain, only results for oral skills are included here.

Study	Measures examined	Significant measures between pre- and post-test	Ratio of significant measures
Lennon (1990)	WPM unpruned, WPM pruned, repetitions/TU, self-corrections/TU, filled pauses/TU, % of repeated and self-corrected words, total unfilled pause time as % of total time of delivery, total filled pause time as % of total time of delivery, MLR between pauses, % of TU followed by pause, % of total pause time at all TU boundaries, mean pause time at TU boundaries	Pruned WPM, filled pauses/TU, % of TU followed by pause	3/12

(Continued)

Study	Measures examined	Significant measures between pre- and post-test	Ratio of significant measures
Freed (1995)	NSs' subjective evaluations, raw frequencies of words or semantic units, number of words or semantic units per minute, unfilled pauses, frequency of filled pauses, length of fluent speech runs, repairs, clusters of dysfluencies	Rate of speech	1/8
Juan-Garau and Pérez-Vidal (2007)	Words/CL, words/sentence, grammatical errors, lexical errors, total errors, CL/sentence, dependent clauses/CL, coordination index, type-token ratio, formulas/CL	Words/CL, words/sentence	2/10
Llanes et al. (2012)	SPM, GUI, CL/TU, Err/TU	SPM, GUI	2/4
Serrano et al. (2012)	Syllables per minute, clauses/TU, Guiraud, Err/TU	SPM, Guiraud	2/4
Llanes and Muñoz (2013)	SPM, GUI, CL/TU, Err/TU	SPM	1/4
Huensch and Tracy-Ventura (2017)	Mean syllable duration, speech rate, MLR, mean silent pause duration within ASU, mean silent pause duration between ASU, number of silent pauses per second, number of filled pauses per second, repetitions, corrections	Mean syllable duration, speech rate, mean silent pause duration within ASU, number of silent pauses per second, number of filled pauses per second	5/9
Leonard and Shea (2017)	Syllables per second, % of pausing time, rate of all pauses, ratio of mid-clause pauses, rate of end-of-clause pauses, rate of long pauses, rate of short pauses, rate of unfilled pauses, rate of filled pauses, MLR, errors per 100 words, subordinate CL per TU, mean length of TU, GUI, VocD	Syllables per second, % of pausing time, rate of all pauses, rate of mid-clause pauses, rate of long pauses, rate of unfilled pauses, rate of filled pauses, MLR, errors per 100 words, subordinate CL per TU, mean length of TU, GUI	12/15

Note: ASU: analysis of speech unit; CL: clause; Err: error; GUI: Guiraud's index; MLR: mean length of run; NS: native speaker; TU: T-unit; WPM: words per minute.

7 Long-Term Residence Abroad and SLA: The Case of Cultural Migrants in France

Fanny Forsberg Lundell

Introduction

The field of study abroad is relatively well-explored and has attracted a lot of attention from second language acquisition (SLA) scholars. Closely adjacent to this field, the field of residence abroad has recently emerged (cf. Avarguez *et al.*, 2015; Mitchell *et al.*, 2015). Although study abroad sojourners most often stay for a maximum of one year in their respective host countries, a number of them end up staying for many years or, in some cases, permanently. This population falls between study abroad students and traditional migrants in that they stay in the host community longer than the typical study abroad student, yet their motivation to migrate as well as their duration of stay differ from other migrants. In fact, those who 'reside' abroad constitute a heterogeneous group, including transnational migrants (Regan & Diskin, 2015), i.e. those individuals who stay for a limited amount of time in one country only to move onto another and who do not see mobility as a major obstacle; lifestyle migrants (Benson, 2012), i.e. individuals who move to another country for lifestyle reasons but never necessarily become fully integrated; and cultural migrants (Forsberg Lundell & Bartning, 2015a), i.e. individuals who migrate to a specific host community because they appreciate the culture and language of that community and choose to stay more or less permanently. These latter two groups are similar to political and economic migrants in that they stay for long periods in the community, but differ significantly in terms of motivating factors, as well as social and psychological circumstances.

'Residents' abroad are of particular interest to SLA researchers, especially with respect to high-level second language (L2) proficiency, adult SLA and the role of individual differences. Many studies on

155

adult SLA and ultimate attainment investigate typical migrant populations of economic and political migrants (Abrahamsson & Hyltenstam, 2009; DeKeyser, 2000), with the exception of Donaldson (2015), Kinsella and Singleton (2014) and Moyer (2004). There has also been a bias toward the examination of grammatical competences and maturational constraints, as a means to confirm or refute the Critical Period Hypothesis (CPH). A plausible conclusion is thus that cultural migrants, with their favorable attitudes and often positive social and psychological learning conditions, constitute a highly relevant population that can be studied in order to better understand the limitations and possibilities of adult SLA. The study of cultural migrants allows us to focus on questions such as the possibilities of native-like attainment in an L2, challenging linguistic features, the age factor and individual differences.

Between 2007 and 2012, these questions were investigated in a large-scale research program, specifically with regard to French as an L2. Our research group collected unique data from Swedish long-term residents in France, with host community stays ranging from 5 to 40 years. The data primarily consist of oral productions in different communicative genres and elicited data in the form of vocabulary tests, grammatical judgement (GJ) tests and psychological tests. In the present work, a summary will be provided of some of the most significant results in respect of the linguistic proficiency of these long-term residents in France. This account builds upon already published data (Forsberg Lundell *et al.*, 2014). Additionally, we will provide a thematic analysis of the long-term residents' motivation to learn the L2 and their integration in France. This latter qualitative study allows a deeper understanding of this group's social and psychological circumstances. This chapter is accordingly not one study – instead, it endeavors to examine a population of Swedish cultural migrants in France from several perspectives by complementing our previous investigation of their linguistic proficiency with a more qualitative consideration of the social and psychological issues at play. It should be noted, in addition, that no systematic comparisons have been made thus far of cultural migrants with the other types of migrants mentioned above, either in terms of socio-psychological orientation, or in terms of L2 attainment. This type of comparison would obviously be a relevant way forward, but within the confines of the present chapter, we focus exclusively on cultural migrants, contrasting their linguistic performance with that of advanced university students. The reason for comparing them with advanced university students is that they are also 'advanced' L2 users, although differing from university students with respect to amount of input and daily L2 use. Accordingly, the comparison allows insight into how certain linguistic features are influenced by prolonged stays in the L2 community.

Who are Cultural Migrants? A Description of an L2 User Population

In this chapter, cultural migrants, as opposed to economic or political migrants, are considered to be individuals who have chosen of their own accord to move to another country where they are learning the target language for cultural and personal reasons. This is a label that we proposed in Forsberg Lundell and Bartning (2015a) in order to account for a category of migrant that is not often described in the literature. It is necessary to clarify more specifically what is meant by 'cultural'. It is a well-known fact that 'culture' is among the most difficult concepts to define. In the present chapter, culture will be used in its anthropological sense, referring to habits, mentalities, traditions, etc., as opposed to culture in an artistic sense. As is clear from research in anthropology and ethnology, cultures are constantly changing and continuously influencing each other. Thus, it can be quite troublesome to define characteristic features of one single culture. However, our interview data make it quite clear that a 'typical French culture' or 'a typical French identity' is a psychological reality for many of our participants. As a consequence, it should be made clear that we will not attempt to define 'French culture' in this chapter; however, this concept will be frequently referenced as it is a reality, albeit vague and subjective, for our participants. The data show that the participants appreciate certain aspects of life in France, which they deem pertinent to French culture and which are often presented in contrast to what is referred to as Swedish culture or way of life. This is thus how the term 'cultural' is used in the present chapter. How do we then define a person as a cultural migrant, as opposed to a lifestyle migrant or transnational? It should be noted that these categories are not mutually exclusive; however, one kind of orientation should be considered predominant. In the present dataset, the motive for migration, and thus predominant migratory orientation, has been determined through questions in the interviews and through short socio-biographical questionnaires. These questions targeted motives for language learning, motives for migration and attitudes toward the host community, and allowed us to explore their primary motive of migration as 'cultural'. A more detailed description of our specific population of Swedish cultural migrants in Paris will be provided in the following.

The population in the present study: Swedish cultural migrants in Paris

The group of participants reported on in this chapter can be described according to the following characteristics. They are all late learners of L2 French, in that they began learning the French language after puberty. The ages of onset vary greatly, ranging from 13 to 21 years. Their age of arrival in France was between 17 and 25 years and their age at the time of the study was between 25 and 60 years. Their length of residence ranged between 5 and 40 years. All had completed secondary education, and the majority had also received a university degree. In their private lives, the vast majority of them had a French partner. When asked about their motives for migration, they frequently mentioned: to learn the French language, Francophile interests and romantic reasons in some cases. A small number of them are study abroad students who decided to stay, but the majority came directly after finishing secondary education in Sweden. This final profile implies that some of the participants received their university degrees in France. The results to be presented are thus based on a specific population of cultural migrants – Swedes in Paris – and we do not know to what extent these results can be generalized to other populations and contexts. In the following sections, more detailed descriptions will be provided on the specific dataset that we have used for our quantitative and qualitative studies.

Quantitative Aspects of L2 Learning: Linguistic Proficiency and Nativelikeness in Cultural Migrants

Study abroad researchers are mainly interested in the benefits of studying abroad compared to a domestic setting, as well as the identification and explanation of linguistic features that develop in a naturalistic setting. Study abroad students are also often compared to control groups of native speakers (NSs), which has led to the conclusion that these students do not reach the levels of native control groups, in particular when it comes to sociolinguistic competence and pragmatics (cf. Regan *et al.*, 2009). However, this comparison with NSs does not lie at the heart of study abroad research. Instead, it is the benefits of studying abroad as compared to a domestic setting that are the main focus for study abroad researchers. More recently, study abroad researchers have become increasingly interested in individual variation in study abroad learning outcomes, focusing not only on group comparisons between different settings, but also on comparisons between different individuals in study abroad settings (e.g. Arvidsson *et al.*, 2018; Mitchell *et al.*, 2015).

When studying cultural migrants, e.g. long-term residents in the host community, other questions arise. As stated in the introduction, the linguistic proficiency of cultural migrants is of particular interest to researchers interested in adult SLA and ultimate attainment. In that same vein, it can be interesting to compare them with lower proficiency levels, which also serve as a benchmark. This latter comparison was used in Forsberg Lundell *et al.* (2014). Two groups of cultural migrants, divided according to age at the time of recording and length of residence (LOR) (Groups 2 and 3), were compared with a group of advanced university students with more years of formal French studies, all of whom had also lived in France, albeit for much shorter periods of time (Group 1). All of these groups were compared to a control group of NSs, half of which was composed of younger speakers, and the other half of older speakers, as a means to match the groups of cultural migrants. All in all, 107,770 words were included in the present spoken dataset. Details on the participants are provided in Table 7.1.

Table 7.1 Participants in the quantitative study

Groups	n	Years of French studies	Length of residence in France (LOR)	Age of recording	Total number of words in informant speech
Group 1. French as a foreign language learners	10	6–12	1–2	19–34	22,502
Group 2. Junior cultural migrants	10	2–6	5–15	25–30	28,210
Group 3. Senior cultural migrants	10	2–6	15–40	45–60	32,278
Group 4. Native speakers (junior and senior)	10	–	–	25–35 45–60	24,780
Total no. of words					107,770

The starting point for our study was a revision of Bartning and Schlyter's (2004) developmental stage model for L2 French. In this model, which was based on data from 80 upper secondary school and university students in the Interfra and Lund corpora, Bartning and Schlyter proposed six different stages, ranging from elementary to highly advanced with respect to the acquisition of French morphosyntax and discourse. After collecting data from long-term residents in France, it quickly became apparent that they could not be classified according to the existing six-stage model and that the model was in need of revision. More specifically, it became clear that morphosyntactic criteria alone could not account for development at these levels, necessitating other criteria pertaining to the domains of vocabulary and fluency.

Two additional stages were proposed, eventually leading to the decision to investigate certain features that had not yet been included in Bartning and Schlyter's (2004) model. In connection to this work, we were inspired not only by the developmental stage model, but also by Abrahamsson and Hyltenstam (2009) and Hyltenstam and Abrahamsson's (2003) work on 'near-native' speakers. Hyltenstam and Abrahamsson (2003) define the near-NS as someone who is perceived as an NS in everyday conversation, but whose production does not evidence native-likeness in all respects when scrutinized in more detail. We assumed that among our long-term cultural migrants, we would find both near-NSs and speakers who are not perceived as native, but whose level can still be categorized as more advanced than that of university students as a result of prolonged exposure to spoken French. This led us to pose the following research questions:

(1) Do we find evidence for the existence of two highly advanced, yet distinct, stages in L2 French? That is, apart from the passing criterion, are there features that converge to create a 'highly proficient user' profile and a near-native profile? Does it follow from the passing criterion that speakers from the near-native level have:
   - fewer morphosyntactic deviances (MSDs)?
   - longer preambles and rhemes (discourse complexity)?
   - more lexical formulaic sequences (LFS)?
   - a significantly higher proportion of low-frequency words?
   - longer mean length of run (MLR) in fluency?
   - a higher speaking rate?
(2) Is it possible to reach nativelike spoken proficiency in an L2 as a 'late' learner?

Methodology

The first step in conducting this analysis was to put all recorded interviews through a listener test. Abrahamsson and Hyltenstam's (2009) near-NS is defined by the fact that she/he passes as an NS when judged by other NSs. The same methodology used by Abrahamsson and Hyltenstam was therefore used in our test. Ten NS evaluators were asked to evaluate the 40 informants from the four groups (see Table 7.1) according to nativelikeness. The judges were instructed to listen to extracts of 20–30 seconds from the informants' interviews.[1] The extracts were taken from the middle of the interviews where no information was revealed about the origin of the informants. The judges were asked to then choose between the following options:

(a) this person has French as her/his mother tongue, and she/he comes from the Paris region;
(b) this person has French as her/his mother tongue, and she/he does not come from the Paris region;
(c) this person does not have French as her/his mother tongue.

The judges were only allowed to listen to the extracts once and were asked to evaluate the certainty of their answers on a scale from 1 to 3 points. The native judges were all from the Paris region. They were between the ages of 25 and 40. Each of them had a post-secondary education and worked either in the education system, business or as technicians. Many of them had knowledge of foreign languages, ranging from one to even three. None of the judges, however, had any knowledge of Swedish, which was a criterion. They were recruited through a French research assistant who identified them through her social circles and based on the criteria given (25–40 years old, had not studied linguistics, no knowledge of Swedish, completed secondary studies). In line with Abrahamsson and Hyltenstam (2009), our definition of the 'pass' criterion is a person judged as a native by at least six out of the ten native judges.

After having implemented the listener test, the non-native participants were placed in three stages. The first stage, Stage 6, corresponded to the most advanced stage in Bartning and Schlyter's (2004) model. It only contains university students, but as can be seen in Table 7.2, there are only nine participants, as opposed to the original ten university students. This tenth student actually passed as an NS and was consequently placed in Stage 8. About half of the cultural migrants were placed in Stage 8, i.e. they passed as NSs when evaluated by NSs of French. This result, in and of itself, is quite encouraging for adult L2 learners, provided that 'passing as a native' is the desired goal. In any case, it points to the high-level proficiency that these long-term residents had acquired. The other half (eleven participants) were placed in Stage 7, a stage which we propose denotes individuals who can be placed somewhere between an advanced formal learner and a near-NS. They are speakers who have considerable LOR, perceived elaborated oral production, but who do not pass as NSs.

Table 7.2 The new division of proficiency levels in stages

Stage 6. The advanced superior stage: Nine speakers who are advanced university students, but who do not have the same linguistic resources as those in Stages 7 and 8, most certainly due to shorter LORs in a French-speaking country.
Stage 7. The highly proficient L2 user stage: Eleven speakers who have a considerable LOR (5–35 years) in France and whose productions are often more elaborate (as shown in Bartning et al., 2009), but who do NOT pass as natives.
Stage 8. The near-native stage: Ten speakers who have the same characteristics as those in Stage 7, but who also passed as natives in the listener test (called 'near-natives').
Native speakers: Ten native speakers (all the NSs of Group 4 passed as NSs).

Having divided the participants along the new stages, the next step was to investigate whether a detailed linguistic analysis would support the existence of two new, distinct stages above Stage 6. The linguistic categories investigated were the following:

- MSDs
- Discursive complexity
- Lexical richness

- LFS
- Fluency

Linguistic categories

Due to limited space, the linguistic categories cannot be presented in complete detail here. The choice of categories was based on earlier studies on very advanced speakers, among others Bartning *et al.* (2009).

Morphosyntactic deviances/100 words

The number of morphosyntactic errors per 100 words was counted. The following are examples of structures included.

(1) Subject-verb agreement (il y a *des cambrioleurs qui *vient* [viennent]) ['there are thieves who come* (singular)']
(2) Tense, mode, aspect (TMA): A broad category for simplification patterns or deviant rules in the tense system: e.g. *imparfait* instead of *passé composé* in past tense contexts (au bout d'un an *je rentrais* (for *je suis rentrée* en Suède) ['at the end of a year I was going back [for 'I went back'] to Sweden']), *passé composé* for pluperfect; indicative instead of subjunctive; problems with auxiliaries (*avoir* 'have' instead of *être* 'be').
(3) The noun phrase: Gender agreement and gender assignment of determiners, e.g. j'ai pas *un* [une] *image très romantique* ('I don't have a (*masc.) very romantic picture'), and gender agreement of adjectives (in different positions: *une *petit (petite) fille, la table *vert (verte), une ville *italien (italienne)* [a small (*masc.) girl, the green (*masc.) table, an Italian (*masc.) city]).

Discursive complexity: Number of words in the preamble (pre-front field)

For the study of discursive complexity, we used a modified model of Morel and Danon-Boileau's (1998) model, *le paragraphe oral*, here labelled as the 'extended clause'. This model accounts for the long pre-front fields that are characteristic of oral French. For our calculation of discursive complexity, we counted the number of words in the pre-front field, since a higher number of constituents has proven to be indicative of nativelikeness (cf. Conway, 2005) (see Figure 7.1).

Lexical richness (proportion of infrequent words)

The method used to measure lexical richness is the lexical oral production profile (LOPP), which is presented in Lindqvist *et al.* (2011). It is a frequency-based measure, which is inspired by the lexical frequency profile (Laufer & Nation, 1995). While the lexical frequency profile is developed for written language, the LOPP method is, as its name suggests, extended to spoken language. The method consists of dividing a

Extended clause				
	Inner clause = rheme			
Pre-front field	Front field	Verbal field	End field	Post-end field
et par contre / la Suède en général / ce qui m'a choquée le plus (and on the other hand / in Sweden in general / what shocked me the most)	c'est l'environnement (NS) ('is the environment')			

Figure 7.1 The extended clause. Source: Our modification of Morel and Danon-Boileau (1998).

speaker's words into different frequency bands: Band 1, Band 2, Band 3 and Off-list. The frequency bands were created on the basis of the Corpaix corpus (Campione *et al.*, 2005). The profile is seen as the proportions of lemmas in the different frequency bands, e.g. Band 1: 95%, Band 2: 2%, Band 3: 1%, Off-list: 2%. The general assumption is that a relatively high proportion of low-frequency words is indicative of a rich vocabulary (cf. Laufer & Nation, 1995). One would thus expect that very advanced L2 users have a higher proportion of lemmas in Band 3 and Off-list than less advanced learners.

Lexical formulaic sequences

The present study makes use of Erman and Warren's (2000) original categorization of prefabs (their term for formulaic sequence [FS]), which was modified slightly in Erman *et al.* (2015). For a problematization of the identification of FSs, see Forsberg (2010) and Granger and Paquot (2008). Sequences can be classified into lexical and qualifier FSs, but we will only focus on LFSs since they have proven to be the most interesting for the study of high-level L2 use.

LFSs incorporate at least one content word. They are used for extra-linguistic reference and denote actions (such as *faire la fête* 'to party'), states (*avoir peur* 'to be scared'), entities (*chef d'entreprise* 'company leader') and so on.

With regard to the practical identification of these sequences, Erman and Warren (2000) make use of the criterion 'restricted exchangeability'. In order for a sequence to qualify as a prefab according to their terminology, exchanging one of the words for a synonymous word must always result in a change of meaning or a loss of idiomaticity (Erman & Warren, 2000: 32).

The first step in identification is to find the LFSs that meet the restricted exchangeability criterion. This is then complemented by searches on Google.fr. The Google tests are carried out following a specific procedure. To test the extent to which restricted exchangeability applies to a sequence, an analogous sequence is created, which has been subject to one of several modifications, e.g. one of the words is exchanged for a synonymous word or one of the words is exchanged for an antonymous word (e.g. *ça marche mal* 'it works bad' instead of *ça marche bien* 'it works well'). In addition, for a sequence to be considered formulaic, it has to appear at least twice as frequently on Google as any of the modified versions, in order to provide some sort of measure of nativelike preference. Frequency is considered as a criterion for 'conventional' status.

Fluency: Mean length of run

Fluency can be measured in many different ways. In the present study, fluency is measured through MLR, which corresponds to the mean number of words between two silent pauses – a silent pause being defined as exceeding 25 milliseconds. This analysis is inspired by that conducted by Towell *et al.* (1996).

Results

In this section, we present an overview of the results that our linguistic analysis yielded with respect to the different categories. Table 7.3 shows the results regarding morphosyntax per stage. Starting with MSDs, the non-parametric analysis of variance (ANOVA) test (Kruskal–Wallis) showed significant differences between the four groups ($p < 0.001$). Next, Dunn's post-hoc test showed no significant differences in MSDs between the different non-native speaker (NNS) Stages 6–8. However, significant differences were shown between all the NNS stages (6–8) as opposed to the NSs in this domain (between Stage 6 and NS [$p < 0.01$], between Stage 7 and NS [$p < 0.01$] and between Stage 8 and NS [$p < 0.05$]). Thus, it seems that morphosyntax is a differentiating criterion between NNS and NS production. However, morphosyntax does not allow us to separate participants into separate advanced stages.

Table 7.3 MSDs per 100 words

Stage	MSDs/100 words (group mean)	SD
Stage 6	0.39	0.20
Stage 7	0.31	0.20
Stage 8	0.22	0.20
Native speakers	0.02	0.03

With regard to the mean length of preambles, Table 7.4 shows that the NS group had a higher mean value (3.21) than the NNS groups (3.01, 2.87 and 2.90, respectively). The highest individual mean values were found in the NS group. However, no significant differences between

Table 7.4 Mean of words/preamble

Stage	Mean	SD
Stage 6	3.01	0.46
Stage 7	2.87	0.33
Stage 8	2.90	0.40
Native speakers	3.21	0.58

stages were found according to the ANOVA ($F_{3,36}$ = 1,359, p = 0.271). Thus, there are no quantitative differences between the groups.

Table 7.5 indicates a progression in the use of LFSs from Stage 6 up to the NSs. The ANOVA test shows significant differences between the four groups ($F_{3,36}$ = 7.05, p = 0.001). The post hoc test (LSD) yields the following differences: between Groups 6 and 7 (p = 0.034), between Groups 6 and 8 (p = 0.020), between Group 6 and NS (p < 0.001), between Group 7 and NS (p = 0.015) and between Group 8 and NS (p = 0.034), but no significant difference between Groups 7 and 8 (p = 0.763). This provides evidence of stages above Stage 6, in that both Stage 7 and Stage 8 produce significantly more FSs than Stage 6. It is also important to note that a difference exists between Stage 8 and the NSs, suggesting FSs as an efficient measure of nativelikeness.

Table 7.5 Lexical FS/100 words

Stage	Mean	SD
Stage 6	1.84	0.87
Stage 7	2.90	0.93
Stage 8	3.30	1.02
Native speakers	4.08	0.98

Another result was the lack of significant difference between Stages 7 and 8, although the figures seem to point toward an increase in LFSs. It was therefore decided to proceed toward a linear regression analysis, which was carried out in order to examine the increase in LFSs across the stages. Stage (independent variable), seen as a longitudinal development from Stage 6 to NS, significantly predicted an increase in the proportion of FSs (dependent variable) β = 0.634, $t(38)$ = 4.46, p < 0.001 and accounted for 34.4% of the variance in the proportion of FSs, i.e. R^2 = 0.344. The regression analysis suggests that there is, in fact, an increase up to the NS level.

With respect to lexical richness, Table 7.6 shows that the proportion of high-frequency lemmas (Band 1) is higher at the less advanced stage and then decreases with each succeeding proficiency level. Looking at the proportions of low-frequency vocabulary (Band 3 + Off-list), it is obvious that as proficiency increases, so does the proportion of advanced vocabulary: The informants who passed as NSs in the listener test (Stage 8) also display the highest proportion of low-frequency vocabulary. As expected, the learners in Stage 6 have the lowest proportion. In order to investigate whether these differences are statistically significant, we ran an ANOVA test, which showed that there were significant differences between the four stages ($F_{3,36}$ = 16,86, p < 0.001). The post hoc test (LSD) shows that there are significant differences between Stages 6 and 7 (p = 0.034), Stages 6 and 8 (p = 0.008), Stage 6 and NS (p < 0.001), Stage 7 and NS (p < 0.001) and between Stage 8 and NS (p < 0.001). There is no significant difference between Stages 7 and 8 (0.509). The results are thus very similar to those of FSs, which lends further support for a stage beyond Stage 6, given that both Stage 7 and Stage 8 produce significantly more non-frequent words than Stage 6. However, this same lack of difference (as for FSs) between Stages 7 and 8 was shown. Notwithstanding, since the figures in Table 7.6 seem to indicate a clear increase along the stages, as is the case for LFSs, we also carried out a linear regression analysis of the lexical profile data. Stage (independent variable), seen as a longitudinal development from Stage 6 to NS, significantly predicted an increase in the proportion of infrequent words β = 1.41, $t(38)$ = 6.56, p < 0.001 and accounted for 53.1% of the variance in the proportion of infrequent words (dependent variable), i.e. R^2 = 0.531. Finally, it should also be noted that the most advanced NNSs failed to produce as many non-frequent words as the NSs, evidencing the difficulty of this domain for NNSs.

Table 7.6 The lexical profiles of the stages (%)

Stage	Band 1	Band 2	Band 3	Off-list	Band 3 + Off-list
Stage 6	94.33	1.95	0.65	3.14	3.72
Stage 7	93.36	1.92	0.87	3.85	4.72
Stage 8	92.91	2.00	0.69	4.40	5.09
NSs	90.02	2.72	1.12	6.15	7.27

As regards fluency, we investigated MLR. This measure yielded significant differences between Stage 6 and the other stages (LSD, Stages 6 and 7, p = 0.006, Stages 6 and 8, p = 0.004 and Stages 6 and NS, p = 0.005) according to an ANOVA ($F_{3,36}$ = 4,338, p = 0.01), whereas the differences between the highly proficient L2 users, the near-natives and the NSs did not prove significant. It can thus be concluded that native-likeness appears to be attainable for this fluency measure. It should, however, be emphasized, as pointed out previously, that fluency can be measured in a number of ways, this being just one of the measures (Table 7.7). For a discussion of different fluency measures, see De Jong *et al.* (2013).

Table 7.7 Mean length of run at the different developmental stages

Stage	Mean	SD
Stage 6	5.52	1.19
Stage 7	9.05	2.11
Stage 8	9.25	2.52
Native speakers	9.23	3.83

Note: Mean number of words between two silent pauses (silent pause = 25 milliseconds).

Summing up linguistic proficiency and nativelikeness in cultural migrants

Stages 6 and 7 are separated by fluency, FSs and lexical richness, which confirms the status of these measures as beneficial when it comes to the characterization of high-level L2 proficiency. It has been made clear that prolonged residency abroad has a significant impact on the mastery of these features. Long-term residents are more fluent, idiomatic and have a more sophisticated vocabulary than advanced university students. Although not unexpected, this should be considered as a key finding of Forsberg Lundell *et al.* (2014). This 'abroad setting' effect on fluency coincides with that of Freed *et al.* (2004), in which the study abroad setting led to higher gains in fluency than the 'domestic setting'. Other study abroad studies have also found lexical gains (e.g. Foster, 2009) and morphosyntactic gains (e.g. Howard, 2001) (although findings appear mixed for morphosyntax in study abroad according to Llanes [2011]). It would, however, be interesting to compare shorter residence abroad (typical study abroad students) with longer residence abroad (cultural migrants), using the same categories of analysis, in order to gain a better understanding of the effect of long-term exposure on these same linguistic categories.

Stages 7 and 8 – the two new stages – are only separated by the listener test, but regression analyses show a trend for both formulaic language and lexical richness, so it is plausible that these two stages are not only dependent on phonology (which is what is presumably measured by the listener test), but also on lexical measures. It would indeed be interesting to repeat this study with a larger dataset in order to verify the generalizability of the results and to identify a clearer pattern.

Furthermore, it was demonstrated that participants in Stage 8 (the near-native stage) differ from NSs with respect to use of FSs, lexical richness and morphosyntactic accuracy (mainly noun phrase agreement). As a consequence, even the most advanced group of long-term residents did not perform according to NS norms in all respects.

However, it is worth mentioning that the dataset contains individual profiles, who did perform in a nativelike manner on all of these measures (cf. Forsberg Lundell & Bartning, 2015b). In order to explain this, it is necessary to turn to studies on individual differences, which can have a stronger impact in a naturalistic language learning setting, where learners need to take advantage of opportunities, handle emotional constraints and challenges and deal with input of many different kinds. Within study abroad research, individual differences is a burgeoning subfield (see Arvidsson *et al.*, 2018; Iwasaki, this volume). With respect to long-term residents, Forsberg Lundell (2013) found that personality and language aptitude are associated with productive knowledge of collocations. It appears that the field of residence abroad, as well as study abroad, is in need of further research on the effects of individual differences. This need has also been highlighted for example by Moyer (2014), who discussed the underestimated importance of socio-psychological orientation for the acquisition of phonology.

Qualitative Aspects of L2 Learning: Language Learning Motivation and Integration of Cultural Migrants

As stated in the previous section, our cultural migrants can be distinguished from advanced university students in terms of more nativelike performance on several linguistic measures. This is not surprising, given that they have spent more time in the host communities than the student participants. One could therefore assume that the length and intensity of exposure play a major role here, which is the argument from usage-based approaches to language learning (e.g. Ellis, 2003). Nevertheless, it is acknowledged that not all long-term residents reach these high levels of proficiency, and we suspect that the favorable socio-psychological profile of the cultural migrants contributed to their L2 success. In order to gain a better understanding of the socio-psychological orientation of our cultural migrants, which presumably affects their language learning, a small-scale thematic analysis (cf. Braun & Clark, 2006) was conducted on their interviews. This study should, however, be seen as an exploratory starting point for further analysis and can be considered as presenting only interesting tendencies within this group of L2 users.

This qualitative study is based on a subset of five life story interviews, recorded between 2004 and 2007 in Paris. These interviews are taken from the same dataset as those discussed in Forsberg Lundell *et al.* (2014). The five Swedish first language (L1) participants were between 26 and 32 years old at the time of recording and had LORs of between 5 and 14 years. The interviews were semi-structured and conducted with an NS of French, contracted for the purpose of data collection. All of the interviews follow the same script, dealing with questions related to studies, work, hobbies, family life, life in France, differences between France and Sweden and the migratory experience. The selection of interview questions was primarily based on the script for the semi-structured interviews used by the InterFra-corpus (https://www.su.se/romklass/interfra), with the addition of questions relating to migratory experience and life in France. The choice of questions obviously guides the choice of conversation topics. Nevertheless, since the interviews are semi-structured, the questions can be seen as open-ended, and some participants will focus more on our chosen themes (see below) than others. For the purpose of the present study, the thematic analysis focused on the following main themes: Learning the French language and Integration in France. The themes were chosen for several reasons: the interview script rendered them present in the actual interviews and their obvious connection to the socio-psychological orientation of the participants. Furthermore, different sub-themes emerged with respect to these themes. The analysis did not include quantification, but can be seen as an exploration of emerging sub-themes in the interviews. All examples were checked for intersubjectivity with another SLA researcher, also working on L2 French.

Learning the French language

Since the participants' stories revolve around their lives in France and their experiences related to moving to another country, learning French was an expected theme, especially given that many of the participants had clearly put a lot of time and effort into learning the language. According to the participants, language learning is by no means easy, though essential. Within this theme, two sub-themes were identified as particularly characteristic of the speakers' narratives: agency and effort and valorization of the native French norm.

Agency and effort

In order to characterize the learners' approach to language learning, the concept of agency (cf. Bandura, 2002) appears appropriate. 'To be an agent is to intentionally influence one's functioning and life circumstances' (Bandura, 2002: 270). There are three modes of agency: personal agency, proxy agency and social agency. In our case, personal agency is relevant, which means that influence is exercised individually. Some of the most striking examples come from Tea, a 25-year-old dancer at the time of recording, who had spent five and a half years in France. She reports studying French at university level in order to reach a higher level of mastery, despite already being a high-proficient speaker. Her primary concerns with French revolve around having an accent. This has to do with the fact that she has experienced being judged because of her accent.

> je fais des études par correspondance. des études de français pour vraiment apprendre le français. parce que j'en ai marre de 'ouais, vous venez d'où/vous avez un petit accent'. [I do distance studies of French to really learn French, 'cause I'm sick and tired of 'oh, where are you from, you have a slight accent'.] (Tea, 25 years, 5.5 years in France)

I: tu disais que tu voulais effacer l'accent? [You said you wanted to get rid of the accent?]

E: oui [yes]

I: pourquoi? [why?]

E: parce que je trouve pas ça très joli, ça fait quand même cinq ans que j'habite en France. et j'en ai marre qu'on me pose la question tout de suite. [Because I don't find it very pretty, and I've lived in France for five years and I'm sick and tired of people immediately asking me that question.] (Tea, 25 years, 5.5 years in France)

Finally, the interviewer questions why she is studying French in the first place (referencing her relatively high proficiency). He wonders if she really needs additional classes and she agrees with him to some extent, but says that her primary motive is to feel good about herself and that fully mastering the French language has an intrinsic value for her.

I: est-ce que tu crois que t'as vraiment besoin? à/au niveau où tu es? [Do you really think that's necessary? At your level?]

E: ben le problème c'est que ben/peut-être pas/mais pour moi. [Well, the problem is that maybe not, but for my own sake.] (Tea, 25 years, 5.5 years in France)

Another participant, Christine, 30 years old, who has lived in France for seven and a half years, also stresses that she still makes an effort to learn French. In her case, it is through a French boyfriend that she continues to learn, or 'master' in her own words. She also speaks about the difficult experience she has had, starting to study at a French university, which also implies a certain level of 'mastery'. Like Tea, she sees mastery of the French language as an important goal, which is well worth the effort.

I: t'as arrêté d'apprendre le français? [Have you stopped learning French?]

E: ah si si, je l'apprends quand même. [No, no, I'm still learning.]

I: tu continues à… [You're continuing to…]

E: oui voilà. parce que j'ai quand même mon copain là depuis un an et demi et avec lui j'essaie de perfectionner un peu plus. [Yes indeed, 'cause now I've had a boyfriend for one and a half years and I'm trying to improve more with him.]

> donc deux ans après j'ai commencé à étudier la musique donc à l'université. donc ça c'était plus dur […] ça a été un perfectionnement on va dire. […] c'était très dur, mais euh je regrette pas. [So two years later, I started studying music at the university and that was harder. Let's say that it really improved. It was very hard, but I don't regret it.] (Christine, 30 years, 7.5 years in France)

Another interesting aspect is the fact that several participants engaged in other activities, with the learning of French as a natural by-product. Coco speaks of how joining a French basketball team helped her learn French. However, Coco's basketball seems slightly more incidental than Saga's bartending, where Saga justifies her choice to work with the fact that 'you're paid to speak'. Both Coco and Saga assume agency over their social and professional development, although Saga takes it one step further by considering how her work can improve her language skills.

E: heureusement je commençais à jouer au basket dans une équipe à la Sorbonne. et là/il y a que des Français. je crois qu'il y a un Allemand aussi. tout le monde parlait français/et moi je parlais pas un mot. ben il fallait bien que j'apprenne. [Luckily I started to play basketball on a team at the Sorbonne and there are only French people on that team. I think there's one German too. Everybody spoke French and I didn't speak a word. Well. I had to learn.] (Coco, 24 years, five years in France)

Saga, speaking of a former job as a bartender:

je trouve que c'est un très bon outil quand tu vas apprendre une langue, parce qu'on est un peu payé pour parler, [...] donc c'était aussi une manière de développer mon français. [I think it's a really good tool when you are going to learn a language, 'cause in some way you're paid to speak. So, it was also a way of improving my French.] (Saga, 26 years, seven years in France)

Valorization of the native French norm

In several cases, when talking about learning the French language, it is notable that the participants have a clear impression of a French native norm that they want to accommodate to, which in this case is exemplified by Tea. Additionally, Tea expresses that she prefers being taught by an NS, advocating that 'he knows the language better'. Through the words of this French learner, it is thus made very clear that a French norm exists and that it is best represented by a NS.

I: mis à part ton accent qu'est-ce que tu sens que tu dois encore améliorer? [Apart from your accent, what would you like to improve?]
E: la grammaire. je fais plein de fautes. je connais pas le subjonctif. je connais pas la différence entre le passé composé et l'imparfait. donc il y a des choses à améliorer quand même. [...] mais c'est vrai que j'ai besoin de quelqu'un pour me corriger. [The grammar. I make a lot of mistakes, I don't know the subjunctive I don't know the difference between *passé composé* and *imparfait*. So there are things that need to be improved. But I really need somebody who can correct me.]

E: après, le problème c'était que le prof /il était/c'était un Suédois. donc je préfère un Français/il connaît mieux la langue. [Then, the problem was that the teacher was a Swede. I prefer a Frenchman, he knows the language better.] (Tea, 25 years, 5.5 years in France)

Integration in France

The participants talk at certain points about their migratory experiences and some of them spontaneously hone in on how they perceive their own integration into French society. Here, a key sub-theme is their integrative motivation.

Integrative motivation

In the relevant passages in the data, there are many cases where it is possible to discern an apparent integrative motivation (cf. Gardner, 1988). This should be considered one of the foremost defining features of the 'cultural migrant': she/he is not just interested in travelling around, like the transnational, but has chosen a specific country and community to live in. It is interesting to observe the level of consciousness that the participants have with respect to integration and what strategies they have used. Saga speaks about the difficulties of 'really wanting to integrate', but also about avoiding co-nationals in order to achieve these goals of integration.

c'était plus difficile pour moi/c'était la deuxième fois. donc je suis rentrée en Suède pendant six mois. et puis je suis retournée en France. et là c'était plus difficile dans le sens où mes ambitions étaient plus grandes/parce que **je voulais vraiment m'intégrer**. Et ça c'était vraiment plus dur. [It was more difficult for me, it was the second time round. I went back to Sweden for six months. And then I returned to France. And there, it was more difficult since my ambitions were higher/I really wanted to integrate. And that was much harder.] (Saga, 26 years, 7.5 years in France)

mais aussi que je voulais vraiment apprendre le français. et pour apprendre le français, je sentais **qu'il fallait que j'évite de parler anglais/et le suédois**. donc je n'ai pas cherché les/cherché les endroits où je savais que je pouvais faire des amis/suédois ou/ou anglophones. **j'ai vraiment cherché/à faire des amis français**. [and also because I really wanted to learn French. And to learn French, I felt that I had to avoid speaking English and Swedish. So I did not go to places where I knew I could make Swedish or Anglophone friends. I really tried to make French friends.] (Saga, 26 years, 7.5 years in France)

The participants also speak about their identities, and one even mentions the relationship between identity and French citizenship. From these pieces of discourse, the impression is given that these participants have a strong French identity or, at least, a strong desire to have a French identity. Christine reports feeling bicultural, but she tends to feel more at ease in France. Vanessa, who has spent 14 years in France, speaks about the application process to become a French citizen. Initially, she did it for practical reasons, but later on she reports having felt that it was more of a personal choice. She describes this as wanting to feel like a part of French society and that becoming a French citizen would contribute to that.

> j'ai développé une partie de moi qui est française/et une partie qui est suédoise. [...] **mais maintenant/maintenant je me sens plus à l'aise en France.** [I have developed a part of me which is French and one part which is Swedish. But now, I feel more at ease in France.] (Christine, 30 years, 7.5 years in France)

> E: juste après l'entretien j'étais vraiment motivée. **je voulais vraiment avoir la nationalité française.** je voulais pouvoir voter. [...] j'avais fait la demande au départ pour passer des concours pour pouvoir être titularisée. [...] mais après l'entretien c'était même pas ça. **c'était pour moi. je voulais sentir que je faisais partie de la société française** enfin être citoyenne de... [Just after the interview I was very motivated. I really wanted to become a French citizen. At first I had done the application in order to pass entrance exams, to acquire my professional title, but after the interview, it was not even that. It was for my own sake. I wanted to feel that I was part of French society, you know, be a citizen of...] (Vanessa, 32 years, 14 years in France)

Summing up: Qualitative aspects on L2 learning – Language learning motivation and integration

Through this brief analysis, we have been able to highlight some motivational and attitudinal characteristics of the cultural migrants investigated. Through the thematic analysis, it has been made clear that these cultural migrants are characterized by agency and effort when it comes to learning French, as well as when it comes to integrating into French society. Agency is closely linked to self-regulation, which is one of the most important factors for adult SLA, according to Moyer (2014). The data also point to the importance of social networks for successful L2 learning, an expanding subfield within current study abroad research (e.g. Dewey, 2017). Furthermore, it points to an interesting link between agency and social networks, which, as such, is not surprising. With the examples of Coco and Saga joining a basketball team and becoming a bartender, respectively, which are two activities that provided valuable networks and possibilities to speak the language, possible evidence is given which points in this direction. Interestingly, Kinginger (2008) and Mitchell *et al.* (2015) have made similar observations for study abroad students. It has also been noted that several of the interviewees have a strong integrative motivation and sense of French identity. These are not questions that they have been forced to answer in a questionnaire. These are simply the words of participants when they voluntarily speak about their migratory experiences and lives in France. It is possible to argue that the points of view expressed in the interviews are essentialist when discussing culture and identity. Nonetheless, it is important to emphasize that the participants themselves frequently honed in on these topics. As previously stated, the choice of the researcher is only to talk about migratory experience, France and Sweden, and the perceivable differences of moving from one country to another. It should also be highlighted that these differences may be more important to this specific category of migrant, who has personally chosen to move to France, often as a result of a particular appreciation for the French language and what they consider French.

Nevertheless, we need to be clear about the fact that not all cultural migrants are as successful in creating social networks and in being agents of their language learning and integration, which further evidences the need for more studies on individual differences in long-term residents.

Conclusions and Future Directions

This chapter has presented a quantitative analysis of the linguistic proficiency of our cultural migrants and a qualitative analysis of their motivation and attitudes toward integration. It is likely that the results from the qualitative analysis may shed light on the quantitative results, which measure the participants' linguistic proficiencies, although no systematic relationship has been investigated here. A good example of how such a relationship could be demonstrated can be found in Mougeon and Rehner (2015) who investigated the relationship between longitudinal development of sociolinguistic competence (although not in study abroad) and what they call 'engagement portraits', which include various measures of language use, exposure and attitudes. In any case, cultural migrants tend to perform very well in both spoken production and on linguistic tests, although not always as well as NSs. Consequently, as a population, they offer us valuable insights into adult SLA. We only touched upon individual variation in this chapter, but it has been suggested that these variations constitute a promising subfield for further investigation. One of the most crucial questions for SLA research continues to be: why are outcomes so different in adult SLA, and even potentially enhanced in migratory contexts? The research of Jean-Marc Dewaele and colleagues on individual factors in SLA (e.g. Dewaele, 2005, 2012) could be further extended to encompass migratory contexts, which has been done recently, such as, for example, Hammer and Dewaele (2015) and Paniciacci and Dewaele (2017).

As has been discussed in several current studies in the field, both in study abroad and high-level L2 proficiency, agency and self-regulation appear to be very important (e.g. Chirkov *et al.*, 2007) in the study of individual factors and their impact on L2 learning in naturalistic contexts. Furthermore, the thematic analysis of the cultural migrants' narratives has also shown that integrative motivation is clearly present. In recent years, Gardner's integrative motivation (e.g. Gardner, 1988) has often been discarded in motivational research in favor of Dörnyei's (2009) L2 Motivational Self System. The L2 Motivational Self System is very useful in many instructional settings and in settings of English as a lingua franca. However, in a migratory context, the integrative motive is still likely to be useful, and the data analyzed here suggest that integrative motivation was an important driving force for our participants.

Furthermore, the study of cultural migrants has clear implications for the state of the art with respect to adult SLA and possibilities of nativelikeness. To date, an important body of research on adult SLA has been oriented toward the CPH, and CPH researchers have found rigorous evidence for differences between L1 and L2 speakers on the levels of morphosyntactic and phonetic intuition. Nevertheless, one could argue that there is a strong bias toward perceptive skills and very little research on actual performance. Therefore, there is an observable gap when it comes to studies investigating nativelikeness in both performance and communicative adequacy. As mentioned in the introduction to this chapter, populations that have been investigated in CPH research are often political or economic migrants. Motives for migration and the impact of social and psychological circumstances have rarely been discussed, with the exception of Moyer's (2004, 2013, 2014) work. It is important to note that the field of SLA is still a young field and that, to date, a large variety of populations have not been investigated. It is plausible that studies within the field of residence abroad constitute an interesting complement to current studies on ultimate attainment, nativelikeness and adult SLA. In the following, we offer some suggestions that would contribute to our understanding of varying outcomes in adult SLA:

(1) *Research in a large variety of migration contexts with a variety of L1/ L2 pairings.* The role of social context, both on a micro and macro level, is in need of further investigation. When context is taken more into account, it is likely that current theories of SLA will need to be reconsidered and reconceptualized.

(2) *Combining linguistic with social-psychological approaches.* Individual variation is likely to be more important in a naturalistic/ migratory context than in a formal context, which makes it necessary to combine measures of linguistic development with social and psychological variables in order to understand development.

(3) *Combining quantitative and qualitative approaches.* Research on individual differences is likely to benefit from mixed-methods designs that will enable us to draw robust conclusions, while providing us at the same time with a more fine-grained understanding of language learning and the migratory experience.

(4) *Focus on the possibilities of long-term, late-onset L2 learners to attain nativelike communicative adequacy.* As discussed above, much of the research on adult SLA has focused on the deficiencies of adult SLA. Furthermore, these deficiencies are often very subtle, targeting phenomena that most likely do not have a direct impact on communication. Our research on cultural migrants suggests that it may be time for a change of perspective. By shifting interest toward context, communicative abilities will be more important than knowledge of language. Conversation analysis and other interactionist approaches would be interesting to explore in order to gain further understanding of the communicative aspects of the linguistic proficiency of adult migrants.

In summary, this chapter has shown that L2 development continues beyond the advanced university student and that possibilities for development exist also when study abroad is replaced by residence abroad. This, however, depends on a complex combination of social and psychological factors, whose relation to L2 attainment remains unexplored.

Note

(1)   The same duration as the extracts in Abrahamsson and Hyltenstam's (2009) study.

References

Abrahamsson, N. and Hyltenstam, K. (2009) Age of L2 acquisition and degree of native-likeness – listener perception vs. linguistic scrutiny. *Language Learning* 58 (3), 249–306.

Arvidsson, K., Eyckmans, J., Rosiers, A. and Forsberg Lundell, F. (2018) Self-perceived linguistic progress, target language use and personality development during study abroad. *Study Abroad Research in Second Language Acquisition and International Education* 3 (1), 144–166.

Avarguez, S., Bilger, M., Buscail, L., Harle, A. and Lagarde, C. (2015) Au-delà du séjour linguistique : le cas des Britanniques implantées dans les Pyrénées-Orientales : aspects culturels et linguistiques. *Cahiers AFLS* 19 (2), 48–69.

Bandura, A. (2002) Social cognitive theory in a cultural context. *Applied Psychology* 51 (2), 269–290.

Bartning, I. and Schlyter, S. (2004) Itinéraires acquisitionnels et stades de développement en français L2. *Journal of French Language Studies* 14 (3), 281–299.

Bartning, I., Forsberg, F. and Hancock, V. (2009) Resources and obstacles in very advanced L2 French. Formulaic language, information structure and morphosyntax. *EUROSLA Yearbook* 9, 185–211.

Benson, M. (2012) How culturally significant imaginings are translated into lifestyle migration. *Journal of Ethnic and Migration Studies* 38 (10), 1681–1696.

Braun, V. and Clarke, V. (2006) Using thematic analysis in psychology. *Qualitative Research in Psychology* 3 (2), 77–101.

Campione, E., Véronis, J. and Deulofeu, J. (2005) The French corpus. In E. Cresti and M. Moneglia (eds) *C-ORAL-ROM, Integrated Reference Corpora for Spoken Romance Languages* (pp. 111–134). Amsterdam: Benjamins.

Chirkov, V., Vansteenkiste, M., Tao, R. and Lynch, M. (2007) The role of self-determined relations and goals for study abroad in the adaptation of international students. *International Journal of Intercultural Relations* 31 (2), 199–222.

Conway, A. (2005) *Le paragraphe oral en français L1, suédois L1 et français L2*. Études romanes de Lund 73. Lund: Lund University Press.

DeKeyser, R. (2000) The robustness of critical period effects in second language acquisition. *Studies in Second Language Acquisition* 22 (4), 499–533.

De Jong, N., Steinel, M.P., Florijn, A., Schoonen, R. and Hulstijn, J. (2013) Linguistic skills and speaking fluency in a second language. *Applied Psycholinguistics* 5, 893–916.

Dewaele, J.-M. (2005) Investigating the psychological and emotional dimensions in instructed language learning: Obstacles and possibilities. *The Modern Language Journal* 89 (3), 367–380.

Dewaele, J.-M. (2012) Learner-internal psychological factors. In J. Herschensohn and M. Young-Scholten (eds) *The Cambridge Handbook of Second Language Acquisition* (pp. 159–179). Cambridge: Cambridge University Press.

Dewey, D. (2017) Measuring social interaction during study abroad: Quantitative methods and challenges. *System* 71, 49–59.

Donaldson, B. (2015) *Ne*-deletion in near-native French: Aspects of L2 sociolinguistic competence. Paper presented at EUROSLA 2015, Aix-en-Provence.

Dörnyei, Z. (2009) The L2 motivational self system. In Z. Dörnyei and E. Ushioda (eds) *Motivation, Language Identity and the L2 Self* (pp. 9–42). Bristol: Multilingual Matters.

Ellis, N.C. (2003) Constructions, chunking and connectionism: The emergence of second language structure. In C. Doughty and M. Long (eds) *The Handbook of Second Language Acquisition* (pp. 33–68). Oxford: Blackwell.

Erman, B. and Warren, B. (2000) The idiom principle and the open choice principle. *Text* 20 (1), 29–62.

Erman, B., Denke, A., Fant, L. and Forsberg Lundell, F. (2015) Nativelike expression in the speech of long-residency L2 users: A study of multiword structures in L2 English, French and Spanish. *International Journal of Applied Linguistics* 25 (2), 160–182.

Forsberg, F. (2010) Using conventional sequences in L2 French. *International Review of Applied Linguistics* 48 (1), 25–50.

Forsberg Lundell, F. (2013) Qué significa pasar por nativo? Un estudio exploratorio sobre la actuación oral de usuarios muy avanzados de español y francés como segundas lenguas. *Studia Neophilologica* 85 (1), 89–108.

Forsberg Lundell, F. and Bartning, I. (eds) (2015a) *Cultural Migrants and Optimal Language Acquisition*. Bristol: Multilingual Matters.

Forsberg Lundell, F. and Bartning, I. (2015b) Successful profiles in high-level L2 French: *c'est un choix de vie*. In F. Forsberg Lundell and I. Bartning (eds) *Cultural Migrants and Optimal Language Acquisition* (pp. 59–82). Bristol: Multilingual Matters.

Forsberg Lundell, F., Bartning, I., Engel, H., Hancock, V., Lindqvist, C. and Gudmundson, A. (2014) Beyond advanced stages in high-level L2 French. *Journal of French Language Studies* 24 (2), 255–280.

Foster, P. (2009) Lexical diversity and native-like selection: The bonus of studying abroad. In B. Richards, M.H. Daller, D. Malvern, P. Meara, J. Milton and J. Treffers-Daller (eds) *Vocabulary Studies in First and Second Language Acquisition* (pp. 91–106). New York: Palgrave Macmillan.

Freed, B., Segalowitz, N. and Dewey, D. (2004) Context of learning and second language fluency in French: Comparing regular classroom, study abroad, and intensive domestic immersion programs. *Studies in Second Language Acquisition* 26 (2), 275–301.

Gardner, R.C. (1988) The socio-educational model of second language learning: Assumptions, findings, and issues. *Language Learning* 38 (1), 101–126.

Granger, S. and Paquot, M. (2008) Disentangling the phraseological web. In S. Granger and F. Meunier (eds) *Phraseology: An Interdisciplinary Perspective* (pp. 27–49). Amsterdam/Philadelphia, PA: Benjamins.

Hammer, K. and Dewaele, J.-M. (2015) Acculturation as the key to ultimate attainment? In F. Forsberg Lundell and I. Bartning (eds) *Cultural Migrants and Optimal Language Acquisition* (pp. 178–202). Bristol: Multilingual Matters.

Howard, M. (2001) The effects of study abroad on the L2 learner's structural skills: Evidence from advanced learners of French. *EUROSLA Yearbook* 1, 123–141.

Hyltenstam, K. and Abrahamsson, N. (2003) Maturational constraints in SLA. In C. Doughty, and M. Long (eds) *The Handbook of Second Language Acquisition* (pp. 539–588). Oxford: Blackwell.

Kinginger, C. (2008) Language learning in study abroad: Case studies of Americans in France. *The Modern Language Journal* 92 (1), 1–124.

Kinsella, C. and Singleton, D. (2014) Much more than age. *Applied Linguistics* 35 (4), 441–462.

Laufer, B. and Nation, P. (1995) Vocabulary size and use: Lexical richness in L2 written production. *Applied Linguistics* 16 (3), 307–322.

Lindqvist, C., Bardel, C. and Gudmundson, A. (2011) Lexical richness in the advanced learner's oral production of French and Italian L2. *International Review of Applied Linguistics* 49 (3), 221–240.

Llanes, À. (2011) The many faces of study abroad: An update on the research on L2 gains emerged during a study abroad experience. *International Journal of Multilingualism* 8 (3), 189–215.

Mitchell, R., McManus, K. and Tracy-Ventura, N. (2015) Placement type and language learning during residence abroad. In R. Mitchell, N. Tracy-Ventura and K. McManus (eds) *Social Interaction, Identity and Language Learning during Residence Abroad* (pp. 115–138). EUROSLA Monograph Series 4. Amsterdam: European Second Language Association.

Morel, M.-A. and Danon-Boileau, L. (1998) *La Grammaire de l'Intonation. L'Exemple du Français*. Paris: Ophrys.

Mougeon, F. and Rehner, K. (2015) Engagement portraits and (socio)linguistic performance: A transversal and longitudinal study of advanced L2 learners. *Studies in Second Language Acquisition* 37 (3), 425–256.

Moyer, A. (2004) *Age, Accent and Experience in Second Language Acquisition: An Integrated Approach to Critical Period Inquiry*. Clevedon: Multilingual Matters.

Moyer, A. (2013) *Foreign Accent: The Phenomenon of Non-Native Speech*. Cambridge: Cambridge University Press.

Moyer, A. (2014) Exceptional outcomes in L2 phonology: The critical factors of learner engagement and self-regulation. *Applied Linguistics* 35 (4), 418–440.

Paniciacci, A. and Dewaele, J.-M. (2017) 'A voice from elsewhere': Acculturation, personality and migrants' self-perceptions across languages and cultures. *International Journal of Multilingualism* 14 (4), 219–436.

Regan, V. and Diskin, C. (2015) Migratory experience and second language acquisition among Polish and Chinese migrants in Dublin, Ireland. In F. Forsberg Lundell and I. Bartning (eds) *Cultural Migrants and Optimal Language Acquisition* (pp. 137–177). Bristol: Multilingual Matters.

Regan, V., Howard, M. and Lemée, I. (2009) *The Acquisition of Sociolinguistic Competence in a Study Abroad Setting*. Bristol: Multilingual Matters.

Towell, R., Hawkins, R. and Bazergui, N. (1996) The development of fluency in advanced learners of French. *Applied Linguistics* 17 (1), 84–119.

8 What First Exposure Studies of Input can Contribute to Study Abroad Research

Rebekah Rast

Introduction

For decades, researchers in the field of second language acquisition (SLA) have debated the extent to which linguistic input plays a role in SLA. Some theories have claimed a crucial role for innateness, often leaving input in its wake, while others have insisted that input is the driver of acquisition. In recent years, research has gradually moved in the direction of 'input matters'. From the work of Doughty (1991), who argues that second language (L2) instruction makes a difference, to the edited volume of Piske and Young-Scholten (2009), which carries the title *Input Matters in SLA*, the message is that exposure to the language being learned constitutes an essential component of foreign language acquisition regardless of whether the language learning context is instructed or not. In SLA research conducted in study abroad (SA) contexts, the issue of input or 'language contact' is crucial because learners abroad find themselves in host countries where language contact is potentially much more intensive and 'present' in a way that is different from the foreign language classroom. The ambient language input is available to them in a variety of forms, and programs need to understand what learners are doing with this input.

First exposure studies in the field of SLA have homed in on this question of input, finding ways to tease apart the effects of the input with respect to other variables, such as the learner's first language (L1) or learner properties such as motivation or attention. These studies are beginning to paint a clearer picture of what learners at the initial stages of language acquisition do with the language input they receive (the 'uptake' that potentially becomes 'intake'), contributing useful information to the debate about the role of the input in language learning. The methodology and tools developed by first exposure studies are applicable to SA studies that seek a more focused approach to what learners are doing with the input encountered abroad. By drawing on first exposure studies, research in an SA context can begin to match the input of the learners' environment with input processing, comprehension and intake to the learners' language systems.

This chapter has two principal aims, both of which concern input in the SA context. Firstly, it describes the goals of first exposure studies, including what they are able to tell us about the input and what learners do with this input, regardless of the learning context. Secondly, it describes more precisely several studies that demonstrate the methods and tools used to document and investigate how input can be observed and measured, and makes suggestions about how SLA research in an SA context might go about measuring input and its effects on acquisition during an SA experience. Beginning with a brief overview of how the construct 'input' is viewed from the perspective of several theoretical frameworks, the chapter addresses these two aims by introducing the reader to first exposure studies that measure input and the role it plays in language development, and concluding with some practical applications for SLA research in the SA context with respect to documenting and measuring input and observing how input converts into intake in foreign language learning.

Input in Theories of SLA

A plethora of approaches, frameworks, models and theories have developed over time in the common goal to better understand how individuals (children and adults) make use of the language input to which they are exposed and how they learn languages beyond their first. The research presented here takes a psycholinguistic approach to SLA. This in no way undermines the importance of research from other perspectives, especially given the focus of this volume, SLA in SA contexts. Research from sociocultural and sociolinguistic perspectives is particularly relevant for SA studies, and should be embraced. Cognitive and social processes work together in language acquisition, and a balance between cognitive and social SLA research is necessary (Larsen-Freeman, 2007; Tarone, 2007). In some cases, they can be studied together, but in other cases, studying the different processes independently is beneficial. The research we present here focuses primarily on the role of linguistic 'input' in foreign language learning and the ways in which learners have been found to benefit from the input to which they are exposed. We take a close look at research projects that investigate the role of input from the very first moments of contact with a new target language (TL), studies that seek to disentangle variables, such as input, L1 knowledge and other L2 knowledge, in language learning. In this way, the studies follow a more traditionally cognitive approach to SLA as opposed to a social one.

As mentioned above, decades of research in SLA have confirmed the common-sense assumption that language acquisition requires exposure to linguistic input (Doughty, 1991; Pica, 1991), and there is now consensus in the field that 'input matters' (Piske & Young-Scholten, 2009). Important questions remain, however: What does this 'input' entail? How much and what type of input is needed? What conditions are ideal for helping learners make use of the input they encounter? The characterization and the role of linguistic input in SLA have been at the core of ongoing debates in the domain of cognitive SLA research. For decades, on one side of the debate is the nativist/generativist/Universal Grammar (UG) tradition, while on the other are frameworks that have in common their opposition to UG theory, such as the emergentist and usage-based perspectives. A third and more recent approach is the learner-variety model, an interactionist-functionalist approach to SLA. Although some similarities between these theoretical frameworks can be found, their claims about input and its role in language acquisition differ.

Within the domain of generative-based linguistic theory of SLA, numerous models and hypotheses can be found, differing generally in their views regarding access to UG, the component of the language faculty that is innate to humans (Chomsky, 1957), and the role of the L1 in SLA or, more recently, the role of the L1 and an L2 in third language (L3) acquisition (García Mayo & Rothman, 2012). One of the most prominent hypotheses within the generativist tradition is the Full Transfer/Full Access hypothesis, which takes a strong L1 transfer and full access to UG stance (Schwartz & Sprouse, 1996). In this model, a language learner comes to the task of SLA with UG values (abstract syntactic rules) set for the L1 grammar, and the L2 learner has access to UG; this is the 'L2 initial state' as Schwartz and Sprouse define it. If the L2 input includes a feature that matches that of the L1 grammar system, the input will confirm the initial system already in place. If the L2 input feature differs from the L1 system, the input will need to 'trigger' a change in the initial state of the system. In an overly simplified explanation of the theory, acquisition takes place when a confirmation or change in the linguistic system occurs. Another important aspect of a generative-based approach is that input is not simply viewed as the raw language of the environment, but also as information provided by one internal system to another. For instance, phonological information extracted by the linguistic system from the sounds of the L2 environment may be processed at the phonological level of representation. The output of this process may then serve as 'input' to another internal level of representation, such as the morphosyntactic level (Carroll, 2001; Sharwood Smith, 2014). Hence, depending on one's approach, 'input' refers to the language in the environment or to an internal mental construct.[1] With respect to the 'input' that concerns us in this chapter, that of the environment, generative-based research has had a reputation for 'disregarding' input (De Bot, 2015). Recently, however, following a long period of focusing more on the nature of the involvement of UG and L1 transfer, Rankin and Unsworth (2016) suggest that generative research in SLA may be moving toward more detailed analyses of the input encountered by learners. Such an evolution would be welcome by all researchers interested in input and its relation to acquisition.

Emergentist frameworks, on the other hand, grew out of psycholinguistic approaches to L1 acquisition that have consistently defined input as the ambient language of the learner's environment (e.g. Clark, 2009). From the emergentist and usage-based perspectives, the frequency and distribution of items and constructions in the input, as well as the frequency of usage, are crucial to acquisition (Ellis, 2002; Tomasello, 2003). Learning a language is considered equivalent to acquiring a complex cognitive skill, which involves the building of an automatized skills set and the constant restructuring of internal representations as language develops. It follows that studies investigate how learners use the language units and constructions found in the input. They examine, for instance, syntactic environments in the productions of learners, such as whether nouns are used as subjects or objects in certain environments, or whether nouns follow or precede adjectives or possessive pronouns. From this perspective, our stored knowledge consists of information about the frequency with which we have encountered specific items in various syntactic frames in the input, and this information plays an important role in how we understand and produce utterances in real-life communication.

Finally, the learner-variety approach can be traced to both functionalist (Klein, 2012) and interactionist approaches to SLA in the European tradition (Corder, 1967; Pekarek Doehler, 2000; Perdue, 1993).[2] In line with emergentist thinking, the learner-variety approach crosses the cognitive-interactionist lines by claiming that communication is key to language learning, that crucial information is present in the input and that learners use the language constituted in negotiation with their interlocutors, as well their own knowledge and cognitive capacities, to analyze this input. A clear difference between the two approaches, however, lies in the fact that emergentism originates in L1 acquisition theory, whereas the learner-varieties approach developed through research that set out to account for subsequent language learning. From the learner-varieties perspective, L2 learners are 'experienced communicators' from the outset, and thus, they develop simple and transparent form-to-function mappings based on general semantic and pragmatic principles (Dimroth, 2018; Klein & Perdue, 1992, 1997). It is the input that contains the information needed to develop these organizational principles when learning a new language. For example, the organizational principle 'Controller First' is considered a universal principle whereby beginner learners place the noun phrase with the highest control in first position in an utterance regardless of their L1 or the language being learned (Klein & Perdue, 1992, 1997). These types of principles are considered to constrain the way speakers arrange items in an utterance, and it is the learner's ongoing analysis of the input within these constraints that leads to language acquisition. According to this approach to SLA, the 'L2 initial state' is not limited to a full transfer of the L1. In order to better understand how organizational principles, pragmatic constraints and other information in the input converge in the mind of the learner, we need to understand, in addition to individual variability such as attention and motivation, how learners, both consciously and unconsciously, work on and analyze the input they encounter.

As can be seen from these descriptions, assumptions about the quantity and quality of input needed for language acquisition, as well as other components that interact with the input, depend largely on one's theoretical perspective. This theoretical information is important to keep in mind as we consider how to analyze language input encountered by learners in a variety of forms and contexts.

First Exposure Studies in SLA

In order to analyze the input and observe its relation to uptake, intake and eventually acquisition, we need to be able to disentangle input effects from the effects of other factors, a challenge that first exposure studies have embraced. One way to do this is to start from the very beginning, from the very first moment of contact with the TL to be learned, and to observe and document what absolute beginners do with the input to which they are exposed. This methodological approach, which spans theoretical frameworks, involves 'first exposure' studies 'in which data are collected from the very first moment of contact with the TL and within the first seconds, minutes and hours of subsequent exposure, and in which all TL input is controlled' (Rast, 2008: 29). First exposure studies set out to better understand the role of the input, the L1 and other factors by documenting the input in its entirety. In this way, the input can be regularly compared with learner performance on tasks in the TL to assess how the input, as distinct from other factors, affects language learning. Exposure can be measured in a variety of ways with respect to performance on TL tasks: (1) upon absolute first contact with the TL; (2) after a given length of time of exposure, i.e. the first few seconds, minutes or hours of contact with the TL; (3) after a controlled number of exposures to a selection of TL items; or (4) a combination of these. Learner performance can be tested through a variety of means, such as lexical decision, word recognition, sentence repetitions, grammaticality judgments, picture verification and various production and narration tasks, as well as by means of psycholinguistic experiments and measures of neurolinguistic activity (for overviews and collections of first exposure research, see Carroll [2013], Han & Rast [2014] and Indefrey & Gullberg [2010]).

First exposure studies from a range of theoretical frameworks have appeared in the past decade. Some have investigated spontaneous input and learning 'in the wild' (e.g. Gullberg *et al.*, 2012; Han & Liu, 2013), while others have developed more structured paradigms using classroom settings or computer-based techniques (e.g. Carroll, 2014; Rast, 2008; Shoemaker & Rast, 2013). Many statistical learning studies are also recognized as 'first exposure' in the SLA literature, even though the input is realized through the creation of artificial languages (e.g. Hudson Kam, 2009; Saffran *et al.*, 1996). These latter studies provide pertinent and useful information about what language learners do when exposed to new sound patterns, how they process the new linguistic information and what they recognize as 'language' or 'words' in the early stages of exposure, all different aspects of the language learning process. We also make a distinction here between 'natural' language learning environments and 'instructed' ones. The former refers to the first exposure studies in which participants were exposed to language in a controlled, yet fairly natural setting (e.g. viewing a video) and were not explicitly told that they would (or should) learn anything. Studies in instructed settings, on the other hand, refer to those in which participants were 'learners' and the expectation of learning language during language classes was understood. This distinction is an important one for the SA context in that both environment types are common and studied in language acquisition research focusing on linguistic gains during SA (e.g. DeKeyser, 2010; Howard, 2011). An important question for this research in SA contexts is how the input can be observed in these environments and measured against linguistic gains. We will return to this question in the section on practical applications for research in SA environments.

One of the primary areas of investigation in first exposure studies, and one that may be of particular interest to both researchers and learners in an SA context, is that of 'word learning'.[3] Word learning, or vocabulary building, is a complex process at the heart of developing a system of communication in and through language and is one of the great challenges for SA students in their host environment. For decades, the study of vocabulary acquisition was hidden behind the emphasis placed on the study of grammar. As Meara (2009: xii) points out, '[...] learning a vocabulary is much more than the acquisition of a list of unorganized words'. Vocabulary studies since the 1990s (following the publication of Nation's [1990] *Teaching and Learning Vocabulary*) have flourished, and implications for educational practice and policy have become increasingly apparent in areas such as SA, literacy and language assessment. In language acquisition studies, we are particularly interested in the processes involved in word learning for the simple reason that understanding these processes will help guide not only researchers in theory building, but also practitioners in language teaching. In what follows, a selection of sample data from research conducted on word learning in first exposure studies is described in order to provide insights into not only vocabulary building, but also the construction of a new morphosyntactic system. We begin with studies conducted outside of the classroom space, contexts that resemble, to some extent, many SA contexts, and follow up with studies conducted in a classroom setting, which parallel the instructed element of some SA programs.

Word Learning: First Exposure Studies in a 'Natural' Setting

From the perspective of psycholinguistic research, to complement the work conducted by statistical learning experts on word learning, a series of studies carried out at the Max Planck Institute (Nijmegen) opted for a more 'ecological' learning situation in that participants encountered real-language input in the form of a weather forecast. The first of these studies (Zwitserlood *et al.*, 1994/2000) investigated initial exposure (15 minutes) to Mandarin Chinese by native speakers of Dutch. The objective of the study was to discover under what conditions learners could recognize certain elements in the TL input and attribute meaning to them. Results showed that the frequency with which words were used by the Mandarin native speaker, in conjunction with the use of visual highlighting, had an effect on the recognition of words and their meaning. In addition, they found that participants were able to categorize as non-words (i.e. words impossible in Mandarin) those items that had correct Mandarin segments in an incorrect position in the syllable. Zwitserlood *et al.* (1994/2000: 12) conclude that, 'the striking result from our experiments is that our listeners, although in the traditional sense "understand" very little, can detect important regularities of the unknown language on the basis of so little input'. They showed that after only 15 minutes of exposure to Mandarin, their Dutch participants were able to recognize whether or not a combination of Mandarin elements constitutes a Mandarin word or not. The sensitivity of their participants to elements of the linguistic input on which they were asked to focus their attention is quite remarkable and highlights the importance of the input in the successful completion of the task, one of the first steps in word learning: to extract a sequence of sounds from the speech stream and recognize the sequence as a word that belongs to the TL in question.

Expanding on and elaborating the methodology of the Zwitserlood *et al.* study, Dimroth *et al.* (2006) and Gullberg *et al.* (2012) used very small amounts of totally controlled language input to investigate what learners are capable of doing with a new linguistic system at first exposure. In these studies, participants (native speakers of Dutch) with no knowledge of Mandarin were exposed to a seven-minute videotape in Mandarin (a weather forecast). Participants were given no instruction or training, and were simply asked to watch the video. They were not asked to interact with the input, nor were they asked to try to learn something.

Following the video session, a series of post-exposure tasks were administered. Gullberg *et al.* (2012) report on the results of a word recognition task and a sound-to-picture matching task. Taken together, the results of the tasks reveal that the frequency of items in the input resulted in a positive effect on word recognition and an ability to map meaning to form when accompanied by gesture. In other words, when items were more frequent and gesture (e.g. pointing) was used in the video, this configuration helped learners comprehend new Chinese words. The study concludes that participants were capable of extracting useful information from a novel speech stream despite the fact that no meaning could be attached to lexical items in the input based on prior linguistic knowledge (there were no cognates in the input). Ristin-Kaufmann and Gullberg (2014) replicated the Gullberg *et al.* (2012) study, this time using the same Mandarin videotape with groups of native speakers of Swiss-German. They also found that seven minutes was sufficient for participants to generalize their newly acquired phonotactic knowledge to reject non-words in the TL. Again, as with the Zwitserlood *et al.* study on focused tasks, participants 'learned' something about TL words with remarkably little exposure to TL input.

In another study from the same data collection, Gullberg *et al.* (2010) also found that Dutch native speaker participants were capable of extracting possible Mandarin word forms, again after only 7–14 minutes of exposure to the weather forecast video input in Mandarin (those exposed to 14 minutes of input viewed the video twice). They also found that participants could extract possible phonotactic constraints, and that with gestural support they were even able to extract sound-referent pairings. Based on an exploratory neural connectivity analysis using functional magnetic resonance imaging (fMRI), results provide evidence of pre-existing and learning-induced neural differences between learners who were more or less successful at word recognition after only 14 minutes of exposure to the novel language. Exposure alone affects our neural structures with respect to language.

Taken together, these studies reveal that adult learners have a remarkable capacity to process aspects of the novel TL speech stream after very little exposure to the TL. These results are important for SLA research, regardless of theoretical framework and context. If learners can extract words from the speech stream and recognize them as belonging to the TL after such little exposure to the novel language, this confirms a very strong language learning capacity in the adult learner that appears to be dependent on language exposure. This scenario has important implications for SA programs in that it confirms the need to guarantee regular exposure to the host language. It also suggests that even passive language activities, such as listening to the radio or watching TV, can be useful for building form-meaning mappings, the basis for word learning, comprehension and production, and begs for further investigation into what types of exposure are most effective for word learning when abroad.

Another series of first exposure studies examined the effect of 'spontaneous input' in the auditory and/or written modality (Han & Peverly, 2007; Park, 2011). In a study of 'natural auditory input', Han and Liu (2013), for example, studied L1 English and L1 Japanese *ab initio* participants exposed to L2 Chinese. The Chinese input was presented in the form of ten videos showing people either ordering food in a restaurant or bargaining in a shop. Participants were asked to answer questions and perform tasks either during or after viewing the video. One focus of Han and Liu's investigation was to observe the extent to which absolute beginners were able to process input for form and meaning. Their results with respect to processing form show that regardless of the L1–TL combination, learners were 'only able to minimally scratch the surface of the input' (Han & Liu, 2013: 160). Results concerning their participants' ability to process naturalistic input for meaning, however, revealed that the comprehension level achieved was quite high (above 60% of the input). The authors attribute this performance to a top-down processing strategy: the participants were found to use their prior experience and knowledge of the world (cued by the visuals in the videos) to comprehend the input. These results, once again, confirm the remarkable capacity of L2 learners to process the input and make sense of it, even after such limited exposure. They also confirm that L2 users, even at the initial stages, make use of prior knowledge about the world to decipher and negotiate the input, an assumption made in the learner-varieties approach, and one that is important for SA studies in which students are confronted with real-life communication.

Although methods and results differ from study to study, a pattern is developing in the first exposure findings. Learners act on their input immediately upon first exposure, and they manage to perceive, segment and comprehend aspects of the input within only minutes and hours of exposure. This sensitivity to the input is observed in the settings discussed here, where the nature of the input ranges from artificial to experimental (weather forecast) to fairly authentic (a YouTube video of a restaurant scene in China). It is these results that are useful for the SA context and for all research on language input. The input does matter, and we are gradually beginning to understand how, when and why it matters, as we will see in the following sections.

Word Learning: First Exposure Studies in an 'Instructed' Setting

Much first exposure research has been conducted in the classroom for the simple reason that controlling, documenting and observing the input is much easier in an instructed setting (i.e. in the classroom) than in a natural one (i.e. outside of the classroom). In a series of first exposure studies conducted within the learner-varieties framework, word learning at the initial stages of instructed SLA (ISLA) has been investigated.

In ISLA input studies in particular, an important focus has been placed on the investigation of input properties or properties of input patterns. In the area of word learning, two properties have been the focus of numerous studies: frequency and transparency. The notion of 'frequency' breaks down into type and token frequencies of words, constructions and structures in the input. Token frequencies are the number of occurrences of the linguistic element, whereas type frequencies refer to the number of patterns in which a linguistic element appears in the input. Take, for example, the word 'cars' in English. If the word 'car(s)' appears 51 times in the input, the token frequency is 51. If the plural marker –s appears in the input attached to seven distinct nouns (e.g. cars, stores and chairs), its type frequency is seven (see Ellis & Collins [2009] for a more detailed description of frequency). As such, both type and token frequencies can be calculated in any given dataset, and tools exist for doing this automatically (e.g. CHILDES [MacWhinney, 2000]). Researchers calculate exact frequencies or refer to categories of frequency, such as 'very frequent' or zero-frequency ('absent' from the input).

The second property, 'transparency', involves a comparison between the learners' L1 and the TL. This comparison often results in 'transparency' being confounded with 'cognate' in that many transparent words are cognates, as in the pair 'information' (English) and *información* (Spanish). While these two words are considered cognates from the perspective of historical linguistics, the psycholinguist is interested in knowing whether the speaker-hearer forms a link between them. To test this, a transparency test is conducted with first exposure participants in which they hear words in the TL and are asked to translate them as best they can into their L1 (for examples, see Rast [2006] and Valentini & Grassi [2016]). In this way, the researcher is able to identify which words in the TL will likely be comprehended by the learners of the study based on L1 (and perhaps other L2) knowledge. As with frequency, categories are allotted for transparency, such as 'very transparent' or not at all transparent ('opaque').

Word learning: Breaking into the speech stream, sentence repetition

One of the initial first exposure studies conducted in the classroom is reported in Rast and Dommergues (2003) and Rast (2008). The study used a sentence repetition task designed to investigate learners' ability to extract words from a novel language speech stream at first exposure, to observe their development over time and to identify the factors that helped learners extract words and learn them. In the study, French native speakers ($n = 8$) learning Polish for the first time received eight hours of instruction from a native speaker of Polish. The sentence repetition task was administered after four hours of instruction and again after eight hours. The task was also administered to a control group of French native speakers with a similar profile to the learners of the study, with no prior exposure to Polish or another Slavic language, for baseline data (zero hours of instruction). Participants were asked to listen to sentences recorded by a native speaker of Polish and repeat the sentences as best they could. An example sentence is provided in the following:

Polish (TL):	*Po polsku mówi ona dobrze.*
	in Polish speaks she well
French (L1):	'Elle parle bien le polonais'.
	she speaks well the Polish
English translation:	'She speaks Polish well'.

The data were analyzed in terms of 'correct' repetitions, based on two criteria:

(1) The number of syllables in the repeated word had to be the same as the number of syllables found in the original word to be repeated.
(2) Only one phoneme per syllable could be repeated incorrectly.

If a repetition did not meet these two criteria, as determined by a native Polish speaker, it was not counted as a 'correct repetition'.

Numerous variables were the focus of observation, including overall time of exposure to Polish, word length, word stress, phonemic distance (between French and Polish phonemes), word position in a sentence, lexical transparency and frequency of a word in the input. Results revealed strong effects of several of these variables on participants' ability to extract words from the speech stream and repeat them, in particular with respect to the position of a word in the sentence, word stress, phonemic distance and lexical transparency. In short, participants repeated words correctly according to a number of parameters with respect to the position of words in a sentence, more short than long words in initial position and more long than short words in final position. It is important to note that these two factors (word position and length) are unrelated to L1 influence, and therefore suggest that learners rely not only on their L1 knowledge but also on other, possibly universal, cognitive factors when faced with a TL task such as repetition. At the phonological level, results revealed that more phonemically familiar than unfamiliar words were correctly repeated, especially when in initial and final positions and when stressed. In other words, stressed Polish words in initial and final positions that comprised only L1 sounds were better repeated than those comprising sounds that are foreign to the learner's L1. This result confirms a strong role for the L1 when it comes to the correct perception and articulation of speech sounds in a novel language. In sum, the sentence repetition data reveal a robust role for the L1 when learners are asked to act on their input at the initial stages of SLA, yet one that is balanced with other factors that appear to be part of the learner's cognitive make-up.

Finally, with respect to the two important input variables, frequency and transparency, findings were revealing. Results showed an important role for transparency: more 'very transparent' words were correctly repeated than 'opaque' or 'fairly transparent' words. For frequency, an unexpected finding revealed the lack of frequency effect after four hours of instruction. An effect of frequency was only observed after eight hours of instruction, suggesting that frequency takes time to kick in.[4] This is an important finding for SLA research and one that has implications for language learning in an SA context in that it raises the important question of how much exposure is needed for learning to happen. This result is intriguing and begs for future research on the effects of frequency in contexts such as natural SA settings, where exposure is tightly intertwined with real-life communication and interaction. The study of transparency and frequency in the input and their effect on comprehension and production will continue to be an important area for future research in both instructed and natural language learning settings. In particular, the question that needs to be addressed is to what extent a transparent item serves as bootstrapping in the comprehension of an utterance. In other words, learners may use transparency in interesting ways that may help them learn new structures. SLA researchers need to better understand these processes, and studies in SA environments may well be able to contribute pertinent data concerning learners' reliance on transparency – both successful and unsuccessful attempts at communication – when they have no other means to express a thought (Rast, 2010).

Word learning: Extracting words from the speech stream, word recognition

Although the sentence repetition task discussed above responded to some questions about how learners break into a novel speech stream, Shoemaker and Rast (2013) took these questions a step further. They developed more fine-tuned methodologies in the form of a word recognition task, again in an instructed setting, to test these findings for perception only, dropping the 'production' requirement inherent in a sentence repetition task. The variables word position, transparency and frequency were the focus of the follow-up study.

Participants of this study resembled those of the Rast and Dommergues (2003) study. Native speakers of French ($n = 18$) who had no prior contact with Polish or another Slavic language received 6.5 hours of Polish instruction.[5] The new study developed a word recognition task with a list of 16 words in Polish compiled according to the two input properties mentioned above, transparency and frequency. Two categories of transparency were established: 'opaque' (no correct translations) and 'transparent' (50% correct translations). Each test word was also classified for frequency: 'absent' from the classroom input or 'frequent' if the word appeared more than 20 times in the classroom input. This frequency-transparency classification system resulted in four categories: transparent/frequent; transparent/absent; opaque/frequent; and opaque/absent. Four test words were assigned to each of the four categories (16 test words), test sentences were created with an equal distribution of these four words across sentences and each of the 16 test words appeared in three different positions: initial, medial and final. Distracter sentences, in which no target words appeared, were included in the task as well. The task was administered before the first Polish lesson and again after 6.5 hours of instruction. Learners listened to a Polish sentence followed by a Polish word, and were asked to indicate whether or not the word was part of the sentence they had heard. In this way, participants were not asked to produce language during the task, an important difference from the repetition task described earlier.

As with the sentence repetition task, accuracy results confirmed the powerful role of transparency when extracting words from the speech stream at this early stage, with transparent words recognized more often than opaque words at both test times. An effect of position (words in middle position were recognized less often than items in initial or final position) was found in the word recognition data at absolute first exposure to Polish (before instruction) and after 6.5 hours of instruction. Finally, frequency effects were not found, once again suggesting that frequency did not necessarily help participants learn the new words. This said, learners improved in their recognition of opaque words, whether frequent or not, and a significant effect of overall exposure to the TL was found, meaning that, after only 6.5 hours of exposure, learners showed significant improvement in their ability to extract words from the speech stream. This suggests that learners may have acquired phonological information about Polish that allowed them to better segment the signal. As mentioned earlier, such results underline the importance of regular exposure to linguistic input in language learning, even receptive input, and argue strongly in favor of the extensive language exposure that SA programs provide. Within this exposure, properties of the input, such as transparency and frequency, can be observed and analyzed, rendering them useful tools of measurement for SA research that seeks to better understand the effects of language contact on language gains.

A subsequent word recognition study was conducted within a larger European cross-linguistic project titled 'Varieties of Initial Learners in Language Acquisition' (VILLA).[6] This project allowed for observation of not only exposure effects but also L1 effects in that it controlled, recorded and documented the input in a cross-linguistic study of the acquisition of

Polish by native speakers of Dutch, English, French, German and Italian from the moment of first exposure through the first 14 hours of classroom exposure (over two weeks).[7]

The VILLA word recognition task closely followed the design used in Shoemaker and Rast (2013); however, words in the new task appeared only in sentence-medial position (not in initial or final positions), as Shoemaker and Rast had already established that the middle position posed the greatest challenge for the recognition of Polish words by native speakers of French. The two input properties studied were, once again, transparency and frequency. Analyses of the word recognition task to date are based on data collected from one group in each country, with the exception of England: French ($n = 17$), Dutch ($n = 19$), German ($n = 20$) and Italian ($n = 17$).[8]

The same frequency-transparency classification system of four categories in Shoemaker and Rast (2013) was used to design the VILLA word recognition task, and procedures were the same. Although learners were tested at slightly different time intervals from the Shoemaker and Rast study, the first test was also administered before Polish instruction began (T1). They were then tested again after 7.5 hours of input (T2) and after a total of 13.5 hours of input (T3).

Analyses of accuracy in the cross-linguistic dataset show complex interactions between variables (van Bergen *et al.*, 2014). With respect to the input properties studied, transparency and frequency, both expected and unexpected outcomes were observed. Firstly, a strong effect of frequency was found in the VILLA version of the task at T2 and T3, with frequent words better extracted than absent words. This result, although not in line with findings reported in Shoemaker and Rast (2013), corresponds to the findings reported in Rast and Dommergues (2003) where a frequency effect was observed after eight hours of exposure (but not yet at four hours). Taken together, these results suggest that frequency, as measured in hours, requires approximately seven to eight hours of overall exposure before learners begin to build lasting mental representations of the individual lexical entries to which they were exposed. This result suggests that something other than frequency of the words themselves may be responsible for the initial learning that takes place, as suggested by Carroll (2012) and Shoemaker and Rast (2013). This is encouraging if, in fact, overall exposure accompanies word learning. Based on these findings, the picture of receptive language learning processes is becoming clearer. Learners appear to acquire, quite rapidly, prosodic and segmental information specific to the TL, which helps them segment the speech stream and eventually leads to word learning. Once this prosodic and segmental information is in place, word learning perhaps becomes faster. These results introduce an important question for SA: To what extent is a focus on prosodic and segmental information important for learners on SA programs and for a potential increase in the efficiency and speed of the language learning process? An interesting SA study might involve observing two groups of learners, one that receives focus on prosodic and segmental information (i.e. pronunciation or phonetic training) and one that does not. Do such instructional practices aid learners in processing not only classroom input, but also the input of the host environment? Might such a classroom experience make learners more sensitive to the sounds of the host language and potentially more able to process these sounds, especially at the initial stages?

Across the L1 groups, transparency showed strong effects; performance on transparent words was better than performance on opaque words at all time periods, a finding that confirms results from the previously conducted experiments mentioned above (Rast & Dommergues, 2003; Shoemaker & Rast, 2013), as well as other first exposure research (Carroll, 2012; Han & Liu, 2013). It is also interesting, and perhaps surprising, to note that no interaction was found between frequency and transparency in the word recognition data of VILLA. In other words, the transparency effect was strong regardless of whether the word appeared in the input or not, and the effect (or not) of frequency did not depend on whether the target word was transparent or opaque. This finding suggests a strong role for the L1 in the process of extracting words from the input. In terms of word learning, clearly extracting meaning from a string of sounds (e.g. through lexical transparency, which allows for form-meaning mapping) helps learners recognize words in a new language, a first step in compiling a new lexicon. Although frequency effects were not observed immediately, they appear to be quite strong after seven to eight hours of exposure, suggesting that 'familiarity' with words in terms of their frequency, even if opaque, eventually provides a benefit to word learning.

What do these results tell us about the input? They tell us that learners gradually make use of input over time. Immediate input in and of itself may not be particularly helpful, but when the input is cumulative, consistent and regular, frequency effects become significant, an observation described and explained in detail by usage-based research (Ellis & Wulff, 2015). At the same time, we observe that the input converted to intake, that is, the input taken in by the learner, does not work alone. Learners do not simply regurgitate the ambient language they have heard. As experienced communicators, they combine their L1 knowledge and the knowledge they have about how language works with the input to segment the speech stream and extract words and language units from the flow of speech, eventually comprehending and producing language based on the linguistic information they have extracted from the input. In order to better understand the next steps of word learning, let us look at how the input affects the building of a new grammatical system and initial oral productions.

Word learning: Grammatical information and oral production

We have observed how beginning language learners break into the TL speech stream and extract words from a flow of unfamiliar speech. We have seen how transparency helps learners identify word boundaries and, hence, take in TL information that would otherwise be difficult, if not impossible, to grasp. We have also seen how frequency seems to play a minimal role in this process at the very beginning and becomes increasingly important with extended exposure to the language being learned. We have observed these effects in learners exposed to only 14 hours of input or less. These results are important for SA studies because they speak to the crucial nature of the input. Without a doubt, learners need to go through these perceptual processes in language learning before they can begin to comprehend, produce and combine novel words, and in order to do this they need sufficient language exposure, an element that SA programs can provide. Given this language exposure, we still need to understand how learners engage with the TL input in interaction and begin to use words to communicate in the new language. The VILLA project investigated oral production as well, examining how learners not only learned the basic forms of lexical items and how to combine them, but also how they learned language-specific grammatical structures, such as inflectional morphology, and began to use them in their own speech.

One study within the project that is particularly relevant to research conducted specifically on formal instruction in the SA context investigates the effects of two types of input exposure on French native speakers' development of nominal morphology in TL Polish (Latos, forthcoming). Unlike French, Polish has a rich system of nominal morphology, two numbers, three genders and seven cases, encoded in inflectional endings. One group of French speakers ($n = 17$) received instruction using a 'meaning-based' (MB) approach in which the input was rich in morphological forms, but forms were not highlighted or emphasized. The other group ($n = 19$) received instruction through a 'form-based' (FB) approach in which the input, also morphologically rich, contained highlighted forms and received emphasis by the instructor in both oral and written modalities. In both conditions, the instructor provided no metalinguistic information about Polish grammar, and only Polish was used in the classroom. Following the 14-hour course, learners met individually with a native speaker of Polish for a Route Direction task that involved looking at a map and telling the interlocutor in Polish how to go from point X to point Y.

Latos (forthcoming) carefully examined the input patterns to which the two groups were exposed and compared them with the learners' oral productions elicited by the task. The detailed analysis of the word *ulic-* ('street') in the two input datasets revealed that, although the Polish instructor intended to use words and forms with similar degrees of frequency in both teaching conditions, she in fact did not always do this. The two groups were exposed to four declined forms of *ulic-* (nominative, accusative, locative and instrumental) with identical temporal distribution, that is, with a gradual introduction of inflectional forms at the same rate. The input differed, however, in token frequency and token distribution. After 14 hours of instruction, when the learners took the Route Direction task, the MB group had been exposed to 269 noun tokens of *ulic-* and the FB group 326 tokens, a difference of 57 tokens. A closer analysis revealed that the instructor used a more balanced distribution of forms with the FB group than she did with the MB group. The distribution of forms in the MB input was nominative (54%), locative (23%), accusative (12%) and instrumental (11%), whereas the FB input exhibited nominative (30%), accusative (29%), locative (25%) and instrumental (16%). If one takes the input into account, the results of the study reveal interesting differences. Learners of the MB group produced the word *ulic-* almost exclusively with the nominative ending at a rate of 87%, whereas the FB group used a wider variety of endings, with accusative being the most frequent (62%) and nominative at 30%. In sum, the FB group received a more varied input than the MB group, and after only 14 hours of contact, the oral productions of the FB group contained a larger variety of inflected forms than those of the MB group. Although the productions of the FB learners were also more accurate than those of the MB group, the crucial point here is that the morphological richness of the learners' productions matched the morphological richness of the input. The strong influence of the input on the learners' speech in the TL is thus confirmed. Not only do these results speak clearly to an important role for the input in SLA, but they also help us understand this role. If learning a foreign language were simply a matter of setting an L1 value to an L2 value based on evidence in the input, such differences in learner productions would be difficult to account for. In the case of Latos' study, learners' took in the forms to which they were exposed, analyzed them with respect to their own knowledge and experience, and produced language that can be described as similar to the type of input they received. This type of meticulous focus on the input is a requirement for moving forward in our understanding of the influence of language contact on language learning.

Finally, another study within the VILLA project investigated learner productions, also after 14 hours of instruction. The goal of this study was to elicit fairly free productions from learners during a communication-based task. The task used was the Finite Story, a film-retelling task (Dimroth, 2012). The short five-minute animated movie, which visually recounts the story of three protagonists (Mr Blue, Mr Red and Mr Green), comprises 31 film segments intended to elicit narrations that require speakers to be particularly explicit and not to leave out information, hence pushing learners to use an atypical information structure. The story involves three neighbors who are sleeping when the roof of their apartment building catches fire. They gradually become aware of the fire and go through a series of steps from trying to notify the fire brigade to waiting for the fire engine to arrive so they can jump and be saved. In the input of the VILLA project, learners regularly encountered a number of carefully selected lexical items that were needed to perform the task. In contrast, some words and structures that could have been helpful for this task never appeared in the input, leaving the learners to fend for themselves when trying to communicate. Learners retold the story individually to a Polish listener as they watched each segment of the movie.

Dimroth (2018) analyzed the productions of Italian and German native speakers of the VILLA project. Overall, she identified support for input-driven factors in the learner production data, as well as for individual creative constructions. Creative word combinations were quite common, such as in the following example of an utterance produced by a native speaker of Italian:

> *to jest muzyka, **telefon muzyka*** (A IT-15)
> this is music, telephone music
> 'The telephone is ringing'. (Dimroth, 2018: 15)

Such structures provide us with an indication of what learners pick up from the input to use in communication. In this example, we see the creativity of the learner who, faced with the Polish equivalent being absent from their lexical repertoire, needs to find another means to communicate the meaning of a telephone 'ringing' and uses *muzyka* in the case. We also observe the use of the copular structure in this example ('this is music'). VILLA learners often produced copula structures in contexts where the copula is not native-like (e.g. Saturno, 2015), an indication of how learners go about using aspects of the input to create new structures that they have not encountered in that exact form in the input.

In terms of grammatical structures, Dimroth identified a variety of verb forms and combinations, including finite verbs combined with other finite verbs (non-target like in Polish), as in the following utterance by a native speaker of German:

> *pan niebieski robi śpi* (A GE-05)
> Mr. Blue do3rd-SG sleep3rd-SG
> 'Mr. Blue is sleeping'.

This example provides evidence of how learners create constructions based on bits and pieces of the language of the input (e.g. Polish equivalents of 'do' and 'sleep'), but never combined in this manner. Such an example shows that input alone is insufficient and that learners do not merely imitate the input they hear. Rather, the input combines with knowledge, attention, memory and other factors in the act of language production.

Closely analyzing the input relative to what the learner does with the input, as in the above analyses, provides us with further insights into the language learning process. Studies of input in all contexts need to look carefully at this relation between the input and the learners' analysis of the input as observed through tasks such as the ones discussed in this chapter. Although first exposure studies have the advantage of being able to control the input from the very beginning, they generally observe language learning in tightly controlled conditions, which may at times compromise the ecology of the study. SA studies are by nature more ecological, and the data can be collected from a wide variety of TL contacts, reflecting the real-life nature of the input. SA studies have identified and described this reality in quite some detail (e.g. Wilkinson, 1998). The following section will address these issues and provide some practical applications for research in an SA context that seeks to better understand the role of language contact in the language learning of students in SA programs. Understanding this role implies an understanding of issues, such as input properties (e.g. frequency and transparency); intensity and regularity of exposure; types of input; the link between input, comprehension and intake; and finally, the transition from intake to production.

Practical Applications for Research in SA Environments

Overall, the first exposure studies discussed in this chapter took on the challenge of measuring language exposure and learning over a limited period of time by means of strictly controlled input that was recorded from the moment of first contact. The findings reveal the impressive language learning that takes place, even at the very initial stages of SLA and ISLA, and the important role of the input in this language learning. These studies confirm the need to further investigate what the learners' input looks like and how it converts to intake in a variety of learning contexts, including one of the most input-intensive settings, that of the SA experience.

Researchers working in an SA context are well aware of the challenges involved in controlling and measuring language contact during SA. Students' language experience is generally more 'in the wild' insofar as they are living in a host community with a host language, where a range of factors determines the quality and quantity of input. In some situations, for instance, a learner receives input passively (e.g. watching TV), whereas in others the learner is actively engaged in conversational interactions, requiring ongoing negotiation of the input with the interlocutor(s). These interactions may be transactional (e.g. ordering coffee) or communicative (real creative language interaction), and they may involve different degrees of exposure in terms of quantity and frequency. Learners in SA contexts also often take language classes, such that understanding the role of instructed input abroad is also important.

An 'input' study therefore needs to carefully consider and describe the situation of the students (e.g. Dewey *et al.*, 2014; Kinginger, 2008, 2009; Kinginger *et al.*, 2016; Segalowitz & Freed, 2004). Are they living with a host family or in a dormitory, with native speakers of the TL language, speakers of their L1 or non-native speakers of the TL with other L1s? If they live with a host family, do they spend time with the host family, during meals for instance? If they spend time together, does the host family speak (and use) the L1 of the students or only the host language? What is the level of engagement of the host family? How creative is the input? Wilkinson (1998), for example, describes how some families use a question-response routine similar to the input found in classrooms. Are the students also receiving formal instruction while on SA? To what extent is their input contact through native speakers or other learners?

During classroom instruction, input can easily be recorded, documented and analyzed, as shown in ISLA studies reported in this chapter; however, in SA, the language contact outside of the classroom will need to be accounted for as well, whether first exposure or not. In the past, documenting the input and learners' 'local engagement' in the SA context has often involved student logs or questionnaires, such as the language contact profile (LCP) (e.g. Freed *et al.* [2004]; also see Hernández [2016] for a modified LCP used on a weekly basis). The LCP has recently been criticized, however, primarily due to the self-reporting nature of the questionnaire. Relying on students to report accurate information about their language contact and engagement is problematic for a variety of reasons, including limitations in recalling frequency and intensity of language use, the lack of objectivity of their self-perceptions and the lack of third-party validation (Fernández & Gates-Tapia, 2017). Learner shadowing, in which a third party reports on conversational activity, proposed as a complement or alternative to self-reporting, has been found to increase reliability (e.g. Mitchell *et al.*, 2017). These new techniques for measuring exposure are indeed welcome improvements. However, they still fail to capture the precise nature of the input that students encounter when abroad and their uptake relative to this input. For this reason, having participants carry recorders with them for a pre-specified length of time to track the input may be an interesting solution (see Kinginger *et al.* [2016] for an example of video recordings of conversational interactions during SA). Given the intensively controlled nature of such a project, appropriate consent forms and procedures, as well as sufficient funds, will be necessary. Although such research projects are complex and require extensive preparation, they promise innovative contributions to extant research in order to advance our understanding of language learning in all contexts. With respect to input studies, Flege (2009) stated this very clearly:

In sum, more and better research will be needed to determine if, as some claim, input is relatively unimportant in L2 learning. To adequately assess the role of L2 input, the input that learners of an L2 actually receive must be assessed more accurately. Measuring L2 input may be impossible, but better estimates of L2 input can and must be obtained. Doing this will require the expenditure of substantial resources (time, money, creativity). For this to happen, researchers must first decide to *give L2 input a chance* to explain variation in L2 learning. (Flege, 2009: 190; original emphasis)

In order for studies to provide clear information about input and the link between input, perception, segmentation, intake and eventually production, decisions need to be made well before the onset of the project about how the input will be recorded and documented in any of the above situations.

For full control of the SA input in the way first exposure studies have been conducted, one approach would be to establish an SA context in which the learners are new to the host language (true beginners) and are exposed to both instructed classroom input and ambient input outside of the classroom. The instructed input can be documented by following methods and techniques described in this chapter. For a full documentation of the ambient input, however, a new methodology is needed, one that would involve learners recording the input they are exposed to from the very beginning of their stay and over a designated period of time, such as one full day or several days so that the input can be matched to their uptake. This approach guarantees control over prior knowledge of the TL (minimal previous exposure) and the input, which in turn will result in a dataset that can contribute to research on what learners do with the input they receive, what they take in and how this activity potentially leads to language acquisition.

For full control of the SA input that is not based on first exposure, another approach is feasible. The methodology would involve conducting a study in which participants are tested for their proficiency level at the onset of the project, and the input is carefully documented from the moment of this onset point. This scenario is reminiscent of 'intervention' studies conducted in the 1980s and 1990s, in which a group of learners is exposed to an 'input treatment' (e.g. Doughty, 1991; Doughty & Williams, 1998; Long, 1983; Sharwood Smith, 1993), while a control group receives no treatment. This methodology requires careful benchmarking of learner proficiency in the TL, specifically in the linguistic domains to be investigated in the research. Once established, this onset level provides a benchmark of proficiency against which language gains relative to the input can be measured. Numerous SA studies have identified ways to measure proficiency level at the onset of the SA experience (e.g. see studies reported in Pérez-Vidal [2014]) and can easily be applied to controlled input studies. Comparisons between participants' performances of the two groups has led to observations and claims about the effects of the input treatment on language acquisition. This approach, again, requires learners' recording their language exposure over a day or several days. Tools proposed by first exposure research for preparing the data collection and transcribing, analyzing and interpreting the data can also be applied to these studies. Such an approach would allow for a close study of the wide-ranging input outside the classroom, the learners' uptake and the effects of the exposure and how the learner engages with the exposure during a specified period of time on language acquisition.

Once the participant proficiency level has been determined (either first exposure or by means of a proficiency test) and the input has been recorded over a pre-specified period of time, in the classroom and/or outside the classroom by a researcher, a third party (in the case of shadowing) or the learner, and documented, a next step is to compare the input to learner performance on specially designed tasks that elicit or test specific TL features and properties of the input over a predetermined period of time. Although first exposure studies currently propose a limited number of tasks as described above in the analysis of word learning, a wide range of tasks may be used depending on the project's research questions and hypotheses. The SALA project (Pérez-Vidal, 2014), for example, provides rich information about tasks used in the SA context to measure performance, as do many other SA studies (e.g. Dewey *et al.*, 2014; Faretta-Stutenberg & Morgan-Short, 2018). Making predictions about the properties of the input before the onset of the study, as first exposure studies have done with frequency and transparency, is an important step when comparing the input and learner performance. Predictions about the input can be made based on prior research findings, pilot studies and corpora of language frequencies (Paquot & Gries, 2019). Finally, tasks need to be administered at well-defined time intervals to ensure a precise observation of how and when different phases of the acquisition process take place.

Selecting participants for these input studies also requires special attention. One possibility is to track a small number of learners through case studies, allowing for a meticulous qualitative analysis of the language learning processes relative to the input. Rast (2008), for example, observed the language development of two learners with similar linguistic profiles exposed to the same input at first exposure. Learners at different proficiency levels exposed to the same quantity of input in terms of length of time (e.g. calculated in hours) could also be compared, as could the same learners at different times during the stay abroad (e.g. upon arrival, after two weeks and again after two months). These comparisons would allow us not only to observe how learner language and a learner's interaction with the input develop over time, but also how the input to the learner may differ depending on proficiency level. For instance, does a newly arrived learner cope differently with the input than a learner who has been abroad for several weeks, and does the input to the learner evolve over time in terms of complexity?

Finally, and simply as a reminder, detailed information about study participants should be collected: the traditional biographical data (age, gender, etc.), as well as language background information, such as L1 and other L2 knowledge and experience, and individual variability, from learners' working memory capacity to their motivation for learning the host language (see e.g. Li *et al.*, 2006). As Rast (2008) discovered from two first exposure case studies, the interlanguage of the two learners, who had similar linguistic, educational and socioeconomic profiles and were exposed to the same foreign language input, developed quite differently. The variation in performance on TL tasks could not be explained by differences in proficiency level, input received or the learners' L1 or other L2s. Something else had to account for these differences. Collecting individual differences data allows for a more complete analysis of learner development when making comparisons of this kind.

Conclusion

SLA researchers working on input at first exposure and those working on input in an SA context have in common the objective to better understand what the input encountered by learners looks like, what learners do with the input and, ultimately, what role the input plays in foreign language learning. The controlled nature of first exposure studies has allowed for the development of ways to measure input and compare it with learner performance at various time intervals. Indeed, such studies have the advantage of being able to provide an unusually precise description of what the input looks like. This chapter has highlighted and provided examples of first exposure research studies that offer a methodological model that we argue can be applied and extended to an SA context.

We have seen what first exposure studies can tell us about the actual input that learners at the initial stages of acquisition might encounter in a variety of settings. The input can be collected, documented and described, and we have seen how first exposure studies have done this and how they identified and kept constant, for measurement purposes, the properties of the input, such as frequency and transparency. We have also observed how studies compare specific aspects of the input to the performance of learners on a variety of language tasks, including the tools used to do this, such as the receptive tasks of repetition and recognition, and production tasks such as film retelling. We have seen how these studies observe how learners combine their input with knowledge of their L1 and knowledge of information structure, and how language works in communication to engage in productive communication. Practical applications have also been offered as to how input can be recorded and documented in an SA environment, with a view to establishing large datasets of input to the SA learner. These samples of first exposure studies demonstrate a methodology that can be used by researchers working in an SA context to document and investigate the role of the language contact in the language development of students abroad.

First exposure research has provided empirical evidence that 'input matters' in foreign language acquisition, an important overall finding for SA programs that expect language learning to happen, and therefore need to guarantee useful host language exposure for their students. The premise of SA is indeed that the change of input exposure conditions is the key to successful language learning (Howard, 2011). In order to understand the nature of this input, first exposure studies have developed tools to closely investigate what linguistic input looks like and what learners do with the input they encounter. The results of this investigation not only inform first exposure research about what learners do in the early stages, but also indicate important paths for future research in SA and other contexts concerning how much and what kind of exposure is needed for learning to happen. In principle, learners in an SA context are no different from learners in other contexts; it is, rather, the environments and the duration of the stay abroad that affect exposure and learners' engagement with that exposure. Pursuing research on the effects of language contact in real-life communicative settings during SA opens the way to new perspectives on how learners negotiate their input. Such an approach by researchers working in an SA context would necessarily constitute a strong contribution to the field of SLA.

Acknowledgments

I would like to thank Jonas Granfeldt, Marianne Gullberg and Martin Howard for inviting me to participate in the COST Action event 'Study Abroad Research in European Perspective', hosted by Mykolas Romeris University, Vilnius, Lithuania, in October 2016, which triggered reflection and discussions about the work presented in the chapter. I would also like to extend a sincere thank you to Martin Howard for his support during the writing of this chapter, and to my two reviewers for their extensive and helpful comments on several versions of this chapter. All errors and omissions are my own.

Notes

(1) Carroll (2001) distinguishes between these concepts, using 'stimulus' to refer to the external linguistic environment and 'input', as well as 'intake', to refer to a mental construct.
(2) The learner-varieties approach also makes use of and builds on aspects of North American interactionist research, such as the work of Gass (1997), Pica (1994) and VanPatten (1996).

(3) It is worth noting that in the psycholinguistic literature, the term 'word' is prob-lematic, as it refers to various types of structures across language systems (Lieven, 2010). For our purposes, we borrow Carroll's (2013) definition of a 'word', that is, a sequence of speech sounds, combined in such a way that the hearer of the word can map meaning to the sound sequence.

(4) Other studies, such as Slobin (1985), have also identified a gradual effect of frequency in language acquisition, implying that frequency in language contact does not follow the simple formula of 'the more the better'.

(5) This research was supported by a grant from the *Programme d'Aide à la Recherche Innovante* (2011–2012), University of Paris 8, St.-Denis, France.

(6) The VILLA project received financial support from the 'Open Research Area in Europe for the Social Sciences': ANR in France, DFG in Germany and NWO in the Netherlands. The UK team received additional support from the British Academy, the Italian team from a PRIN grant and the French team from the *Structures Formelles du Langage* lab (CNRS) and the University of Paris 8.

(7) See Dimroth *et al.* (2013) and Rast (2017) for detailed information about the methodology.

(8) The English native speaker data from the UK were not available at the time of analysis and have not yet been incorporated into the results of the word recognition task.

References

Carroll, S. (2001) *Input and Evidence: The Raw Material of Second Language Acquisition.* Amsterdam: Benjamins.

Carroll, S. (2012) Segmentation on first exposure to an L2: Evidence for knowledge-driven, top-down processing. In K. Braunmüller, C. Gabriel and B. Hänel-Faulhaber (eds) *HSM13 Multilingual Individuals and Multilingual Societies* (pp. 23–45). Amsterdam: Benjamins.

Carroll, S. (2013) Introduction to the special issue: Aspects of word learning on first expo-sure to a second language. *Second Language Research* 29 (2), 131–144.

Carroll, S. (2014) Processing 'words' in early-stage foreign language acquisition: A com-parison of first exposure and low proficiency learners. In Z.-H. Han and R. Rast (eds) *First Exposure to a Second Language: Learners' Initial Input Processing* (pp. 107–138). Cambridge: Cambridge University Press.

Chomsky, N. (1957) *Syntactic Structures.* The Hague: Mouton.

Clark, E. (2009) *First Language Acquisition* (2nd rev. edn). Cambridge: Cambridge Uni-versity Press.

Corder, S.P. (1967) The significance of learners' errors. *International Review of Applied Linguistics* 5 (4), 161–170.

De Bot, K. (2015) Moving where? A reaction to Slabakova et al. (2014). *Applied Linguistics* 36, 261–264.

DeKeyser, R.M. (2010) Monitoring processes in Spanish as a SL during study abroad. *Foreign Language Annals* 43, 80–92.

Dewey, D., Bown, J., Baker, W., Martinsen, R., Gold, C. and Eggett, D. (2014) Language use in six study abroad programs: An exploratory analysis of possible predictors. *Language Learning* 64 (1), 36–71.

Dimroth, C. (2012) Videoclips zur Elizitation von Erzählungen: Methodische Überle-gungen und einige Ergebnisse am Beispiel der 'FiniteStory'. In B. Ahrenholz (ed.) *Einblicke in die Zweitspracherwerbsforschung und ihre methodischen Verfahren* (pp. 77–98). Berlin: Mouton de Gruyter.

Dimroth, C. (2018) Beyond statistical learning: Communication principles and language internal factors shape grammar in child and adult beginners learning Polish through controlled exposure. *Language Learning* 58, 117–150.

Dimroth, C., Gullberg, M., Indefrey, P. and Roberts, L. (2006) The effects of exposure to an unknown L2+. Annual Report. Max Planck Institute for Psycholinguistics, Nijmegen.

Dimroth, C., Rast, R., Starren, M. and Watorek, M. (2013) Methods for studying a new language under controlled input conditions: The VILLA project. *EUROSLA Yearbook* 13, 109–138.

Doughty, C. (1991) Second language instruction does make a difference: Evidence from an empirical study of SL relativization. *Studies in Second Language Acquisition* 13, 431–469.

Doughty, C. and Williams, J. (eds) (1998) *Focus on Form in Classroom Second Language Acquisition*. Cambridge: Cambridge University Press.

Ellis, N.C. (2002) Frequency effects in language processing: A review with implications for theories of implicit and explicit language acquisition. *Studies in Second Language Acquisition* 24, 143–188.

Ellis, N.C. and Collins, L. (2009) Input and second language acquisition: The roles of frequency, form, and function: Introduction to the Special Issue. *The Modern Language Journal* 93, 329–335.

Ellis, N.C. and Wulff, S. (2015) Second language acquisition. In E. Dabrowska and D. Divjak (eds) *Handbook of Cognitive Linguistics* (pp. 409–432). Berlin: Mouton de Gruyter.

Faretta-Stutenberg, M. and Morgan-Short, K. (2018) The interplay of individual differences and context of learning in behavioral and neurocognitive second language development. *Second Language Research* 34 (1), 67–101.

Fernández, J. and Gates Tapia, A. (2017) An appraisal of the Language Contact Profile as a tool to research local engagement in study abroad. *Study Abroad Research in Second Language Acquisition and International Education* 1 (2), 248–276.

Flege, J. (2009) Give input a chance! In T. Piske and M. Young-Scholten (eds) *Input Matters in SLA* (pp. 175–190). Bristol: Multilingual Matters.

Freed, B.F., Dewey, D., Segalowitz, N. and Halter, R. (2004) The language contact profile. *Studies in Second Language Acquisition* 26 (2), 349–356.

García Mayo, M.P. and Rothman, J. (2012) L3 morphosyntax in the generative tradition: The initial stages and beyond. In J. Cabrelli Amaro, S. Flynn and J. Rothman (eds) *Third Language Acquisition in Adulthood* (pp. 9–32). Amsterdam: Benjamins.

Gass, S. (1997) *Input, Interaction, and the Second Language Learner*. Mahwah, NJ: Lawrence Erlbaum Associates.

Gullberg, M., Roberts, L., Dimroth, C., Veroude, K. and Indefrey, P. (2010) Adult language learning after minimal exposure to an unknown natural language. *Language Learning* 60 (Suppl. 2), 5–24.

Gullberg, M., Roberts, L. and Dimroth, C. (2012) What word-level knowledge can adult learners acquire after minimal exposure to a new language? *International Review of Applied Linguistics* 50, 239–276.

Han, Z-H. and Peverly, S. (2007) Input processing: A study of ab initio learners with multilingual backgrounds. *International Journal of Multilingualism* 4 (1), 17–37.

Han, Z-H. and Liu, Z.H. (2013) Input processing of Chinese by ab initio learners. *Second Language Research* 29 (9), 145–164.

Han, Z-H. and Rast, R. (2014) Introduction: First exposure, input processing, and theorizing. In Z.-H. Han and R. Rast (eds) *First Exposure to a Second Language: Learners' Initial Input Processing* (pp. 1–6). Cambridge: Cambridge University Press.

Hernández, T.A. (2016) Short-term study abroad: Perspectives on speaking gains and language contact. *Applied Language Learning* 26 (1), 39–64.

Howard, M. (2011) Lessons from the world of SLA on the impact of learning context in L2 acquisition: Insights from study abroad research. In P. Trévisiol-Okamura and G. Komur-Thilloy (eds) *Discours, Acquisition et Didactique des Langues: Les Termes d'un Dialogue* (pp. 87–101). Paris: Orizons.

Hudson Kam, C.L. (2009) More than words: Adults learn probabilities over categories and relationships between them. *Language Learning and Development: The Official Journal of the Society for Language Development* 5, 115–145.

Indefrey, P. and Gullberg, M. (2010) The early stages of language learning: Introduction. *Language Learning* 60 (Suppl. 2), 1–4.

Kinginger, C. (2008) Language learning in study abroad: Case studies of Americans in France. *The Modern Language Journal* 91, 1–124. Monograph.

Kinginger, C. (2009) *Language Learning and Study Abroad: A Critical Reading of Research*. London: Palgrave Macmillan.

Kinginger, C., Wu, Q., Lee, S.-H. and Tan, D. (2016) The short-term homestay as a context for language learning: Three case studies of high school students and host families. *Study Abroad Research in Second Language Acquisition and International Education* 1 (1), 34–60.

Klein, W. (2012) A way to look at second language acquisition. In M. Watorek, S. Benazzo and M. Hickmann (eds) *Comparative Perspectives to Language Acquisition: Tribute to Clive Perdue* (pp. 23–36). Bristol: Multilingual Matters.

Klein, W. and Perdue, C. (1992) *Utterance Structure: Developing Grammars Again*. Philadelphia, PA: John Benjamins.

Klein, W. and Perdue, C. (1997) The basic variety. Or: Couldn't natural languages be much simpler? *Second Language Research* 13, 301–347.

Larsen-Freeman, D. (2007) Reflecting on the cognitive-social debate in second language acquisition. *The Modern Language Journal* 91, 773–787.

Latos, A. (forthcoming) From input to output: Inflectional morphological features in the oral productions of initial L2 learners exposed to Meaning-based vs. Form-based input. In M. Watorek, A. Arslangul and R. Rast (eds) *Premières Etapes dans l'Acquisition des Langues Etrangères: Dialogue entre Acquisition et Didactique des Langues*. Paris: Presses de l'Inalco.

Li, P., Sepanski, S. and Zhao, X. (2006) Language history questionnaire: A web-based interface for bilingual research. *Behavior Research Methods* 38 (2), 202–210.

Lieven, E. (2010) Language development in a cross-linguistic context. In M. Kail and M. Hickmann (eds) *Language Acquisition across Linguistic and Cognitive Systems* (pp. 91–108). Amsterdam: Benjamins.

Long, M. (1983) Does second language instruction make a difference: A review of the research. *TESOL Quarterly* 15, 359–382.

MacWhinney, B. (2000) *The CHILDES Project: Tools for Analyzing Talk*. Mahwah, NJ: Lawrence Erlbaum Associates.

Meara, P. (2009) Preface. In B. Richards, M. Daller, D. Malvern, P. Meara, J. Milton and J. Treffers-Daller (eds) *Vocabulary Studies in First and Second Language Acquisition: The Interface Between Theory and Application* (pp. xii–xiv). Basingstoke: Palgrave Macmillan.

Mitchell, R., Tracy-Ventura, N. and McManus, K. (2017) *Anglophone Students Abroad. Identity, Social Relationships and Language Learning*. London: Routledge.

Nation, I.S.P. (1990) *Teaching and Learning Vocabulary*. Boston, MA: Heinle and Heinle.

Paquot, M. and S.Th. Gries (eds) (2019) *The Practical Handbook of Corpus Linguistics*. Berlin: Springer.

Park, E.S. (2011) Learner-generated noticing of written L2 input: What do they notice and why? *Language Learning* 61, 146–186.

Pekarek Doehler, S. (2000) Approches interactionnistes de l'acquisition des langues étrangères: Concepts, recherches perspectives. *Acquisition et Interaction en Langue Étrangère* 12, 3–26.

Perdue, C. (ed.) (1993) *Adult Language Acquisition: Cross-Linguistic Perspectives* (Vol. I and II). Cambridge: Cambridge University Press.

Pérez-Vidal, C. (ed.) (2014) *Language Acquisition in Study Abroad and Formal Instruction Contexts*. Amsterdam: John Benjamins.

Pica, T. (1991) Input as a theoretical and research construct: From Corder's original definition to current views. *International Review of Applied Linguistics* 29 (3), 185–196.

Pica, T. (1994) Research on negotiation: What does it reveal about second language learning conditions, processes and outcomes? *Language Learning* 44, 493–527.

Piske, T. and Young-Scholten, M. (eds) (2009) *Input Matters in SLA*. Bristol: Multilingual Matters.

Rankin, T. and Unsworth, S. (2016) Beyond poverty: Engaging with input in generative SLA. *Second Language Research* 32, 563–572.

Rast, R. (2006) Le premier contact avec une nouvelle langue étrangère: Comment s'acquitter d'une tâche de compréhension? *Acquisition et Interaction en Langue Étrangère* 24, 119–147.

Rast, R. (2008) *Foreign Language Input: Initial Processing*. Clevedon: Multilingual Matters.

Rast, R. (2010) The use of prior linguistic knowledge in the early stages of L3 acquisition. *International Review of Applied Linguistics in Language Teaching* 48 (2/3), 159–183.

Rast, R. (2017) Foreign language learning and teaching: From first exposure to first productions. Unpublished manuscript. 'Habilitation à Diriger des Recherches', L'Université Grenoble Alpes, France.

Rast, R. and Dommergues, J.-Y. (2003) Towards a characterisation of saliency on first exposure to a second language. In S. Foster-Cohen and S. Pekarek Doehler (eds) *EUROSLA Yearbook 3* (pp. 131–156). Amsterdam: John Benjamins.

Ristin-Kaufmann, N. and Gullberg, M. (2014) The effects of first exposure to an unknown language at different ages. *Bulletin Suisse de Linguistique Appliquée* 99, 17–29.

Saffran, J.R., Newport, E.L. and Aslin, R.N. (1996) Word segmentation: The role of distributional cues. *Journal of Memory and Language* 35, 606–621.

Saturno, J. (2015) Copular structures in Polish L2. *Linguistica e Filologia* 35, 69–98.

Schwartz, B. and Sprouse, R. (1996) L2 cognitive states and the Full Transfer/Full Access model. *Second Language Research* 12 (1), 40–72.

Segalowitz, N. and Freed, B. (2004) Context, contact, and cognition in oral fluency acquisition: Learning Spanish in At Home and Study Abroad contexts. *Studies in Second Language Acquisition* 26, 173–199.

Sharwood Smith, M. (1993) Input enhancement in instructed SLA: Theoretical bases. *Studies in Second Language Acquisition* 15, 165–180.

Sharwood Smith, M. (2014) Possibilities and limitations of enhancing language input: A MOGUL perspective. In A. Benati, C. Laval and M. Arche (eds) *The Grammar Dimension in Instructed Second Language Learning* (pp. 36–57). London: Bloomsbury.

Shoemaker, E. and Rast, R. (2013) Extracting words from the speech stream at first exposure. *Second Language Research* 29 (2), 165–183.

Slobin, D.I. (1985) Crosslinguistic evidence for the language-making capacity. In D.I. Slobin (ed.) *The Crosslinguistic Study of Language Acquisition: Vol. 2, Theoretical Issues* (pp. 1157–1256). Hillsdale, NJ: Lawrence Erlbaum Associates.

Tarone, E. (2007) Sociolinguistic approaches to second language acquisition research – 1997–2007. *The Modern Language Journal* 91, 837–848.

Tomasello, M. (2003) *Constructing a Language. A Usage-Based Theory of Language Acquisition*. Cambridge MA: Harvard University Press.

Valentini, A. and Grassi, R. (2016) Oltre la frequenza: l'impatto di trasparenza e accento sullo sviluppo lessicale in L2. In L. Corrà (ed.) *Sviluppo della Competenza Lessicale: Acquisizione, Apprendimento, Insegnamento* (pp. 125–143). Rome: Aracne.

van Bergen, G., Rast, R. and Shoemaker, E. (2014) Recognizing lexical forms in the speech stream at first exposure. Paper presented at The European Second Language Association (EUROSLA) Conference 24, York, UK, 4 September.

VanPatten, B. (1996) *Input Processing and Grammar Instruction: Theory and Research*. Norwood, NJ: Ablex.

Wilkinson, S. (1998) On the nature of immersion during Study Abroad: Some participant perspectives. *Frontiers: The Interdisciplinary Journal of Study Abroad* 4, 121–138.

Zwitserlood, P., Klein, W., Liang, J., Perdue, C., Kellerman, E. and Wenk, B. (1994/2000) The first minutes of foreign-language exposure. Unpublished manuscript, Max-Planck-Institute for Psycholinguistics, Nijmegen.

9 Understanding Socialisation and Integration through Social Network Analysis: American and Chinese Students during a Stay Abroad

Rozenn Gautier

Social Network Analysis

The concept of social network has gained in popularity over recent years with the advent of social media such as Facebook and Twitter. However, as Mercklé (2014) explains, social networks were born long before the internet emerged. 'Their existence could in fact be said to be as old as humanity itself: from the moment there are interconnections between individuals and between social entities, there are social networks' (Mercklé, 2014: 191). A social network could therefore be defined simply as a set of social relations maintained by an individual.

An analysis of social networks has traditionally been characterised by two research paradigms (Eve, 2002). The first, considered the dominant paradigm, is the analysis of complete networks (often called social network analysis [SNA]). The second analyses personal networks (or ego-centric networks) and derives from the work of the Manchester School. These two types of analysis use different research methods and pursue different objectives. 'Modern SNA seeks to provide an overall transcription of social data in the form of networks, while in the Manchester School the emphasis is on exploring personal relationships, in a specific sense, that of face-to-face relations [...]' (Eve, 2002: 191).

For Wasserman and Faust (1994), the analysis of social networks as we know it today would not have been possible without Moreno's (1934) work. This researcher initiated the field of study of sociometry (or the measurement of interpersonal relationships in small groups). Moreno developed a method for analysing and visualising the structure of groups, called the sociogram. The analysis of social networks then became increasingly formalised. As Carrington (2014) explains, over time, the analysis of social networks has used an increasing number of techniques borrowed from mathematics. In this way, the language of graphs has developed to become one of the main tools in SNA. A graph is a diagram in which individuals are designated by 'vertices' (or nodes) and are represented by points. The relations between individuals are called 'edges' (or links/lines). Individuals and their relationships are then conceptualised in the form of a matrix in which each row corresponds to a vertex of the graph as well as each column (the rows and columns of the matrix are presented in the same order). In this matrix (called an adjacency matrix), the intersection of a row and a column produces either 0 (when there is no relation between the two vertices) or 1 (in the case of a relationship).[1] Through these matrix analyses and associated matrix calculations, SNA can be applied to a multitude of domains. Two well-known properties used in this kind of analysis are the cohesion and the shape of the network (Borgatti *et al.*, 2009). Cohesion refers to the interconnection of the network according to measures such as density. As for the shape of the network, this indicates areas that are more strongly interconnected or actors that play an important role – measured, for example, by their centrality.

The research presented here focuses on personal network analysis, an approach inherited from Bott (1957) and the Manchester School (Barnes, 1954; Mitchell, 1969), which has now been taken further by other researchers such as Bidart *et al.* (2011). This type of study is concerned with the concept of sociability, which can be defined as all the actual relationships that connect a person to others by interpersonal links (Bidart, 1988). Furthermore, researchers are interested in the socialisation that is seen as the process by which an individual develops interpersonal links with others (Bidart, 2012). Analysis in terms of personal network is concerned with a specific individual (Ego) and relations with the people around him/her (Alter). Such studies not only examine network size and composition but also use certain structural indices (such as density or centrality) specific to the mathematical analysis of adjacency matrices. One aim of personal network analysis is to understand how the structure and composition of interpersonal relationships can influence the behaviour of individuals and vice versa.

Social Networks in a Foreign Community

The experience of individuals who have crossed borders to settle temporarily or permanently in another country has been reported by various authors. Whether it is the experience of the year abroad among European students (de Federico de la Rúa, 2008; Murphy-Lejeune, 2003; Papatsiba, 2003) or other international students (Calinon, 2009; Carnine, 2014; Thamin, 2008; Verdi Rademacher, 2014), living in a foreign community requires adaptation and learning new things. Moving abroad implies a change and requires adapting to a new social system, with all the consequences this can have on an individual. This relational mobility does not necessarily mean having to start the process of sociability from nothing. First, students abroad or migrants have already set up a network in their country of origin and they are by no means novices when it comes to socialisation. Second, they may never completely abandon old friendships or family ties and often continue to maintain them during their experience of mobility (Verdi Rademacher, 2014).

Nevertheless, social integration in a new environment is not immediately guaranteed and the socialisation process involves several stages. During their first contact with the foreign community, students abroad or migrants enter a relational vacuum. In a context of mobility, the way students engage in new social networks can therefore be an interesting indicator of the degree to which they have adapted or integrated. How do they confront the social isolation in which they are initially immersed and how do they weave their social networks in the foreign community? What influences do these personal relationships have on how they adapt to the host country and on different aspects of their development?

Different authors have addressed some of these issues from a variety of perspectives. Murphy-Lejeune (2003) took an anthropological approach as she studied European students' adaptation in a context of mobility. She identified several factors influencing their experiences such as age, level of second language (L2) proficiency, mobility capital, motives, expectations and social activities. Her results showed that these different aspects shape students' experiences of mobility. For some it will be a meaningful experience, for others it will remain a sort of 'non-event' in which the adaptation process has not been activated.

Studies on the sociability of people living in a foreign community have shown that individuals develop differentiated social networks in terms of both structure and composition (Brandes *et al.*, 2008; Carnine, 2014; Lubbers *et al.*, 2010; Verdi Rademacher, 2014). Carnine (2014) analysed the mobility of young French, American and Chinese people in an international context. Her analysis of the compositional aspects of students' personal networks in the context of mobility identified different profiles of adaptation to the host country, linked to different degrees of national identification. Other studies (Brandes *et al.*, 2008; Lubbers *et al.*, 2010) have described migrants' social networks in both qualitative and quantitative terms and reconciled the different dimensions that make up social relations by describing the structure and composition of social networks. These studies are concerned with how social structure is created in a host community in the specific context of migration. In line with this, Martínez García *et al.* (2002) demonstrated that when migrant women in Spain are integrated into networks including more people from the host community, this reduces the risk of a nervous breakdown. Similarly, Doucerain *et al.* (2015) found statistically significant relationships between personal networks and cultural difficulties or acculturation stress. The authors revealed that the larger the size, interconnection and density of personal networks with L2 speakers, the lower the cultural difficulties and acculturation stress observed.

Social Networks in a Study Abroad Context

A range of resources can be conveyed by the structure of personal networks. In order to build a more complete picture of learners' socialisation during study abroad (SA), a number of researchers on L2 acquisition have turned to SNA. Studies on the impact of social networks on acquisition and language use were first popularised by Milroy (1987, 2002). She demonstrated that differences in the structure and nature of social networks directly influence individuals and have an impact on their language practices. She defines the strength of a social network in terms of density and multiplexity. On the one hand, individuals can have multiplex links, which means that they are linked to members of their network in various areas of sociability (the individuals frequented are all at once their friends, co-workers and/or neighbours). And on the other hand, individuals can maintain dense ties in their communities, which implies that the people in their networks know each other. A multiplex and dense network is therefore an indicator of strong social integration.

In the SA context, studies focusing on social networks are relatively rare. Studies in this line (de Bot & Stoessel, 2002; Lybeck, 2002; Wiklund, 2002) have mainly focused on qualitative research, documenting frequency, intensity, multiplexity and/or durability of social interactions and relating them to language use and development. More recently, quantitative research investigating the social networks of learners during SA has also been conducted (Dewey *et al.*, 2013). However, in these different studies, contacts and interactions in the L2 are mainly addressed using retrospective approaches such as questionnaires. As explained by Kinginger (2010) and McManus *et al.* (2014), questionnaire methods involve making generalisations about L2 contacts for the whole stay abroad (often between 10 and 15 weeks). Learners are asked to quantify their contacts after the event, at the end of their stay. The reliability of the details provided therefore remains difficult to assess. These studies generally rely on a single questionnaire to define learners' sociability and to link this to acquisition. Such studies could therefore be improved upon by analysing sociability with multiple data collection tools, thereby allowing data to be triangulated. Moreover, such research observes learners' social networks at one particular point in their stay abroad and over a relatively short period (approximately one semester). To date, there is little longitudinal research on social network development during SA. Furthermore, SNA during SA has been mostly conducted through small-scale case studies (Gautier & Chevrot, 2015; Isabelli-García, 2006) and has mainly investigated American students abroad. Several authors have stressed the importance of broadening the field of knowledge on SA by observing the experiences of diverse national learners (Howard *et al.*, 2013; Kinginger, 2008).

In the research outlined in this chapter, the decision was made to use the concept of social network and its methods of data collection and analysis. Indeed, the tools developed in sociology offer the possibility for fine-grained observation and analysis of social relations. The aim of this study was to demonstrate that social networks developed in an SA context may present contrasting structures and that it is possible to highlight a typology of networks. Moreover, by offering a more precise picture of personal relationships and their dynamics during SA, the focus was also placed on tracing the causes of the development of different types of personal networks over time.

Two sets of questions are the focus of this chapter:

(1) What are the personal network patterns of American and Chinese SA students who travelled to France for a year? And how can structural, compositional and interactional variables highlight contrasting personal network patterns?
(2) What can the different types of personal networks reveal about the experiences abroad?

In this sense, I opted for a longitudinal approach allowing social developments to be monitored over time. My analysis combines qualitative methods with quantitative and structural methods. Certain parts of this analysis are quantified, allowing the use of a 'mixed' method as described by Bidart and Cacciuttolo (2012). This provides detailed elements for analysing personal networks by tracing, in particular, their causes.

Methodology

Participants

The study participants were 29 French foreign language learners, spending two semesters at a university in France. They attended the same course in a university language centre. They had 14–16 hours of French classes per week, including a language and a literature/culture component. The participants' mean age was 21.6 (range: 18–25 years). Half of the students (14) came from the USA (all native English speakers) and the other half (15) were from China (all native Mandarin speakers).

At the beginning of the course, the students' proficiency in French varied slightly; about three quarters of the students were placed at B1 level (intermediate speakers) and the other quarter were placed at B2 level (upper-intermediate speakers) on the Common European Framework of Reference for Languages (CEFR).[2] Three of the learners who were originally placed at B2 level during the first semester advanced to a C1-level class during the second semester.

Procedure

Data for this longitudinal study were collected over a period of nine months, with three major data collection points scheduled in September (Time 1 [T1]), January (Time 2 [T2]) and May (Time 3 [T3]). On each occasion, the learners were met twice and each observation period followed the same process. First, a semi-directed interview was conducted in French, for approximately one hour. Each interview was audio-recorded. Then, the students were given a logbook they had to fill in for the next week. At the end of that week, interviews were conducted with the students about their personal networks. All the interviews were conducted in French on a one-to-one basis between each participant and a French native speaker.

Instruments

Two types of data were used to look into the participants' sociability over the SA period.

A one-week logbook

To get a picture of each participant's personal network, first, a logbook was used as a name generator. As the sociologists Degenne and Forsé (2004) have explained, the choice of name generator depends on the underlying research question. This study aimed to provide a broad view of the participants' sociability and of the different relationships that could be established in the particular context of SA. A name generator was therefore chosen that allowed the closest approach to capture the learners' sociability as experienced on a day-to-day basis. A logbook approach is more natural and less intrusive than direct observation (Fu, 2007) and therefore seemed appropriate. Moreover, as Degenne and Forsé (2004: 25) explain, 'the use of a logbook affords an interesting methodological aspect. It presents a definite advantage over statements that are not based on any physical aid: it can minimise both the distortions of memory and any retrospective rationalisation by participants'.

The participants had to fill in the logbook every day for one week. The question of how long learners are asked to keep a logbook is a sensitive issue. Too short a period could lead to the logbook being insufficiently representative, but over too long a period, the participants could get bored and lose motivation or even give up. In previous surveys using logbooks, the time frame has ranged from 1 week to 100 days (for a review of various logbook studies, see Degenne and Forsé [2004] and Fu [2007]). For this study, the week-long period was agreed upon for two main reasons. First, the logbook could potentially take between 20 and 40 minutes to fill out per day (Fu, 2007), which translates to approximately 2.5–5 hours per week. This seemed to be a reasonable time commitment to ask of the students. Second, other significant studies have also used week-long logbooks to study personal networks (Blanpain & Pan Ké Shon, 1998; Héran, 1988) and produced interesting results within this time frame.

Instructions on how to fill in the log were given orally and a written reminder was present on the front page of the logbook. Learners were asked to keep a record of all face-to-face conversations and phone (or Skype) conversations that they had during the day. The logbook included tables to be completed on each page with the following information: conversation, first name(s) of interlocutor(s), duration, place and language. Learners were requested to fill in the logbook at regular intervals during the day, rather than at one time. This instruction was given by pointing out that the ideal way to fill out the logbook was just after an interaction. Learners were asked not to complete the logbook when they were in class, because the focus of this study was on the interactions that took place outside the classroom in their daily lives. The logbooks were given to the learners at the end of the first meeting in each observation period. Learners were also asked to be as rigorous and accurate as possible when completing the logbook and an initial reading of the data suggests that they followed this instruction. The number of conversations recorded per day for all learners varied from 0 to 57, with an average of 8. This average number of conversations remained relatively constant for each of the three time points (T1: 8.79; T2: 8.39; T3: 7.60) with a slight decrease at T3. The relative stability of the average number of conversations seems to confirm that the students were conscientious in keeping the logbooks in a regular manner.

Following the logbook-keeping week, interviews about personal networks were conducted using the following methodological approach.

Interviews on personal networks and social practices

The duration of the interviews depended on the number of people present in each learner's personal network, but varied from 30 minutes to 1.5 hours. A computer aid was used to guide these interviews, where all the information provided by the learners was recorded. As an initial step, I listed all the people mentioned in the logbook. Then, a series of questions was asked of each individual, which can be summarised as follows.

- Personal characteristics: Age, sex, language used and nationality.
- Location of the relationship: In the host country or in the country of origin.
- Type of relationship: Family, friend, acquaintance, etc.
- How often they saw that person on a 6-point scale, ranging from every day to never. I specified that they had to provide a general frequency for the immediate period.
- Type of activities they shared with that person.
- How long they had known each other.
- People they knew in common. I specified that these should be people who also saw each other without the learner present, in order to narrow down the question and limit the number of individuals listed.

The data extracted from the logbooks and the interviews on personal networks were also supplemented by interviews on social practices that took place prior to the logbook. The objective of these interviews was twofold: providing extensive linguistic material that could then be used to assess the students' progress in French language use, and gathering general impressions of their social practices during their stay in France with a view to a more qualitative approach. For the purpose of this chapter, the analysis will focus only on the social aspects in question. The interviews focused on the learners' accommodation, their daily life, their leisure, their work and their adaptation as well as their friendships and the personal ties they built up in France. Qualitative analysis of the interviews has been chosen here, with the main aim of understanding the students' sociability and how their personal networks were formed.

Analysis

Cluster analysis was used to analyse the personal networks in this study. This multidimensional and descriptive method of analysis consists of grouping objects in such a way that objects in the same cluster are similar with regard to a set of variables characterising the objects. Cluster analysis is therefore a particularly relevant method for interpreting data defined by a large number of variables. For network analysis, certain fundamental elements are involved in observing and comparing the composition of personal networks (Wellman, 2007). The following section outlines the indices used to define the networks in question. The structural and composition variables have been selected by following other work that has been done on social network typologies (Bidart *et al.*, 2011; Brandes *et al.*, 2010; Lubbers *et al.*, 2007).

Structural aspects

This research draws on the sort of mathematical analysis of social networks usually conducted in sociology. In order to establish the structure of the network, many network analysts, and much of the software for manipulating networks, use adjacency matrices. These matrices are used to calculate structural indices such as density and measures of centrality.

- Size and number of ties: An essential criterion is the size of the Ego network, i.e. the total number of Alter cited by Ego. The number of links between the Alter is also a basic indicator of how Alter are connected within the social network.
- Density: The simplest structural parameter is density. It represents the proportion of existing relationships to the number of possible relationships across the network. In a non-directed network, the number of possible links corresponds to $n(n-1)/2$ (with n corresponding to the number of points of the network, i.e. to the number of Alter). For example, in a network comprising 10 Alter, the number of possible links between Alter is 45. If there are 25 links existing in the network, the network density will be 0.55. Density is generally expressed as a proportion, that is to say, 55% in this example. The higher the density, the stronger the cohesion within the Alter' networks.
- Measures of centrality: Centrality is defined by several measures that are complementary to density. In SNA, researchers have observed that some Alter play a 'more important' role than others. Some people may have many contacts within the network while others have very few. Centrality creates the link between the general structure of the network and the specific position of each of its members (Degenne & Forsé, 2004). In this analysis, the most commonly used centrality measures have been taken into account (Bidart *et al.*, 2011; Borgatti *et al.*, 2013), namely betweenness (Freeman, 1979), closeness (Freeman, 1979) and eigenvector centrality (Bonacich, 1972). I will return to the specificities of each of these measures when analysing the results. Density and measures of centrality were calculated using Ucinet software (Borgatti *et al.*, 2002).
- Isolates: When an Alter is not connected to any other network member. This indicator makes it possible to determine whether the network is more or less interconnected.

Compositional aspects

Following Brandes *et al.* (2008) and Lubbers *et al.* (2010), four classes of network members were distinguished based on types of international relations. 'Originals' are members of the network who are from the same country as Ego and live in the country of origin. 'National peers' come from the same country as Ego but live in France. 'Hosts' come from and live in France. 'Transnationals' come from other countries and live in France.

- For each class of network members, the percentage of Alter present in the network was calculated.
- Strength of ties is based on the frequency of interaction, the number of shared activities and the length of the relationship.

Interactional aspects

The two indicators taken into account were the language mostly used in conversations between Ego and his/her Alter and the amount of interaction time reported in the logbook.

Results: Five Different Types of Personal Networks

As explained by Bidart *et al.* (2018), a typology is a way of comparing networks in a systematic manner. In order to explore the characteristics of the networks and compare them in an inductive and systematic way, we used cluster analysis. By looking at all the networks at each of the longitudinal time points, i.e. 29 networks at each observation time (three), giving rise to 87 learner datasets, the cluster analysis led us to adopt five types of network: dense, extended, concentrated, dissociated and eclectic.

- A dense network is highly connected, with high density and is made up of a high number of national peers.
- An extended network has a high number of connections and links but a looser interconnectedness than the dense network.
- A concentrated network has a high betweenness centrality index revealing the presence of some central Alters connected to most of the others.
- A dissociated network refers to networks in which structural indicators are very low, meaning there are separate parts in the network.
- An eclectic network reveals networks with average values on the structural aspects. This type of network is better defined by its composition and interactional values, which are oriented towards L2 speakers.

Before providing more detailed analysis of the different personal networks, Table 9.1 provides a summary of the number of learners present in each network at each data collection point, indicating their nationality and overall level of proficiency in French.

Table 9.1 shows that each type of network was fairly well represented at all three points in time. It also highlights a fairly clear distinction in the socialisation of learners according to their country of origin. Indeed, the dense network was exclusively made up of American learners and the concentrated network only comprised Chinese learners. Two other types, the extended and dissociated networks, had a majority of one of the two nationalities. The extended network was mainly composed of American learners and the dissociated network was largely made up of Chinese

Table 9.1 Number of students in each network according to their level of proficiency and nationality

Network types / Nationality	Level of proficiency	No. learners T1		No. learners T2		No. learners T3		Total
		Am	Ch	Am	Ch	Am	Ch	
Dense	B1	10	–	4	–	2	–	16
Extended	B1/B2	1	–	5	3	8	3	20
Concentrated	B2	–	4	–	4	–	5	13
Dissociated	B1/B2/C1	1	8	1	6	–	7	23
Eclectic	B2/C1	2	3	4	2	4	–	15

learners. The eclectic type had a mixed population in terms of nationality at T1 and T2 and only included Americans at T3. Level of French proficiency seems to have had a less obvious impact. The dense network appeared to be more representative of learners with a relatively low level of French language (B1), while learners with a relatively high level (B2/C1) had eclectic networks. Finally, there were also disparities in the representation of learners at each time. Thus, the dense network comprised a large number of students at T1 (10) and this figure declined considerably at T2 (4) and T3 (2). Conversely, in the extended network, there was only one learner at T1 whereas this number increased at T2 (8) and T3 (11). In the other three types of networks (concentrated, dissociated and eclectic), there were some fluctuations between time points but they were less striking.

A presentation of the five types of network now follows with examples of personal network graphs as illustrations. In the illustrations, Ego network members are represented, with each square representing a member of the network and each line representing a link between two network members. Ego is not represented in the illustrations as he/she is connected to every member and it would therefore make the figure difficult to read. In order to define the learners' sociability, I relied on the indicators that present the strongest or weakest values of all the networks. In the next section, the presentation of the networks will be illustrated by a graph representing one of the learners (selected as an example). Furthermore, each of the quantitative characteristics of the networks will be illustrated by comments made by the learners who developed the same type of network.

Dense networks: The importance of a peer group

Of the 14 Americans in this study, ten had a dense network at T1, but only four retained this type of network at T2 and two at T3. These networks were therefore representative of the beginning of their stay. These American students were all living with a French host family during their time in France.

The dense networks (see Figure 9.1 for an example of a learner graph) had a strong relationship structure with high density, closeness centrality and eigenvector centrality. These three indicators together indicate that interconnection was important, that the paths between members of the network were short and that almost all individuals knew each other. These networks were made up of a significant proportion of national peers and just under a third of their members were hosts. They contained a low proportion of transnationals. The members of the network were new acquaintances since Ego had known them for a short time but saw them frequently. A particularly remarkable aspect of their interactions was that they very often mixed first language (L1) and L2 in the same conversation. The proportion of L1 speakers was higher than that of L2 and consequently their time speaking in the L1 was greater than in the L2.

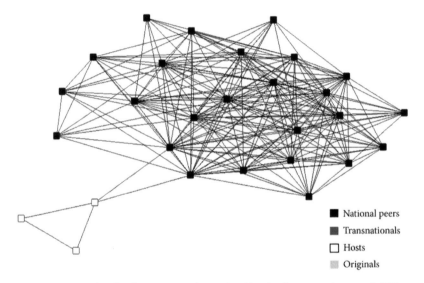

■ National peers
▨ Transnationals
☐ Hosts
▨ Originals

Figure 9.1 Example of a dense network graph – Heather's personal network (T1)

Dense networks: Main motive of the stay abroad and level of proficiency in French

In this type of network, learners often reported some detachment about their stay in France, referring to it as a one-year vacation. Some described the trip as a transition in their lives, allowing them to pause the frantic pace they were experiencing in the USA.

> *Ici c'est comme mes vacances pour tout l'année. Oh oui j'aime beaucoup! Parce que c'est seulement je dois aller seulement au université, c'est tout!*

> This is like being on vacation all year long. Oh, yes, I like it a lot! Because all I have to do is go to university, that's all! (Samantha, T1)[3]

The learners in this type of network had a relatively low level of French compared to the learners in the other networks (this type of network only included learners with level B1 French). Many reported having difficulties with the French language, causing some problems with oral comprehension and expression. For example, in the first interview, Jeff reported what he had understood about his host family's jobs as follows:

> *Ils sont retraités euh mais de temps en temps mon père il aidé ses amis qui travaillent encore. Il fait beaucoup je sais pas euh il y a un semaine il est au sud de France parce qu'il y a un opéra? Et son ami veut qu'il vient et il t'aider? il s'aider? Je comprends pas. Oui ma mère elle est allée au Lyon parce que son ami also euh aussi veut qu'elle vienne là aide elle euh je sais pas qu'elle fait mais elle travaille dans une bureau il y a huit ans elle travaille une bureau je sais pas que elle fait mais elle est allée au Lyon.*

They're retired, er, but from time to time, the father helps his friends who still work. He does a lot, I dunno, er, a week ago, he was in the South of France because there was an opera? And his friend wanted him to come and help? I don't understand. Yeah, the mother, she went to Lyon because her friend, well, wanted her to come and help there too, she, er, I dunno what she does, but she works in an office, she's worked in an office for eight years, I dunno what she does, but she went to Lyon. (Jeff, T1)

Dense networks: Few transnational Alter and a peer group of fellow nationals

Another aspect of this type of network is the low proportion of transnational Alter (people from a foreign country other than their own) compared to other networks. Dense networks included, on average, 7% transnational Alter. The average for the other networks varied between 15.5% and 37%. This low proportion can be explained by the pervasiveness of American students in a very dense group. Emily, who still had a dense network at T2, explained why she preferred relations with American friends as follows:

> *Tous les amis est des États-Unis parce que nous nous avons euh oui nous avons beaucoup les choses similaires c'est facile de avoir amis de États-Unis. Oui c'est facile de faire les relations avec eux. Oui, mais les autres euh Chinois Japonais Ukrainiens euh oui. C'est différent parce que je ne sais pas qu'est ce qui se passe dans le pays.*

All my friends are from the United States because we've got, er, yeah, we've got lots of things in common, it's easy to have friends from the United States. Yeah, it's easy to make the connections with them. Yeah, but the others, like Chinese, Japanese, Ukrainian, er, yeah. It's different because I don't know what things are like in their country. (Emily, T2)

Extended networks: The importance of diverse relationships and experiences

The learners with an extended network were predominantly American (six Chinese learners had this type of network out of the 20 extended networks). These networks were mainly found at T2 and T3.

The extended networks were characterised by a high number of links and members. The eigenvector centrality was low, indicating that the individuals strongly connected to the other members of the network had few connections with one another. The network structure was fairly loose with a large number of isolated Alter and a low closeness centrality, meaning that the paths between individuals were long. In terms of composition, Ego was related to a significant proportion of national peers and the proportions of the other three types of members were relatively balanced. More than half of the speakers of these networks spoke L1 with Ego; the conversation time in this language was particularly high. However, the average speaking time in the L2 was also relatively high. The learners in these networks had a large number of Alter, such that their speaking time was considerable in both languages (Figure 9.2).

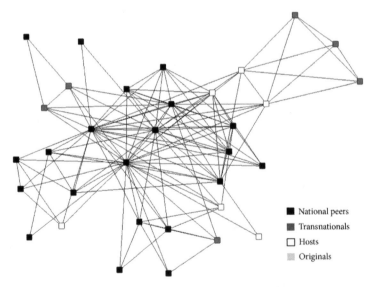

Legend:
- ■ National peers
- ■ Transnationals
- □ Hosts
- ▨ Originals

Figure 9.2 Example of an extended network graph – Kristen's personal network (T3)

The majority of learners in this type of network came to France through an American exchange programme, which often creates strong cohesion between students especially in the early days of their stay. In the second observation phase of this study, the American students who had come to France for only one semester left and new students arrived for the second semester. This tends to be the point at which learners break away from the group of Americans to create other relationships. This was the case for Samantha who referred to American exchange students from the first semester as 'the old groups'.

> *Je connais plus de Français maintenant que les autres groupes, les vieux groupes de notre programme sont partis. Il y a des nouveaux mais mon but c'est de connaitre plusieurs Français et ne parle pas beaucoup avec les Américains parce que je veux améliorer mon français et apprendre plus de la culture français, ce qu'ils font et tout ça.*

> I know more French now than the other groups, the old groups from our programme have left. There are new ones, but my aim is to get to know lots of French people and not to talk much with the Americans because I want to improve my French and learn more about French culture, what they do, and all that. (Samantha, T2)

In this type of network, the connections were quite strong between the Alter, although the density was lower than in the dense networks as the number of links between members in the network was high. Rather than the notion of a reference group, which is characteristic of the dense network, here there was an extensive network of connections. The Alter from different spaces mixed together and the idea that 'my friends' friends are my friends' seemed particularly important. Kristen, for example, felt confident with a small group of friends who then introduced her to other friends. Like most Americans present in this network, she wanted to free herself as much as possible from the American group.

> *C'est un groupe et c'est plus facile pour moi et quelque fois il fait des amis et il fait euh ils font des amis et je peux euh faire des amis comme ça. Ils savent que nous pouvons aller où il n'y a pas beaucoup des Américains et des choses comme ça.*

> It's a group and it's easier for me and sometimes they make friends, er, they make friends, and, er, I can make friends like that. They know places we can go where there aren't many Americans and stuff like that. (Kristen, T3)

In this way, Ego meets the friends of his/her friends and expands his/her network, for example in the case of Melis who explained that she first met a French friend who then introduced her to her friends:

> *En fait j'ai rencontre avec une amie française qui me présenter à ses amies et ça c'est comment je fais des amies françaises. C'est pas facile de rencontrer avec des Français s'il y a un grand groupe d'Américains.*

> Actually, I made a French friend who introduces me to her friends and that's how I make French friends. It is not easy to meet French people if you're in a big group of Americans. (Melis, T3)

Concentrated networks: The importance of a few strong, central relationships

This type of network was representative only of the sociability of Chinese learners. Four learners retained this type of network at all three time points, while one learner had this type of network only at T3.

The concentrated networks were small in size with few links between members. Centrality was high. On the one hand, betweenness centrality was the strongest in these networks among all the others. This indicates that some individuals were central to the network and that they built bridges between individuals. On the other hand, given the small size of the network, closeness and eigenvector centralities also presented high values. This can be explained by the fact that centrality was focused on certain individuals. The proportion of national peers was very high. The frequency of exchanges was low but the number of shared activities was substantial and the members of the network had been known for a long time. The learners communicated in their L1 a lot and the network comprised a high proportion of speakers of this language. The proportion of L2 speakers was low and the conversation time in French was the lowest among all the networks (Figure 9.3).

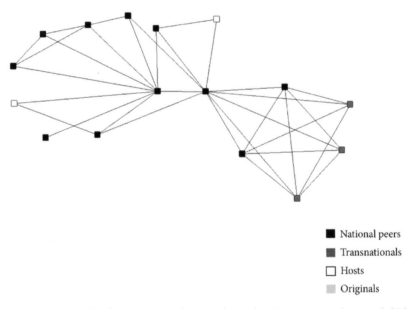

■ National peers
■ Transnationals
□ Hosts
▨ Originals

Figure 9.3 Example of a concentrated network graph – Wen's personal network (T1)

Concentrated networks: Central relationships

In the concentrated networks, Ego gave great importance to some Alter with whom she/he spent more time and/or with whom she/he had a longer-standing relationship. For example, Wen was very close to a friend who arrived in France at the same time. They attended the same university in China before coming, lived in the same residence during their stay and spent a lot of time together. This was also the case for Yaxin at T3, whose relationships were focused around a particular friend. She explained that it was easier for her to share her experience in France with an Alter from China.

> *Elle est fille, elle est chinoise, elle est comme moi on a même expérience. On a beaucoup de choses en commun.*

> She's a girl, she's Chinese, she's like me, we share the same experiences. We have a lot in common. (Yaxin, T3)

The central person could also be a boyfriend, as was the case for Shuyang and Huiyan. They both had Chinese boyfriends whom they met during their stay and who became an important member of their network. They spent a considerable amount of time with their boyfriends and had several relations in common with them, making them central in their respective networks. Shuyang's boyfriend was so important to her that when asked why she was staying in France, she cited him as the primary reason:

> *Je pense que c'est mon copain parce que euh il travaille ici et euh on s'entend bien et euh on s'aime bien on s'aime beaucoup et donc euh je pense que c'est ça euh c'est un raison pour moi de rester en France.*

> I think it's my boyfriend because, er, he works here and we met months ago and, er, we get on well and, er, we like each other a lot, we love each other a lot, and so, er, I think it's that, er, that's a reason for me to stay in France. (Shuyang, T3)

Concentrated networks: Main motive of the stay abroad

The activities of learners in this type of network were very much oriented towards their academic work and their progress in French.

> *Tous les jours je dois aller au CUEF pour étudier et après je rentrer chez moi étudier et la vie euh il n'y a pas des choses spéciales euh arrive.*

> Every day, I have to go to the CUEF to study and after that, I go home to study, and [as for] life, well, nothing special has really, er, happened. (Wen, T2)

They were in France to obtain a qualification and wanted to do everything possible to achieve this goal. Sociability, especially meeting French speakers, therefore seemed a little secondary to them at first. They explained their low level of contact with French by the fact they spent time in places where it was easier to meet Alter from China than Alter hosts. They were aware that they had few relations with French speakers and pushed back the idea of meeting French people to a later stage:

> *J'ai trop d'amis chinois j'ai pas beaucoup d'amis français mais je sais que j'aurai plus d'amis français plus tard je sais si je rentre à la spécialité les camarades sont tous des Français donc c'est obligatoire de faire des amis français mais maintenant c'est pas obligatoire je me sens mieux quand je parle chinois euh c'est comme ça.*

I have too many Chinese friends I don't have many French friends but I know I'll make more French friends later I know if I start studying a subject at university [i.e. as opposed to just following a language course] my fellow students will all be French so I'll have to make French friends, but I don't have to yet and I feel better when I talk Chinese, er, that's just how it is. (Huiyan, T2)

Concentrated networks: Low use of French

In their logbooks, these learners reported less use of French than in any other type of network. On average, the learners spent approximately three hours conversing in French over a week. In other networks, the average conversational time in French ranged from 4.5 to 19 hours. This low use of French in their everyday life could also be observed through the small proportion of speakers who used the L2 in their network (17.1%).

> *Je parle chinois plus que français parce que la plupart de mes amis sont des Chinois donc euh après le cours de temps en temps je communique euh je parle au téléphone avec des amis de ma classe mais la plupart je parle chinois.*

I speak Chinese more than French because most of my friends are Chinese so er after the course from time to time I communicate er I talk on the phone with friends in my class but mostly I speak Chinese. (Wen, T3)

Dissociated networks: Diverse contexts of sociability

Dissociated networks appeared at all three timepoints during the stay and were more representative of Chinese sociability (only two networks of this type were networks where Ego was American). These dissociated networks were marked by a very loose structure. The number of links, the density and the indexes of centrality were weak, indicating that the members were quite dispersed in the network. The large number of isolate Alter can explain this. These learners had dissociated the different parts of their sociability and a large number of individuals were not connected to the network. The high proportion of original Alter explains the high number of isolated individuals. Learners maintained many connections with members from their home country. The proportion of hosts was the lowest among all networks. As a result, speakers of Ego's L1 were very numerous compared to L2 speakers. L1 conversation time was high and four times greater than the time spent talking in French (Figure 9.4).

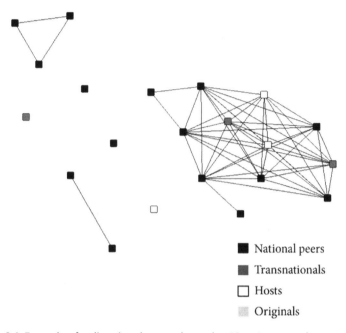

National peers

Transnationals

☐ Hosts

Originals

Figure 9.4 Example of a dissociated network graph – Meng's personal network (T3)

Dissociated networks: High number of isolated Alter

Structural indicators such as density, betweenness centrality and number of links were at their lowest in these networks. No particularly central individual could be identified in the network. There was also no group of particularly interconnected friends and the members of the network were therefore rather dispersed. A possible explanation for these low structural indicators is that the learners had a large number of native Alter in these types of network. These were isolated members of the network because they lived in China and were in fact not linked to any member in France. These Alter were contacted independently by telephone or via the internet. Isolated members were high in number with 11.17 Alter on average connected to no other network member. Similarly, the average percentage of original Alter was high (34.9%), with one third of the members of the network living in China. This was the case, for example, for Rongjie who had been in contact with a few friends with whom she tended to speak several times a month. Every day she would also contact her boyfriend who had remained in China and she would speak to her parents several times a week.

Je pense à la famille beaucoup au fur et à mesure très très souvent main-tenant au début je ne pense pas beaucoup peut-être maintenant il y a des pressions des stress. Je voudrais retourner en Chine oui si possible, rester plusieurs années [en France] c'est une chose très triste pour moi.

I think about my family a lot, more and more, very very often now whereas not so much at first. Maybe now there is stress and pressure. I would like to go back to China if possible, staying several years [in France] is very sad for me. (Rongjie, T3)

Similarly, another student, Lei, called her parents and some of her friends in China every day. Just like Rongjie, she missed her family and her daily life in China.

On vraiment pense à notre famille, à ses parents et on déjà réserve le bil-let d'avion en juin de retourner en Chine donc euh aussitôt que je réserve euh le billet c'est comme ma cœur est déjà volé en Chine.

We really think about our families, our parents, a lot, and we've already booked our plane tickets in June to go back to China, so, er, as soon as I book the ticket, it's like my heart is already flying back to China. (Lei, T2)

These learners had maintained many connections with family and friends in China, whom they contacted on a regular basis. Their contexts of sociability were therefore very divided: on the one hand, there were the members of their networks who were still in China and, on the other, there were their classmates, their neighbours in their residence and a few friends whom they saw alone.

Dissociated networks: Few host Alter

Of all the networks identified, the dissociated type had the lowest proportion of Alter hosts with an average of 5.5%, as opposed to between 10.3% and 32% in the other networks. These learners had difficulty establishing friendships with French speakers. In one case, this was due to the student's shyness and the lack of opportunities to meet French people:

Je pense que le problème pour moi c'est je n'ose pas parler oui ça m'empêche de pratiquer avec les autres j'ai peur de perdre la face que la situation devient de plus en plus mauvais. Je n'ose pas parler avec les autres même si c'est pas en français même en chinois je ne parle pas beaucoup. J'ai pas beaucoup d'occasion pour pratiquer le français et je ne connais pas du tout les autres Français sauf euh trois de cours.

I think the problem for me is that I don't dare speak, yes, it stops me from practising with others, I'm scared of losing face, so the situation gets worse and worse. I don't really dare speak to other people, even if it's not in French, even in Chinese, I don't speak much. I don't get much opportunity to practise French and I don't know any French people except, er, three in class. (Meng, T3)

One student had the opportunity to meet French people through her job in a large fast-food chain. This two-month experience was significant for her. She spoke to me at length and tried to analyse the reasons underpinning what she experienced as a failure of communication with French people:

Le moment quand je trouve c'est difficile de parler c'est pendant mon travail je trouve que mon patron est vraiment courageux de m'embaucher parce que pour moi c'est mon niveau de français pour bien travailler n'est pas suffisant. Ils [ses collègues] sont plutôt euh des personnes euh il n'y a pas beaucoup beaucoup d'étudiants là-bas donc ce sont plutôt des gens qui ont travail déjà depuis longtemps ou depuis un moment dans la société donc euh quand parfois ils parlent même si je comprends ce qu'ils parlent je sais pas comment je peux parler avec eux. Et parfois quand ils parlent j'essaie de parler avec eux mais ça ne marche pas très bien oui c'est pas trop intéressant notre conversation.

The time when I find it hard to talk is at work I think my boss was really brave to hire me because I don't think my level of French is good enough to work well. They [her colleagues] are kind of, er, people, er, there aren't very many students there so these are people who've already been working for a long time or for a while, in society, so, er, sometimes, when they're talking, even if I understand what they're saying, I don't really know how to talk to them. And sometimes when they talk, I try to talk with them, but it doesn't really work, yes, our conversations aren't really interesting. (Xiexuan, T3)

In this excerpt, she expressed the fact that differences in social status seem to have created distance and a lack of mutual understanding of the two different worlds inhabited. On the one hand, Xiexuan was studying French at university and wanted to work in order to make progress in French; on the other hand, her colleagues were living in the completely different reality of full-time work in a fast-food restaurant. Xiexuan also highlighted communication difficulties related to her level of French, which she did not feel was sufficient for her to communicate effectively. Another student foregrounded the same reasons:

Je pense que un peu un peu isolée du monde français je n'ai pas trouvé une bonne un bon moyen pour intégrer la société française j'ai déjà trouvé beaucoup des amis chinois. D'abord, c'est le niveau de français quand des gens parlent vite je ne peux pas comprendre et puis c'est la culture on ne peut pas trouver une chose très intéressante.

I think [as I'm] a little bit isolated from the French world, I've not found a good, a good way to integrate into French society, but I've already found a lot of Chinese friends. First, there's the level of French, when people speak fast I can't understand them and then it's cultural, you can't find something very interesting. (Yapin, T2)

This student reported that while she was in contact with French students in the courses she attended at university, she had not found a way to establish any meaningful dialogue with them. Other students described their difficulties in creating relations with French-speaking classmates in similar terms. Attempts to connect with these classmates failed and so they progressively gave up.

Eclectic networks: The importance of otherness and adaptation

This network was present at all three stages of the survey: two Americans at all three times, two Chinese at T1 and T2, two Americans at T2 and T3 and one Chinese at T1. The eclectic networks had a more heterogeneous structure; the structural indicators presented average values. This indicates that some areas of the network were dense, while others were looser. Some individuals were isolated, others more central. These networks stood apart from other networks by their composition. Ego had a significant proportion of host and transnational Alter and a small proportion of original and national peers. On average, Ego shared few different activities with members of his/her network. The proportion of speakers of French was very high and the conversation time in this language was much higher than in other types of networks (Figure 9.5).

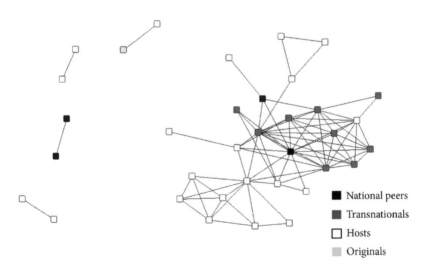

Figure 9.5 Example of an eclectic network graph – Jack's personal network (T3)

Eclectic networks: High number of host and transnational Alter

These networks had the highest proportion of host and transnational Alter among all the networks. About one third of the members were from France (32%) and another third represented transnationals (37%). Some learners mentioned this aspect of their sociability as one of the benefits of their stay in France.

> *C'est l'idée de voir plusieurs nationalités parce qu'aux Etats-Unis tout le monde euh ils s'intègrent dans la culture américaine. Mais ici, j'ai eu l'opportunité de rencontrer beaucoup de gens complètement différents de parler avec eux de connaitre leur culture un petit peu tu vois de faire leur connaissance.*

> It's the idea of meeting several nationalities, because in the United States everybody, er, they become integrated into American culture. But here, I had the opportunity to meet a lot of completely different people, to talk with them, to get to know their culture a little bit, you know, to get to know them. (Kathleen, T3)

As for relations with host Alter, one Chinese student expressed that she had found a better strategy than her other Chinese friends to meet French speakers:

> *Je sais pas si c'est arrogant de dire ça mais je pense que moi je fais mieux qu'eux quand je parle avec des Français ou les autres étrangers j'ai pas peur, je me gêne pas. Je pense grâce à la colocation même si ça se passe pas très bien euh je sais comment parler, commencer parler avec les Français ou les étrangers.*

> I don't know if it's arrogant to say this, but I think I do better than them when I speak with French people or other foreigners, I'm not afraid, I'm not embarrassed. I think, thanks to living in a flat-share, even if it's not going all that well, er I know how to talk, to start talking, with French people or foreigners. (Yaxin, T2)

Among all the networks, the eclectic network presented the lowest rates of Alter from country of origin (9%). They were therefore not completely absent from this type of network, but nonetheless represented a less substantial part of the relationships in question.

Eclectic networks: High conversation time in French

As for spoken languages, the eclectic networks presented extreme results with the lowest average proportion of speakers using the L1 (27.6%) and the highest average for the percentage of speakers using the L2 (58.9%). Similarly, for the conversation time reported in the logbook over a week, the learners in these networks were those who spoke the least in their L1 (4 hours per week) and the most in the L2 (19 hours per week) compared to other networks.

Learners had a high proportion of French speakers in their network, speaking French with more than half the members. One learner noticed a progression in the amount of time she spent speaking French:

> J'ai réalisé en fait l'autre jour que je parle beaucoup français maintenant beaucoup en fait juste avant de me coucher normalement j'appelle ma mère ou j'envoie un texto à mes parents ou ma sœur juste pour parler un peu anglais avec quelqu'un parce que c'est trop bizarre maintenant je parle pas du tout [anglais] c'est plus rare.

> I actually realised the other day that I speak French a lot now, in fact, just before going to bed I tend to call my mother or I send a text message to my parents or my sister just to speak a bit of English with someone, because it's too weird now, I don't speak it at all, it's much more rare. (Meredith, T3)

For some of these students, speaking a lot of French was a goal from the start and they proved fairly intransigent about it. Although they would make some concessions, they tried where possible to avoid speaking their L1:

> Souvent, souvent je parle français, je dois progresser en français j'ai pas le temps pour parler anglais. Et j'ai fait ça j'ai parlé que le français. Mais par exemple avec des étudiants américains qui veulent apprendre parce que j'ai une amie, elle veut apprendre tu vois elle veut pratiquer le français il y a parfois des choses qu'elle ne peut pas dire alors la conversation tourne en anglais je comprends mais ça ne dure pas longtemps.

> Often, often, I speak French, I have to make progress in French, I don't have time to speak English. And I've done that, I've spoken only French. But for example with American students who want to learn, because I have this friend, she wants to learn, you know, she wants to practise French, sometimes there are things she can't say, so the conversation switches to English, which I understand, but it doesn't last long. (Kathleen, T3)

Discussion and Conclusion

Cluster analysis revealed noticeable differences in the way Chinese and American learners structure their network. Indeed, some networks were predominantly representative of American sociability (dense and extended networks) and others of Chinese sociability (concentrated and dissociated networks). In this section, additional analyses will be provided to explain some of these differences.

This study enabled a qualitative approach to analysing sociability, by linking learners' feelings about their stay with different types of networks. In the dense and extended networks mostly represented by Americans, the learners are mostly accommodated in host families. On the other hand, in the concentrated and dissociated networks predominantly represented by the Chinese students, it is more common for them to be housed in university halls of residence. Levels of satisfaction with each type of accommodation tend to be different. Learners living in university residences often feel isolated and report that health conditions are sometimes questionable. American learners, mostly accommodated in French-speaking families, are generally satisfied with the help and support provided by family members. Chinese students staying in university halls, mostly out of town, often feel isolated and insecure. They also deplore the large number of students of the same origin. de Langenhagen (2011) in her survey of Chinese students in Grenoble (France) highlighted this housing difficulty as an urgent problem. Other studies have also shown that accommodation can have a strong influence on adaptation and on the sociability developed in the host country (Allen, 2010; Carnine, 2014; Diao *et al.*, 2011; Wilkinson, 2002).

Additionally, American learners proved to be fairly relaxed when it came to the stakes related to this mobility experience, considering it as a year of vacation. Conversely, most Chinese learners express a strong attachment to academic achievement. These two aspects relating to accommodation and to the motives underpinning the stay seem important for understanding the distinctions between the types of networks. As Carnine (2014) explains, Chinese students' SA can be framed as 'qualification mobility', while for American students' SA, it is more about 'credit mobility'. In this respect, the Chinese prefer long stays where the goal is to obtain a university degree, which will then be valued in their country of origin. Conversely, the USA and France have inter-university agreements and learners are strongly encouraged to study abroad for the purpose of completing their degree. These stays can last one or two semesters.

The eclectic network stands apart from the other four profiles of sociability and seems to represent more successful integration in the host community. The students with this form of network live in heterogeneous types of accommodation, some in flat-sharing arrangements, others in host families and others still in university halls of residence. The learners in these networks, however, seem to have a more reflective attitude both linguistically and socially. They seem to develop strategies to get away from people from the same country of origin and to try to get closer to host Alter. In general, these learners seem more involved in their sociability during their stay in France.

US exchange programmes and Chinese agencies

The Chinese students mostly turn to private agencies in their country in order to prepare their stay in France. These agencies offer them help in choosing the city and host university, guide them through the process of enrolling in French courses and support them through administrative procedures such as applying for a visa. These organisations can also offer services related to the logistics of moving to the country, for example collecting students from the station or finding them accommodation. Different authors (Carnine, 2014; de Langenhagen, 2011) focusing on Chinese learners' stays abroad have pointed to the lucrative nature of these agencies. Even if they can solve the many difficulties related to settling in France (visa, university registration, housing), these agencies do not provide continued support to the students once they have arrived. Different students in the present study sample reported disappointment with these agencies.

Conversely, for American students, exchange programmes have been set up in connection with the host university and offer many services. They take care of all administrative procedures prior to the trip. They offer students accommodation, often in French host families or more rarely in university halls of residence. Programme managers are available to address any questions and in case of problems during the stay. A number of activities and excursions are offered during the stay, so that students can visit different cities in France. The programmes also promote the students' integration by encouraging them to volunteer in associations. American learners pay for this package of services, which provides greater guarantees than those provided by Chinese agencies.

For American and Chinese students, the conditions of their stay in France therefore differ greatly. American learners who come with a university exchange programme find themselves in a relatively comfortable situation, in which they are better prepared, receive more help with the settling-in process and are more supported in their daily lives. Conversely, Chinese learners seem to be left to their own devices during their stay in France.

Differences in mobility capital and in the process of socialisation

The mobility capital described by Murphy-Lejeune (2003) emphasises the importance of previous experience of mobility. In the present sample, most of the Chinese students had never travelled abroad (11 students out of 15), while most of the Americans had already experienced a trip abroad (only 3 students out of 14 had never left the USA). While these stays had sometimes been short (a two- to three-week school trip), American learners had therefore already experienced the social, cultural and linguistic upheaval and dislocation involved in a trip to another country.

In addition, the question of personal predispositions to otherness (Murphy-Lejeune, 2003) may also provide insight into the differences in socialisation observed between Chinese and American learners. Indeed, similarities have been found between French and American networks (Grossetti, 2007). Grossetti shows that there are many structural and compositional convergences between the personal networks developed in France and the USA, whereas recent studies show that the prevalent form of sociability in China is very different than in Western countries. In China, there is a relational culture called *guanxi* in which 'social relations are founded on emotional and instrumental motives. Dyadic, especially affective, links have the potential to facilitate exchanges of services' (Favre, 2014: 94). This relational culture is therefore based on building and maintaining relationships between people with mutual obligations and benefits. As Qi (2013) explains, *guanxi* can be defined by the emphasis on long-term relationships and social norms such as reliability, reciprocity and commitment. Therefore, Bian (2002) explains that resources circulate differently in the personal networks of Chinese people as compared to Western personal networks. Similarly, in her study of American, French and Chinese students in a mobility context, Carnine (2014) observed that Chinese students presented the least heterogeneous networks in terms of nationality.

The study offers an insight into the differences that separate Chinese students from students from Western countries during a stay abroad and the potential impact that these differences may have in terms of personal network development abroad. In addition, it is clear that both travel preparation and living conditions in the country have an impact on how personal networks develop.

In conclusion, this chapter has served primarily as an illustration of longitudinal analysis of personal networks in an SA context. The combination of qualitative and quantitative methods makes it possible to approach students' sociability from different perspectives and thus to increase understanding of how their social relationships are created. This work could be productively extended by analysing how these different types of network influence different areas of learning, such as sociolinguistic, intercultural or pragmatic competence in the L2.

Notes

(1) My intention here is simply to provide a brief introduction to network analysis, highlighting a few key elements of this type of analysis of social relations. For a more detailed review of its origins and theoretical and methodological proponents, see Scott (2000) or Wasserman and Faust (1994).
(2) The French language learning centre assessed the students' proficiency at the beginning of each semester.
(3) Translations are provided as a reading aid to allow non-French speakers understand the content of the interview excerpts; however, they do not attempt to render the linguistic features (approximations, grammatical errors, etc.) of the original French.

References

Allen, H.W. (2010) Interactive contact as linguistic affordance during short-term study abroad: Myth or reality? *Frontiers: The Interdisciplinary Journal of Study Abroad* 19, 1–26.

Barnes, J.A. (1954) Classes sociales et réseaux dans une île de Norvège. Traduit de l'anglais par Jean Grange. *Réseaux* 182, 209–237.

Bian, Y. (2002) Chinese social stratification and social mobility. *Annual Review of Sociology* 28, 91–116.

Bidart, C. (1988) Sociabilités: quelques variables. *Revue Française de Sociologie* 29 (4), 621–648.

Bidart, C. (2012) Réseaux personnels et processus de socialisation. *Idées Économiques et Sociales* 169 (3), 8–15.

Bidart, C. and Cacciuttolo, P. (2012) Combining qualitative, quantitative and structural dimensions in a longitudinal perspective. The case of network influence. *Quality & Quantity* 47 (5), 2495–2515.

Bidart, C., Degenne, A. and Grossetti, M. (2011) *La Vie en Réseau: Dynamique des Relations Sociales*. Paris: Presses Universitaires de France.

Bidart, C., Degenne, A. and Grossetti, M. (2018) Personal networks typologies: A structural approach. *Social Networks* 54, 1–11.

Blanpain, N. and Pan Ké Shon, J.L. (1998) 1983–1997: Les Français se parlent de moins en moins. *INSEE Première* no. 571.

Bonacich, P. (1972) Factoring and weighting approaches to status scores and cliques identification. *Journal of Mathematical Sociology* 2, 113–120.

Borgatti, S.P., Everett, M.G. and Freeman, L.C. (2002) *Ucinet for Windows: Software for Social Network Analysis*. Harvard, MA: Analytic Technologies.

Borgatti, S.P., Mehra, A., Brass, D.J. and Labianca, G. (2009) Network analysis in the social sciences. *Science* 323 (5916), 892–895.

Borgatti, S.P., Everett, M.G. and Johnson, J.C. (2013) *Analyzing Social Networks*. London: Sage.

Bott, E. (1957) *Family and Social Network*. London: Tavistock.

Brandes, U., Lerner, J., Lubbers, M.J., McCarty, C. and Molina, J.L. (2008) Visual statistics for collections of clustered graphs. In *Proceedings of the IEEE Pacific Visualization Symposium (PacificVis '08)* (pp. 47–54). Kyoto. IEEE Computer Society.

Brandes, U., Lerner, J., Lubbers, M.J., McCarty, C., Molina, J.L. and Nagel, U. (2010) Recognizing modes of acculturation in personal networks of migrants. *Procedia – Social and Behavioral Sciences* 4, 4–13.

Calinon, A.-S. (2009) Facteurs linguistiques et sociolinguistiques de l'intégration en milieu multilingue: le cas des immigrants à Montréal. Doctoral thesis, University of Montreal and the University of Franche-Comté.

Carnine, J. (2014) La mobilité estudiantine française, le 'Study Abroad' américain et le 'Liu Xue' chinois: une étude comparative des séjours internationaux au travers des réseaux sociaux et des identifications nationales. Doctoral thesis, Université Jean Jaurès, Toulouse.

Carrington, P.J. (2014) Social network research. In S. Dominguez and B. Hollstein (eds) *Mixed Methods Social Networks Research. Design and Application* (pp. 35–64). New York: Cambridge University Press.

de Bot, K. and Stoessel, S. (2002) Introduction: Language change and social networks. *International Journal of the Sociology of Language* 153, 1–7.

de Federico de la Rúa, A. (2008) Amitiés européennes. Les réseaux transnationaux des étudiants Erasmus. *Informations Sociales* 147 (3), 120–127.

Degenne, A. and Forsé, M. (2004) *Les Réseaux Sociaux*. Paris: Armand Colin.

de Langenhagen, V. (2011) Les représentations des étudiants chinois de français langue étrangère en situation de mobilité étudiante en France. Doctoral thesis, Institut National des Langues et Civilisations Orientales, Paris.

Dewey, D.P., Belnap, R.K. and Hillstrom, R. (2013) Social network development, language use, and language acquisition during study abroad: Arabic language learners' perspectives. *Frontiers: The Interdisciplinary Journal of Study Abroad* 22, 84–110.

Diao, W., Freed, B. and Smith, L. (2011) Confirmed beliefs or false assumptions? A study of home stay experiences in the French study abroad context. *Frontiers: The Interdisciplinary Journal of Study Abroad* 21, 109–142.

Doucerain, M.M., Varnaamkhaasti, R.S., Segalowitz, N. and Ryder, A.G. (2015) Second language social networks and communication-related acculturative stress: The role of interconnectedness. *Frontiers in Psychology* 6, 1–12.

Eve, M. (2002) Deux traditions dans l'analyse des réseaux sociaux. *Réseaux* 115, 183–212.

Favre, G. (2014) Conférence INSNA sur des réseaux sociaux, Xi'an Jiaotong university, Chine, 11-15 juillet 2013. *Bulletin de Méthodologie Sociologique* 122, 87–98.

Freeman, L.C. (1979) Centrality in social networks: Conceptual clarification. *Social Networks* 1, 215–239.

Fu, Y.-C. (2007) Contact diaries: Building archives of actual and comprehensive personal networks. *Field Methods* 19 (2), 194–217.

Gautier, R. and Chevrot, J.-P. (2015) Social network and acquisition of sociolinguistic variation in a study abroad context: A preliminary study. In R. Mitchell, N. Tracy-Ventura and K. McManus (eds) *Social Networking and Second Language Acquisition during Residence /Study Abroad* (pp. 169–184). EUROSLA Monograph Series 4. Amsterdam: European Second Language Association.

Grossetti, M. (2007) Are French networks different? *Social Network* 29, 391–404.

Héran, F. (1988) La sociabilité, une pratique culturelle. *Economie et Statistique* 216 (1), 3–22.

Howard, M., Mougeon, R. and Dewaele, J.-M. (2013) Sociolinguistics and second language acquisition. In R. Bayley, R. Cameron and C. Lucas (eds) *The Oxford Handbook of Sociolinguistics* (pp. 340–359). New York: Oxford University Press.

Isabelli-García, C. (2006) Study abroad social networks, motivation and attitudes: Implications for second language acquisition. In M.A. DuFon and E. Churchill (eds) *Language Learners in Study Abroad Contexts* (pp. 231–258). Clevedon: Multilingual Matters.

Kinginger, C. (2008) Language learning in study abroad: Case studies of Americans in France. *Modern Language Journal* Supplement 92, 1–124.

Kinginger, C. (2010) American students abroad: Negotiation of difference? *Language Teaching* 43, 216–227.

Lubbers, M.J., Molina, J.L. and McCarty, C. (2007) Personal networks and ethnic identifications The case of migrants in Spain. *International Sociology* 22, (6), 721–741.

Lubbers, M.J., Molina, J.L., Lerner, J., Brandes, U., Ávila, J. and McCarty, C. (2010) Longitudinal analysis of personal networks. The case of Argentinean migrants in Spain. *Social Networks* 32 (1), 91–104.

Lybeck, K. (2002) Cultural identification and second language pronunciation of Americans in Norway. *Modern Language Journal* 86 (2), 174–191.

Martínez García, M.F., García Ramírez, M. and Maya Jariego, I. (2002) Social support and locus of control as predictors of psychological well-being in Moroccan and Peruvian immigrant women in Spain. *International Journal of Intercultural Relations* 26, 287–310.

McManus, K., Mitchell, R. and Tracy-Ventura, N. (2014) Understanding insertion and integration in a study abroad context: The case of English-speaking sojourners in France. *Revue Appliquée de Linguistique Appliquée* 19 (2), 97–116.

Mercklé, P. (2014) La 'découverte' des réseaux sociaux. A propos de John A. Barnes et d'une expérience de traduction collaborative. *Réseaux* 182, 187–208.

Milroy, L. (1987) *Language and Social Networks*. Oxford: Blackwell.

Milroy, L. (2002) Social networks. In J. Chambers and N. Schilling-Estes (eds) *Handbook of Language Variation and Change* (pp. 549–572). Oxford: Blackwell.

Mitchell, J.C. (1969) *Social Network in Urban Situations*. Manchester: Manchester University Press.

Moreno, J.L. (1934) *Who Shall Survive. A New Approach to the Problem of Human Inter-relations*. Washington, DC: Nervous and Mental Disease Publishing.

Murphy-Lejeune, E. (2003) *L'Étudiant Européen Voyageur, Un Nouvel Étranger*. Paris: Didier.

Papatsiba, V. (2003) *Des Étudiants Européens. 'Erasmus' et l'Aventure de l'Altérité*. Bern: Peter Lang.

Qi, X. (2013) *Guanxi*, social capital theory and beyond: Toward a globalized social science. *The British Journal of Sociology* 64 (2), 308–324.

Scott, J.C. (2000) *Social Network Analysis. A Handbook*. London: Sage.

Thamin, N. (2008) Dynamiques des répertoires langagiers et identités plurilingues de sujets en situation de mobilité. Doctoral thesis, Université Stendhal, Grenoble.

Verdi Rademacher, M. (2014) Les multiples mobilités de la migration. Le cas des migrants chiliens en France. Doctoral thesis, Ecole des Hautes Etudes en Sciences Sociales, Paris.

Wasserman, S. and Faust, K. (1994) *Social Network Analysis: Methods and Applications*. Cambridge: Cambridge University Press.

Wellman, B. (2007) Challenges in collecting personal network data: The nature of personal network analysis. *Field Methods* 19 (2), 111–115.

Wiklund, I. (2002) Social networks from a sociolinguistic perspective: The relationship between characteristics of the social networks of bilingual adolescents and their language proficiency. *International Journal of the Sociology of Language* 153, 53–92.

Wilkinson, S. (2002) The omnipresent classroom during summer study abroad: American students in conversation with French hosts. *Modern Language Journal* 86, 157–173.

10 Individual Differences in Study Abroad Research: Sources, Processes and Outcomes of Students' Development in Language, Culture and Personhood

Noriko Iwasaki

Introduction

Study abroad (SA) is commonly believed to benefit language learning, yet not all students thrive in SA. Much research has been conducted on SA to tackle this puzzle, with mixed results: 'Virtually the only constant finding' on SA is 'individual variation within each study' (Coleman, 2013: 25). As Kinginger (2015: 7) puts it, 'if there is any consistent finding in this research, it is of inconsistency; individual differences in achievements, often significant, are documented in nearly every study'.

Such variable achievements among students are largely due to enormous differences/variation/variability in various factors, both internal and external to students: their individual characteristics (e.g. motivation, personality, learning styles, language learning aptitude) and SA contexts/experiences (e.g. accommodation, social networks, opportunities for target language use), as well as interactions between internal and external factors. Comparisons between students in SA contexts and those in the classroom in their home country (at-home [AH]) have found that differences in achievement within the SA cohort are more pronounced than in the classroom cohort (e.g. Freed, 1995; Huebner, 1995), and more significant than differences between the groups (DeKeyser, 1991). This is attributable to 'the high degree of freedom students have with regard to how to spend their time, in particular who they talk to, how often, where and about what' (DeKeyser, 2014: 320).

Clearly, individual differences are an important issue in SA. However, understanding findings about individual differences and judging whether or what coherent stories have emerged can be taxing, given researchers' differing use of the term 'individual differences' and different research orientations to 'individual differences'.

On the one hand, the term 'individual differences' in traditional mainstream second language acquisition (SLA) research has been used to refer to individual learners' internal characteristics as the potential source of differing outcomes. Often, the goal of SLA individual difference research is to identify learners' characteristics that predict differential outcomes. The quantitative methodology typically adopted for this purpose involves large samples and aims to provide generalisable results. Researchers may attempt to control variability in predetermined domains, but the emergence of other types of variability can nonetheless cause 'undesirable' noise in otherwise well-designed experimental paradigms.

On the other hand, the term 'individual differences' can also be used interchangeably with other terms, such as variation and variability, to refer to differences observed among different individuals. The main interest is in understanding variations of experiences and outcomes during SA or after SA. These studies usually utilise qualitative data from sources such as diaries and interviews and are analysed qualitatively. There are also studies with a mixed research design whereby the two types of data complement each other.

Whichever approach is taken, another challenge of understanding individual difference research is the variety of variables being considered as source variables and as outcome variables, and the variety of methods for measuring and observing them. 'If there is anything that cannot easily be standardized it is what individual differences to focus on and how' (DeKeyser, 2014: 321).

This chapter's goal is twofold. First, it aims to untangle the differences among approaches taken to investigate individual differences, using summaries of seminal and recent studies in order to better understand the advances to date.[1] In doing so, it describes types of variables considered so far and outlines salient trends. Second, besides presenting summary findings, it seeks reasons for puzzling findings. This feeds into a discussion that relates shifts in the approach to individual differences in SA studies to a shift in focus in applied linguistics, where individualism (learner-centredness) has given way to individuality (person-centredness [Benson, 2019]).

The chapter is organised primarily by research orientation with regard to individual differences. It first reviews studies conducted to investigate pre-SA individual differences as the potential source of SA outcomes, followed by studies focused on illustrating intra-SA differences in processes, such as individuals' experiences, and finally those dealing with the understanding of differences as outcomes. These are not always mutually exclusive, as some studies link learners' outcomes to processes or vice versa.

Pre-SA and Intra-SA Individual Differences as the Source of Differing Outcomes

Pre-SA individual differences as predictors of linguistic outcomes

In mainstream SLA research, so-called individual differences are important learner-internal variables that can predict learning outcomes. Pre-SA individual differences potentially predict differential rates or levels of learning. The goal of this research is to identify the cause–effect relationship and account for the variability in the outcomes. The learner-internal variables considered include language learning aptitude, motivation, anxiety, learner beliefs, personality, willingness to communicate (WTC), learning style, learning strategies and working memory (see Dewaele, 2009; Ellis, 2004). Identifying which learner characteristics predict 'how quickly and how well an individual learner will acquire a new language and which type of instruction would suit them best' is the practical reason behind the interest in individual differences in SLA (Roberts & Meyer, 2012: 1).

Motivated as they often are by the practical goal of assisting students who study abroad, SA researchers are keen to identify predictors of 'successful' outcomes. A similar orientation is seen in research investigating the role of individual differences in students' language learning processes and outcomes.

Besides the learner-internal psychological/cognitive variables, researchers have considered several other characteristics of learners, such as gender, age and experience with foreign language learning. Traditionally, they have examined whether or how learners' pre-SA characteristics predicted their post-SA outcomes (assessed at the end of SA or after SA) by first identifying or measuring SA participants' pre-SA characteristics. The outcome variables examined have primarily been gains in various aspects of target language (L2) competence, particularly oral proficiency, though the range of outcomes examined to assess students' development has widened in recent years.

A seminal series of studies conducted to identify significant predictors of language learning gains utilised a large corpus assembled by the American Council of Teachers of Russian (ACTR). Brecht *et al.* (1993, 1995) studied gains in learning Russian among 658 US-based students who studied in four-month Russian programmes in Russia between 1984 and 1990. The outcome variables were listening, reading and oral proficiency. Oral proficiency was assessed by the oral proficiency interview (OPI), developed by the American Council on the Teaching of Foreign Languages (ACTFL). Brecht *et al.* examined the effects of the variables they considered the most salient, namely, gender, knowledge of other foreign languages, general language learning aptitude as measured by the Modern Language Aptitude Test and pre-SA Russian language proficiency. They found that students with lower pre-SA oral proficiency tended to show larger gains in oral proficiency after SA. The other significant predictors were gender (men showed greater gains), language learning aptitude, pre-SA knowledge of grammar, reading ability and knowledge of other foreign languages.

Davidson (2010) updated Brecht et al.'s (1993) study by examining 1,881 students in two-, four- and nine-month programmes in Russia between 1994 and 2009. He mostly replicated Brecht et al.'s (1993, 1995) results. Among both four-month and nine-month programme students, pre-SA grammatical knowledge, reading comprehension ability and language learning aptitude significantly correlated with their post-SA language gains in listening, reading and speaking. The effect of gender, however, was no longer found. He attributed this to changes in gender roles in Russian society and dedicated pre-programme training. He also noted an observation about 'remarkable levels of variation that occurred among different learners within the study abroad cohort' (Davidson, 2010: 23).

These earlier studies suggested that SA provides contexts conducive to oral proficiency development and that pre-SA grammatical knowledge is among the important predictors for oral gains in language proficiency (see also DeKeyser, 2010). Most early studies examined oral performance (proficiency and fluency) as an outcome variable, reflecting the fact that it is most often examined and it is also where SA students have been reported to gain the most (Llanes, 2011). Investigations of predictors of gains in other types of L2 outcomes are rather scarce.

Llanes et al. (2012), however, examined both written (composition) and spoken (narrative task) production as outcome variables among 24 Spain-based university students. The students had studied English for at least 13 years prior to one-semester SA in the UK. The researchers used a questionnaire to examine the role of various pre-SA and intra-SA factors. The students showed more improvement in speaking (gains in three of four measures: fluency, accuracy and lexical complexity) than in writing (gain in one of four measures: fluency in terms of the number of words per t-unit). In terms of learner-internal factors, student attitudes of high linguistic expectations correlated with gains in lexical complexity, and personal orientation (e.g. towards meeting people from other countries) correlated with lexical complexity in written production. Also significantly related to gains were external factors such as students' majors, living accommodations and the presence or absence of English-speaking people at home.

Examinations of pre-SA individual differences as predictors of gains rarely place the main focus on lexical and grammatical outcomes.

However, Grey *et al.* (2015) focused on the development of accuracy and speed in the lexical and grammatical judgements of 26 advanced-level, US-based university students of Spanish. They studied the role of three types of cognitive capacities as individual differences by measuring the students' working memory (via recalls of auditory-presented sentence-final words), phonological working memory (accuracy in repeating paired non-words) in L1 and phonological working memory in L2. They found that in a five-week SA programme, students showed some improvement in accuracy of grammatical judgement and in accuracy and speed of lexical judgement; however, this improvement was independent of the students' pre-SA working memory or phonological working memory.

Another area of linguistic development examined in relation to individual characteristics is pragmatic competence. Taguchi (2015) examined how pre-SA cross-cultural adaptability related to the production of ten speech acts (e.g. request) in an oral discourse completion test (DCT) among 22 intermediate-level Japanese learners from diverse countries (e.g. Taiwan, US, Korea, Brunei) studying in Japan for 13 weeks. Pre-SA cross-cultural adaptability was significantly related to gains in speech act appropriateness (assessed by native speaker raters). Taguchi attributes the results to the relation between cross-cultural adaptability and the students' cultural integration. Cultural integration potentially gives them ample interactional opportunities and access to pragmatic practice. Notably, Taguchi complemented her quantitative study with an analysis of interviews with two contrasting students that revealed how their intra-SA activities differed. The student with the lowest score in cross-cultural adaptability spent most of her free time sightseeing, while the student with the highest adaptability score joined four clubs, made efforts to build a social network and observed how language was used in real life.

SLA studies of individual differences as predictors of differing outcomes have focused on students' improvement as a group, but many such studies also noted large variations within the group (e.g. Davidson, 2010). Some also found that pre-SA students' characteristics affect their intra-SA contexts and experiences, which in turn affect the outcomes. Hence, it is not SA in itself that influences students' learning, but rather what happens during SA. Many studies therefore examine the role of intra-SA variables, especially language use and social networking during SA.

Intra-SA individual differences as predictors of linguistic outcomes: Language use and social network

Recent studies increasingly regard intra-SA variables (often in addition to pre-SA variables) as the source of differences in outcomes. These variables characterise individuals' context or experience during SA such as the students' language use and social networking during SA. Pre-SA variables, however, also affect intra-SA language use. Below, studies of intra-SA language use and those of social network as predictors for post-SA linguistic outcomes will be reviewed, followed by a review of studies on pre-SA individual differences affecting intra-SA language use.

The primary intra-SA variable considered is language use (also called 'language contact'), operationalised as the amount of time spent on language use during SA, which is commonly believed to be the key to language gains. As early as 1990, Freed (1990) reported the unexpected finding of absence of the effect of both interactive and non-interactive out-of-class language use on learning outcomes in French (oral proficiency, grammatical knowledge and reading comprehension) among 38 US-based university students who studied in France for six weeks. She assessed students' out-of-class language use with an earlier version of the language contact profile (LCP)[2] on which students self-reported the approximate number of hours they spent per day using French in various activities: e.g. speaking French with native speakers (interactive); watching films, reading newspapers and books (non-interactive). Freed found that for the group, the amount of time spent on out-of-class language use was unrelated to gains in oral proficiency (OPI) or grammar and reading comprehension (assessed by a multiple-choice test). However, closer analyses revealed lower-level students' gains were related to interactive language use, whereas higher-level students' gains were related to non-interactive language use. Freed (1990: 475) suggests that '*different types* of linguistic involvement interacts in *different ways* with the processes of language learning at *different stages* in the acquisition process' (my emphasis). Interestingly, she also examined the effect of pre-SA variables (oral proficiency, motivation, attitude towards correctness and language learning aptitude) on this intra-SA variable of out-of-class contact. Students with higher pre-SA proficiency reported more hours of informal language use with native speakers, but the other factors had no significant effects.

Other studies reported similar puzzling findings. Magnan and Back (2007) examined the relationship between students' language use (assessed with a shortened version of Freed *et al.*'s [2004] LCP) and their gains in oral proficiency (OPI).[3] Twenty US-based university students with intermediate-level French spent one semester in France, and as a group, their post-OPIs were rated significantly higher than their pre-OPIs – even though eight students remained at the same level. Their gains were not significantly related to the use of French with locals or to their living arrangements (living with native French speakers or not). Some students reported positive experiences of a homestay and others reported negative experiences, regardless of whether or not they improved. Magnan and Back found that while interaction with US peers in French was negatively correlated with gains, some students greatly benefited from talking with foreign peers (e.g. Serbian, Algerian) who were fluent in French, indicating further variation and complexity in the relation between students' language use and gains.

In addition to language use (LCP), Martinsen (2010) considered another intra-SA variable, namely, the relationship with the host family (according to students' responses on a questionnaire) as a predictor of gains in oral proficiency among 45 US-based students learning Spanish for six weeks in Argentina. He also examined two pre-SA variables: motivation and intercultural sensitivity. The students significantly improved as a group, but the range of outcomes varied; some even showed lower proficiency. He found that the pre-SA level of intercultural sensitivity (measured by the Inventory of Cross-Cultural Sensitivity [ICCS], Cushner, 1986) was the only significant predictor of gains in speech assessed by native speakers' rating. Martinsen speculates that repetitive daily conversation with host families may be insufficient for improvement, and that the quality of interaction may be a more important contributor to improved oral proficiency.

The data obtained through the OPI are also used to assess speaking fluency. Segalowitz and Freed (2004) examined gains in oral performance among 22 SA participants studying Spanish for one semester in Spain by analysing temporal and hesitation phenomena in two-minute audio-recorded segments of the pre- and post-SA OPI data. They examined the effects of the students' out-of-class language use (LCP) as well as their pre-SA cognitive abilities (L2-specific speed and efficiency of lexical access, and speed and efficiency of attention control) on the gains. Once again, SA students' gains were unrelated to their language use except for a negative correlation between gains and time spent speaking with the homestay family. The authors speculate that most homestay interactions might have been short, repetitive exchanges. Having found pre-SA speed and efficiency of lexical access to be related to OPI gains, they suggest that oral gains may depend on pre-SA cognitive readiness.

Despite these studies' counterintuitive finding that the amount of time spent on out-of-class language use does not necessarily relate to gains in oral performance, other studies, such as Hernández (2010), have reported the expected positive influence of intra-SA language use on oral proficiency development. Hernández examined the relationship between pre-SA motivation and language use, and between language use and gains in oral proficiency, among 20 US-based students of Spanish who spent a semester in Spain. He assessed these students' pre-SA integrative and instrumental motivation with a questionnaire, their intra-SA language use (modified LCP) and their oral proficiency assessed by simulated OPI (SOPI, recording responses to pre-recorded questions/instructions). Most (16 of 20) students improved their SOPI scores, and their language use accounted for the gains. Furthermore, pre-SA integrative motivation had a positive effect on language use. Hence, the pre-SA motivation affected intra-SA language use, which in turn influenced the outcome. Speculating on the source of the discrepancies between his and Segalowitz and Freed's (2004) findings, Hernández pointed out that his participants used Spanish more (60.68 hours a week)[4] than Segalowitz and Freed's participants (18 hours per week). Hernández also reported significant variation among his participants (e.g. the time spent speaking Spanish ranged from 3.5 to 42 hours per week).

The studies reviewed above considered oral proficiency the primary outcome variable, but the role of intra-SA language use was also assessed in studies examining gains in other outcomes such as pragmatic competence. Matsumura (2003) examined the development of pragmatic competence (native-like choice of advice strategy assessed by multiple-choice test) among 137 university students from Japan studying English for eight months in Canada. He found the self-reported amount of exposure to have the strongest effect on development, followed by pre-SA proficiency. Taguchi's (2008) examination of pragmatic development (accuracy and speed of comprehending implied meanings in aural refusals and opinions) among 44 Japanese students learning English in the USA showed some effects of out-of-class use of language (modified LCP). Students' gains in comprehension speed were linked to out-of-class time spent reading and speaking, but not to out-of-class time spent writing or listening. The students' gains in comprehension accuracy were not related to language use, however. Taguchi (2008: 57–58) also reported considerable variation among participants in the reported amount of language use for all sub-skill areas, suggesting that opportunities for input and interaction were susceptible to social conditions and learner agency.

Dewey (2007) examined the role of language use (LCP) in vocabulary development among 20 US-based learners of Japanese in three programmes (11-week SA, 9-week domestic immersion [IM] and 13-week at-home-institution instruction [AH]). Both SA and IM students outgained AH students in all three measures of vocabulary (receptive knowledge, depth of vocabulary knowledge and everyday situational vocabulary). Productive language use (speaking/writing activities) facilitated vocabulary development. Among SA students, time spent speaking Japanese correlated with gains in situational vocabulary, and time spent writing in Japanese correlated with gains in depth of vocabulary knowledge.

However, language use did not predict gains in reading comprehension in a study by Dewey (2004) that used the RLCP (a modified LCP for reading and cultural learning) to examine gains in reading (e.g. free recall of texts students had read, self-assessments; reading processes assessed by think-aloud). The participants were 30 US-based students learning Japanese: 15 in an 11-week SA programme in Japan, and 15 in a 9-week IM programme. Only in self-assessments did SA students show greater gains than IM students, and language use and cultural learning did not predict the gains in any of the measures. Dewey attributed the lack of significant correlations to greater variability in the RLCP among SA participants engaging in a wide range of activities.

A study conducted by Díaz-Campos (2004) linked improvement in Spanish pronunciation to L2 use (LCP) regardless of whether students studied at home or abroad. Díaz-Campos assessed the pronunciation of Spanish consonantal segments among US-based students in two pro-grammes (10 students in AH, 27 in 10-week SA in Spain). The AH and SA groups made comparable gains in producing native-like segments. The factors associated with native-like pronunciation were more years of instruction (seven or more), more use of Spanish during AH/SA and gender (females).

Development in writing was examined as part of the Study Abroad and Language Acquisition (SALA) project. Pérez-Vidal and Juan-Garau (2009) examined development in writing among 37 Catalan–Spanish bilingual undergraduates majoring in English, both before SA and after three months of SA in English-speaking countries (mostly the UK). Gains in writing were assessed by five measures: two measures of fluency (words per clause; words per minute), accuracy (errors per word), syntactic complexity (ratio of subordinated clauses) and lexical complexity. After SA, the students as a group showed significant gains in fluency (words per minute) and in lexical complexity. Dividing the group into high and low achievers, Pérez-Vidal and Juan-Garau found that high achiever status was associated with intra-SA factors involving opportunities for contact (e.g. having a job while abroad; developing a wider social network), self-assessment and experien-tial emotions (e.g. having grown more outgoing during SA).

Many studies examining relationships between the amount of intra-SA language use and various linguistic outcomes have reported some-what surprising findings. The reported amount of language use was often not related to gains, sometimes related to gains regardless of whether the students were in AH or SA (e.g. Díaz-Campos, 2004) and even negatively correlated with gains, in the case of time spent with a host family (e.g. Segalowitz & Freed, 2004). Such mixed findings may be partly attribut-able to how language use is quantified. Dewey (2017), arguing that many previous studies utilising LCP have only used the overall total number of hours in their analysis, attaches importance to breaking down how much time is spent on different activities. Meanwhile, Fernández and Gates Tapia (2016) found that some LCP items are unclear to participants, and that the LCP might not capture fluctuations in language use during SA.

Mixed findings could also be explained by the quality of interac-tion, which may itself be linked to another intra-SA variable – the social network. Recent studies increasingly consider social networks as one of the intra-SA variables. Coleman (2015: 42) underscores their significance, stating, 'social networks are crucial to the learning outcomes of study abroad. [...] They represent a major influence on the variability of the study abroad experience'.

Dewey *et al.* (2012: 114) defines the social network as 'a structure comprised of individuals who are connected with others by one or more specific types of interdependency, such as friendship, kinship, or common interests'. It has recently drawn increasing attention, but earlier studies also indicated the importance of the social aspects of students' experience during SA. Ginsberg and Miller (2000), for example, found that among 85 US-based students learning Russian in four-month programmes in Russia, time spent using language did not explain whether or not their oral proficiency (OPI) improved. Instead, their case studies of four students revealed that the difference appeared to be due to the quality of interaction with a small number of locals rather than the quantity of social activity undertaken with locals.

Isabelli-García (2006) attempted to account for variation in students' linguistic gains (SOPI) by examining the relationship between motivation and the development of social networks among four US university students learning Spanish in Argentina for five months. The students' weekly diary entries were used to assess their motivation, attitude to the host culture and social networking. Tom, whose motivation was initially instrumental, experienced a change to integrative motivation through friendships with locals. Another student, Jennifer, failed to establish a social network during SA, which negatively affected her motivation and attitude. Tom's oral proficiency improved, but Jennifer's did not. The students' motivation/attitude affected social network building, which in turn influenced their motivation/attitude.

Dewey et al. (2012) studied the relationship between these two inter-related intra-SA variables, language use (LCP) and self-reported social networking and post-SA self-perceived gains in speaking (based on OPI guidelines) among 204 US university students learning Japanese who spent an average of 8.4 months in Japan. Several factors were found to be significant predictors of gains: one of the social network variables (dispersion, i.e. the number of social groups such as host family and school clubs) and three measures of language use. Two measures (total time speaking Japanese, time speaking Japanese with close native speaker friends) correlated positively with perceived gains, whereas the correlation was negative for the third variable (time spent speaking English with native speakers of Japanese).

Baker-Smemoe et al. (2014) examined seven pre-SA and intra-SA variables, including social networks, to determine predictors of gains in oral proficiency (OPI) among 102 native English speakers who participated in SA of various lengths (8–16 weeks) in Mexico, Spain, France, Egypt, Russia and China. The variables examined were students' age, gender, personality, pre-SA oral proficiency (OPI), pre-SA intercultural sensitivity, social networks and language use (LCP). Dividing the students into 'gainers' who improved their oral proficiency ($n = 57$) and 'non-gainers' who did not ($n = 43$), the authors investigated whether gainers and non-gainers related differently to the examined variables and which variables predicted gains. The gainers differed from the non-gainers in two aspects of social networks: dispersion (gainers were in more groups) and intensity (they forged closer relationships). Considering all the variables, the optimal combination of predictors consisted of pre-SA intercultural sensitivity and two aspects of social networks – high English proficiency among target language friends and decreased network size over time. The authors explain that English-proficient native speakers of the target language likely facilitate L2 learners' entry into local social groups, and the smaller network suggests intense, emotionally closer relationships. The amount of language use played an insignificant role, even when divided into different types of activities.

What is important, then, is the quality of interaction enabled by intense social networks, i.e. 'deeper conversations with close friends' (Baker-Smemoe et al., 2014: 481). Meanwhile, the nature of desirable social networks during SA seems to vary. For instance, the role of English-speaking locals yielded mixed results (i.e. negative consequence of time speaking English with Japanese locals [Dewey et al., 2012] vs. positive consequence of social networking with English-proficient locals [Baker-Smemoe et al., 2014]). Recent advances in technology further complicate social networks and language use. SA itself has changed dramatically; it is no longer an 'immersion' context due to technological advances in telecommunications and globalisation. The ability to sustain one's home network via the internet is a factor that impedes the expansion of social networks (e.g. Coleman & Chafer, 2010; Mitchell, 2015). However, social media like Facebook could also enhance L2 interaction and social networks (Back, 2013).

Other pre-SA and intra-SA factors also affect whether and how well students succeed in building social networks and using the L2. WTC in the L2 is another such variable. Yashima et al. (2004) studied 60 Japanese high school students who studied in the USA, to analyse the relationship between pre-SA attitude/motivation (including WTC) and (1) students' communication with locals (amount and frequency) and (2) their satisfaction with interpersonal relationships during SA. All variables were assessed with a questionnaire. WTC was significantly correlated with the self-reported amount of time spent talking with the host family, and frequency of communication correlated significantly with students' satisfaction with interpersonal relationships.

Dewey et al. (2013) considered several pre-SA and intra-SA variables to discover what factors predict the amount of intra-SA language use (total, in-class, out-of-class, receptive and interactive). The participants were 118 L2 learners in six programmes in Spain, Mexico, France, Russia, China and Egypt. A regression analysis was conducted with measures of personality, OPI ratings, gender, age, programme variables (housing type, programme length, coursework) and social network variables. The most important factor influencing language use (measured via language logs, where students recorded minutes per day spent on specified activities over one week) was the SA programme. When variables related to programmes were removed from the regression equation, the sole predictor for language use (total hours, interactive hours and receptive hours) was age: older learners reported using the language more. The number of native speaker friends was a predictor of the total time spent on out-of-class language use. Personality was a predictor of in-class language use in that more open (curious, imaginative) students reported more L2 use than did less open students. Intercultural sensitivity, often reported to predict language gains in other studies, was not a predictor of any aspect of language use. The authors speculate that the apparent lack of effect of personality on out-of-class hours may be due to greater diversity in out-of-class experience.

Describing language learning as 'part of a much bigger picture', Coleman (2015: 38) urges research on 'whole people and whole lives', suggesting that there exist other important personal outcomes of SA. Indeed, researchers are increasingly interested in studying other types of SA outcomes, most notably in interculturality and identity. Studies focused on intercultural sensitivity are discussed first below.

Pre-SA individual differences as predictors of SA outcomes in intercultural sensitivity

Though the distinction between intercultural sensitivity and intercultural competence is not always clear, Hammer *et al.* (2003: 422) distinguished intercultural sensitivity from intercultural competence by defining the former as 'the ability to discriminate and experience relevant cultural differences' and the latter as 'the ability to think and act in interculturally appropriate ways'. Some researchers have used questionnaires (e.g. the ICCS) to quantitatively assess intercultural sensitivity and determine which pre-SA and/or intra-SA variables predict development in intercultural sensitivity.

Martinsen (2011), who showed that pre-SA intercultural sensitivity predicted gains in speech among 45 US-based students learning Spanish for six weeks in Argentina, also examined pre-SA and intra-SA predictors of students' development of intercultural sensitivity (ICCS). He examined those same students' pre-SA motivation, pre-SA language skills, the intra-SA relationship between student and host family and interaction with native speakers (LCP), and found that the time spent interacting with native speakers predicted the development of intercultural sensitivity.

Williams (2005) examined gains in intercultural sensitivity and adaptability among US-based students in SA and AH programmes. The SA students (*n* = 44) participated in one-semester SA in European countries, Australia, Japan and Mexico. The AH students (*n* = 48) were recruited from business and English courses. SA students showed greater gains, but regardless of whether students studied abroad, intercultural exposure (e.g. number of close friends from another culture, different languages studied) was the sole significant predictor of high scores on intercultural sensitivity and adaptability among various factors considered (e.g. gender, major, religion).

Bloom and Miranda (2015) reported a similar finding on the significance of prior intercultural experience. Their mixed-methods study on intercultural sensitivity change focused on 12 US-based students of Spanish who participated in a summer SA programme in Spain. They did not find significant quantitative change in the students' self-assessment on intercultural sensitivity questionnaires after SA, but this was largely accounted for through qualitative analyses of students' reflective journal entries. When the group was divided into those with less and more prior intercultural experience, they found that the two groups of students had qualitatively different perceptions and experiences, and that less experienced students tended to overestimate their intercultural sensitivity on the questionnaire.

However, pre-SA intercultural experience, such as having lived in another culture, is not always related to intercultural development during SA. Vande Berg *et al.* (2009) compared gains in Intercultural Development Inventory (IDI) scores and oral proficiency (SOPI) among 138 US-based AH students and 968 SA students learning seven different languages (Arabic, Chinese, French, German, Japanese, Russian and Spanish) in programmes of various lengths. The SA students outperformed the AH students in both, but pre-SA experience living, traveling or studying abroad was not associated with intercultural development. Interestingly, SA students who lived with other US or host country students showed significant gains in IDI, while students who lived with host families did not. However, pre-SA IDI scores were highest in the latter group of students, suggesting less room for development. Furthermore, students who reported spending more time with their host families gained more than those who spent less time. This suggests that further investigation may be necessary to understand the nature of intercultural development.

Kinginger (2009: 27) contends that SLA-oriented SA research is often product oriented and aims to uncover a generalisable psycholinguistic process of L2 learning, whereas considering SA as a context variable 'analogous to an experimental treatment' yields puzzling results. Kinginger (2009: 52) remarks that 'individual differences are absorbed in the effort to document group differences, yet their presence must be noted'. Such notes on variation are included in studies reviewed above (e.g. Davidson [2010] and Martinsen [2010] on variation in the outcomes; Hernández [2010] and Taguchi [2008] on variation in how students spent their time). Because of these concerns, some researchers pursue a more process-oriented approach and qualitatively examine students' experiences and activities during SA. Moreover, there is increasing interest in 'differential access to learning opportunities shaped by learners' subjective desires or access to social networks' (Kinginger, 2009: 30).

Individuals' Differing Processes during SA

Variations in homestay experiences

One of the most puzzling aspects of previous studies is the unexpected absence of positive effects of homestay or even the existence of negative effects (e.g. Segalowitz & Freed, 2004). This was also shown by Rivers (1998), who compared 2,224 dormitory placement students and 285 homestay placement students in ACTR data from 1976 to 1994. Homestay students were slightly less likely to exhibit gains in speaking and listening, but more likely to gain in reading.

Many case studies have elucidated the magnitude of variability in students' homestay experiences. Wilkinson (1998a) conducted ethnographic interviews over eight months and contrasted Molise and Ashley, two US-based students learning French. Both seemed prepared for a short four-week SA in France in terms of intercultural experience and language proficiency (though Molise, having immigrated from Cambodia via Thai and Philippine refugee camps, apparently underwent extensive cultural adjustment first-hand). Molise felt lucky to be accepted as a family member in France, but Ashley was disappointed to find her host family was detached and unwelcoming. Molise spoke French daily with the family, but Ashley did not have the same opportunities. Upon encountering unexpected cultural deviations, Molise sought advice and explanations from her host family, whereas Ashley turned to US-based peers. Molise changed her major to French; Ashley dropped her French minor. Wilkinson (1998b: 134) attributes Molise's greater cultural learning in part to her Cambodian-American hybrid identity, which 'weaken[ed] her ties to one particular ethnic group, making it less threatening for her to try on a new identity as a foreigner in France'. Others among Wilkinson's (1998a, 2000) seven participants also experienced discomfort with their homestay families, for example feeling like a tenant. Wilkinson (2000: 40) underscores each student's SA experience as 'unique and dynamic, shaped through myriad personal backgrounds, opportunities, and choices'.

Students' accounts reveal that homestay does not necessarily provide many opportunities to use the L2 in other contexts, either. Tanaka (2007) interviewed Japanese students who had spent twelve weeks studying at a private English school in New Zealand. Most of the 18 students, who stayed with local families, were unable to interact with locals or host families because of their English proficiency or their reserved personality, and only 5 students had positive experiences. Some students could not comprehend the host family's English or were not proficient enough to express themselves. Many merely exchanged simple greetings or had short conversations.

Allen's (2010a) study of 18 US-based university students studying French for six weeks in France also revealed variation in the perspectives and experiences that students described in bi-weekly learning blogs and interviews, reflecting divided perceptions about the helpfulness of inter-action with host families. Allen (2010a: 3, citing Lantolf & Pavlenko, 2001) also highlighted diversity in students' agency, which she considers a 'co-constructed phenomenon wherein individuals continually position themselves in relation to the learning process and learning environment'. Other studies focusing on students' experiences (Kinginger, 2008; Pel-legrino Aveni, 2005) have likewise discussed the homestay environment as a co-constructed phenomenon.

Upon finding a lack of positive or negative effect of homestay, researchers (Martinsen, 2010; Segalowitz & Freed, 2004) have speculated that interaction with a host family may be mostly based on repetitive interaction. In Fernández and Gates Tapia's (2016) comparison of two US-based students studying Spanish for 15 weeks in Argentina, Josh and Erin self-reported similar numbers of hours spent speaking with similar types of interlocutors (host mother and conversation partner). Josh's interaction consisted largely of repetitive, formulaic responses to the host mother's questions, whereas Erin often initiated a range of topics. Likewise, Diao et al. (2018) compared their US-based students, Adam and Sam, whose one semester studying Mandarin in China produced very different outcomes in oral proficiency (SOPI). In their self-recorded din-nertime conversations with host families, Adam relied on his host family for subtopic nomination, while Sam's active nomination of subtopics led to a greater range of subtopics. The authors attributed their respective linguistic gains to the quality of interaction co-constructed by the host parents and the students.

Mealtime interaction with the host family can also facilitate cultural learning (e.g. Kinginger et al., 2016; Lee et al., 2017). Kinginger et al. (2016) studied US-based high school students' mealtime interaction with host families, utilising audio-recorded interaction and interviews with the participants and host family. Lee et al. (2017) utilised audio record-ing of interactions, bi-weekly diaries, interviews and photographs in a longitudinal study on the process through which two US-based homestay students of Chinese learned table etiquette. The study revealed how students learned language, culinary practices and associated ideologies through the interactions.

These studies underscore the importance of closely investigating both SA contexts and students' perceptions, and understanding how the contexts and interactions are co-constructed. Students' agency, which is linked to their motivation, plays a significant role in shaping intra-SA contexts.

Dynamicity/fluidity of individuals' motivation

As Isabelli-García's (2006) study showed, motivation is a dynamic, fluid variable subject to change. In fact, many traditional learner-internal individual difference variables previously treated as static or unchanging are now understood to be fluid and dynamic. Changes in these variables can themselves be objects of inquiry, rather than potential sources of differences in outcomes. Using mixed methods, Allen and Herron (2003) examined changes in linguistic and affective outcomes among 25 US-based university students studying French in a summer programme in France. The students showed gains in oral proficiency (picture description and role play) and listening comprehension. Though the interviews showed no significant quantitative changes in motivation or attitude towards the target culture after SA, they revealed students' language anxiety during SA, due to linguistic insecurity and cultural differences.

Allen (2010b, 2010c) examined the development of motivation among US-based intermediate-level French learners studying in a six-week programme in France (two participants in Allen [2010b] and six in Allen [2010c]). The data included questionnaires, interviews and learning blogs before, during and after SA. Before SA, the students' motives were either linguistically oriented (desire to be proficient in French) or pragmatic (useful for future careers). These motives affected their construction of their social network, the ways they used language, efforts to integrate into host families during SA and their overall motivation. Linguistically oriented students became further motivated to learn and use French, while pragmatically oriented students did not develop language learning motivation but rather saw SA as a cultural and travel experience. The students' agency affected their contexts (e.g. relationship with peers and host family), which further influenced their motivation.

Tarp (2006) examined semi-open questionnaires, semi-structured interviews and diaries of Danish business school students who participated in one- or two-week (short-term) SA in the UK, France, Ireland, Scotland and Spain, to show how individual students' agendas (expectations and purposes of SA) influenced their agency in responding to intervening conditions (e.g. access to and interaction with the foreign culture), leading to differences in their outcomes. Individuals' agency plays an important role in their experiences and outcomes – including the development of intercultural sensitivity.

Individuals' experiences and cultural, sociolinguistic and pragmatic development

To explore how seven US-based, advanced students of Spanish in SA perceived their own intercultural learning during SA, Covert (2014) examined their reflective journals and interviewed them. The students spent a semester in Chile, where they all lived with host families. The participants' lack of knowledge of the Spanish language or culture made them aware of their intercultural incompetence such that they felt awkward and uncomfortable. However, the students also reported purposefully adjusting their language and behaviour in order to conform to local norms. Covert attributes such transformation to the students' personal agency.

Larzén-Östermark (2011) focused on two students, selected from six, in order to shed light on individuals' differing learning experiences. The Finnish university students, both majoring in English, envisaged careers as English teachers. Suvi (female) spent an academic year in Scotland studying Gaelic and Celtic studies and English philology; Mikko (male) worked in a hostel in London for about seven months. Though their aspirations and experiences differed greatly, both felt their greatest gains were in cultural awareness, achieved through interaction with people of multicultural backgrounds – Suvi at a sandwich shop where she worked part-time, and Mikko at the hostel where he held a managerial post with six subordinates of various ethnic backgrounds. Suvi learned about the importance of making cultural differences overt and negotiable; Mikko became aware of the importance of acknowledging prejudices and making efforts to reduce them.

Jackson's (2013) longitudinal examination of the 'whole person' development of Kingston, a university student from Hong Kong who studied in Canada for a year, focused on his intercultural sensitivity (IDI and other data including conversations, field notes and essays) from pre-SA, ending after a one-semester course on intercultural transition in Hong Kong. Kingston tended to overestimate his intercultural sensitivity (IDI scores), interacted mostly with people sharing his own ethnicity and had limited development during SA. However, the post-SA guided critical reflection prompted awareness of his reluctance to change during SA and the realisation that he had failed to take advantage of opportunities. It was the post-SA guided critical reflection that developed his intercultural sensitivity and eventually transformed him.

These studies focused on small numbers of individuals and qualitatively analysed their experiences and growth. Such outcome variables as intercultural sensitivity can be elusive, but the studies elucidated different processes by which students developed intercultural sensitivity. In-depth longitudinal qualitative studies have likewise illuminated students' experiences and their sociolinguistic and pragmatic development.

In a longitudinal ethnographic study, Siegal (1995) focused specifically on individual differences in experiences with the use of honorifics in Japanese. She compared two contrasting students studying Japanese in Japan: Arina (a university student from Hungary) and Mary (a Japanese teacher from New Zealand). Conducted over 18 months, the study utilised several types of data (e.g. learning journals, interviews, field observation) to illustrate the experiences in Japan that informed these students' perceptions of honorific language, and the way they used honorifics in Japan. Their use of honorifics was linked to their presentation of self and their experiences. Attempting to maintain face as a scholar, Mary misused the modal marker *deshoo* 'isn't it', believing erroneously that it expresses politeness. Arina, after participating in a public event where she observed how Japanese speakers use different registers for specific purposes, had incorporated honorifics into her repertoire.

Hassall (2015) reported on the development of understanding and use of address forms in Indonesian by contrasting Ross and Amy, two Australian university students who studied Indonesian in a summer programme. In Indonesian, kinship terms (e.g. *Bapak* 'father' and *Ibu* 'mother') are used in place of the pronoun 'you' depending on context, while the pronoun *anda* 'you', introduced in the textbook, is rarely used. Hassall utilised pre- and post-tests and interviews to assess students' development bi-weekly. Ross, a homestay *ab initio* learner of Indonesian, took advantage of mediation and support from an intermediate-level fellow student also staying with Ross's host family. By speaking Indonesian with his hosts, Ross learned to use kinship terms and dropped the use of *anda*. Unlike Ross, who engaged in social interaction with locals, Amy felt alienated in the unfamiliar environment (which Hassall attributed to her low proficiency and gender) and maintained her identity as a formal learner, retaining the use of *anda* and regarding kinship terms solely as vocative terms.

These studies revealed that each individual's sociolinguistic and pragmatic development was affected by both individuals' experience and identity, leading to their differing outcomes. We turn next to studies that illustrate variations in such sociolinguistic and pragmatic outcomes.

Variations in Individuals' Outcomes

Sociolinguistic and pragmatic outcomes

Sociolinguistic awareness and the acquisition of sociolinguistic variation are considered more susceptible to the benefits of the naturalistic exposure available during SA than is grammatical or lexical development. Yet, as we saw above, students' intra-SA experiences and dispositions vary, and their post-SA sociolinguistic and pragmatic outcomes vary greatly. Howard (2012) observed individual differences in the development and outcomes of five Ireland-based university advanced learners of French who spent a year in France. He analysed the students' use of a range of variable features of French that differed in the degree of (in)formality, including negative *ne* deletion and *nous/on* variation in referring to 'we' in pre-SA, post-SA and one-year delayed post-SA sociolinguistic interviews. He found that in their pre-SA interviews, the students already differed considerably in their use of informal variants, suggesting that some had learned informal variants in the classroom. The students used more informal variants in post-SA interviews to varying degrees, and generally retained the use of informal variants one year after SA, but to varying degrees (i.e. some decreased use of some informal variants, while others increased use of some informal variants). The study highlighted the value of close-up analyses of individuals.

The use of plain (informal) and polite (formal) sentence-ending styles among learners of Japanese has also been extensively studied. Iwasaki (2010) studied five US-based students' use of these styles by comparing their pre-SA OPI with post-SA OPI conducted after they spent a year in Japan. Though earlier studies (e.g. Marriott, 1995) had reported overuse of the plain style with university instructors (with whom the polite style is expected) or a haphazard mix of the two styles among Australian secondary school students, Iwasaki found that only two students appeared to overuse the plain style. Moreover, style shifts by these five students' were mostly consistent with the styles' social meanings, suggesting that they were making choices about using the styles. Though Iwasaki (2010) did not examine the students' experiences during SA, Iwasaki (2011) cast light on four of the five students' experiences and their interpretations of those experiences, conveyed in retrospective interviews. They had developed their understanding of the styles via diverse experiences and had chosen to use the styles to present their preferred identities in each context, sometimes knowingly diverging from the norm.

Students' sociolinguistic and pragmatic outcomes partly reflect the students' agency and (preferred) identities. Post-SA students deliberately diverge from the pragmatic norm at times. Kinginger and Farrell (2004) reported that Benjamin, a US-based student who wished to appear polite, preferred to use the formal French *vous* 'you' even with peers, while another student, Bill, preferred to use the informal *tu*, regarding it as a marker of his personality. These students took part in Kinginger's (2008) extensive, thorough mixed-methods study on 24 US-based students learning French in France for an academic year. Kinginger examined various aspects of their linguistic development, utilising various pre- and post-SA tests and collecting qualitative data via journals and interviews over the year of SA participation. She explored case histories of six students in depth based on their journals and interviews. The combination of quantitative linguistic assessments and detailed analyses of the students' experiences and stances uncovered the complex relationship between their intra-SA experiences/perceptions and their language learning outcomes. Not only were the students' environments (e.g. homestay) and case histories highly variable, but their dispositions towards language learning and SA also differed widely, affected by the dominant discourses about SA in the USA. The students' outcomes in language learning were attributed to all of these factors.

Changes in sense of selves and L2 identities

Attention is increasingly being drawn to each student's experience, stance and identities. Students' motivations, affects and anxieties influence their outcomes and are tied to their image of self. Pellegrino Aveni (2005) investigated 76 US-based university students studying Russian in

Russia for either four months or an academic year, and selected six students who provided a large amount of information (narrative journals, interviews and questionnaires). She illustrated how inextricably each student's self and sense of security were intertwined with his or her language use. The students coped with anxiety triggered by threats to their self-presentation, arising from both learner-internal sources (e.g. their own attitudes towards self) and external, social-environmental cues. However, the author reported that many enhanced their internal security, which in turn enabled them to participate more actively in interactions.

Benson *et al.* (2012, 2013) focused on SA students' narratives and their identity development. Benson *et al.* (2013: 127) summarised the findings of the 2012 study, stating that whereas 'study abroad programmes provide a context to scaffold second language identity and its development', individuals' L2 identities are equally influential in their own understandings of their SA experiences. Benson *et al.* (2013) report on narratives by Siri and Janice, both English teacher education students from Hong Kong, who each spent a semester in an English-speaking country (Australia and the UK, respectively). Their SA experiences contrasted most in terms of their engagement in interaction with local people (especially their host families). Their contrasting levels of engagement led Janice to develop her L2 identity while Siri's development stagnated. Siri, who described her personality as very shy and passive, made no effort to learn; hence, her SA experience reinforced her Hong Kong identity. In contrast, Janice began to perceive herself as an English user, rather than just a learner. According to Benson *et al.*, the students' SA experiences and viewpoints are a consequence of both individuality, shaped by pre-SA experiences, goals and expectations, and identity. The uniqueness of these experiences also conditions individual differences in the outcomes of SA.

Discussion and Conclusion

The puzzles of SA have gradually been cracked. No single 'individual difference' variable, internal or external, can predict students' outcomes, not only because multiple variables interact with each other, but also because many of the variables are dynamic and subject to change. For this reason (among others), comparisons between SA and AH as the control are no longer emphasised (Marijuan & Sanz, 2018). The crucial factor in intra-SA change is each student's own agency. Hence, positioning SA students as 'language learners' is problematic – in at least two respects. First, individuals studying abroad are not passive learners whose outcome is subject to the context, but individuals who act in given environments according to their goals. Second, their goals are by no means limited to language learning.

SA research on individual differences/variations reveals shifts of orientation in methodologies and the treatment of individuals that mirror the

changes in applied linguistics discussed by Benson (2019). Early research on
SA, focused on mainstream SLA 'individual differences', aimed to discover
whether and which attributes of individual learners would predict successful SA, with linguistic development as the primary criterion for 'success'.
As the research goal was to provide generalisable, statistically significant
results, quantitative studies examined groups (categorised according to
their attributes). In this process, each individual learner became a 'generalised abstract entity' or 'an abstraction, a simplified representation of
personification of the learning process, devoid of any truly individual and
social dimension' (Riley, 2003: 96, cited in Benson, 2019). This paradoxical
approach, dubbed 'SLA individualism', treats constructs such as motivation as attributes of individuals rather than relationships between individuals and their social contexts (Toohey & Norton, 2003: 58).

As SLA research increasingly shifts its focus to social orientation, individuals' language learning has come to be regarded as a social process in a
social context. Though this chapter's review has not dealt with the theoretical frameworks employed in the summarised studies, the methodological
shifts point to shifts in commonly adopted theoretical orientations as well,
that is, from linguistically and/or cognitively oriented theories to socially
oriented theoretical frameworks (especially sociocultural theory). The
resulting intense focus on individuals in turn requires qualitative approaches
to research, as seen in the SA research above (see also Jackson, 2017).

Benson (2019) argues that applied linguistics is now entering the era
of 'person-centredness', whereby language learners are seen as 'people'
within a social conception of individuality, just as Coleman (2013) advo-
cates consideration of 'whole people, whole lives' in SA research. Also, a
renewed conceptualisation of 'success' in SA positions students as more
than just 'language learners': their successes can be manifested variously,
including in heightened intercultural sensitivity, enhanced sense of self
and renewed identities. Students and SA contexts both vary widely, and
the individuals involved (with their motivation, agency, sense of self and
identities) interact with various contexts. As Coleman (2015: 37) puts it,
'all [these] divergent external factors interact with the individual's changing identities, goals and motivations, the social encounters, language use,
and physical and virtual networks [...] and the sheer serendipity of what
happens during a foreign sojourn'.

SA research has advanced. We now have a better understanding of the
complexity of the individual in a social context. Mixed-methods studies
(e.g. Kinginger, 2008) are very revealing, and the consolidation of results
from well-designed, large-scale quantitative studies (e.g. Dewey *et al.*,
2012, 2013) and from intensive qualitative studies enables us to identify
common issues, such as the importance of the social networks that enable
high-quality interaction, and the vital role of agency. The recent special
issue of the journal *System*, titled 'Methodological Diversity and Innovation in Study Abroad Research' (De Costa *et al.*, 2017), also features

some case studies and other innovative methodologies. The knowledge gained through diversified methodologies has deepened understanding of the complexity of the individuals in SA contexts.

Many taken-for-granted assumptions about SA are unsupported, and recent studies have explained why. Homestay does not always provide environments conducive to students' development. In terms of linguistic gains (and perhaps also for personal development), it is the quality of interaction that matters, rather than the amount of time spent with the host family. Importantly, homestay experience and interaction are co-constructed phenomena.

However, current research is unquestionably limited, especially in terms of individual research participants' characteristics: country of origin, race, ethnicity, socioeconomic background, cultural/linguistic heritage and so on (Marijuan & Sanz, 2018). Most studies deal with (Caucasian) university students based in the USA or Europe, or European or East Asian students whose destinations are English-speaking countries. Undoubtedly, this is partially due to two facts: only studies reported in English are widely read and included here, and university students are a population to which researchers have easy access.

SA often leads to significant renegotiation of identity, which is expected to diverge depending on who the participant is (e.g. Anya [2011] on black students; Jing-Schmidt et al. [2016] on heritage students). Identity renegotiation in turn affects experiences and outcomes. The effect of gender on linguistic outcomes was not found significant in Russian SA (Davidson, 2010), but gender is nonetheless reported to affect students' experiences and social networks, and little is known about Lesbian, Gay, Bisexual, Transgender, Queer (LGBTQ) individuals' SA experiences (see Marijuan & Sanz, 2018). Exploring individuals' experiences and development with attention to little-studied student characteristics may further our understanding of diversity, of the reality of individuals' SA experiences and possibly of commonly shared issues affecting the development of their language, culture and personhood.

Notes

(1) In her comprehensive critical review of earlier SA research, Kinginger (2009) also discusses important observations about individual differences.
(2) The LCP used in this study was an adapted version of the LCP used by Day (1985).
(3) The assessment instruments (e.g. LCP, OPI) used to collect the data are named in parentheses.
(4) The LCP used by Segalowitz and Freed (2004) and Hernández' (2010) modified LCP included a similar range of interactive and non-interactive activities.

References

Allen, H.W. (2010a) Interactive contact as linguistic affordance during short-term study abroad: Myth or reality? *Frontiers: The Interdisciplinary Journal of Study Abroad* 19, 1–26.

Allen, H.W. (2010b) Language-learning motivation during short-term study abroad: An activity theory perspective. *Foreign Language Annals* 43 (1), 27–49.

Allen, H.W. (2010c) What shapes short-term study abroad experiences? A comparative case study of students' motives and goals. *Journal of Studies in International Education* 14 (5), 452–470.

Allen, H.W. and Herron, C. (2003) A mixed-methodology investigation of the linguistic and affective outcomes of summer study abroad. *Foreign Language Annals* 36 (3), 370–385.

Anya, U. (2011) Connecting with communities of learners and speakers: Integrative ideals, experiences, and motivations of successful black second language learners. *Foreign Language Annals* 44 (3), 441-466.

Back, M. (2013) Using Facebook data to analyze learner interaction during study abroad. *Foreign Language Annals* 46 (3), 377–401.

Baker-Smemoe, W., Dewey, D.P., Bown, J. and Martinsen, R.A. (2014) Variables affecting L2 gains during study abroad. *Foreign Language Annals* 47 (3), 464-486.

Benson, P. (2019) Ways of seeing: The individual and the social in applied linguistics research methodologies. *Language Teaching* 52 (1), 60–70.

Benson, P., Barkhuizen, G., Bodycott, P. and Brown, J. (2012) Study abroad and the development of second language identities. *Applied Linguistics Review* 3 (1), 173–193.

Benson, P., Barkhuizen, G., Bodycott, P. and Brown, J. (2013) *Second Language Identity in Narratives of Study Abroad*. Basingstoke: Palgrave Macmillan.

Bloom, M. and Miranda, A. (2015) Intercultural sensitivity through short-term study abroad. *Language and Intercultural Communication* 15 (4), 567–580.

Brecht, R., Davidson, D. and Ginsberg, R.B. (1993) *Predictors of Foreign Language Gain during Study Abroad*. Washington, DC: The National Foreign Language Center.

Brecht, R., Davidson, D. and Ginsberg, R.B. (1995) Predictors of foreign language gain during study abroad. In B. Freed (ed.) *Second Language Acquisition in a Study Abroad Context* (pp. 37–66). Amsterdam/Philadelphia, PA: Benjamins.

Coleman, J.A. (2013) Researching whole people and whole lives. In C. Kinginger (ed.) *Social and Cultural Aspects of Language Learning in Study Abroad* (pp. 17–46). Amsterdam/Philadelphia, PA: Benjamins.

Coleman, J.A. (2015) Social circles during residence abroad: What students do, and who with. In R. Mitchell, N. Tracy-Ventura and K. McManus (eds) *Social Interaction, Identity and Language Learning during Residence Abroad* (pp. 33–50). EUROSLA Monograph Series 4. Amsterdam: European Second Language Association. See http://www.eurosla.org/eurosla-monograph-series-2/social-interaction-identity-and-language-learning-during-residence-abroad/ (accessed 5 April 2018).

Coleman, J.A. and Chafer, T. (2010) Study abroad and the internet: Physical and virtual context in an era of expanding telecommunications. *Frontiers: The Interdisciplinary Journal of Study Abroad* 19, 151–167.

Covert, H.H. (2014) Stories of personal agency: Undergraduate students' perceptions of developing intercultural competence during a semester abroad in Chile. *Journal of Studies in International Education* 18 (2), 162–179.

Cushner, K. (1986) *Human Diversity in Action: Developing Multicultural Competencies for the Classroom*. New York: McGraw Hill.

Davidson, D.E. (2010) Study abroad: When, how long, and with what results? New data from the Russian front. *Foreign Language Annals* 43 (1), 6–26.

Day, R. (1985) The use of the target language in context and second language proficiency. In S. Gass and C. Madden (eds) *Input in Second Language Acquisition* (pp. 257–271). Rowley, MA: Newbury House.

De Costa, P.I., Rawal, H. and Zaykovskaya, I. (2017) Editorial introduction: Methodological diversity and innovation in study abroad research. *System* 71, 1–6.

DeKeyser, R. (1991) The semester overseas: What difference does it make? *ADFL Bulletin* 22 (2), 42–48.

DeKeyser, R. (2010) Monitoring processes in Spanish as a second language during a study abroad program. *Foreign Language Annals* 43 (1), 80–92.

DeKeyser, R. (2014) Methodological considerations about research on language development during study abroad. In C. Pérez-Vidal (ed.) *Language Acquisition in Study Abroad and Formal Instruction Contexts* (pp. 313–326). Amsterdam/Philadelphia, PA: Benjamins.

Dewaele, J.-M. (2009) Individual differences in second language acquisition. In W.C. Ritchie and T.K. Bhatia (eds) *The New Handbook of Second Language Acquisition* (pp. 623–646). Bingley: Emerald.

Dewey, D.P. (2004) A comparison of reading development by learners of Japanese in intensive domestic immersion and study abroad contexts. *Studies in Second Language Acquisition* 26, 303–327.

Dewey, D.P. (2007) Japanese vocabulary acquisition by learners in three contexts. *Frontiers: The Interdisciplinary Journal of Study Abroad* 15, 127–148.

Dewey, D.P. (2017) Measuring social interaction during study abroad: Quantitative methods and challenges. *System* 71, 49–59.

Dewey, D.P., Bown, J., Baker, W., Martinsen, R.A., Gold, C. and Eggett, D. (2013) Language use in six study abroad programs: An exploratory analysis of possible predictors. *Language Learning* 64 (1), 36–71.

Dewey, D.P., Bown, J. and Eggett, D. (2012) Japanese language proficiency, social networking, and language use during study abroad: Learners' perspectives. *Canadian Modern Language Review* 68 (2), 111–137.

Diao, W., Donovan, A. and Malone, M. (2018) Oral language development among Mandarin learners in Chinese homestays. *Study Abroad Research in Second Language Acquisition and International Education* 3 (1), 32–57.

Díaz-Campos, M. (2004) Context of learning in the acquisition of Spanish second language phonology. *Studies in Second Language Acquisition* 26 (2), 249–273.

Ellis, R. (2004) Individual differences in second language acquisition. In A. Davies and C. Elder (eds) *The Handbook of Applied Linguistics* (pp. 525–551). Oxford: Blackwell.

Fernández, J. and Gates Tapia, A.M. (2016) An appraisal of the Language Contact Profile as a tool to research local engagement in study abroad. *Study Abroad Research in Second Language Acquisition and International Education* 1 (2), 248–276.

Freed, B.F. (1990) Language learning in a study abroad context: The effects of interactive and non-interactive out-of-class contact on grammatical achievement and oral proficiency. In J.E. Alatis (ed.) *Linguistics, Language Teaching, and Language Acquisition. The Interdependence of Theory, Practice and Research* (pp. 459–477). Washington, DC: Georgetown University Press.

Freed, B.F. (1995) What makes us think that students who study abroad become fluent? In B.F. Freed (ed.) *Second Language Acquisition in a Study Abroad Context* (pp. 123–48). Amsterdam/Philadelphia, PA: John Benjamins.

Freed, B.F., Dewey, D.P., Segalowitz, N. and Halter, R. (2004) The language contact profile. *Studies in Second Language Acquisition* 26 (2), 349–356.

Ginsberg, R. and Miller, L. (2000) What do they do? Activities of students during study abroad. In R.D. Lambert and E. Shohamy (eds) *Language Policy and Pedagogy: Essays in Honor of A. Ronald Walton* (pp. 237–260). Amsterdam/Philadelphia, PA: Benjamins.

Grey, S., Cox, J.G., Serafini, E.J. and Sanz, C. (2015) The role of individual differences in the study abroad context: Cognitive capacity and language development during short-term intensive language exposure. *The Modern Language Journal* 99 (1), 137–157.

Hammer, M.R., Bennett, M.J. and Wiseman, R. (2003) Measuring intercultural sensitivity: The Intercultural Development Inventory. *International Journal of Intercultural Relations* 27 (4), 421–443.

Hassall, T. (2015) Individual variation in L2 study-abroad outcomes: A case study from Indonesian pragmatics. *Multilingua* 34 (1), 33–59.

Hernández, T.A. (2010) The relationship among motivation, interaction, and the development of second language oral proficiency in a study-abroad context. *The Modern
Language Journal* 94 (4), 600–617.

Howard, M. (2012) The advanced learner's sociolinguistic profile: On issues of individual
differences, second language exposure conditions, and type of sociolinguistic variable.
The Modern Language Journal 96 (1), 20–33.

Huebner, T. (1995) The effects of overseas language programs: Report on a case study
of an intensive Japanese course. In B. Freed (ed.) *Second Language Acquisition
in a Study Abroad Context* (pp. 171–193). Amsterdam/Philadelphia, PA: John
Benjamins.

Isabelli-García, C. (2006) Study abroad social networks, motivation and attitudes:
Implications for second language acquisition. In M.A. DuFon and E. Churchill (eds)
Language Learners in Study Abroad Contexts (pp. 231–258). Clevedon: Multilingual
Matters.

Iwasaki, N. (2010) Style shifts among Japanese learners before and after study abroad in
Japan: Becoming active social agents in Japanese. *Applied Linguistics* 31 (1), 45–71.

Iwasaki, N. (2011) Learning L2 Japanese 'politeness' and 'impoliteness': Young American
men's dilemmas during study abroad. *Japanese Language and Literature* 45, 67–106.

Jackson, J. (2013) The transformation of 'a frog in the well': A path to a more intercultural, global mindset. In C. Kinginger (ed.) *Social and Cultural Aspects of Language
Learning in Study Abroad* (pp. 179–204). Amsterdam/Philadelphia, PA: Benjamins.

Jackson, J. (2017) Commentary 3: Case studies of study abroad: Making sense of developmental trajectories. *System* 71, 122–124.

Jing-Schmidt, Z., Chen, J.-Y. and Zhang, Z. (2016) Identity development in the ancestral
homeland: A Chinese heritage perspective. *The Modern Language Journal* 100 (4),
797–812.

Kinginger, C. (2008) Language learning in study abroad: Case studies of Americans in
France. *The Modern Language Journal* Monograph issue, 92 (S.1), 1–124.

Kinginger, C. (2009) *Language Learning and Study Abroad: A Critical Reading of
Research*. Basingstoke: Palgrave Macmillan.

Kinginger, C. (2015) Student mobility and identity-related language learning. *Intercultural
Education* 26 (1), 6–15.

Kinginger, C. and Farrell, K. (2004) Assessing development of meta-pragmatic awareness
in study abroad. *Frontiers: The Interdisciplinary Journal of Study Abroad* 10, 19–42.

Kinginger, C., Lee, S.-H., Wu, Q. and Tan, D. (2016) Contextualized language practices as
sites for learning: Mealtime talk in short-term Chinese homestays. *Applied Linguistics*
37 (5), 716–740.

Lantolf, J.P. and Pavlenko, A. (2001) (S)econd (L)anguage (A)ctivity theory: Understanding second language learners as people. In M. Breen (ed.) *Learner Contributions to
Language Learning: New Directions in Research* (pp. 141–158). London: Longman.

Larzén-Östermark, E. (2011) Intercultural sojourns as educational experiences: A narrative study of the outcomes of Finnish student teachers' language-practice periods in
Britain. *Scandinavian Journal of Educational Research* 55 (5), 455–473.

Lee, S.-H., Wu, Q., Di, C. and Kinginger, C. (2017) Learning to eat politely at the Chinese
homestay dinner table: Two contrasting case studies. *Foreign Language Annals* 50
(1), 135–158.

Llanes, À. (2011) The many faces of study abroad: An update on the research on L2 gains
emerged during a study abroad experience. *International Journal of Multilingualism*
8 (3), 189–215.

Llanes, À., Tragant, E. and Serrano, R. (2012) The role of individual differences in a study
abroad experience: The case of Erasmus students. *International Journal of Multilingualism* 9 (3), 318–342.

Magnan, S.S. and Back, M. (2007) Social interaction and linguistic gain during study
abroad. *Foreign Language Annals* 40 (1), 43–61.

Marijuan, S. and Sanz, C. (2018) Expanding boundaries: Current and new directions in study abroad research and practice. *Foreign Language Annals* 51 (1), 185–204.

Marriott, H. (1995) The acquisition of politeness patterns by exchange students in Japan. In B. Freed (ed.) *Second Language Acquisition in a Study Abroad Context* (pp. 197–224). Amsterdam/Philadelphia, PA: Benjamins.

Martinsen, R.A. (2010) Short-term study abroad: Predicting changes in oral skills. *Foreign Language Annals* 43 (3), 504–530.

Martinsen, R. (2011) Predicting changes in cultural sensitivity among students of Spanish during short-term study abroad. *Hispania* 94 (1), 121–141.

Matsumura, S. (2003) Modelling the relationships among interlanguage pragmatic development, L2 proficiency, and exposure to L2. *Applied Linguistics* 24 (4), 465–491.

Mitchell, R. (2015) The development of social relations during residence abroad. *Innovation in Language Learning and Teaching* 9 (1), 22–33.

Pellegrino Aveni, V. (2005) *Study Abroad and Second Language Use: Constructing Self.* Cambridge: Cambridge University Press.

Pérez-Vidal, C. and Juan-Garau, M. (2009) The effect of study abroad (SA) on written performance. In L. Roberts, D. Véronique, A.C. Nilsol and M. Tellier (eds) *EUROSLA Yearbook* (pp. 269–295). Amsterdam: Benjamins.

Riley, P. (2003) Self-access as access to 'self': Cultural variation in the notions of the self and personhood. In D. Palfreyman and R. Smith (eds) *Learner Autonomy across Cultures: Language Education Perspectives* (pp. 92–109). Basingstoke: Palgrave Macmillan.

Rivers, W.P. (1998) Is being there enough? The effects of homestay placements on language gain during study abroad. *Foreign Language Annals* 31 (4), 492–500.

Roberts, L. and Meyer, A. (2012) Individual differences in second language learning: Introduction. *Language Learning* 62 (s2), 1–4.

Segalowitz, N. and Freed, B.F. (2004) Context, contact, and cognition in oral fluency acquisition. *Studies in Second Language Acquisition* 26, 173–199.

Siegal, M. (1995) Individual differences and study abroad: Women learning Japanese in Japan. In B. Freed (ed.) *Second Language Acquisition in a Study Abroad Context* (pp. 225–244). Amsterdam/Philadelphia, PA: Benjamins.

Taguchi, N. (2008) Cognition, language contact, and the development of pragmatic comprehension in a study-abroad context. *Language Learning* 58 (1), 33–71.

Taguchi, N. (2015) Cross-cultural adaptability and development of speech act production in study abroad. *International Journal of Applied Linguistics* 25 (3), 343–365.

Tanaka, K. (2007) Japanese students' contact with English outside the classroom during study abroad. *New Zealand Studies in Applied Linguistics* 13 (1), 36–54.

Tarp, G. (2006) Student perspectives in short-term study programmes abroad: A grounded theory study. In M. Byram and A. Feng (eds) *Living and Studying Abroad: Research and Practice* (pp. 157–185). Clevedon: Multilingual Matters.

Toohey, K. and B. Norton (2003) Learner autonomy as agency in sociocultural settings. In D. Palfreyman and R.C. Smith (eds) *Learner Autonomy across Cultures: Language Education Perspectives* (pp. 58–74). Basingstoke: Palgrave Macmillan.

Vande Berg, M., Connor-Linton, J. and Paige, R.M. (2009) The Georgetown consortium project: Interventions for student learning abroad. *Frontiers: The Interdisciplinary Journal of Study Abroad* 18, 1–75.

Wilkinson, S. (1998a) Study abroad from the participants' perspective: A challenge to common beliefs. *Foreign Language Annals* 31 (1), 23–39.

Wilkinson, S. (1998b) On the nature of immersion during study abroad: Some participant perspectives. *Frontiers: The Interdisciplinary Journal of Study Abroad* 4, 121–138.

Wilkinson, S. (2000) Emerging questions about study abroad. *ADFL Bulletin* 32 (1), 36–41.

Williams, T.R. (2005) Exploring the impact of study abroad on students' intercultural communication skills: Adaptability and sensitivity. *Journal of Studies in International Education* 9 (4), 356–371.

Yashima, T., Zenuk-Nishide, L. and Shimizu, K. (2004) The influence of attitudes and affect on willingness to communicate and second language communication. *Language Learning* 54 (1), 119–152.

11 Four Questions for the Next Generation of Study Abroad Researchers

Celeste Kinginger

Introduction

In an overview article prepared well over 20 years ago, Coleman (1997) lamented the absence of research-generated knowledge about language learning in study abroad. In the place of a scientific approach, he argued, the profession was relying on the fond memories of senior colleagues and on age-old folklore about the richness and productivity of a sojourn abroad for language students. A new species of deep water dinosaur fish, the 'coelacanth', had recently been discovered, providing Coleman (1997: 2) with an apt metaphor for the state of affairs in the UK as he saw it: 'even in this environment where the pedagogical coelacanth lurks in many an academic backwater [...] there can be few domains where misinformation is so frequent and unsupported allegations so frequently unchallenged'.

More recently, scholars have noted the tenacity of these beliefs or their variants. DeKeyser (2010: 89), for example, decries the pervasive notion that language development in study abroad settings is a magical formula making possible a process of 'easy learning'. In a study examining Turkish students' beliefs about language learning in an English-speaking environment, Güvendir (2017) found that the participants' expectations for gains in language ability were somewhat unrealistic due to the persistence of these myths. In a study titled 'Don Quixote meets *ser* and *estar*', Polio and Zyzik (2009) take issue with a perennial problem in curriculum design, namely the recruitment of study abroad as a rationale to neglect the language-related needs of students in advanced literature courses. In this case, the American students in question were believed to have overcome any linguistic challenges, having sojourned in Spanish-speaking locales. However, and although they were expected to grapple with the intricacies of Cervantes' major work, they were still struggling with a basic, although thorny, grammatical issue: the choice and use of the copula 'to be'. It seems fairly clear that students, educators and language curriculum designers continue to overestimate the power of study abroad to enhance learning, and that many do not follow developments in research on this phenomenon or do not have access to these findings.

Yet, over the past several decades, research on language and culture learning in study abroad settings has yielded many important insights. For example, we now know that while study abroad can in principle lead to language learning in every domain, in comparison to classroom instruction it is generally more useful for the development of abilities related to social interaction than for mastery of grammatical subtleties such as the choice between *ser* and *estar*. We have examined the extent to which identities claimed by or ascribed to students can shape their experiences and achievements in both positive and negative ways (e.g. Kinginger, 2008). Significant individual differences in learning outcomes have been documented, and their sources have been explored with an array of increasingly sophisticated quantitative and qualitative approaches. In attempting to understand the degree to which students are in fact actively engaged in relevant activity, researchers have moved beyond the calendar diary (Ginsberg & Miller, 2000), to the more systematic Language Contact Profile (Freed *et al.*, 2004) and from there to social network documentation and analysis (Dewey *et al.*, 2012; Isabelli-García, 2006; McManus *et al.*, 2014).

In a comprehensive review of the literature then available (Kinginger, 2009), one of the conclusions reached was that, with a few exceptions, such as the work of the American Council on the Teaching of Russian (e.g. Davidson, 2010), study abroad research was largely a piecemeal affair involving small-scale studies with convenience samples of students from the researchers' own institutions. Today, the field is benefiting from the findings of several larger-scale, collaborative efforts. Among these are the Study Abroad and Language Acquisition (SALA) project examining the development of English language skills in Spanish–Catalan bilinguals (e.g. Pérez-Vidal, 2014); the Languages and Social Networks Abroad (LANGSNAP) project investigating social integration and the learning of French and Spanish by British university students (e.g. Mitchell *et al.*, 2017); the multinational Intercultural Resources for Erasmus Students and their Teachers (IEREST) project developing and testing research-based materials to enhance the educational value of study abroad (Beaven & Borghetti, 2016); and of course, the current European Cooperation in Science and Technology (COST)-funded 'Study Abroad Research in European Perspective' (SAREP) project, led by Martin Howard, to advance the field through dialogue among interested scholars and the generation of cohesive, yet cross-disciplinary studies.

It would seem that study abroad research in applied linguistics and language education is indeed emerging as a scholarly domain with its own identity, a journal (*Study Abroad Research in Second Language Acquisition and International Education*) and designation as a special interest group of the *Association Internationale de Linguistique Appliquée* (AILA). This is, in short, a reasonably good time to take a step back and reflect on some of the broader questions that should be taken into consideration as the research proceeds. Before doing so, however, it is necessary to issue a caveat: My main interest is, and has been for a long time, in understanding the qualities of study abroad experiences. On the one hand, this interest stems from considerable experience in reading the findings of quantitative studies where the amplification of individual differences in study abroad is evident (Huebner, 1995) but rarely well explained. In the interest of socially just education, it has always seemed to me that we need to know why some students succeed and others apparently do not, whether the answer has to do with the nature of their experiences, their dispositions toward learning or the instruments we recruit for assessment. On the other hand, my own research has been informed by Vygotskian sociocultural theory, an approach to understanding cognition as a historical process mediated by psychological tools, the most salient of which is language (Lantolf & Thorne, 2006). To recall, Vygotsky's genetic method called for observing the processes by which cognition is formed, rather than simply registering the products of this development, and for doing so while bearing in mind the dialectical relationship between mind, society and social history (Poehner *et al.*, 2018). Scholars in this tradition are drawn by the theory toward investigating educational quality, and how, for instance, micro-level phenomena under scrutiny are shaped by, and help to shape, lives and societies in the much longer term.

This chapter poses four questions about future research on language learning in study abroad, with candidate responses where possible. These questions have emerged from my familiarity with the study abroad literature which, it must be acknowledged, is influenced and limited by my location as a scholar in the USA. First is a question about historical time, routinely obscured in our literature reviews and interpretive efforts. How shall we take account of students' rapidly evolving, technology-enhanced communicative environments, of the spread of English as a *lingua mundi*, of changes in the middle-class family as a form of social order or of the increasing force exerted on subjectivity by neoliberal and consumerist ideals – all of which have real or potential effects on the study abroad experience? Second is a question about chronological scope. Why are there so few truly longitudinal studies examining the enduring influence of language study abroad on learners' lives? Third is a question about perspective. Why do so many projects focus exclusively on student novices, ignoring the views of their hosts, and therefore often yielding instantiation of the very ethnocentrism we are attempting to reduce? Last but by no means least is a question about meaningful impact. How can the findings of our research serve to inform policy, shape curricula and enhance program design?

Historical Time

As noted by Coleman (2013: 27), in principle at least, 'planets, genes, carcinomas, or dropsophilia melanogaster will behave the same in 2008 as in 1998. Not so with humans in a social context'. As a literary historian by training, Coleman expressed quite reasonable discomfort with the neglect of historical time underlying many literature reviews in study abroad research. The unquestioned assumption appears to be that studies from, for example, the 1990s, yield results that are directly comparable to those of contemporary investigations, as if larger shifts in the purpose or nature of this experience are insignificant. This is an important observation that deserves to be considered in further detail. On one level, demographic information is useful: for example, a snapshot of changes in American study abroad may be derived from the statistics published in the Institute of International Education's Open Doors reports (Institute of International Education, 2004, 2017a, 2017b). While the number of students going abroad has increased steadily over the past decades, the length of these sojourns and their academic focus have changed. From 1985 to 2016, the number of American students undertaking an entire academic or calendar year of study abroad dropped from 17.7% to 2.3%. In 1985, the percentage of students abroad who were foreign language majors was 16.7; in the 2017 report, foreign language has been merged with international studies to yield a percentage of 7.4. Today, according to the 2017 report, most students going abroad are majoring in science, technology, engineering and mathematics (STEM) fields (25.2%), business (20.9%) and social sciences (17.1%).

Thus, the typical contemporary American study abroad sojourn does not involve a student embarking on a full year of in-country study with language learning expressly prioritized. Many study abroad researchers have acknowledged these very obvious changes, and have set out to document the language-related value of brief in-country sojourns (e.g. Martinsen, 2010; Reynolds-Case, 2013). In this sense, the research has evolved with the times to meet contemporary needs. On another level, however, there has been insufficient recognition of changes in the qualities of study abroad, whether short or longer term, as an environment for language learning. As candidates for reflection on this question, I propose the development of personalized, technology-enhanced communicative environments, the transformation of the middle-class family as a form of social order and accompanying changes in routine pedagogical practices at home (e.g. the rarity of shared meals), the spread of English as a *lingua mundi* and the rise of neoliberal, consumerist ideals as they impact education.

Students' use of technology has been noted in study abroad research for many years. As early as 1995, Twombly (1995) described the tendency of US-based female students in Costa Rica to block out the sounds of catcalling on the street with the then ubiquitous Walkman (an individual sound system). Later, in Knight and Schmidt-Rinehart's (2002) survey of host perspectives, the homestay mothers pointed out that the use of computer-based communication technology slowed or prevented students' integration into local practices. In my own 2008 study of American students in France, one of the focal students, 'Deirdre', reported spending nearly all of her spare time in front of a computer screen exchanging messages with her family and boyfriend at home. In the interval since then, in common usage the term 'social networking' has lost its original meaning and now refers primarily to computer or mobile device-mediated interaction. The above-mentioned LANGSNAP project (Mitchell *et al.*, 2017) aimed to capture the everyday linguistic practices of contemporary study abroad in relation to language learning. The study followed 56 British students majoring in French or Spanish using Language Engagement and Social Networks questionnaires and various measures of language development. Among the major findings of this research is that study abroad today is 'a multilingual and intercultural experience, involving virtual as well as face-to-face relationships, and the maintenance of long-term social relations alongside those created during the sojourn itself' (McManus *et al.*, 2014: 112). Clearly, study abroad researchers have no choice but to acknowledge the widespread use of personalized communicative environments, and seek the means to turn these to the advantage of learning (e.g. Godwin-Jones, 2016). For instance, prior to their sojourns, students can be encouraged to engage in online communities related to those they will join and to follow the local news media to discover the perspectives of their hosts (Goertler, 2015). They can also participate in formal telecollaborative exchanges designed to provide sheltered access to socially consequential second language (L2) interactions and opportunities to begin crafting an appropriate L2-mediated identity (Kinginger, 2016).

Another notable change in societal practices that may impact the homestay component of study abroad programs has been the evolution of the middle-class family as a form of social order. Ochs and Kremer-Sadlik (2013), along with a multidisciplinary team of scholars, conducted an ethnographic study of 32 Los Angeles families with working parents and two school-age children. The study found that the pressures of long work and commuting hours, along with multiple after-school activities, meant that the families were rarely together at home at the same time. According to the scan-sampling data, during the few hours when the families were in fact at home, they congregated as families only an average of 14.5% of at-home time. Due to these pressures, family dinners, once the site of 'repeated rites of passage to adult discourse' (Blum-Kulka, 1994: 45), had become rare and fragmented. The ritual of family mealtime has been replaced by refrigerators and cupboards stocked with prepackaged convenience foods, such as pizza and Gogurts, eaten whenever children are hungry. Although we cannot generalize from these findings to the practices of other societies, we do know that the family mealtime ritual has traditionally been a key site for the socialization of student guests abroad (e.g. Cook, 2008; DuFon, 2006).

At least one case study (Lee *et al.*, 2017) has documented an orientation similar to that of the Los Angeles families adopted by a hosting household in Shanghai. In this case, the family respected the letter of the law in that they did, indeed, provide meals for their American guest, 'Kevin'. However, the spirit of the law was not respected: no doubt in part because Kevin displayed poor mastery of Chinese table etiquette, he took his meals at his own table in the company of a laptop computer, behind a wall separating him from the room where the hosts dined in front of the television. As a result, Kevin received no instruction in local manners apart from warnings about food waste. The research team was struck by Kevin's apparent indifference regarding the social as opposed to the strictly utilitarian aspects of food consumption in his homestay. This suggests that if the typically middle-class students who study abroad have been brought up in a home with little routine family interaction, they may not be prepared to profit from such interaction if it is expected, and they may not miss it if it is not. Thus, we cannot assume that programs including homestays involve socializing interactions around ritual family gatherings.

For Anglophone language learners, the spread of English as a *lingua mundi* also has consequences for language learning in study abroad. English is the official language of instruction in many institutions abroad, such that even if students are enrolled in local universities this participation may not enhance their language proficiency. English is also the *de facto* shared lingua franca among international student groups throughout the world. There is some evidence that the broader problem of being excluded from important conversations identified by the American Academy of Arts and Sciences (2017) may be reflected in study abroad contexts as well, for example when American classmates are considered dispreferred conversation partners because, without language learning experience, they lack empathy for those who struggle with English and fail to accommodate their interlocutors (Kalocsai, 2009). No doubt, the spread of English also has multifarious consequences for all students of languages other than English.

Finally, it is important to consider how the spread of neoliberal ideals has impacted the imagination of study abroad participants and parents. In a nutshell, neoliberalism is an ever-expanding, transnational mode of economic rationality characterized by privatization, deregulation and the withdrawal of nation states from responsibility for civic well-being. As described by Gill and Scharff (2011: 5), neoliberalism 'sees market exchange as an ethic unto itself, and it holds that the social good will be maximized by maximizing the reach and frequency of market transactions'. Further, it is a 'mobile, calculated technology for governing subjects who are constituted as self-managing, autonomous, and enterprising'. As critiqued by Kubota (2016), the translation of these notions for evaluating the worth of study abroad yields an emphasis on the competitiveness of the individual in the global employment marketplace. Specifically, 'a neoliberal social imaginary constructs an image of the neoliberal subject as equipped with communication skills, a global mindset, and intercultural competence' (Kubota, 2016: 349).

What is obscured in this portrayal is the fact that contemporary study abroad remains at least partially rooted in the Grand Tour tradition (Gore, 2005); in other words, it is the domain of the privileged striving middle or upper middle classes who expect to enjoy the consumption of educational experiences. The development of communication skills or intercultural competence is an effortful, occasionally quite challenging process. Yet, the promotion of study abroad, in the USA at least, usually emphasizes leisure or adventure over learning or effort of any kind (Doerr, 2012). To Google Image study abroad is to find photo after photo of students jumping for joy on beaches or exotic backdrops, skydiving, bungee jumping or riding elephants. Privileged students who can afford study abroad are explicitly primed to expect magical 'easy learning' (DeKeyser, 2010: 89). What is worse, of course, is the neoliberal tendency to gloss over fundamental social inequality and injustice. International educational experiences are not, by any means, available to every student, regardless of how self-managing or enterprising he or she may be. According to Kubota's (2016: 355) analysis, in fact study abroad 'reflects and reinforces gender, race, ethnic, geographical and socioeconomic inequalities'. Clearly, it is important for language educators and researchers to provide realistic guidance countering popular ideologies of study abroad while also understanding and critiquing inherent problems in the accessibility of international education and actively advocating for inclusion and diversity.

Chronological Scope

In the fields of applied linguistics and language education, scholars are increasingly aware of the need for a longer research time frame for study abroad research. The post-sojourn experience has recently been identified as a 'new frontier' (Plews, 2016). The great majority of research on language learning in study abroad involves pre- and post-measures of outcomes or qualitative investigation of processes taking place during the sojourn proper. Results are limited to short-term effects, and 'conclusions concerning long-term linguistic or intercultural effects, sustained shifts in individual perspectives or identity, or potential extended community benefits can be drawn only with caution from most SA research or remain indeterminable or speculative' (Plews, 2016: 2).

We know very little about the re-entry process when language students return to their domestic campus (c.f. Lee & Kinginger, 2018), and even less about the destinies of committed language learners once they complete their undergraduate studies and move on to graduate work or professional pursuits. Anecdotal evidence shows that some programs explicitly welcome, include and support study abroad veterans expressly in order to bolster the size and cohesion of their local L2 community (Cagle, 2011). In other cases, students find that there are few relevant courses they can choose upon their return in order to continue developing their proficiency or that advanced courses assume advanced literacy and neglect their language-related needs (Polio & Zyzik, 2009). Only a few studies have examined specific questions relevant to the extended afterlife of language study abroad, such as the extent and nature of attrition in language ability (Jiménez-Jiménez, 2004) or the growth in the sophistication of language beliefs (Amuzie & Winke, 2009). An important exception is the expansion of data collection and analysis for the above-mentioned LANGSNAP project from a two- to a five-year period, allowing research into the long-term evolution of foreign language proficiency under various conditions (Huensch *et al.*, 2019; Tracy-Ventura & Huensch, 2018).

Meanwhile, in fields outside or adjacent to language education, American scholars have conducted a variety of survey-based studies to document the long-term impact of study abroad in meeting broadly defined educational goals. A sojourn abroad has been shown to enhance academic focus among returning students (Hadis, 2005) and to promote the development of intercultural competence (Rexeisen *et al.*, 2008; Salisbury *et al.*, 2013). Several projects have also demonstrated that study abroad helps students in various fields to orient toward international careers (Franklin, 2010; Orahood *et al.*, 2004). The Institute for the International Education of Students (IES) surveyed five decades of IES alumni (Dwyer, 2004) demonstrating that the experience abroad had a long-term impact on students' later academic achievement, career direction and intercultural and personal development (Norris & Gillespie, 2009).

Among the most influential of these studies is the SAGE project investigating the influence of study abroad on 'global engagement' among alumni using a mixed-methods 'tracer' design alongside life story interviews with randomly selected participants (Paige *et al.*, 2009). Five dimensions of global engagement were investigated in the study: domestic or international civic engagement, knowledge production, philanthropy, social entrepreneurship and voluntary simplicity. A total of 6,391 alumni of 22 programs were surveyed after a period of time ranging from 3 to 45 years, and 63 interviews explored the meaning of global engagement for particular individuals. The findings of the study present compelling evidence for the impact of study abroad in that a significant proportion of the group surveyed had become globally engaged, productive members of society who were civically involved, practiced environmentally aware lifestyles and made contributions of labor or financial resources to philanthropic causes. The study also found that participants pursued graduate education at a higher rate than that of the general undergraduate population. A similar project was carried out with a control group of students who had not studied abroad, and a sixth dimension of global engagement (internationally oriented leisure activities) by Murphy *et al.* (2014). Participants were 1,283 alumni of the University of Wisconsin (1980–2010), including 270 who had gone abroad during their undergraduate years. Findings showed no difference between the groups for social entrepreneurship or knowledge production, generally higher levels of global engagement for the study abroad group on other dimensions and a strikingly higher propensity for the study abroad group to be involved in internationally oriented leisure activities.

Given the overall decline in support for language study in the USA and the challenges that contemporary American language learners tend to encounter while abroad, it is hardly surprising to find that the focus of larger-scale research on long-term impacts has turned away from language to consider other, more readily demonstrable benefits of study abroad. Language does appear in these studies, but in an ancillary role as a skill or a support for internationally oriented leisure activity (Murphy *et al.*, 2014). There is no consideration of the extent to which language *per se*, especially in its pragmatic dimensions, offers access to intercultural awareness (Agar, 1994). In the SAGE study, meanwhile, language fluency is listed as the top domain mentioned by students in response to an open-ended question about impact (Fry *et al.*, 2009: 29). Similarly, in the IES survey, alumni indicated that 'Enhanced ability to speak foreign language (sic.) used in the workplace' as one of the most important results of their experience abroad (Norris & Gillespie, 2009: 386). Moreover, 'respondents who participated in IES programs conducted solely in a foreign language were 62% more likely to have developed global careers than participants of programs taught exclusively in English' (Norris & Gillespie, 2009: 391). Foreign language proficiency clearly retains some importance in the estimation of study abroad participants, and clearly presents advantages for internationally oriented careers. However, since the recent large-scale research on study abroad does not prioritize language, it provides few insights specifically useful to language educators.

In response to this situation, along with colleagues within and outside my home institution, we have recently launched a mixed-methods tracer study similar in design to the SAGE investigation but with an explicit focus on language. Titled 'The Careers of Language Study Abroad Alumni', and funded by the US Department of Education, the three-year project will involve a large-scale survey of former language learners abroad at any career stage followed by life history interviews with selected willing participants. The survey, designed in collaboration with the American Council for International Education, will gather information on the extent to which foreign language ability developed at the post-secondary level is valued, recognized and cultivated across the lifespan, and the extent to which this ability offers personal and professional opportunities and satisfaction. It will also investigate if and how language ability is supported after study abroad, and the advantages that these learners enjoy as well as the barriers they face. The survey will be promoted and delivered to users by the Forum on Education Abroad, the main US-based professional organization for study abroad providers and administrators, with over 800 institutional members. If, as we hope, the survey attracts a large number of respondents of varying ages, results will include findings concerning changes in the perceived long-term value of study abroad for language learning over the past several decades.

In its second phase, the project will involve life history interviews semi-structured around the themes of the larger study, namely the significance of language ability after graduation and in the longer term, the specific role of study abroad, forces that either help or hinder language development, and the pleasures and satisfaction or frustrations involved in the pursuit of language ability. They will also inquire about antecedents to study abroad, that is, events or conditions experienced during the participants' youth that inspired them to pursue international education in general and language proficiency in particular. In addition, participants will be asked to recount any specific memorable incidents or learning episodes involving the pragmatic aspects of the language(s) they have studied. Combining the rigor of a carefully conducted quantitative survey with the richly representative autobiographical data only available from face-to-face qualitative interviews, we hope to assemble a comprehensive portrait of the US post-sojourn experience from the point of view of participants.

Perspective

This point of view of participants, however, is not the only perspective of interest. I have, in the past, regularly argued that while students' comments are valuable, students are not necessarily the most reliable informants for qualitative research on study abroad. Yet, many qualitative studies, including some of my own, rely exclusively on the observations, in interviews or diaries, of novice interactants who do not necessarily understand the motives or general, culturally derived dispositions of their interlocutors. With few exceptions (e.g. Knight & Schmidt-Rinehart, 2002), the opinions of hosts tend to be absent from the literature. As a result, misunderstandings that may be rooted in key cultural differences are represented from a naïve perspective that may serve to perpetuate the very ethnocentrism that study abroad and associated research are intended to overcome. Having already outlined this problem in other publications (e.g. Kinginger, 2010, 2019), here I will dwell on the advantages and challenges of a more inclusive approach, one in which the views of local hosts, teachers and program administrators are heard.

In an effort to practice what we have lately been preaching on this matter, my research team has endeavored to design projects expressly including hosts and local teachers as participants as we investigate the development of Chinese language abilities in China. Our first project examined a summer intensive exchange program for high school students. The program director, Dali Tan, was recruited as a member of the research team to help in data collection and to share her wisdom and knowledge of the program. All parties were interviewed, and the main data consist of transcribed audio recordings of mealtime interactions. Our findings have been published as a study of dinner table talk *per se* (Kinginger *et al.*, 2016a), and also as a series of three contrasting case studies (Kinginger *et al.*, 2016b). By including the voices of host families in particular, we have been able to discover the specific value that hosts attribute to their experience. For example, we know that the parents appreciated a temporary 'sibling-like' relationship for their only children, and that homestay discussions yielded insights to help all parties overcome stereotypes, such as the Chinese views that American schooling is lax and non-competitive or that the preparation of American food involves no effort. In the case of successful homestay experiences, we learned of the host parents' and siblings' affection or admiration for their guests. In the case of at least one relatively less successful experience ('Henry' in Kinginger *et al.*, 2016b), had we interviewed the student only, we would never have learned about the intense care his hosts had taken to plan and to offer myriad learning experiences, including special meals, short trips and local outings, most of which were refused.

In subsequent work, Lee (2017) carried out a longitudinal study of two learners of Chinese, with data collected across classroom and study abroad experiences over several years. The above-cited study from this dissertation (Lee *et al.*, 2017) similarly illustrates the importance of the host family perspective in interpreting homestay practices. To recall, one of the participants in this study was excluded from the family dining space and asked to consume his meals alone. How can this be explained? If we ask only the student, 'Kevin', the response is not particularly revealing, because he does not seem to have noticed that there was anything amiss. However, if we pose this question to the host mother, a more credible explanation emerges. Specifically, Kevin did not display mastery of hygienic eating, plunging his rice-covered chopsticks into the communal dishes, thereby polluting them and rendering them inedible by others. Having unsuccessfully attempted to reprimand Kevin and teach him to eat properly by deliberately and slowly removing each grain of rice, bit by bit, from a communal dish, for the sake of avoiding food waste, she began to serve him separately. Although somewhat banal in nature, this example clearly demonstrates how a basic misunderstanding can lead to an unfortunate withdrawal of the learning opportunities afforded to all parties during routine mealtime interactions.

For all of the advantages presented in research including the voices of local participants, it must be acknowledged that this may not be strictly necessary if researchers are themselves either members of the host community or are highly familiar with it. It is also the case that recruitment can pose significant challenges, since it is necessary to obtain consent both from students and from host families or others who are involved. In our experience thus far, it can be frustrating to have consent from a particular student, but not from the corresponding hosts, or vice versa. Obtaining informed consent in accordance with a university's board of ethics can also be complicated if any relevant parties, including host family children, are not yet legally defined as adults. These difficulties present a risk of reducing the scope of studies already of small scale. In the case of a large-scale study such as the above-described survey of language study abroad alumni, recruiting hosts to join the project might be possible in principle, but would be costly and present significant logistical difficulties.

Impact

A final question concerns the impact of research on language learning in study abroad. Now that this domain has become an identifiable subfield with significant achievements relevant to language educators, program directors, policymakers, students and parents, how can we communicate these findings beyond our own journals and conference venues such that they make a difference? How can we demonstrate the unique learning opportunities available to language learners abroad in order to attract investment of time, effort and financial resources to support international education for a broader population of students and in order to enhance the quality and not just the amount of study abroad?

One clearly accessible avenue is the development, testing and showcasing of effective pedagogies based on the findings of research. For example, the above-mentioned IEREST project (Beaven & Borghetti, 2016) is an example of a successful effort to translate research on intercultural competence into modules that students and teachers can take up and use to enhance the European Region Action Scheme for the Mobility of University Students (Erasmus) experience. Similar efforts with a clear focus on language would likely also meet with success. Researchers investigating language learning in study abroad have a responsibility to share their findings and their implications with the broader profession of language educators, through participation in association meetings and publication in journals addressed to teachers and curriculum designers.

Another possibility is to reach out to organizations of international educators outside but adjacent to our field. In my own case, working with provider organizations or with professional organizations such as the Forum on Education Abroad has been a singularly rewarding experience in which it has been clear throughout that expertise on language learning is very much in demand for the development of practical applications and curricula. The Forum on Education Abroad, for example, establishes national standards for the design and implementation of study abroad in the USA including recommendations for language education that must be informed by insights from the most recent and therefore the most relevant research.

Conclusion

In composing this chapter, I have taken advantage of an opportunity to reflect on a variety of themes relevant to the future of research on language learning in study abroad contexts. I have argued for greater attention, both for research itself and for the interpretation of findings, to sociohistorical forces shaping the study abroad experience. These include the ubiquity of personalized communicative environments, the evolution of the middle-class family as a form of social order, the spread of English as a *lingua mundi* and the growing prominence of the neoliberal social imaginary. I have commented on the dearth of longitudinal scope in the study abroad knowledge base, and introduced a newly launched study intended to begin filling this gap. I have updated a theme in my other writing to do with problems of perspective in the qualitative literature, particularly an exclusive focus on students' points of view and an associated disregard for the voices of others. Finally, I have asked a sincere question, to which I cannot provide an answer relevant to all, about the educational and societal impact of this research. My hope is that these reflections will be taken for what they are, namely, an opinion about the current state and desired future of study abroad research, albeit a relatively well informed one, emerging from a particular interpretive stance.

References

Agar, M. (1994) *Language Shock: Understanding the Culture of Conversation.* New York: William Morrow and Company.

American Academy of Arts and Sciences (2017) *America's Languages: Investing in Language Education for the 21st Century.* Cambridge, MA: American Academy of Arts and Sciences.

Amuzie, G. and Winke, P. (2009) Changes in language learning beliefs as a result of study abroad. *System* 37, 366–379.

Beaven, A. and Borghetti, C. (2016) Interculturality in study abroad. *Language and Intercultural Communication* 16, 313–317.

Blum-Kulka, S. (1994) The dynamics of family dinner talk: Cultural contexts for children's passages to adult discourse. *Research on Language and Social Interaction* 1, 1–50.

Cagle, L. (2011) Community building: Study abroad and the small German program. *Die Unterrichtspraxis* 44, 12–19.

Coleman, J.A. (1997) Residence abroad within language study. *Language Teaching* 30, 1–20.

Coleman, J.A. (2013) Researching whole people and whole lives. In C. Kinginger (ed.) *Social and Cultural Aspects of Language Learning in Study Abroad* (pp. 17–46). Amsterdam/Philadelphia, PA: Benjamins.

Cook, H. (2008) *Socializing Identities through Speech Style: Learners of Japanese as a Foreign Language*. Bristol: Multilingual Matters.

Davidson, D. (2010) Study abroad: When, how long, and with what results? New data from the Russian front. *Foreign Language Annals* 43, 6–26.

DeKeyser, R. (2010) Monitoring processes in Spanish as a second language during a study abroad program. *Foreign Language Annals* 43, 80–92.

Dewey, D., Bown, J. and Eggett, D. (2012) Japanese language proficiency, social networking, and language use during study abroad. *The Canadian Modern Language Review* 68, 111–137.

Doerr, N. (2012) Study abroad as 'adventure': Globalist construction of host-home hierarchy and governed adventurer subjects. *Critical Discourse Studies* 9, 257–268.

DuFon, M.A. (2006) The socialization of taste during study abroad in Indonesia. In M.A. DuFon and E. Churchill (eds) *Language Learners in Study Abroad Contexts* (pp. 91–119). Clevedon: Multilingual Matters.

Dwyer, M.M. (2004) Charting the impact of studying abroad. *International Educator* 13, 14–17/19–20.

Franklin, K. (2010) Long-term career impact and professional applicability of the study abroad experience. *Frontiers: The Interdisciplinary Journal of Study Abroad* 19, 169–190.

Freed, B., Dewey, D., Segalowitz, N. and Halter, F. (2004) The Language Contact Profile. *Studies in Second Language Acquisition* 26, 349–356.

Fry, G.W., Paige, R.M., Jon, J., Dillow, J. and Nam, K. (2009) Study abroad and its transformative power (CIEE Occasional Paper 32). See https://www.researchgate.net/publication/242678434_Study_Abroad_and_its_Transformative_Power_OCCASIONAL_PAPERS_On_International_Educational_Exchange32 (accessed 31 March 2019).

Gill, R. and Scharff, C. (eds) (2011) *New Femininities: Postfeminism, Neoliberalism and Subjectivity*. Basingstoke: Palgrave Macmillan.

Ginsberg, R. and Miller, L. (2000) What do they do? Activities of students during study abroad. In R. Lambert and E. Shohamy (eds) *Language Policy and Pedagogy: Essays in Honor of A. Ronald Walton* (pp. 237–260). Amsterdam/Philadelphia, PA: Benjamins.

Godwin-Jones, R. (2016) Integrating technology into study abroad. *Language Learning and Technology* 20, 1–20.

Goertler, S. (2015) Study abroad and technology: Friend or enemy? See http://fltmag.com/study-abroad-and-technology/ (accessed 31 March 2019).

Gore, J. (2005) *Dominant Beliefs and Alternative Voices: Discourse, Belief, and Gender in American Study Abroad*. New York: Routledge.

Güvendir, E. (2017) Turkish students and their experiences during a short-term summer visit to the US. *Study Abroad Research in Second Language Acquisition and International Education* 2, 21–52.

Hadis, B.F. (2005) Why are they better students when they come back? Determinants of academic focusing gains in the study abroad experience. *Frontiers: The Interdisciplinary Journal of Study Abroad* 11, 57–70.

Huebner, T. (1995) The effects of overseas language programs: Report on a case study of an intensive Japanese course. In B. Freed (ed.) *Second Language Acquisition in a Study Abroad Context* (pp. 171–194). Amsterdam/Philadelphia, PA: Benjamins.

Huensch, A., Tracy-Ventura, N., Bridges, J. and Cuesta, J. (2019) Variables affecting the maintenance of L2 proficiency and fluency four years post-study abroad. *Study Abroad Research in Second Language Acquisition and International Education* 4 (1), 96–125.

Institute of International Education (2004) Open doors 2004 fast facts. See http://www.iie.org/opendoors.iienetwork.org/ (accessed 1 July 2005).

Institute of International Education (2017a) Fields of study of US study abroad students, 2005/06-2015/16. *Fields of Study.* See https://www.iie.org/Research-and-Insights/Open -Doors/Data/US-Study-Abroad/Fields-of-Study (accessed 31 March 2019).

Institute of International Education (2017b) Duration of US study abroad, 2005/06– 2015/16. *Duration of Study Abroad.* See https://www.iie.org/Research-and-Insights/ Open-Doors/Data/US-Study-Abroad/Duration-of-Study-Abroad (accessed 31 March 2019).

Isabelli-García, C. (2006) Study abroad and social networks, motivation, and attitudes: Implications for SLA. In M. DuFon and E. Churchill (eds) *Language Learners in Study Abroad Contexts* (pp. 231–258). Clevedon: Multilingual Matters.

Jiménez-Jiménez, A. (2004) Linguistic and psychological dimensions of second language attrition during and after a study abroad experience. Unpublished doctoral thesis, The Pennsylvania State University.

Kalocsai, K. (2009) Erasmus exchange students: A behind-the scenes view into an ELF community of practice. *Apples – Journal of Applied Language Studies* 1, 25–49.

Kinginger, C. (2008) *Language Learning in Study Abroad: Case Studies of Americans in France.* Modern Language Journal, 92, Monograph.

Kinginger, C. (2009) *Language Learning and Study Abroad: A Critical Reading of Research.* Basingstoke: Palgrave Macmillan.

Kinginger, C. (2010) American students abroad: Negotiation of difference? *Language Teaching* 43, 216–227.

Kinginger, C. (2016) Telecollaboration and student mobility for language learning. In S. Jager, M. Kurek and B. O'Rourke (eds) *New Directions in Telecollaborative Research and Practice: Selected Papers from the Second Conference on Telecollaboration in Higher Education* (pp. 19–29). Research-publishing.net. See https://doi.org/10.14705/ rpnet.2016.telecollab2016.487 (accessed 31 March 2019).

Kinginger, C. (2019) Overcoming ethnocentrism in research on language learning abroad. In M. Fuchs, Y. Loiseau, and S. Rai (eds) *Study Abroad: Traditions, Directions, and Innovations* (pp. 15–28). New York: Modern Language Association.

Kinginger, C., Lee, H.-S., Wu, Q. and Tan, D. (2016a) Contextualized language practices as sites for learning: Mealtime talk in short-term Chinese homestays. *Applied Linguistics* 37, 716–740.

Kinginger, C., Wu, Q., Lee, H.-S. and Tan, D. (2016b) The short-term homestay as a context for language learning: Three case studies of high school students and host families. *Study Abroad Research in Second Language Acquisition and International Education* 1, 34–60.

Knight, S. and Schmidt-Rinehart, B. (2002) Enhancing the homestay: Study abroad from the host family's perspective. *Foreign Language Annals* 35, 190–201.

Kubota, R. (2016) The social imaginary of study abroad: Complexities and contradictions. *The Language Learning Journal* 44, 347–357.

Lantolf, J. and Thorne, S. (2006) *Sociocultural Theory and the Genesis of Second Language Development.* Oxford: Oxford University Press.

Lee, H.-S. (2017) Learning Chinese in and beyond study abroad: Two case studies of language learning processes. Unpublished doctoral thesis, The Pennsylvania State University.

Lee, H.-S. and Kinginger, C. (2018) Narrative remembering of intercultural encounters: An activity-theoretic study of language program reintegration after study abroad. *Modern Language Journal* 102, 578–593.

Lee, H.-S., Wu, Q., Di, C. and Kinginger, C. (2017) Learning to eat politely at the Chinese homestay dinner table: Two contrasting case studies. *Foreign Language Annals* 50, 135–158.

Martinsen, R. (2010) Short-term study abroad: Predicting changes in oral skills. *Foreign Language Annals* 43, 504–530.

McManus, K., Mitchell, R. and Tracy-Ventura, N. (2014) Understanding insertion and integration in a study abroad context: The case of English-speaking sojourners in France. *Revue Française de Linguistique Appliquée* 19, 97–116.

Mitchell, R., Tracy-Ventura, N. and McManus, K. (2017) *Anglophone Students Abroad: Identity, Social Relationships and Language Learning.* London: Routledge.

Murphy, D., Sahakyan, N., Yong-Yi, D. and Magnan, S. (2014) The impact of study abroad on the global engagement of university graduates. *Frontiers: The Interdisciplinary Journal of Study Abroad* 24, 1–23.

Norris, E. and Gillespie, J. (2009) How study abroad shapes global careers: Evidence from the United States. *Journal of Studies in International Education* 13, 382–397.

Ochs, E. and Kremer-Sadlik, T. (2013) *Fast-Forward Family: Home, Work, and Relationships in Middle-Class America.* Berkeley, CA: University of California Press.

Orahood, T., Kruze, L. and Pearson, D. (2004) The impact of study abroad on business students' career goals. *Frontiers: The Interdisciplinary Journal of Study Abroad* 10, 117–130.

Paige, R.M., Fry, G.W., Stallman, E.M., Josic, J. and Jon, J. (2009) Study abroad for global engagement: The long-term impact of mobility experiences. *Intercultural Education* 20 (S1–2), S29–44.

Pérez-Vidal, C. (2014) *Language Acquisition in Study Abroad and Formal Instruction Contexts.* Amsterdam/Philadelphia, PA: Benjamins.

Plews, J. (2016) The post-sojourn in study abroad research – another frontier. *Comparative and International Education/Éducation Comparée et Internationale* 42 (2). See http://ir.lib.uwo.ca/cie-eci/vol45/iss2/1 (accessed 31 March 2019).

Poehner, M., Kinginger, C., Van Compernolle, R. and Lantolf, J. (2018) Pursuing Vygotsky's dialectical approach to pedagogy and development: A response to Kellogg. *Applied Linguistics* 39, 429–433.

Polio, C. and Zyzik, E. (2009) Don Quixote meets *ser* and *estar*: Multiple perspectives on language learning in Spanish literature classes. *Modern Language Journal* 93, 550–569.

Rexeisen, R.J., Anderson, P.H., Lawton, L. and Hubbard, A.C. (2008) Study abroad and intercultural development: A longitudinal study. *Frontiers: The Interdisciplinary Journal of Study Abroad* 17, 1–20.

Reynolds-Case, A. (2013) The value of short-term study abroad: An increase in students' cultural and pragmatic competence. *Foreign Language Annals* 46, 311–322.

Salisbury, M.H., An, B.P. and Pascarella, E.T. (2013) The effect of study abroad on intercultural competence among undergraduate college students. *Journal of Student Affairs Research and Practice* 50, 1–20.

Tracy-Ventura, N. and Huensch, A. (2018) The potential of publicly shared longitudinal learner corpora in SLA research. In A. Gudmestad and A. Edmonds (eds) *Critical Reflections on Data in Second Language Acquisition* (pp. 149–170). Amsterdam/Philadelphia, PA: Benjamins.

Twombly, S. (1995) Piropos and friendship: Gender and culture clash in study abroad. *Frontiers: The Interdisciplinary Journal of Study Abroad* 1, 1–27.

Index